Benoît Vermander
The Encounter of Chinese and Western Philosophies

Benoît Vermander

The Encounter of Chinese and Western Philosophies

A Critique

DE GRUYTER

ISBN 978-3-11-221476-3
e-ISBN (PDF) 978-3-11-079911-8
e-ISBN (EPUB) 978-3-11-079920-0
DOI https://doi.org/10.1515/9783110799118

This work is licensed under the Creative Commons Attribution 4.0 International License (CC BY 4.0). For details go to https://creativecommons.org/licenses/cc-by/4.0/

Creative Commons license terms for re-use do not apply to any content (such as graphs, figures, photos, excerpts, etc.) not original to the Open Access publication and further permission may be required from the rights holder. The obligation to research and clear permission lies solely with the party re-using the material.

Library of Congress Control Number: 2023937087

Bibliographic information published by the Deutsche Nationalbibliothek
The Deutsche Nationalbibliothek lists this publication in the Deutsche Nationalbibliografie; detailed bibliographic data are available on the Internet at http://dnb.dnb.de.

© 2025 the author(s), published by Walter de Gruyter GmbH, Berlin/Boston.
This volume is text- and page-identical with the hardback published in 2023.
This book is published open access at www.degruyter.com.

Cover image: Benoît Vermander
Printing and binding: CPI books GmbH, Leck

www.degruyter.com

Acknowledgments

A significant part of the present book's argument has been shaped by my teaching at Fudan University since 2009 and by the stimulating interactions that took place here over these years. My gratitude goes first to Bai Tongdong 白彤东 who invited me to participate in the Master's Degree "Chinese Philosophy in English" that our School of Philosophy started in 2011. From that time on, I have taught every year in this program a semester-long course, centered on the spiritual dimension and on the rhetorical structures of ancient Chinese classics. This gave me the opportunity to meet with students of very diverse geographical origins and academic backgrounds. Through their questions and remarks, they actively participated in the elaboration of the ideas exposed in this work. Among my colleagues at Fudan, I also wish to thank in a special way Li Tiangang 李天纲, Xie Jing 谢晶, Sun Xiangchen 孙向晨, Zhang Qingxiong 张庆熊, Yao Dali 姚大力, Li Hongtu 李宏图, Zhang Shuangli 张双利, Yu Zhejun 郁喆隽, Cai Qinghua 才清华, Chen Jia 陈佳, Xu Bo 徐波 and Huang Bei 黄蓓 for the insights and knowledge shared over the years.

In addition, although my courses on comparative spirituality and on religious anthropology, intended for Chinese students, bear only partly upon the content of this book, their preparation and delivery helped me to dig further into the way various disciplines and currents interact in the present-day Chinese intellectual landscape. Among the former doctoral students whose input was particularly valuable and who also acted as research assistants I own a special debt to Chen Jiaren 陈嘉仁, and also to Jin Shunhua 金舜华 and Wang Ziming 王子铭.

Over an extended period of time, I have also benefited from exchanges with, notably, Anne Cheng, Yolaine Escande, John Lagerwey, Béatrice L'Haridon, Michel Masson, Thierry Meynard, Élisabeth Rochat de la Vallée, Nicolas Standaert and Edmond Ryden. For inputs of various lengths and natures, I also wish to mention with gratitude the names of Fiorella Allio, Guillaume Dutournier, Julie Gary, Luce Giard, Guo Ke 郭可, Roberte Hamayon, Marc Kalinowski, Heup Young Kim, Lu Jin 鲁进, Roland Meynet, Chloë Starr, Xie Hua 谢华, Min Jung You, and Zhang Liang 张靓.

It is in the Society of Jesus that I found access to Chinese classics, and it will come as no surprise to find the names of the late Claude Larre, Yves Raguin and Jean Lefeuvre mentioned here among the ones of those who shared with me a particular access to the treasures of ancient China. Two other Jesuits shaped my way of reading and interpreting texts, and I remember them with a particular feeling of thankfulness: François Marty and Paul Beauchamp.

I wish to mention here two of my Chinese teachers: at Sichuan Normal University, Professor Du Daosheng 杜道生, cousin of Guo Moruo 郭沫若, nurtured in me a fascination for Chinese lexicography that had been awakened already by what I knew of the editorial enterprise of the *Dictionnaire Ricci* endeavord by the Ricci Institute, a research center I would join shortly after benefiting from Professor Du's teaching. Also in Chengdu, Li Jinyuan 李金远 taught me not only the art of Chinese painting but also the one of merging into one meditative reading, lived experience, and artistic expression. I also fondly remember the support and kindness constantly shown to me by Vincent Shen Qingsong 沈青松 from the time I first met him in Taiwan (it was in 1994, two years after my arrival there) till his premature departure in 2018.

Chapter 4 draws in good part on an earlier essay, "Encoding the Way: Ritual Ethos and Textual Patterns in China" published in *Geschichte der Philologien* (61/62, 2022, p. 5–31). In its fourth section, Chapter 6 contains some material from "Self-Examination, Discernment, and Decision Making: Criss-crossing the Confucian and Ignatian Traditions" published in *Journal of Management, Spirituality & Religion* (19[5], October 2022, p. 522–545). Permission to reproduce these materials is gratefully acknowledged. Besides, in Chapter 4 and in the third section of Chapter 5 I summarize and rework propositions first developed in *Comment lire les classiques chinois?* (Les Belles Lettres, 2022).

Two anonymous readers gave valuable suggestions on a first draft of this volume. I am most indebted to Paul Kim Hosle for a careful reading of the manuscript, which has resulted in many editorial improvements.

Finally, my gratitude goes to an anonymous benefactor and to the Hochschule für Philosophie München for helping in making this book an Open Access publication.

Fudan University, March 2023

Contents

Acknowledgments —— V

Introduction —— 1

Part I: **The Limits of an Encounter**

Chapter 1
The Gardens of Philosophy —— 13
    Mapping and Mappers —— 13
    Cosmos and "The-World-as-It-Is" —— 22
    Permanence and Process —— 29
    Non-Dual Cognition versus Dualist Reasoning —— 32
    Correlations and/or Substances —— 35
    Does Transcendence Matter? —— 47
    The Otherness That Lies Within —— 55

Chapter 2
"Rectifying Names" —— 58
    Di, Tian, Shen, Guishen, Shenming… —— 58
    Lexical Disputations: Five Notions —— 66
    What's in a Name? —— 74

Chapter 3
Philosophical Narratives in (and about) China —— 82
    The May Fourth Movement as a Philosophical Event —— 84
    Recreating Philosophy —— 89
    The Beijing Model —— 100
    The Shanghai Variant: A "Dual Ontology" —— 111

Part II: **Reimagining the Engagement**

Chapter 4
Encoding the Way —— 127
    Ritual, Language, and Text —— 128
    Three Characteristics of Early Chinese *Wen* —— 134

From "Texts" to "Classics" —— 142
Attentiveness: The Reader as Ritual Practitioner —— 145

Chapter 5
Comparative Classics, Comparative Philosophy —— 152
From Notions to Motions —— 152
Models of Dialogue —— 155
Modes of Reading —— 165
Beyond Comparative Classics —— 179

Chapter 6
Exploring New Gardens —— 185
Ritual: Terms, Issues and Styles —— 185
Confucian Meritocracy: Between Authoritarianism and Democracy —— 192
Thinking about Thoughtlessness —— 199
Phronesis in the Confucian and Ignatian Traditions —— 211

Conclusion —— 228

References —— 233

Abbreviations —— 249

Note on Citations and Translations —— 250

Index of Authors and Works —— 252

Index of Subjects —— 256

Introduction

A long time ago, asserts the *Laozi*,¹ people in one village could hear the cries of dogs and roosters in the adjacent settlement, and yet the idea of visiting each other never occurred to them (*Daodejing* 80). Are we dealing here with descriptive or prescriptive prose? The text may nostalgically refer to the past, as my rephrasing implies, or, alternatively, it speaks of a utopian country, in which (suggests the same stanza) travel, weapons, machinery and even the art of writing would be considered as suspect.

Ancient Chinese thinkers were insisting on a point that the *Laozi's* micro-parable illustrates in its own fashion: only after one's way of behaving and thinking has "settled", has fully matured, should one endeavor to move further along the road. Streams, notes Mencius 孟子 (372–289 BCE), fill every hollow they meet along the way before flowing on to the sea. Similarly, when devoting yourself to the art of studying (*xue* 學), you need to go *deeper* before you go *further*, i.e., you must get to the bottom of each of the difficulties met in the course of your exploration. After an issue has been thoroughly dealt with, one can shift to another topic (*Mencius* 4B.18 and 7 A.24). The Confucian thinker Yang Xiong 揚雄 (53 BCE–18 CE) extends the analogy to all natural phenomena, thus strengthening further its intellectual and spiritual significance: the wild goose proceeds "like water" (*you shui* 猶水) in the sense that, rather than trying to cover all the surrounding territory, it goes only towards certain directions and it lands only in certain locations. Besides, "a tree develops its branching by [first] stabilizing its roots. It proceeds the way water does!" (Yang Xiong, *Exemplary Sayings* [*Fayan* 法言] 1.14).²

As illustrated by our representative examples above, Chinese philosophy is not spontaneously "comparative"; it does not travel from one village to another so as to look at the neighbors' dogs and roosters. These animals are evoked in another adage of Mencius: when dogs or roosters escape from the farm, one knows which direction to go searching. Conversely, whoever has lost her heart-mind (*xin* 心) has also lost the reference point from which to start the quest. Thus, "the way of learning through apprenticeship" (*xuewen zhi dao* 學問之道) is to resort to a teacher who will provide us with the guidance we need as we search for the heart we lost – "and that's it! [*er yi yi* 而已矣]", concludes Mencius (*Mencius*

---

1 Also called *Daodejing* (i.e., *The Classic of the Way and [Its] Virtue [Potency]*). As the sections of this seminal work are extremely short, I name them "stanzas" (following Levi 2018 and others) rather than "chapters".
2 For the rules applying to quotes and translations throughout this volume, see the Appendix "Note on Citations and Translations."

Open Access. © 2023 the author(s), published by De Gruyter. This work is licensed under the Creative Commons Attribution 4.0 International License. https://doi.org/10.1515/9783110799118-002

6 A.11). Rather than walking at random, we need to firmly adhere to the path the teacher has opened in front of us.

Even if they may sound unduly constraining, Laozi's and Mencius' precepts constitute a useful reminder: one does not circulate with impunity from one philosophy, from one wisdom, from one culture to another, as one would tour a country. The displacement must be triggered by a *necessity* experienced in the innermost. Following the way of water, a philosophy that wants to be comparative in scope should not proceed further as long as it has not probed deeper. In other words, a philosophy that extends over very vast areas may prove to be shallow.

For ancient Chinese thinkers, the art of studying was certainly not equivalent to accumulating knowledge. Rather, it was akin to exert the virtue of attentiveness till the truth being reached or the phenomenon being observed had been *tasted* by the students, till they were able to integrate what they had learnt into deliberation and conduct. What it meant to "study" already constituted a subject of meditation.[3]

Keeping in mind the lessons drawn from this opening, I will now ponder over the criticisms that Kant had addressed to "scholasticism". What at first glance may seem to be a rather disconcerting detour will eventually lead us to formulate the first proposition of the present work: inviting the Chinese and Western traditions into fruitful dialogue requires to carry out a detailed, at times critical appraisal of the way in which they are usually put into relation. I thus endeavor in this book a "critique" in the traditional meaning of the term: an inquiry led in order to better discern the conditions presiding over the shaping, validity, limitations or fallacies of a given body of discourses and assumptions. As stated by Foucault, "critique is not a matter of saying that things are not right as they are. It is a matter of pointing out on what kinds of assumptions, what kinds of familiar, unchallenged, unconsidered modes of thought the practices that we accept rest" (Foucault 1988, 154). Kant's critique of scholasticism will inspire the framing of my own questions as to the way comparative philosophy is understood and practiced today, for the present endeavor might suffer from limitations similar to the ones that Kant was pinpointing in the philosophical enterprise of his time. When complemented by a text-based appreciation of what "study" was entailing for ancient Chinese thinkers, this questioning will help us to find novel ways "to develop our branching by stabilizing our roots", to appropriate the analogy suggested by Yang Xiong.

Philosophizing (*philosophieren*) is by no means a laudatory term in Kant's vocabulary. It is synonymous with "repeating one's lesson". Kant's criticism of phil-

---

[3] What "studying [learning]" was meant for, and how to apply oneself to study, became a lasting topic of debate in classical China. Summarizing how a disagreement with the scholar Geng Dingxiang 耿定向 (1524–1596) evolved into a full-fledged quarrel, Li Zhi 李贽 (1527–1602) explained: "Geng Dingxiang and I argued over learning" (Lu 2020, 217).

osophical *learning*, which led him to formulate the "conceptus cosmicus" (*Weltbegriff*) of a philosophical endeavor and to contrast it with the "scholastic concept" (*Schulbegriff*),[4] maintains a relevance that goes beyond the schools and traditions (specifically the one of Christian Wolff) he had in mind at the time. Philosophy, says Kant, cannot be learnt. Whereas the "scholastic concept" is turned towards the logical perfection of a given system of knowledge, the cosmic concept orients the philosopher towards the ultimate ends of human reason (*teleologia rationis humanae*) so she may operate a breakthrough through the dense forest of knowledge systems (*KrV*, B867/AA 3: 542.26 f.).

Kant's *conceptus cosmicus* is not akin to an understanding of philosophy in a "cosmopolitan" sense, as some translations and interpretations would imply. It rather suggests that philosophy (and, in fact, every particular science) is a "universe" of cognition in which each part of the whole as well as the form taken by the articulation of these parts are dynamically subordinated to the end(s) that this universe assigns to itself. Two levels need to be distinguished here. The first one has to do with the mindset that triggers subjective rational activity: if someone has grasped something actively, "generating" it from her capacity to exercise reason and following the guiding idea that grounds the unity of the field of knowledge that she is investigating, then, she has entered the domain of philosophical activity as Kant envisions it. Conversely, if she has integrated the exact same content passively, for instance by following the cursus provided by an academic institution, such person has merely "learned, and is a plaster cast of a human being" (*KrV*, B864/AA 3: 541.11; transl. Fugate 2019, 569). However (and we enter here a second level of Kant's discussion), the building of a system of cognition through the activity of reason is not enough for accessing the *conceptus cosmicus* of what philosophy ought to be: "Philosophy as a world concept is the idea of the philosophy or philosophical doctrine that would be known and taught by the ideal philosopher" (Fugate 2019, 575). Such "ideal" doctrine is to be understood as a system of wisdom based on the idea of the necessary unity of all ends. It is not enough to think rationally and independently: you need to think *teleologically*. Said otherwise, you need to formulate what Kant elsewhere calls reflective teleological judgments – judgments informed by ends that are both necessary and universal. By contrast, the scholastic philosopher deals with the method and the ends

---

[4] "Bis dahin ist aber der Begriff von Philosophie nur ein Schulbegriff, nämlich von einem System der Erkenntnis, die nur als Wissenschaft gesucht wird, ohne etwas mehr als die systematische Einheit dieses Wissens, mithin die logische Vollkommenheit der Erkenntnis zum Zwecke zu haben. Es gibt aber noch einen Weltbegriff (*conceptus cosmicus*), der dieser Benennung jederzeit zum Grunde beleget hat, vornehmlich wenn man ihn gleichsam personifizierte, und in dem Ideal des Philosophen sich als ein Urbild vorstellte" (*KrV*, B866/AA 3: 542.19–26).

of *particular* domains of cognition without referring to their use by (and to their location vis-à-vis) other fields.

So as to insert Kant's discussion into the perspective that this book will develop, we need to put the former in context. The term "scholastic philosophy" is primarily applied to Medieval European philosophy, and, by extension, to movements and thinkers grounding their own endeavors into a reinterpretation of its principles and methods ("neo-scholastics"). The legitimacy of applying this term to other cultural contexts than Medieval Europe (Song-Ming philosophy or Tibetan Buddhism for instance) has been debated. Several thinkers have found such cultural decontextualization useful for formalizing the relationships between textual canons and their interpreting communities in various intellectual and religious settings.[5] And indeed, taken as a tool for comparative studies, the concept of "scholasticism" may rightly encompass all philosophies taught in the schools. "Schools" (universities or other institutions) have always been prone to privilege a given textual corpus that serves as the key reference-point for the debates in which teachers and students alike are engaged.

At the same time, Medieval scholasticism was characterized not only by the privileged reference to a given *corpus* but also by a method for exploiting its resources, namely the *quaestio disputata*. Though elliptical, Kant's criticism applies not only to the closure of the corpus to be taught, but also to the failure of the scholastic method to draw the freedom and the will of the interlocutors into the question at stake. Based on the dialectic of pro and contra, the *quaestio disputata* – a pedagogical device heavily favored by Medieval theological schools – relies on the demonstrative syllogism of Aristotle's *Organon*, seeking thereby to shape theology into a given form of science. The strengths of the method are obvious:

> Students were trained to see both sides of a problem, to learn the viewpoint of the ancient philosophers (the 'authorities') with regard to it, to argue on behalf of their own opinion, and to answer objections to it. [...] The masters found the "question" form an excellent one in which to express their views. [...] Even their published commentaries, which are sometimes literal exposition of the prescribed text, frequently took the question form, the commented text serving simply as the occasion for raising certain problems.
>
> (Maurer 1982 [1962], 91–92)

However, the scholastic method of argumentation (the *sed contra dicitur* opposed to the opening *videtur quod non*) must implement a founding principle, which constitutes the major premise of the syllogism, with the issue to be resolved being exposed within the minor premise. Per se, the *disputatio* requests that the principle

---

5 See especially Cabezon (1998); Tiles (2000).

belongs to the order of the question to be solved. At the same time, ensuring its validity means that said principle should derive from a higher one. The term of the process could have been met when considering the Being *qua* Being, but Aristotle had clearly stated that what comes first is absolutely out of the process of proof (Aristotle, *Met.* Γ3, 1005b; Γ4, 1006a). This is exactly why scholasticism, insofar as it was attempting "a methodological and philosophical demonstration of Christian theology as inherently rational and consistent" (Price 1992,120) was ultimately to meet with almost inextricable difficulties.

Still, it would be excessive to consider the *disputatio* as the only dialogic mode present within the scholastic tradition. The latter possessed, at least potentially, alternative ways of anchoring the truth-seeking process into dialogue and non-formalized discussion, ways that could have engaged scholastic philosophy into new venues, and that were to bear fruits a long time after the demise of the scholastic endeavor. Of particular importance here are the considerations on the life of Christ found in the third part of the *Summa Theologica:* the *modo conversationis* is what characterizes Jesus' active life, states Thomas Aquinas (*ST* III, q. 40), and this mode of familiar conversation, typical of Jesus' style of teaching (*familiariter cum hominibus conversando*), is the adequate way to convey to one's public "the truths that have been contemplated (*contemplata*)" (*ST* III, q. 40 a 1. Resp.). In other words, "conversation" is the process through which active life and contemplative life are united into one. This development should not be seen as peripheral within the scope of the *Summa.* Through his analysis of Christ's way of proceeding, described as dialogical in style and nature, Thomas captures the best of an earlier theological style, more spiritual and introspective, the freedom and plasticity of which might have corrected the logical excesses of latter-day scholasticism.[6] No tradition that maintains the ability to bring interlocutors together, to enable them to reflect and debate as a community, could ever be a fully closed system: its openings, sometimes even its contradictions define its dialogic potential.

Again, it might come as a surprise that a book focused on Chinese philosophy[7] and its current engagement with the Western tradition ponders over European

---

[6] This reading of the Quaestio 40 is developed by Theobald (2007), notably in 421 ff. and 465. See also Vermander (2011).

[7] I will not debate whether "Chinese thought" is "philosophy" (one may usefully refer to a recent summary of the discussion in Rošker 2021, 1–7). Lexical confrontations around the topic have proven to be more confusing than helpful. Nothing in my view goes against the use of the word "philosophy" in Chinese context; but I am conscious that this remains a sensitive issue, due to the anchorage of the term into the Greco-Latin tradition. I use indiscriminately the terms of "philosophy", "thought", "thought system", "wisdom system". I agree with Carine Defoort when she suggests that different ways of articulating structures and procedures of thought can be ap-

Medieval scholasticism. However, the fact of locating exchanges and breakthroughs within the framework of a canon and of the various interpretative strategies it allows is even more characteristic of the Chinese "philosophizing" that starts with the Eastern Han dynasty (25–220) than of Western scholasticism. The ever-evolving exegesis of the state-sanctioned Classics[8] was going along the systematization of thought traditions. In this regard, the ambitious endeavors of Zhu Xi 朱熹 (1130–1200) and of Thomas Aquinas (1225–1274) offer comparable features. For mentioning just one example, the epistolary exchanges of Zhu Xi and Lu Jiuyuan 陸九淵 (1139–1192) about the way to articulate the notions of "supreme polarity" (*taiji* 太極) and "non-polarity" (*wuji* 無極) are in many respects akin to a *disputatio*, by their argumentative style as well as by the publicity given to the debate (Darrobers and Dutournier 2012).

I am already sketching here a mode of philosophical rapprochement that does not start by comparing or contrasting concepts and worldviews. Rather, it first focuses on the way various traditions relate to their canons and inscribe thought processes into social settings. A *formal* rapprochement, so to speak – and yet, one that is certainly very significant. We reflect and debate within textual and societal frameworks, and their deciphering is part of the process of understanding, interpreting – and comparing.

The attention to be given to such textual and social anchoring is part of the philosophical endeavor proper. When Gadamer, in *Truth and Method*, reflects upon what it means to "understand" and "interpret", he starts with the analysis of a concrete historical situation: that which, in the second half of the 18th century and especially in the first half of the nineteenth, translated the methods employed in the natural sciences into a paradigm through which to judge the progress recorded in the knowledge of humankind, its moral nature and its social setting. Gadamer's considerations on our relation to the classics are anchored in this historical recovery, which leads him to circulate from one period to another and yet always brings him back to the rupture from which he begins his inquiry. Likewise (to quote a very different work), in *The Order of Things*, Michel Foucault endeavors to move away from a reflection centered on the meaning of what a given subject may express towards an investigation bearing on the mental systems by which

---

proached as "family resemblances", as Wittgenstein puts it (Defoort 2001, 407). Debates on lexical options are often red herrings.

8 I will write "Classics" when referring exclusively to texts included in a state-sanctioned canon ("The Four Books and Five Classics"), opting for "classics" when the term is used in a more general sense. The distinction has its importance: The *Zhuangzi* and the *Daodejing* are "classics" but not "Classics". As I generally refer to texts that were largely commented upon – independently from their canonical status – I will privilege the writing "classics" throughout this book.

ideas are produced. But Foucault needs to proceed through a long historical wandering which begins in the 16th century and takes us through several *epistemes* and the transformations that affect them over time. It is the historical study of these epistemes and their transformations that explains how "Man" was constructed both as a sovereign *subject* and as an *object* of knowledge.

Although of infinitely more modest size and ambition, this work is inspired by the way of proceeding initiated by Gadamer and Foucault. It will revisit a historical phenomenon – the encounter between Chinese and Western philosophy after the re-opening of the latter in the 1980s – and, when needed, will turn towards the "prehistory" of this phenomenon, i.e., the intellectual cross-fertilization that happened from the beginning of the seventeenth century till the first half of the twentieth. It recognizes that only an interdisciplinary approach and a reflective review of such historical developments can assess their significance. It does not stop with the analysis of sequential events. Rather, it relies on it to unfold questions about what it means to mutually understand each other (*intercompréhension*) – about the conditions under which mutual understanding takes place – and also about the way "comparative philosophy" is conducted today. And this is where we meet again with Kant's *Weltbegriff* and *Schulbegriff*: "Comparative philosophy", as I will describe its unfolding for the last 40 years or so in the Chinese-Western context, has evolved into a scholastic endeavor. Again, let us not immediately take the term in too pejorative a fashion. Scholasticism, as Kant fully recognizes, should not be the object of a caricature: it is concerned with the formal perfection of a domain of cognition, even if it does not operate the jump that (Kantian) philosophy dares to make when it enters its "world concept": to investigate the source, the nature and the boundaries of all cognition from an architectonic perspective. We will thus pay respectful attention to the way East-West comparative philosophy proceeds, and notably to its frequent reliance on the commentarial approach of the classics – an archetypal scholastic endeavor if there is one. However, we may occasionally also meet with expressions of "scholasticism" that, by *philosophizing*, by mostly arguing over terms and textual interpretations, somehow hinder our access to investigative, unfettered thinking.

There are three ways of approaching Chinese philosophy from a comparative viewpoint. The first one starts from a set of questions that crisscross times and cultures – say, around the proclivities that human nature may or not contain, or about the ideal ruler or political regime, or yet on matters of self-cultivation, its methods and ultimate goals. It unfolds an array of hypotheses and answers which, partly divide, partly gather on common grounds a shortlist of Chinese and non-Chinese thinkers. The second approach elects to contrast the basic tenets of Chinese thought with another set of axioms, often with the avowed objective to liberate the understanding of Chinese thinking from the framework of concepts and presuppositions anchored in the Western tradition (and such work also means to liberate Western thinking from the same presuppositions). The third one pragmatically studies the dynamics of reactions and interactions awakened by one of the successive encounters between the Chinese canon and other canonical traditions, encounters that took place alongside the progressive introduction into China of, first, Buddhist/Indian metaphysical and logical vocabulary and syntax, second, Western categories of thought and beliefs in their various, sometimes conflicting expressions.

Undertaken with due caution, each of these approaches proves to be fruitful. And they tend to complement each other, even though their respective proponents are prompt to find faults in their counterparts' designs and presuppositions. Still, there are trends in comparative philosophy as elsewhere. For the last 40 years or so, a specific version of the second approach has awakened a considerable interest, generating an impressive amount of literature. One of the goals that this book assigns to itself is to assess its results, and to do so from the standpoint that critical distance suggests. I will mainly ponder over the contrast often suggested between Chinese "correlative thinking" (or similar expressions) and Western "ontology", and I will question its accuracy and relevance. While recognizing how important it is to contrast traditions and systems taken as a whole, I will also suggest hermeneutical strategies that avoid the trap of swiftly "essentializing" the thought structures under study.

Let me here roughly summarize the mainstream understanding of the Sino-Western variant of comparative philosophy, as I understand its premise, as well as the reasons that make me write this book in response:

In the grand narratives of intellectual history sketched in a number of Western and Chinese accounts,[9] "Western thought" effectively starts (begins its journey towards world prominence, so to speak) around the time of Plato, to whom Aristotle offers both correctives and continuation, and then develops in an almost straight line that runs through Cicero, Augustine, Thomas Aquinas, Descartes ... before finding a kind of double apex in Kant and Hegel. The latter may constitute the "apotheosis" of Western thought, both in the sense that it signals a further culmination just after the one already achieved by Kant and in that it announces an inevitable "decay", which may also be described as a welcome metamorphosis, though Heidegger is sometimes tasked with the same role. Thinkers as diverse as Nietzsche, Wittgenstein, Whitehead, Dewey or Bergson (and, later on, Foucault/Deleuze, at least for some of the authors whom we will comment) testify

---

9 I will identify some of these accounts in Chapters 1 to 3, and give at the same time more diversified and nuanced portrayals of them.

to a (praiseworthy) work of deconstruction within the Western tradition itself. From its origins onwards, the latter would have relied upon the building-up of an *ontology*, which not only presupposes the existence of a master-category (Being, induced by the features of the family of languages within which Western thought developed), but also its assumption into a substantialist view of reality that puts "relations" and "processes" into a subordinate position. The same view explains the primacy given to the autonomy of individual beings, including human subjects. Various thought systems extended these premises into the logical, theological or yet political realms.

In contrast, according to the same meta-narrative, ancient Chinese thought originated from divinatory speculations that led (a) to stress the *fluidity* of all phenomena and forms of life, (b) to focus on the *relationships* governing the passage from one state of matter (and one state of affairs) to another, (c) to describe the *patterns* of cosmic and social existence by establishing correlations among the various spheres of existence, and ultimately (d) to determine how to *best adapt* (individually and collectively) to these overarching patterns. Challenged by the irruption of a thought syntax (and a correlated lexicon) imported from India, Chinese thought was eventually able to rephrase its original intuitions. It did so partly thanks to the fact that Buddhist thought was also arguing for the *inanity* of all substantified "beings" (though by following another path than the one traveled in ancient China), and, for another part, thanks to the inventiveness displayed in the use of ancient concepts such as *li* 理 (patterns), and *qi* 氣 (energy, fluid, or even matter). Chinese thought thus progressively systematized its intuitions and concepts into syntheses embracing all the levels of existence and intellectual speculation. The political and gnoseological commotions brought in by the shaping of unbalanced relationships with the West led two or three generations of Chinese philosophers to reconsider their own tradition primarily through concepts and methods rooted in Western philosophy. The current task rather lies in recapturing the premises proper to Chinese thought, so as to build upon the resources they offer or, at least, to live and think in the tension that the reference to a "dual ontology" necessarily triggers.[10]

---

[10] I will discuss the notion of "dual ontology" in Chapter 3. Its promoters do not consider its use contradictory with the Western origin of the term "ontology" per se, as they contrast two ways of perceiving and conceptualizing phenomena. This is reinforced by the fact that the usual Chinese translation of the term "ontology" (*bentilun* 本體論) is sometimes used as a direct equivalent of the technical term used by the "Western" philosopher whose work is translated, and sometimes as referring to a China-specific concept: "Instead of a study of being, *bentilun* is a study of *ben* (root, origin) and *ti* (stem, body) of things" (Li and Cauvel 2006, 40; see also Rošker 2021, 36–38).

This meta-narrative deciphers texts, partly in function of concepts that it extracts from their reading (but sometimes takes out of context), partly according to notions that are not found in these texts and are superimposed over them. It constructs syntheses, equivalences and oppositions that are somehow too well balanced for not triggering questioning. Besides, the concept of "Chinese philosophy" supported by the said vision sometimes refers to the thought developed until around the demise of the Western Han (2000 years ago), sometimes to the various stages of intellectual reformulation that China underwent after it entered into contact with Buddhism and, more largely, with Indian texts and reasoning. In the same way, "Western philosophy" may refer to the Greek source and its Roman subsidiary, or else to the philosophical developments that occurred from Augustine onwards, as if Greek and Semitic sources had entered naturally into fusion. In such reconstructions, Indian and biblical ways of sensing and reasoning are extremely difficult to appreciate and assess independently, due to the fact that they are primarily located vis-à-vis the "Chinese" and "Western" sources that they have respectively contributed to renew and shape.

As I see the task at hand, the critique of such positions is a preliminary for tackling the following question: in today's context, what style of cross-cultural philosophical engagement should be imagined and fostered? Cross-cultural philosophical dialogue is indeed indispensable to the revival of philosophies that could be both local and genuinely dialogic, if not "cosmopolitan".

The first two chapters will focus upon the dominant model propounded by Western sinologists when it comes to comparing the Western philosophical tradition with the Chinese one. I will detail its main topics and assertions before dealing with lexical and translation issues, crucial for the appreciation of Chinese thought. The third chapter will shift to Chinese narratives about local, comparative and global philosophies, notably assessing its self-positioning vis-à-vis Western authors, topics and concepts. A second part will follow, also composed of three chapters. It will attempt at articulating the conditions under which Chinese philosophy can meaningfully cross-fertilize with other traditions in global debates and endeavors. Chapter 4 will offer a general reading of ancient Chinese classics, alternative to the one that presently dominates the landscape described in Chapters 1 to 3. In Chapter 5, I will harness the results and insights already gathered, offering a kind of blueprint as to the way to positively draw upon different philosophical traditions to engage common questions and pursue shared endeavors. A last chapter will present four cases of ongoing transcultural philosophical dialogues and the promises they bear, while my conclusion will attempt to recapitulate our journey and to open up further perspectives.

Part I: **The Limits of an Encounter**

Chapter 1
The Gardens of Philosophy

Let us imagine Chinese and Western philosophical traditions as *gardens*, each of them displaying its distinctive style and ornaments. You may also visualize two parks facing each other, with various enclosures in their midst – rock garden or rose garden according to the case. This is more or less how sinologists or comparative philosophers envision their field of study. Comparative philosophy is akin to landscaping: it watches over two premises located in the same resort, the one mirroring the other (which being the mirror of which depending upon your vantage point). The two cannot be separated one from the other since the concepts mobilized for describing the first are to be understood in reference to the second. What I call here "the Western blueprint" corresponds to the representation of our philosophical gardens as endeavored by Western scholars, a representation that largely depends (as we will see in our second chapter) upon the manufacturing of a specific lexicon. In parallel, the third chapter will describe the Chinese contribution to the same landscaping operation. These are not two concurrent representations: Chinese and Western academics often share common interests in creating a mirror-image of their traditions, even if their perspectives differ in other respects.

Mapping and Mappers

The general design of our twin parks is easy to describe: the Castle of Comparative Philosophy provides the two of them with a common entrance. From there, one can take a turn to the left and go through eight Chinese-inspired landmarks, from which one contemplates their Western counterparts on the other side of the resort. Alternatively, one can start on the right and enjoy the opposite view. In both cases, the circuit leads to the gardens of Process Philosophy. Table 1 shows a general map of the resort so as to guide us throughout the wanderings that will follow.

Tab. 1: The Twin Gardens of Chinese and Western Philosophies

Entry Door: Castle of Comparative Philosophy	
On the Chinese side	**On the Western side**
The-World-as-it-is	Cosmos
Becoming	Permanence
Non-Dual Cognition	Dualistic Reasoning
Correlative Thinking	Substance
Analogies/Aesthetic	Theory/Dialectic
Examples	Taxonomies
Immanence	Transcendence/Universalism
Plurality of Meanings	Rational Ethos
Gardens of Process Philosophy – Exit Door	

This mapping is inspired by a book published in 1995 by David L. Hall and Roger T. Ames, *Anticipating China*.[11] Roger Ames (b. 1947) and David Hall (1937–2001) have exerted much influence in the field of Chinese-Western philosophy, and have been joined by many colleagues and students. They themselves followed the path opened up by a few predecessors, notably A.C. Graham (1919–1991). Together with David Hall and Henry Rosemont Jr. (1934–2017), Roger Ames has been and remains the most influential spokesman of a current that reads Chinese philosophy in the light of a worldview influenced by American pragmatism and process philosophy. His personal and institutional contribution to the field (the latter operating notably through the journals *Philosophy East and West* and *China Review International* as well as through two book series at the State University of New York Press, which include a number of groundbreaking studies) has contributed to define anew the field of East-West comparative philosophy.

A number of collective volumes testify to the central position that the vision pioneered by Graham, Ames, Hall or Rosemont has acquired. The collection of essays entitled *One Corner of the Square. Essays on the Philosophy of Roger T. Ames*, published in 2021, constitutes a remarkable example of this trend. The editors, Ian M. Sullivan and Joshua Mason, summarize the achievements of Ames and like-minded colleagues as follows:

---

[11] I slightly changed the structure of *Anticipating China*'s expository structure by amalgamating Sections 5 and 6 and Sections 8 and 9 of the first chapter.

> Bringing rigorous attention to the philosophical background implied by early translations of key Chinese ideas, these scholars sought to present Chinese philosophy "on its own terms." With a reflective methodology that produced creative translations revealing new ways of conceiving the cosmos, knowledge, and ethics, Ames and his collaborators have brought Chinese philosophical traditions away from orientalist projections and into constructive cross-cultural dialogue on critical issues of our time. This has meant rooting out the metaphysical and epistemological ideals that are part of mainstream Euro-American philosophy's very language, and self-consciously employing a vocabulary with a bit less semantic baggage.
>
> (Sullivan and Mason 2021, xvi)

Presenting Chinese philosophy on its own terms is indeed what all students of Chinese philosophy writing in another language ought to do, and this necessarily entails to deal with a number of translation issues regarding lexicon, syntax and context. In many respects the 1687 *Confucius Sinarum Philosophus*, the first published translation of three of the Four Books[12] was already doing just that: the Jesuits Philippe Couplet, Christian Wolfgang Herdrich, Prospero Intorcetta and François de Rougemont had grounded their efforts upon the manuscript translations of their predecessors, undertaken for almost a century at that time (Meynard 2011). The enthusiasm they showed for the doctrine of Confucius is well documented, and they made their fervor spread throughout Europe. Fostered by Jesuit Relations and translations, a China-generated shift in episteme questioned the consistency of spheres of knowledge (biblical chronology, logic and metaphysics, the distinction between human wisdom and biblical revelation) that were previously thought unbreakable from Christianity considered not only as a faith but as an overarching knowledge system. The translation endeavor continued almost uninterrupted, progressively enriched by the number of languages in which it took place, as well as by the variety of viewpoints of the ones who undertook it – Catholics, Protestants, Russian Orthodox, and fervently anticlerical scholars...

The Genealogy of the Comparative Endeavor

From the start, and for good part of its development, the sinological endeavor has been comparative and self-reflective. During the 17th and 18th century, translations of Chinese classics allowed for inchoate attempts at comparative theology, anticipating the way the continuation of the translation endeavor framed the debate on the methods and goals of comparative philosophy during the 20th century. In fact, the questions raised in the West as to the nature and implications of the Chi-

---

12 It included the *Analects*, the *Great Learning* and the *Doctrine of the Mean*, omitting the *Mencius*.

nese *Weltanschauung* were more or less the same in both cases. These successive attempts defined the way Sinology started to delineate its field and methods. Somehow, a "hermeneutical triangle" was drawn by the correlative shaping of sinological knowledge, the comparative reading of classics, and preliminary attempts at doing, first, comparative theology, and, later on, comparative philosophy.

It is true that the hermeneutic triangle drawn by Sinology, the cross-reading of the classics and comparative theology/philosophy was left largely unexploited during the 19th century and the beginning of the 20th century. Its exploration, from the 1920s onwards, was attempted again by modern Chinese philosophers, through ways and means utterly different from the ones privileged by their predecessors (we will come back to this in the course of Chapter 3). The Western canon that these philosophers were dealing with had largely changed, both modified and enriched by 19th-century philosophers. In contrast, the frontiers of the Chinese canon had remained strikingly constant. It was rather its relevancy that had become object of debate and anguish.

Still, exceptions to the "decay of the comparative endeavor" undergone during one century and half can be easily found, notably in the work of some great translators. Legge's dealings with the Taoist classics constitute a case in point, brilliantly analyzed by Girardot:

> The issue of Taoism at the end of the nineteenth century was two-fold. From one perspective, it could be carefully defined, classified and tamed as a textual object or sacred book-religion by Müller and Legge's relatively reverent and civil methods of comparison. Yet in the sense suggested by Giles' more overtly suspicious, combative and non-comparative approach, it could be made to disappear altogether as a 'religion' by being reduced to other fragmented, though ostensibly more 'objective' and 'natural', philological and historical categories. [...] Whereas before, as a missionary, [Legge], as the discoverer of a Chinese Sky God, had been viciously attacked by other more conservative missionaries on theological grounds, now, as a professional scholar, he was assaulted for the same findings by Sinologists who were profoundly disturbed by the ambiguity and fragmentary nature of the textual evidence. [...] Sinology after Leggism was mostly satisfied with what was taken as the manifest secularity and rationality of the Classical Confucian canon – principles that were ironically also based largely on Legge's translation of the Classic.
>
> (Girardot 1999, 116–117)

What was indeed at stake in Legge's attempt was its ultimate feasibility and legitimacy: could one associate into the same "hermeneutical triangle" Sinology, the cross-study of classics and comparative theology? The boldness of this attempt could only alienate him from the majority of the missionaries as well as from the quasi-totality of the sinologists. Till today, questions similar to the ones Legge and his contradictors dealt with continue to crisscross academia.

Let me remark that, if these questions were framed in theological terms, the term "comparative theology" was not in use yet. Still, from Ricci to Legge, the endeavor was comparative. From the start, Jesuit narratives were providing evidences that religious traditions and political systems observed in Europe were a product of history rather than being inscribed in nature, and (most importantly) that remarkable civilizational achievements could take shape and evolve on bases other than those of the Mediterranean and European civilizations. Confucianism in particular provided the model of a "civil religion" based on reason and guarantor of social order without being bound to the dogmas of the Christian religion. Descriptions of Chinese political and technological practices were similarly deconstructing the codes of Western knowledge. Recalling these well-known historical facts may help us to put into perspective present attempts at presenting Chinese thought "on its own terms". It is necessary to come back to the genealogy that has shaped a field of knowledge when trying to assess the most recent contributions that have taken place within it.

Additionally, I do not think that former translations and discussions of Chinese texts were all rooted in "orientalist projections" – far from it. One wonders whether it is not rather the insistence of present-day Comparatists on "differences", exclusive from a recognition of any commonality, that is not, in essence, orientalist. Edward Slingerland has labeled "neo-Orientalism" the claim of "radical otherness" (Slingerland 2013, 6–10). In another contribution, Slingerland calls Ames' and Hall's enterprise "constructivist". He describes it as inspired by a "normative mission" and ultimately working in "the theological mode" (Slingerland 2019, 291–294). In fact, Slingerland's analysis anticipates some of the critical remarks I will develop in the course of this chapter (see notably Slingerland 2019, 33–50). I found it necessary to take up the subject again, and this for the following reasons: Slingerland focuses his analysis on the supposed "Holism" that good part of present-day comparative philosophy finds in the Chinese tradition, and convincingly shows that such representation is misleading. At the same time, his discussion centers upon the mind-body relationship, using arguments taken mainly from cognitive sciences. While agreeing with most of its conclusions, I have tried to analyze what is at stake in the debate from within the realm of comparative philosophy, working from textual evidences (both Chinese and Western) to a greater extent that Slingerland's excellent book endeavors to do.

Going one step further: in the paragraph already quoted, Sullivan and Mason underline the need for "creative translations". All (good) translations are necessarily creative in some respects – although "creativity" meets with its limits when it applies to the art of conveying a body of thought and experiences into another language and culture. As we will see in Chapter 2, the real question is to decide whether Chinese ancient texts do or do not need to be rendered by means of a highly specialized lexicon, purposefully – and creatively – shaped for the field. I will argue for the contrary thesis, for reasons that will be presented in due time.

Towards a Post-comparative Philosophy?

The vision that Sullivan and Mason sketch opens up another important issue. Ames has insights to contribute both to the framing of the questions associated with it and to their potential resolution (see notably Ames 2010 and 2011): how do the goal of "presenting Chinese philosophy on its own terms" and the one to engage "into constructive cross-cultural dialogue on critical issues of our time" articulate one with the other? Does not the restitution of the original concepts and approaches of a given body of thought rather make it less easy to find points of engagement with another tradition? Does it not complicate the dialogue rather than allow for a conversation? Additionally, who is going to decide that such or such system of thought has been presented "on its own terms" when it is necessarily done in a language and in a time that differs to the extreme from the ones of its elaboration? And are not the "terms" into which we introduce the system fatally modeled on the questions (and conclusions) we had in mind from the start? The current overarching reference to pragmatism and process philosophy (fields associated with a very specific lexical range) certainly raises such a suspicion. However, it would be both unfair and unwise to transform a mere suspicion into a definitive criticism. Let us unfold the questions I just formulated throughout the course of this book. Our two last chapters will be dealing again with the conditions under which comparative philosophy can be both scrupulous and creative.

So as to better assess how central has become the perspective sketched in the preceding paragraphs, this for sinology as well as for comparative philosophy, we need to explore a bit further the contributions that have paced the field. Besides the volume of essays edited by Joshua Mason and Ian M. Sullivan, other collections enrich the terms of the debate. For instance, an issue of the journal *Frontiers of Philosophy in China* dated from December 2012 contains an interesting response by Ames to some of the objections its works have raised: Ames locates his intellectual project into the "evolutionary process" through which the Confucian thought has been commented and enriched from one generation to another till the present time, when it is now ready to play a prominent role on the world stage. In other words, Confucians studies are meant to become an essential component for the endeavor sometimes dubbed "world philosophy". Among still other contributions, Behuniak has edited a Festschrift in homage to Ames that helps to assess the importance of the latter in the shaping of present-day comparatist enterprises (Behuniak 2018). Also, a direct engagement between Ames and some contemporary Chinese philosophers is provided by a volume edited by Zhao Dunhua and George F. McLean, conjointly published by the Department of Philosophy of Peking University and the Council for Research in Values and Philosophy (Zhao and McLean 2007). In this volume, one contribution at least (the one by Kelly James Clark) engages into a factual discussion of Ames' denial of the theistic dimension of Chinese ancient Confucianism, a point we will discuss in the next chapter.

Differing from the position of Ames and Hall, *The Philosophical Challenge from China*, edited by Brian Bruya, makes a plea for intercultural (inter-philosophical, one might say) borrowings, this independently from the context where ideas originated, handling concepts and insights "in a way that exploits the inherent plasticity of all ideas" (Bruya 2015, xvii). In parallel, Ma and Van Brakel recognize the way the Western tradition has presently framed the philosophical landscape, and they advocate for a cautious way of dissociating the reading of Chinese text from such tradition, a way that would avoid the traps set by universalism and relativism alike (Ma and Van Brakel 2016). For these authors and like-minded ones, "universalism is impossible, but that does not mean we are enclosed in one conceptual scheme (relativism), for we are always involved with an indefinite number of conceptual schemes, but they do not add up to one overarching scheme" (Møllgaard 2021, 383[13]).

In the course of our inquiry, I will allude to other attempts at doing comparative philosophy with a focus on Chinese resources, among them the ones of Yuk Hui (*Art and Cosmotechnics*, 2020), Jana Rošker (*Interpreting Chinese Philosophy*, 2021) and Fabian Heubel (*Was ist chinesische Philosophie?*, 2021).[14] Whatever the divergences that may exist from one version to another, these attempts may be loosely classified into a larger perspective: the one that aims at grounding a "post-comparative" philosophy (Moeller 2018, 42) informed by the conviction that philosophy "is, in essence, not a tool for finding truth, but rather a means for an endless search for constantly changing truths" (Rošker 2021, 139). I am not sure I fully agree with the package of assumptions that governs such endeavor. In what follows, I will rather try to unfold a dialogic style grounded upon the *experiential* and *teleological* dimensions of philosophical thinking: if my attempt is

---

13 See also the debate between Møllgaard (2005) and Ames (2005).
14 Heubel (2021) challenges at length the positions developed by François Jullien and (on the opposite side) Jean-François Billeter. In this book I have avoided discussing these authors: this would not have significantly enriched the discussion as I frame it. The works debated in this chapter follow a line that is often similar to the one of Jullien, even if they do so in a markedly different style. Besides, the argumentative style proper to François Jullien has made discussions bearing upon his argument generally inconclusive. One can identify the issues at stake by referring to Jullien (2009, 2015); Billeter (2006) and Keck (2009).

"post-comparative", it is only in that it subordinates comparisons to the undertaking of tasks to be identified in the context of a cross-cultural community. I will detail the enterprise throughout Chapters 4 to 6, once I have elucidated the context in which comparative philosophy is practiced today.

We are now ready to leave the map for the territory, in other words, to go for a walk around the main landmarks that define the current-day dominant understanding of the Chinese-Western engagement. We will follow the map already sketched, and we will refer not only to Ames and Hall's above-mentioned book but also to writers who have joined them in their endeavor – or sometimes have developed a distinct voice. While presenting as faithfully as possible the arguments at stake, I will hint at the difficulties I perceive. Some of these difficulties I will deal with in this chapter. I will keep others for the discussion I develop from Chapter 2 onwards.

The Castle of Comparative Philosophy

We enter our gardens through the castle where "Comparative Philosophy" lies half-sleeping. Comparative philosophy has not fully awakened yet: she remains closely wrapped in the mantle of "Sameness", which prevents her from breathing and extending her limbs at ease. "Sameness" is the garb that Comparative Philosophy needs to get rid of:

> In the enterprise of comparative philosophy, difference is more interesting than similarity. That is, the contrasting presuppositions of the Chinese and Anglo-European traditions are [...] a presently more fruitful subject of philosophic reflection than are the shared assumptions.
>
> (Hall and Ames 1987, 5)

Is this remark self-evident? Behuniak challenges it to some extent. Still, he intends less at correcting the assertion than at bending it:

> If the next turn is a re-turn to appreciating sameness, with an eye toward moderating some of the more controversial claims that Hall and Ames have made, then I think the field is going in circles. The next turn, I believe, must be to rise above sameness and difference, to cycle beyond comparison altogether, and to embrace that "sort of commonality" that Hall and Ames promised at the outset – one that unites contemporary thinkers in a culturally complex but shared world. [...] At this juncture, sameness and difference have become the Scylla and Charybdis through which comparative philosophers must cross, and those attempting passage watchfully scrutinize one another.
>
> (Behuniak 2001, 5)

I bring the challenge one step further: in my view, sameness is as interesting as differences are. One might even argue that similarities are more enlightening than differences: similarities may point towards some essential facts – for instance, that reason, moral sense and/or other faculties obey universal patterns, the human brain being wired accordingly. Or else, they may confirm to us that the number of questions around which the mind and human communities revolves is necessarily limited. Pierre Hadot says: "In the final analysis, there are relatively few possible attitudes with respect to our existence, and, irrespective of historical influence, different civilizations have been led to similar attitudes" (Hadot 1995, 699[15]). In contrast, differences could be attributed to historical or cultural "accidents", and thus take the status of *curiosa*.

I would not enter so far into this line of reasoning. I would rather argue that, *a priori, sameness and differences are equally interesting and meaningful*. I do not argue here that the human mind functions necessarily according to the same pattern everywhere, or that the number of existential questions is pretty limited – though these are obviously more than mere hypotheses. Still, such assertions probably need serious reformulation. I argue that privileging difference over similarity blurs how we deal with basic questions on cognition and the human condition.

When doing comparison, we do not wish to focus on sameness or difference per se. We rather try not to dwell on "constructed sameness" or "constructed differences", as both of them constitute a trap: they erase or highlight this or that aspect of a given textual corpus so as to strategically oppose (or, conversely, identify) it with another corpus. For instance, one may want to "prove" that the ancient Chinese had benefited from God's "natural revelation", even without the support of biblical scriptures (this is "constructed sameness"). Or, conversely, one wishes to establish that the whole of Chinese thinking is governed by the ideas of "immanence" and "process", which are essentially foreign to the classical Western toolbox ("constructed difference"). As a consequence, the commentator may conveniently forget some texts (sometimes considered apocryphal, without any serious basis[16]) or yet decide upon lexical rectifications when it comes to some key concepts. Our discussion on lexical issues (Chapter 2) will provide ample examples of such constructivist approach.

---

15 I follow here the modified translation of this passage offered by Force (2011), 17.
16 Herbert Giles' hypotheses as to the dating of the *Laozi* constitute a celebrated example of such ill-grounded suspicions (Girardot 1999).

Cosmos and "The-World-as-It-Is"

Let us start our wandering by the Western bank, and visit first a landmark that presents itself as a microcosm, i.e., modeled on the cosmos. The concept of "Cosmos", write Hall and Ames, refers to *world-order*, the latter emerging from an initial state of chaos, through the imposition of laws that engineer a state of permanence (of rest). Both the original chaos and the body of laws that overcomes it are variously described from one variant of the "Western narrative" to another (*Genesis* is not the *Theogony* is not the *Timaeus*). In all cases, *mythologizing* (telling stories about the Origin) will lead to *philosophizing* (a specific world-order will be accounted for through the unearthing of organizing "principles", this last notion giving rise to the one of causation). "The central components of the concept of 'rationality' are grounded in the myths of origins to which the founders of the Hellenic and Hebraic traditions appealed" (Hall and Ames 1995, 11).

It is more difficult to characterize the Chinese-style landmark facing the Western bank: Hall and Ames approach it on the negative mode. Some cosmogonic myths, they concede, are given written expression during the Han dynasty. However, these accounts do not speak of the emergence of a cosmos but rather of a multiplicity of phenomena. Accordingly, there is no belief in a single-ordered-world; while Greece privileges rest, permanence and causation, "the Chinese 'world-as-such' […] requires no external principle or agency to account for it" (Hall and Ames 1995, 185). Frederick W. Mote offers a partly similar argument when he writes: "The genuine Chinese cosmogony is that of organismic process, meaning that all the parts of the entire cosmos belong to one organic whole and that they all interact as participants in one spontaneously self-generating life process" (Mote 1989, 15).

Here, I will not deal with the reconstruction of the "Western" narrative as described above. Still, let me make a passing observation on *Genesis* I, as we will come back to this text later in the course of this chapter: the *tohû wabohû* of the Hebrew is much more similar to the desolation of a wasteland than to the Greek "chaos": if disordered, the latter abounds in resources and energies (Beauchamp 2005 [1969], 161–163). Accordingly, the first and the second give rise to very different world orders. As there are "chaos" and "chaos", there are also "order" and "order".

Now, what does the Chinese "world-as-such" look like, and to what extent is it justified to say, as Hall and Ames do, that (1) it does not take the shape of a specific world-order; (2) is not characterized by permanence; (3) does not give rise to the notion of causality; and (4) is not the result of any agency external to it? The last point would warrant further specification: Ames' and Hall's statement sometimes implies that the universe is not submitted to any agency at all – that all things happen of themselves –, and, in other places, that it is not submitted to any agency external to it.

First, let me stress the fact that cosmogonies had been spreading early and everywhere in the territory today called China. They were comprising a number of variants, making the study of Chinese mythology as rich as the one undertaken in any territory of the world.[17] In fact, tackling mainly Hall's and Ames' accounts, Paul Goldin has already successfully deconstructed "the myth that China has no creation myth" (Goldin 2008), and has illustrated the pervasiveness of stories such as the ones of Pangu and Nüwa as well as the cosmogonic echoes found in the *Laozi* and the *Zhuangzi*, among others. However, my account differs slightly from Goldin's: I see Chinese creation myths (the existence of which cannot be doubted) as having been somehow *displaced* from one setting to another. This thesis requires a few developments:

Chinese and Roman civilizations shared a common trait: orthodoxies (Confucian orthodoxy in the Chinese case) soon privileged historical narratives over cosmological ones. The real birth of the (civilized) world had to coincide with the apparition of the Sage Emperors in one case, with the founding of Rome (Livy's *Ab Urbe condita* comes to mind) in the other. The Roman motto is "From the foundation of Rome onwards...", and not "from the creation of the world onwards..." The Confucian narrative is very close to such a perspective: the surge of civilization provides one with the adequate historical and moral vantage point. In contrast, Indian and Greek cultures gave prominence to a storytelling more cosmic than political. Said otherwise, in the case of China and Roma, the moral-political imperative (history is the ultimate moral and political teacher) selected heavily among available narratives. And yet, in China, notwithstanding the way the Confucian tradition and the state apparatus proceeded to erase mythological narratives, cosmogonic stories and topics can still be found in abundance. *Zhuangzi, Huainanzi, Shanhaijing*,[18] the *Songs of Chu* (*Chuci* 楚辞) were not inventing the stories of origins that they narrate. Rather, they re-tell them, conferring upon them a given interpretation, the way Greek philosophers were also doing. The way *Zhuangzi* proceeded with mythological narratives is especially noteworthy, and we will find occasions to illustrate this point. Even in the Confucian literature, myths are constantly reworked: whoever did the editing of the *Classic of Odes* gave us a precious

---

[17] Among a rich literature on the subject, cf. Birrell (1993); Le Blanc and Mathieu (2008); Granet (1994 [1926]).

[18] "[In the first five chapters of the *Shanhaijing*], for each mountain details are given [...] about the form of its gods and the nature of appropriate sacrifices. Most of these gods are animal-human hybrids. [...] It is in effect the earliest example of a 'register of sacrifices' (*sidian* 祀典)" (Lagerwey 2000, 13).

repertoire of stories that take the ordering of the world as their leitmotiv. In the *Mencius* (*Teng wen gong* 滕文公 – 3 A.4 and 3B.9), the shaping of a cosmic order is akin to ridding the world of flooding waters, excessive vegetation, and harmful beasts. Later works collect popular versions of myths still circulating. Let us think for instance of the *Forgotten Tales* (*Shiyiji* 拾遺記): if its compiler, Wang Jia 王嘉, died in 390 CE, it is most unlikely that he forged the stories that he claims to be part of an oral tradition not entirely recorded by the classics. We are rather in presence of mythical variants, as all mythological corpuses, oral and/or written, deal with various versions of foundational stories and develop in the process through which they solve the contradictions fostered by the narrative effervescence. The substance and details of the variants found in the *Forgotten Tales* agree with the hints provided by the *Shanhaijing*, the *Zhuangzi* or yet the *Tianwen* 天問 chapter of the *Songs of Chu*, among others.

In all the texts that I mentioned the story of Yu the Great (*Da Yu* 大禹), the tamer of the Great Flood, stands prominent. Marcel Granet has retraced the quasi-omnipresence of this figure in the chain of myths that grounds the representations (and later on, the philosophical and social constructions) of ancient China (Granet 1994 [1926]). If one looks for a story narrating the passage from "Chaos" to "Cosmos", a story as strongly articulated as the ones found in the so-called Western narratives, none will offer more striking features than this one. One may object that the story of Yu the Great does not speak about the creation of the world properly speaking but merely about a "Flood myth", as there exists one in so many civilizations. However, the Yu narrative operates a projection from *creation* to *re-creation*. And this for an obvious reason: *cosmic and political orders in China could not be separated.* On the one hand, the ordering of the cosmos is a prerequisite for the establishment and consolidation of the political realm. On the other hand, a well-ordered government concurs to the maintaining of cosmic order, notably by the fact that it sustains the performance of the appropriate rituals – and performing rituals, assert Xunzi and other authors, is the task that humankind must accomplish so as to ensure cosmic harmony.[19]

So, can we support the idea of an opposition between a "cosmos", on the one hand, and a world deprived of order – the one thousand things being "just there" –, on the other hand? Decidedly not. The world, in China, obeys laws without which things would fall apart. Let us come back to the story of Yu the Great, the hero who worked unceasingly to go from the chaos of the Flood to the cosmic-political order that guarantees the subsistence of "All Things Under Heaven

---

[19] Besides the main textual source on the subject, Xunzi's *Lilun* 禮論 treatise, one may refer to the interpretation of this text and related ones offered by Sato (2010).

[tianxia 天下]".²⁰ His labors are eventually rewarded by a heavenly revelation, namely, the "Universal Pattern" that orders the world. I am alluding here to the *Hongfan* 洪範 chapter of the *Classic of Documents* (*Hongfan: Great Plan, Universal Pattern*), one of the oldest sections of this Classic. It presents all phenomena (natural elements, behaviors, political matters, calendar, sources of happiness and unhappiness) in combinations based on the numbers five and nine:

> When Gun fought the Great Flood, he upset the Five elements. This provoked *Di* 帝²¹ to great anger and as a result he did not share with him the great Plan [Universal Pattern] in its Nine sections. Because of this, the fundamental principles were lost and Gun was forced into exile, where he died. It fell to Yu to rise up and to take on the mantle of this task, whereupon Heaven [*Tian* 天] shared with Yu the Great Plan and its Nine sections. And so it was that everything was again in order.
> (*Classic of Documents, Hongfan.* Translation Palmer 2014, 94, modified)

The text continues with a description of the phenomenal world (its building blocks being constituted by Elements, Human conducts, Course of events, Understanding) that proceeds on the basis of a numerological grid. The composition of the *Hongfan* chapter appears so rigorous that some Russian formalists have speculated on its number of characters, which would have been calculated in such a way as to place them within a magic square (Volkov 1991). If the very high antiquity that the tradition assigns to it is in no way plausible, the opinion that locates the writing of this work at a much later period (2ⁿᵈ or 1ˢᵗ century BCE) is hardly founded either. We can (cautiously) follow Artiémiï Karapétiants when he integrates this short treatise into the layer of texts that the Zhou dynasty presented as a synthesis of the thought of the vanquished Shang in order to better claim and control their inheritance – which would indeed place it among the oldest texts of the *Documents* (Karapétiants 1991). This passion for numbering (the character *shu* 數 refers both to numbers and natural laws), this quest for the patterns organizing the world in all its dimensions, material and spiritual, though numerological speculations will assert itself till at least the Han dynasty (taking novel expressions later on), which goes radically against the very idea of an "a-cosmos".

Said otherwise, Chinese thought was as much preoccupied as Ancient Greece was by the transition from Chaos to Cosmos, and both civilizations were trying to

---

20 "This term referred mainly to all the land under the name of the Son of Heaven and the right to rule on such land. The ancient Chinese held that the rule of senior officials was over their enfeoffed land, and that of dukes and princes was over feudal states. [...] The term has later evolved to refer to the whole nation or the whole world" (Wang and Han 2021, vol. "History", entry "Tianxia").
21 In Chapter 2, I will comment upon the figure of this god. Note already that this passage assimilates *Di* with *Tian.*

identify (through very different means) the laws by which a stable cosmic and political universe was able to subside. The famous story of the death of Chaos (*Hundun*)²² in *Zhuangzi* 7.7 is a philosophical meditation about whether such transition is commendable:

> The Ruler of the Southern Ocean was Shu, the Ruler of the Northern Ocean was Hu, and the Ruler of the Centre was Chaos. Shu and Hu were continually meeting in the land of Chaos. Chaos was treating them very well. They consulted together how they might repay his kindness, and said, "Men all have seven orifices so as to see, hear, eat and breathe. Only he alone is without them. Let us try to chisel some." Accordingly, they chiseled one orifice per day; and on the seventh day Chaos died.
>
> (*Zhuangzi* 7.7)

This reworking of an ancient myth speaks of the demise of Chaos, vanquished by Order. Contrary to his Confucian counterparts, Zhuangzi laments the fact, while stating that such demise happened through the imposing of distinctions, differentiations, of which the seven orifices pierced into the face of Chaos constitute the symbol. In other words, Zhuangzi confers a new meaning to a cosmogonic story that speaks of how the chaos of the origins gave way to an organized cosmos (a story also evoked in the *Shanhaijing*, the *Zuozhuan*²³ and the *Huainanzi*, among other ancient texts). The analysis of other foundational mythical stories, notably the one of Shennong 神農, the Divine Farmer, would reinforce this conclusion (cf. notably Ode 245; *Huainanzi* XIX, 1). As a matter of fact, the notion of "Chaos" in its philosophical sense is firmly asserted by the *Liezi* 列子 in its *Tianrui* 天瑞 ("Happy Omens") chapter: "By *Hundun*, one means that the multitude of things formed a confused mass and that nothing distinguished them from one another [渾淪者，言萬物相渾淪而未相離也]" (*Liezi* 1.2).²⁴ Such indistinction could not but be overcome, whatever the appreciation one may pass on the disappearance of Chaos.

For the authors of *Anticipating China*, the Chinese "dynamic sense of order" would not occur from any act of separating, but rather from "the energy of change within chaos itself", which implies that "order is always richly vague" (Hall and

---

22 The ramifications of the *Hundun* myth have also been traced by Granet (1994 [1926]) and these stories read as a counterpart of the ones dedicated to Yu the Great: the Yu storyline is about ordering and civilizing, *Hundun*'s speaks of a return to the original Chaos.
23 The *Zuozhuan* (or *Zuo Tradition, Commentary of Zuo*) is an historical chronicle that runs from 722 to 468 BCE. An authoritative English translation is provided by Stephen Durrant, Wai-yee Li, and David Schaberg (2016).
24 I will make a limited or subordinate use of the *Liezi* throughout this book, because of the issues that bear on the dating of this text.

Ames 1995, 231). Let me just oppose to this the cosmogony found at the very beginning of the third chapter of the *Huainanzi*, and the reader may reach her own conclusions.

> Before heaven and earth took shape, the world lay huddled in on itself, chaotic, turbid, elusive: this was the great beginning. The Dao arose in an immense void which engendered extent and duration, from which the primordial breath was born. As this breath acquired limits and contours, its aerial and ethereal parts refined to form the sky, its heavy and cloudy parts coagulated to form the earth. The merging of the aerial and the subtle came more easily than the accretion of heaviness and turmoil, so the sky took shape before the earth stabilized.
>
> The essences of heaven and earth united to constitute yin and yang, those of yin and yang came together to form the four seasons, and those of the four seasons were disseminated to produce the multitude of beings. Fire arose from an accumulation of hot breaths of the yang, while from the epitome of fire arose the sun. The water formed by condensation of the cold breaths of yin and its quintessence was the moon. As for the quintessences produced by a dispersion of the breaths of the sun and the moon, they engendered the stars and the sidereal markers. The sun, the moon, the stars and the sidereal markers went up to the sky; the waters, the dust and the silt were deposited on the earth.
>
> Long ago, during the struggles between Gonggong and Zhuanxu for sovereign power, Gonggong shook Mount Disjoint in fury, shattering the heavenly pillar and causing the earth's anchor to break. The sky tilted northwest, causing the sun, moon, stars and star markers to slide in that direction; on land, a depression formed in the south-east towards which water, dust and silt converged.[25]
>
> (*Huainanzi* 3, 1–3, with reference to Kalinowski 2022, 2–5)

Still, one point needs to be conceded to Ames and Hall: one senses in our texts the prescience of a continued presence of the original Chaos, and such presence is not necessarily threatening: it does speak of the original vital influx. One may legitimately say, as Ames and Hall do, that the representation of *Hundun* has to do with the idea of a "foetal beginning" (Hall and Ames 1995, 190). Chapter 7 of the *Huainanzi* illustrates this point. But the same chapter also shows that growth is a process of ordering: the description of the embryonic process offered by this chapter culminates in the apparition of a new human being in the tenth month. This apparition is akin to the surge of a new expression of the One: in Chinese numerology, if number Nine corresponds to the total of all the parts of a compound, the Ten operates the return to the One.

Besides, attitudes vis-à-vis the "order" to be shaped registered from one author to another vary greatly. The nostalgia of an "a-cosmic" world found in the *Laozi, Zhuangzi, Liezi* (and in some passages of the *Huainanzi*) has political undertones:

---

[25] See a summary of the debates on such cosmologies within the *Huainanzi* (notably in its Chapter 2) and on the nature of their connection with the *Zhuangzi*, in Puett (2000).

it shows distaste towards a social order based on distinctions, principles and linguistic mastery. In contrast, Confucians see operations such as dividing, numbering, naming, ordering or hierarchizing as grounding the civilizational process itself. Still, recognize all ancient thinkers, though with varying inflections, such operations entail what we would call "alienation", a multifaceted phenomenon that they describe and understand in all its dimensions: political alienation; alienation from the original "stuff" (the matter that inscribes humankind into the chain of all sentient beings); and alienation from inner freedom. While extolling the passage from chaos to order (which several books of the *Book of Rites* (*Liji*禮記) both justify and narrate) and showcasing its impact on the political and gnoseological realm ("naming" grounds both knowledge and the art of governance – Cf. *Analects* 13.3, 17.9 *et passim*), many Confucians cannot but share in the nostalgia exhibited by their Daoist counterparts: "ordering the world" has a cost. Xunzi constitutes an exception: describing Ritual as the conduit by which the natural (*xing* 性) is transformed into an artifice (*wei* 偽), he attributes to the latter term an eminently positive meaning. It is indeed artificial to establish distinctions among beings and conditions, and, likewise, it is artificial to legitimize these distinctions through a ritual anchorage. At the same time, it is not only necessary but also moral and beneficial to do so, for the artifice ensures the existence and the continuity of the social body. "To divide" (*fen* 分) and "to civilize" (*jiaohua* 教化) are joint processes. Civilization demands ritualization, and ritualization is about ordering, putting things in order through the distinctions we institutionalize.

Till now, I have examined only the foundational oppositions that Hall and Ames construe between the Western civilization based on the passage from chaos to cosmos, and the Chinese world, which "does not depend upon the belief that the totality of things constitutes a single-ordered world" (Hall and Ames 1995, 11–12). This basic divide, continue the authors, invalidates the idea of "causality" (in its Aristotelian meaning) in China. It also accounts for the preference displayed towards "permanence" and "rest" in the Western world, while China privileges the dynamism inherent to a focus on "processes". Another consequence of the divide is that a "world-as-it-is" conception (the one developed in China) dispenses with the very idea of a creative agency. These are all-important theses. Although I just challenged the thesis according to which Chinese thought describes the world as a "a-cosmos", which already leads us to consider the related propositions with some distance, some of these propositions do trigger extremely helpful insights, and all of them need to receive careful consideration. I will examine them as we continue to circulate from one "landmark" to another in our wandering throughout the gardens of philosophy.

Permanence and Process

On the Western side, our second enclosure is dedicated to "Rest and Permanence". In contrast, its Chinese counterpart focuses on "Dynamism and Process". Rest and Permanence have a privileged relationship to *logos*, which progressively won in respectability over both *mythos* and *historia*. The prominence earned by *logos* went together with "a forgetting of the mythical sources of rational speculation" (Hall and Ames 1995, 14[26]). Such speculation turned increasingly into an investigation of *physis* (or *natura*). "*Physis* was to be accounted for by recourse to *logos*. [...] Two other fundamental turnings helped to guarantee the preference for permanence over the flux of human experience. The first is the dualism of soul and body [...] and the second, of course, the ontological dualism introduced by Parmenides" (Hall and Ames 1995, 19). Our authors then relate such dualism to the separation between quantitative considerations (numerical ordering of things) and qualitative ones. Mathematical speculations were also responsible for the doctrine according to which "Only Being is".

The principal task I here assign to myself lies in questioning not the construction of the Western model attempted by our authors but rather of its Chinese counterpart. Still, a few words about the Western model may be in order. First, reference to the so-called Western "dualism" flattens a variety of representations and modes of thinking. In the Greek, Latin and Semitic worlds, thinking through ternary divisions was as natural a thought process as was the recourse to binary oppositions. Even if Paul of Tarsus was indeed deeply influenced by the Platonic concept of the soul,[27] the Paulinian distinction between body, spirit and soul has its antecedents and filiation – which showcases the tension, continuous in the Western tradition, between Greek and Semitic anthropological and gnoseological schemes. Augustine makes the research of a ternary, quasi-trinitarian structure of reality a systematic endeavor (O'Daly 1987). Besides individual examples, one may think of ternary foundational divisions present in the Western tradition such as the one between feelings, intellect and will.

Second, if there has been at any time a "preference for permanence over the flux of human experience", the fact (which, in my view, remains dubious in itself) is a feature of modern European thought rather than of European classical worldview and speculations. The latter were attaching much importance to phenomenal transformations as experienced and registered in everyday life. In classical poetry

---

[26] As just seen, the same book denies or at least minimizes the presence of cosmogonic myths in Chinese thought.
[27] See for instance El-Kaisy and Dillon (2009).

for instance, the idea of "time" was not spontaneously associated with the one of "eternity" but rather with daily or seasonal rhythms:

> For the Homeric Greeks time was not homogenous; it had quality; it differed at large for the whole world within the horizon. There are all the changes of the day from dawn to the end of night, all the changes of the year from beginning of spring on through summer, autumn, and winter. For the Romans time was weather, weather time, *tempus, tempestas*; and *mauvais temps*, etc. Whatever came man could neither bring nor avert. Neither chaotic nor mechanically regular, it appeared to be the work of other minds, and above all of the power in the sky, Zeus.
>
> (Onians 1988 [1951], 411)

It might be our modes of reading that often decide upon the "preferences" manifested by a certain culture or time, while said culture or period nurtured a variety of aesthetic and philosophical apprehensions.

Third, speaking of a "preference for permanence" should not preclude one to scrutinize what has been said about "Process" within the Western tradition. Whitehead did not introduce the term of Process and similar ones into Western philosophy (we will reconsider, at the end of this chapter, the question of the nature of the novelty brought in by Whitehead and like-minded thinkers). The study by Aristotle of both *Energeia* and *Kinesis* is certainly not located on the margins of his system. Divine noetic activity is described by Aristotle in terms of process (divine thinking is "thinking of thinking"), even if such activity is happening in and for all eternity, Aristotle does not hesitate to speak of thought activity in the context of eternity (see *Met.* 1075a2), And, when it comes to humankind, the process of thinking means *to think as God thinks*, even if we, human beings, attain this state only in a struggle that unfolds through the varied elements in our nature (Mulhern and Mulhern 1968).

In contrast with the so-called Western tradition, Ames and other authors describe Chinese thought as putting the stress on processes inscribed into the natural (and, for Confucians, educational) realm, which forbids it to apprehend reality in terms of permanence and of "being". As they understand them, these characteristics are partly a result of linguistic determinations.

I argue that, while it indeed focuses on the description of *processes* (the ones through which cosmic and social order are created and maintained), Chinese ancient thought manifests a strong propensity to prefer "permanence" and "rest" above all things. The term of "rest" largely corresponds to the character *jing* 靜, a central notion of the *Laozi.* The same Classic (and many others) speak of "permanence" through the use of the sinograms *heng* 恆 / *chang* 常.[28] Let us consider Stanza 16 of the L*aozi:*

> Whoever reaches the extreme of vacuity [*xu* 虛] is established in stillness. All beings are activating themselves, I contemplate [*guan* 觀] the return [*fu* 復]. Every living thing multiplies, and each of them returns to its root. To return to one's root, this is called Stillness [*jing* 靜], which is [also] called fulfilling [*fu* 復] one's destiny.[29] Fulfilling destiny is the constant [*chang* 常] [law]. To know the constant [law] is called Illumination.
> 致虛極，守靜篤。萬物並作，吾以觀復。夫物芸芸，各復歸其根。歸根曰靜，是謂復命。復命曰常，知常曰明。
>
> (*Laozi* 16)

What is contemplated can indeed be characterized as a *process:* the "return" (*fu*). At the same time, such contemplation unveils the "constant" (*chang*), in the sense that the process is unceasing, and such realization is akin to the obtention of "stillness" (rest). This goes beyond a mere opposition between "process" and "permanence".

Most of the commentaries on the *Yijing* would reveal the same *circularity* (rather than *opposition*) between rest and permanence. No doubt, the *Yijing* attempts to describe the way in which phenomena necessarily follow each other and arrange themselves. It is, in the extreme, a mathematics of all possible phenomena, based on the idea that everything only exists in exchange, passage, fluidity: gradation is another name for contrast, and a logic of *transformations* governs the universe. At the same time, if the transformations affecting all phenomena are scrutinized through the minutiae intrinsic to Chinese mantic speculations, the goal is always to find constant laws among such apparent variety, and thus to uncover the paradoxical permanence of all things.

With varying intensity, such perspective can be found in all schools and authors. It permeates cosmology and it also extends to the political realm (I have already stressed how vain it is to try to separate the two domains). What does the concept of *wu-wei* 無為 (non-action) refer to if not the capacity to stay at rest in the middle of surrounding transformations? The mystical tone of the Stanza 16 of *Laozi*, quoted above, finds a political parallel in the *Analects* of Confucius:

---

[28] During the time of the Emperor Liu Heng 劉恆 (203–157 BCE),, the character *heng* 恆 was taboo and substituted by *chang* 常. Although the taboo was lifted afterwards, expressions such as *chang dao* 常道 had become so common that they remained unchanged. The concept of *heng* is theorized in the *Hengxian* 瓦先, a text part of the Shanghai Museum collection of excavated bamboo slips. See Ding 2016.

[29] "Fulfilling" and "coming back to one's origin" constitute one and the same operation.

> The Master said, "One who governs by means of virtue (*de* 德) may be compared to the North Celestial Pole (*beichen* 北辰), which remains in its place and all the stars pay homage to it."
> 子曰:「为政以德，譬如北辰，居其所而众星共之。」
>
> (*Analects* 2.1. Translation Ni 2017, 94)

I would then suggest that, in the Western tradition (if the term can be retained), "rest" is often thought of in terms of process (as shown by the approach of the divine noetic activity in Aristotle), while, in the Chinese case, the apprehension of the process that governs all processes (i. e., the law of succession and return as described by the *Yijing*) leads one to enter into rest and permanence.

When dealing at a later stage with the question of "being", I will not deny, of course, the importance of linguistic determinisms: Chinese language does not possess strict equivalences of concepts and grammatical forms such as "to be" or "being" (though ancient Chinese is not lacking in tools playing the role fulfilled by copular verbs in other languages). However, at various instances in the course of this book, I will endeavor to illustrate the fact that Chinese philosophy is essentially "experiential" and that its genius lies in coming up with ways to break through the prison house of language, which relativizes terminological issues. Additionally, later in this chapter I will discuss the use of *you* 有 and *wu* 無, examining whether these two characters can be legitimately related to notions such as, respectively, "being" and "non-being" (see Hall and Ames 1995, 195).

Non-Dual Cognition versus Dualist Reasoning

The Western side of our next pair of landmarks offers a view on Zeno's and Parmenides' speculations, as both philosophers opened up the divide between reason, on the one hand, and sensitive experience, on the other hand. In contrast, "classical culture in China developed without these hard and fast dualisms. [...] Chinese thinkers were not forced to become obsessed with the goal of providing a rational account of motion and change" (Hall and Ames 1995, 33). The same authors relate this topic to a discussion around two all-important characters: *li* 理 (which points at *patterns* in things and events), a character that "does not entail the distinction between the intelligible and the sensible world which has had such prominence in the Western world" (Hall and Ames 1995, 213); and *xiang* 象 (usually translated as "image" or "figure") through which "what is imaged is the process" (Hall and Ames 1995, 218).

I have already warmed against the danger of seeing "dualism" everywhere in Western thought, a propensity that translates into "reverse orientalism", as Slingerland labels it. Besides, I think that Chinese thinking was alert to the gap that may exist between the fact of "seeing", "sensing" something, on the one hand, and the one of giving a reasoned account of the phenomenon observed, on the other hand. The point of attention lies elsewhere; ancient Chinese thinkers were focusing upon the process of observation and contemplation *as a self-transforming process*. "Observing water is an art [*guan shui you shu* 觀水有術]", Mencius exclaims (7 A.24): you need to "perceive" what is below the surface, to go beyond (or behind) the senses so as to enter into the "subtle" (*wei* 微), into what is barely perceptible. The overcoming of ordinary perceptions, which are informed by interests and emotions (an operation indispensable to enter another level of cognition) is also propounded by Zhuangzi when he recommends to practice "the fasting of the heart [*xin zhai* 心齋]" (*Zhuangzi* 4.2), i.e., a distancing from the "codes" (*fu* 符) that the heart-mind imposes upon spontaneous perceptions. Still in the *Zhuangzi*, the famous apologue of Butcher Ding (this royal officer in charge of preparing the sacrifices carves a beef without ever blunting his knife because he focuses on the "inner", on the hidden articulations of the animal) offers a similar recommendation (*Zhuangzi* 3.2). Spiritual in nature, the focus chosen by Chinese thinkers differs from the one elected by the early Greek scientific texts that Ames and Hall make use of, but this does not weigh upon the point at stake; Chinese classics certainly do not identify perception and reality. Actually, they *were* "obsessed with the goal of providing a rational account of motion and change", for this is exactly the goal that manticology was fixing for itself:

> The development of divinatory techniques and procedures has led, following the development of manticology, to the increasingly rigorous rationalization of artificially produced configurations, from the confused starry cracks of primitive scapulomancy to standardized half-H tracings of the divination on turtle plastron, from them to the configurations of the numerological hexagrams, and finally to the algebraic configurations of the *Yijing* hexagrams.
> (Vandermeersch 2013, 113)

Texts anchored in the divinatory tradition were revealing to their readers and listeners the patterns through which to understand the data provided by sensory observation, and this according to laws that were constant, as these laws were meant to predict how transformations would succeed one to another. This path was differing from the one followed by "Western" science, but it was precluding neither a taking of distance from sensory observations, nor a formalization of the data compiled by the observer – in fact, divinatory techniques were first and foremost formalizing the data that practitioners were gathering.

It is at this stage that a discussion on the characters *li* and *xiang* can take place. I have no basic objection against the interpretation that *Anticipating China* and related works offer of these two concepts, but we need to apprehend them in their historical developments. *Li* can be first translated as "pattern" or "motive", as exemplified by the following canonical sentence, central to the understanding of the *Yijing:*

> [The Sage] looking up, contemplates the heavenly signs [*tianwen*], and, looking down, scrutinizes the earthly patterns [*dili*].
> 仰以觀於天文，俯以察於地理。
>
> (*Xici* 繫辭 I.4).[30]

Here, *wen* and *li* are almost synonymous, and refer to the way phenomena are adjusted into patterns. This differs in several respects from the meaning that Zhu Xi (for whom things take shape through the encounter between a "principle" – *li* – and "material breath" – *qi*) will assign to the term. Zhu Xi's meaning cannot be used retrospectively for understanding ancient texts. As is also the case with Western concepts, Chinese characters unfold their signification from one author to another, and are sometimes loaded with new meanings in the course of intellectual history.

As to the character *xiang*, it is first and foremost a term that takes its meaning from the system constituted by the original diagrams of the *Yijing* and their commentaries: each hexagram (*gua* 卦) calls for a weighing (*tuan* 彖) and a figurative reading as an "image" (*xiang* 象). The *Yijing* delivers the images, the archetypes (*xiang*) on which the forms (*xing*) are modeled: "Images take shape in Heaven. Forms take shape on Earth. Thus, transformations and evolutions are made visible [在天成象，在地成形，變化見矣]" (*Yijing, Xici* Commentary, 1.1).

In this respect, I am not sure that it is absolutely correct to say that "what is imaged is the process". More exactly, what is imaged *through the passage from one image to another* is the process. Even if their apparition is transitory, images proper have a kind of stability, the same way that "forms" (the form taken by a man or by a mountain) are both transient and fixed. *In fact, the "Process" in its origin can never be fully imaged or imagined.* "Perfect image has no shape [大象無形]", asserts *Laozi* 41. As to the *Huainanzi*, it takes the description of the Way as a prototype of its own textual composition: the Way is both fixed and elusive. Similarly, the reciprocal production of squares and circle investigated by Chinese mathematical treatises (notably the *Nine Chapters on the Art of Mathematics* [*Jiuzhang yishu* 九章算術]) reveals that "different forms evolve into one another, ending and beginning like a circle, *of which no one can trace an outline* [以不同形相嬗也，終

---

[30] The *Xici* can be considered as the most important commentary among the ones gathered into the "Ten Wings" (*Shiyi* 十翼), the first collection of commentaries on the Hexagrams, now an integral part of the *Yijing* proper.

始若環，莫得其倫]" (*HNZ* 7.7 – translation Major et al. 2010, 250[31]). The constant shift between patterns suggests that the Origin evoked by the text can never be fully "imaged", never be "grasped".

Correlations and/or Substances

This leads us to our fourth twin landmarks. They contrast the triumph of the "substance" in the West with the one of "correlative thinking" in China. This latest term has gained a central position in the discussion of ancient Chinese philosophy:

> Chinese thinking depends upon a species of analogy which may be called "correlative thinking." Correlative thinking, as it is found both in classical Chinese "cosmologies" (the *Yijing* (Book of the Changes), Daoism, the Yin-Yang school) [...], involves the association of image or concept-cluster related by meaningful disposition rather than physical causation. Correlative thinking is a species of spontaneous thinking grounded in informal and ad hoc analogical procedures presupposing both association and differentiation. The regulative element in this modality of thinking is shared patterns of culture and tradition rather than common assumptions about causal necessity.
> (Hall and Ames 1998, 3)

Let us illustrate the above presentation of correlative thinking: analogical reasoning based on the observation of the four seasons as well as complex divination procedures were providing ideal representations of the way to tame natural forces and, concurrently, to organize the socio-political system. Agricultural activities could not be separated from human and religious duties taken in their entirety, as shown by this excerpt of the *Guanzi*, the final editing of which took place around 26 BCE, though it gathers texts written between the 4th and the 1st century BCE:

> [In Spring] repair and clean the places of the spirit, and respectfully pray that decay be blocked; venerate the upright yang, put in order the dikes, hoe and plant the fields, erect bridges, repair canals, roof the houses and fix the plumbing; resolve grievances and pardon the guilty, bringing into communication the four quarters. Then the soft breezes and sweet rains will come, the hundred families will be long-lived, and the hundred insects will be abundant.
> 修除神位，謹禱獘梗，宗正陽，治隄防，耕芸樹藝。正津梁，修溝瀆，甃屋行水，解怨赦罪，通四方。然則柔風甘雨乃至。百姓乃壽，百蟲乃蕃。
> (*Guanzi* 管子, *Sishi* 四時. Translation Shaughnessy 2007, 508)

---

31 On the *Huainanzi's* principles of composition, see Vermander (2021a).

As can be seen, the text associates seasonal occurrences, agricultural activities and political dominant political/religious duties, according to a sophisticated system of analogies. China has indeed developed a specific style of "correlative thinking". Yet, I will develop three reasons for disputing, at least to some extent, this opposition between the centrality of the "substance" in the West against the focus upon "correlation" in China. The first one has to do with the historical background of Chinese "correlative thinking", which will relativize its applicability to the whole of ancient classics and alter the representation given of it. The second is based upon what I will call "the essential relationality" of the Greek concept of "substance". The third one derives from the challenge I intend to bring to the opposition drawn at the beginning of this section, notably by rehabilitating the notion of "causality" in the Chinese context.

Scholars working on correlative cosmology, i.e., on the establishment of a systemic relationships among phenomena according to the relatedness (*lun* 倫) of their structures have shown special interest towards the development of Chinese numerology (Granet 1999 [1934], 101–126; Graham 1986; Shaughnessy 2007). If correlative thinking and numerology are indeed strongly related, then, correlative thinking is certainly neither "spontaneous" nor "informal". It is actually difficult to imagine a way of proceeding more codified than the Chinese establishment of correlations.

At the same time, numerology and correlative thinking should not be fully equated. Actually, the importance given to numerology may have led into two directions. The first one was the early development of mathematical operations. As an illustration, the decimal-based calculation table found in the Tsinghua bamboo slips collection, dated c. 300 BCE, organizes a set of operations on a number basis that extends from ¼ to 8,100. It makes use of the principles of commutativity and distributivity, allows the user to make divisions, and even to extract the square root of certain numbers (Feng 2017).

The second direction induced by the focus on numerology was indeed leading towards speculations inspired by correlative thinking. Correlative cosmology was systematized in the late Warring States and the early imperial periods. In her study on cosmology and musical harmony, E. Brindley dates the shift from a social/psychological conception of harmony to the insertion of the theme into a correlative cosmology "from within a period starting from around 325 BCE" (Brindley 2012, 16). Numerological concerns predate correlative cosmology, but the latter grounded its developments on the former. I actually think that *numerology* is more foundational than *correlative thinking* and can be found independently from a full development of the latter. Analogies depend upon numbering, not numbering upon analogies. This changes the nature of this cultural trait as represented by Hall and Ames.

This is not the place to give a full account of the way "numbers" (*shu*) were conceived of in ancient China. However, one may stress the following: numbers were possessing a qualitative value – Granet points towards "an extreme respect for numerical symbols that combines with extreme indifference for any quantitative notion" (Granet 1999 [1934], note 230). Among other phenomena, they could indicate: the array of impressions felt by the ear or the eye (Five); the surge of life energy (Seven); the completion of a process as well as the sum of the parts of a given territory (Nine). Therefore, numbers were expressing the ordering of reality. At the same time, they were always referring to their origin, the One (*yi* 一) that begets the ten thousand (*wan* 萬) manifestations of this same reality, privileging a stress on organic continuity over the formalism of numerical combinations. The One being seen as the primordial unity and the Two as the couple within the One, not fully separated from it yet, the Three was the first number *stricto sensu*. All system of classifications were referred to the Three, on the basis of which both the square and the circle were computed (Granet 1999 [1934], 237–242). Special attention was also given to alternation between odd and even numbers, equated to the one intervening in the yin/yang rhythm in all phenomena. The first decennial series eventually organized the scale of meanings given to all numbers from One to Nine (Ten being seen as a return to the One). Texts from the early Han period testify to the culmination of all numbers in Nine (sum) and its derivatives (essentially 81) and/or Ten (completion and return), while earlier texts show that alternative numberings ordered on a "Base Seven" were sometimes privileged. Such representations were going along the development of methods of computation.

Michael Puett has been among the ones who have argued for a late and subordinate status of correlative thinking in the history of ancient Chinese thought:

> Correlative cosmology was not an assumption at all-even in the early Han. It was rather a claim, and one that was hotly debated. There was thus a strong self-consciousness at the time that other people did not accept correlative ways of thinking. And what I would like to argue here is that was also a strong self-consciousness of the fact that some of the earlier texts-including those authored by figures recognized as great sages did not use correlative ways of thinking either. There was, in short, a concern precisely with the disjunction [...] between earlier texts and the correlative cosmology that some Han figures were using to interpret those texts.
>
> (Puett 2000, 29–30[32])

As Puett frames it, the contemporary debate on both the pervasiveness of correlative thinking and on its complex association with cosmogonies is blurred by the

---

[32] In this article, Puett amalgamates rather quickly "correlative thinking", "cosmologies" and "cosmogonies".

fact that some scholars find cosmogonies "unfaithful" to their representation of what Chinese thought is or at least ought to be, while other scholars (such as Charles Le Blanc) much value this literary genre and the teachings it delivers – a proof among others that sinological controversies remain heavily loaded with theological undertones. Contrary to Puett, I think that a full-fledged system of correlative thinking did appear before the Han. There is no reason to doubt the traditional attribution of such system (as based on the yin-yang alternation) to the figure of Zou Yan 鄒衍 (305–240 BCE). I read the *Zhuangzi* as a proof of the influence of such systematizations of earlier speculations and as a pointed criticism against it. The following passage illustrates the nature of such criticism:

> One and Speech are two; two and one are three. Going on from this, even the most skillful cannot reach the end, and how much less can the mass of the people! Therefore, from non-existence we speak of existence till we arrive at three; from existence to existence, to how many should we reach? Let us not proceed then, since that is it.
> 一與言為二，二與一為三。自此以往，巧歷不能得，而況其凡乎！故自無適有，以至於三，而況自有適有乎！無適焉，因是已。
>
> (*Zhuangzi* 2.9)

Thus, my own historical sequencing would read as follows:

Before the Warring States: there is coexistence of, on the one hand, a mantological/numerological system and, on the other hand, a corpus of traditional mythologies that comprise cosmogonies. The mantological system, though based on correlations, is not yet anchored in an overarching "correlative cosmology". And very few traces of both (if any) can be found in the *Analects*, or even, later on, in *Mencius* and *Xunzi*.

Towards the middle of the Warring States, a specific school of correlative thinking takes shape and becomes widespread. Though close to the School of the Dao, the most notable interpreters of the later (Laozi, Zhuangzi) aim criticisms at a vision that puts into a grid the various dimensions of reality, hindering the immediacy of our lived experiences, from which illumination arises.

The apex of systematic correlative thinking may have happened slightly before the Han period: The text that pushes analogical reasoning to the furthest was undoubtedly the *Lüshi Chunqiu* 呂氏春秋, compiled around 239 BCE. As the events registered during the Han dynasty unfolded, political and moral considerations severely limited the influence of correlative thinking in its full systematicity, notably because such way of reasoning practically subordinated the autonomy of the sovereign to the pre-ordained working of the cosmos in a way that could not but awaken the suspicion of the Han rulers (the eventual demise of Liu An 劉安, the patron of the *Huainanzi* editorial enterprise, can be understood in this light). Later on, the

"Mystic learning [xuanxue 玄學]" School[33] developed a new way of reading the classics that displaced their interpretation from the cosmological realm to what I provisionally call the "metaphysical" or "ontological" domain.

What we can infer from the previous discussion is that Chinese thought cannot be reduced to one single way of envisioning reality and of "framing" it into a grid. Correlative thinking exercised a paramount influence in Chinese intellectual history but it also was the object of criticisms. Eventually, these criticisms triggered speculations that renewed both the interpretation of ancient writings and the framework by which to understand and conceptualize phenomenal reality.

Let us now turn towards the primacy given to "substance" in the West, contrasted to the one given to "relationality" and "correlation" in China. A glance at Aristotle's approach of the subject will again warn us against oversimplified presentations: "substance" is said of individuals ("no universal term is the name of a substance" [*Met.* 1041a4]), while "universals" are *formally* defined as the essential qualities shared by a set of individuals.[34] While perception by the senses gives us access to (necessarily) individual substances, universals are *abstracted* from singulars. "Abstraction" and "relations" are notions that are better understood when related to each other: it is in the *Categories* that Aristotle discusses relations and enumerates their particularities. Among them: (a) the very definition of a relation (parenting or slavery for instance) makes reference to something else than one of the terms it includes; (b) all *relata* convert; (c) since what is perceptible (or is susceptible to be known) is simultaneous with its being perceived (or known), perception and knowledge are relations (their *relata* coexist with them); (d) substances *in the relation of perception* do not exist before they are perceived; and, since its definition make reference to an "another", the process of abstraction satisfies Aristotle's criteria for being a relation. Aristotle's universals being abstractions, universals are real *without being separate substances*. They possess independent, substantial being only in the mode of "as if". The fact that they have the structure of relations ensures that they cannot exist apart in their own right. This analysis of the very process of cognition cannot but lead us to the following conclusion:

> Relations have their starring role in the *Metaphysics*. Note Aristotle's metaphysical vocabulary: matter-form, substance-accident, universal-particular, species-individual etc. all have a relational structure. [...] This relational structure gives a way for universals to signify real features of the world without being separate substances [...] A universal is an abstraction. That is, strictly, it is an *abstractum* abstracted from *abstrahendum*. Once again, we have two *relata*,

---

33 Lynn (2022) prefers to translate this expression by "Arcane Studies".
34 Technically speaking, a universal is a property that can be a constituent of more than one substance. Cf. Armstrong (1978), esp. 89–91.

the *abstractum* and the *abstrahendum*, being related by a relation, abstraction. Neither exists on its own, yet each can be taken as if it did and can serve as subjects in the sciences.
(Bäck 2008, 10)

In simpler terms: (1) Perception is of substances; knowledge of universals, i.e., of relations; (2) Aristotle's philosophy is no more centered on substance than on relation. It needs to make use of the totality of its toolbox, but it certainly gives a prominent role to relations in the way it envisions the cognitive process. I suggest that a similar kind of balance can be found in Chinese thought; even if reality is first apprehended in terms of relations, "things" to be related have their own way of "subsiding". In this light, let us look again at the *Hongfan* chapter:

> First, the Five Elements. 1: Water. 2: Fire. 3: Wood. 4: Metal. 5: Earth. Water: it moistens and goes down. The fire: it blazes and it rises. Wood: it bends and straightens. Metal: it gives way and it changes. The earth: it sows and bears fruit. What moistens and descends gives salt. What flames and rises gives bitterness. What bends and straightens gives acid. What gives way and changes gives acridity. What sows and bears fruit is sweet.
> 一，五行：一曰水，二曰火，三曰木，四曰金，五曰土。水曰潤下，火曰炎上，木曰曲直，金曰革，土爰稼穡。潤下作鹹，炎上作苦，曲直作酸，從革作辛，稼穡作甘。
> (*Classic of Documents, Hongfan*)

Beyond the grid of correlations detailed here, one senses that the entities associated within the system possess some kind of "nature", that they exhibit intrinsic qualities. There is no reason to privilege either the fact that they are associated into a framework of correlations or else the qualities that are theirs.

> There is nothing wrong to demonstrate that Chinese philosophy focuses on process and change, but it is not necessary to infer from here that it has to be non-substantial. Following Aristotle's relation between categorical being and potential/actual being, change itself should assume something that is changing. Substantialism and metaphysics of process do not have to be opposite.
> (Yu 2014, 148)

As Aristotle would imply, "substance" and "relations" can be understood only throughout the relationality that make one and the other term mutually intelligible.

One may venture to add that dogmatic elaborations on the Trinity accomplished a further and decisive step when they put relationality at the heart of substance itself: approaching God as "one substance" in "three persons" is akin to defining the divine substance according to the continuous flow of exchange that constitutes the "divine economy": in God, "relations" are not "accidents", as they still were in Aristotle's *Categories*. "Relation in God is not as an accident in a subject, but is the divine essence itself. [...] A 'divine person' signifies a relation as subsistent" (Thomas Aquinas, *ST* I, q. 29.4).³⁵

Causality in Chinese Thinking

We remember that the quotation with which I opened this section was contrasting "substances" to "correlative thinking", before stating that the latter had been preventing the rise of the idea of causal necessity. The time has come to confront the question of "causality" in China. For Hall and Ames:

> Correlative thinking is effectively a nonlogical procedure in the sense that it is not based upon [...] causal implications or entailments or anything like the sort one finds in Aristotelian or modern Western logics. [...] The correlative indifference of correlative thinking to logical analysis means that the ambiguity, vagueness and incoherence associable with images and metaphors are carried over into the more formal elements of thought.
> (Hall and Ames 1995, 124)

I will come back to the supposed "vagueness" of Chinese thought later on. Here, I focus on the following question: does ancient China ignore causation? As one knows, any phenomenon or process has many causes (every language conveys in its own way the fact that a given thing or event has been caused by a previous factor). China certainly ignores the very specific effort of thought that has led to the definition of the Aristotelian material, formal, efficient, and final "causes". Let us note however that Aristotle intended much less to develop a formal system of causation than to illustrate how he was anchoring metaphysics into the quest for the "final cause": philosophy is wisdom insofar as it reflects on the cause as an *end*. And this teleological orientation is also a way to consider together *being* and *becoming*, thus avoiding to be caught in the static contemplation of substances (see *Met.* A). As rightly stressed by Jiyuan Yu:

> [For Aristotle,] the Prime Mover imparts motion not because it is an active agent which causes motion in a physical way, but because "it is the object of desire and the object of thought", and "it produces motion by being loved" (*Metaphysics* 1072a25–29, b3) All things are moved by the Prime Mover because each of them has a natural desire or impulse for being eternal and for going beyond one's short existence. The continuous motion is not by an external cause that

---

35 The way by which to reach this definition or a similar one as well as the implications to be drawn from it differ from one theologian to another, though differences are often more terminological than properly dogmatic. Cross (2002) offers a remarkable overview of the issue, from Gregory of Nyssa till Thomas Aquinas and Duns Scott.

stays at the end of the process. Rather, it is the actualization of this intrinsic pursuit for eternity.

(Yu 2014, 141)

Chinese texts evidently look for what may have "caused" such or such misfortune for instance. Historical writings relate a military defeat to the fact that a sovereign has ignored the Mandate of Heaven, has gone against ritual rules, or has been ill-advised. There is a difference before finding a causal explanation "irrational" (and then unconvincing) and asserting that no causal explanation has been provided for. Obviously, China does not ignore the "why". Taken as face value, Ames' and Hall's proposition sounds surprising when considering the debating style of Chinese thinkers. The one of them who takes most pain to argue logically, through a step-by-step procedure, is probably Mozi. Let me quote an excerpt of one of the (chronologically) first writings of the collection that bears his name, i.e., the first of the three treatises on *Condemning Offensive Warfare:*

> Now, if there is one man who enters another's orchard or garden and steals his peaches and plums, all who hear about it condemn him. If those above who conduct government get hold of him, then they punish him. Why is this? Because it is by harming the other that he benefits himself. When it comes to stealing another's dogs, hogs, chickens and suckling pigs, his unrighteousness is greater than entering the other's orchard or garden and stealing his peaches and plums. What is the reason for this? Because his harming the other is much greater, his lack of benevolence and righteousness is even greater, and the crime more serious [...] When it comes to killing an innocent man, seizing his clothes and fur garments, and taking his spear and sword, the lack of righteousness is greater again than entering another's animal enclosure and taking his horses and oxen. What is the reason for this? It is because the loss to the other is even greater.
>
> (Mozi, *Fei Gong, Shang* 非攻 上. Translation Johnston 2010, 167)

There is no need, I think, to comment upon the careful hierarchizing of causes and effects that Mozi, in this text and many others, intends to bring to the light of the day.

As to Mencius, he makes indeed an extensive use of correlative or, simply, analogical reasoning. *Mencius* 6 A.2, a passage centered on analogies between water and human nature, is a case in point. However, Mencius' argument is to be understood in a wider context: water, for ancient China, was more than a metaphorical vehicle. It was, in many respects, the reality best able to reveal the characteristics of the Way. The observation of water was allowing one to experience how the Way sustains the world. Sarah Allan has convincingly shown that the meditation upon water was transformational of behaviors and attitudes (Allan 1997). Besides, argue some commentators, correlative reasoning may have its own logical rules, which is based on *frequency:*

> *Good* correlative reasoning assigns things into categories using *strong* correlations, and *bad* correlative reasoning assigns things into categories using *weak* correlations. Whether a correlation is strong or weak depends, in turn, upon how frequently the thing being categorized is expected to occur together with the things to which it is being correlated.
>
> (Jones 2016, 202)

In any case, and even when putting aside Jones' line of argumentation, our first observation (the primacy given to water, seen as being, more than a mere metaphor, the closest expression of the One and the Dao) is probably more relevant than the second one (the logical structuring of correlative reasoning): I plead for a special status of "water metaphors" in ancient China – as is the case for the ones having to do with fire and light in the Greek context. In both cases, these elements relate to a geographical/existential milieu that becomes the privileged setting of thought experience.

Another point needs careful consideration: does the use of examples and images (very frequent also in Western philosophical writings) always testify to analogical reasoning? Certainly not. For instance, Mencius writes:

> I have a liking for fish, and I also have a liking for bear's paws. If I cannot have the two, I will let the fish go, and choose the bear's paws. I have a liking for life, and I also have a liking for righteousness [justice]. If I cannot have the two, I will let life go, and choose righteousness. I like life indeed, but there is that which I like more than life, and therefore, I will not seek to possess it at any price. I loathe death indeed, but there is that which I loathe more than death, and therefore there are risks that I will not avoid to take.
> 孟子曰：「魚，我所欲也；熊掌，亦我所欲也，二者不可得兼，舍魚而取熊掌者也。生，亦我所欲也；義，亦我所欲也，二者不可得兼，舍生而取義者也。生亦我所欲，所欲有甚於生者，故不為苟得也；死亦我所惡，所惡有甚於死者，故患有所不辟也。」
>
> (*Mencius* 6 A.10)

Mencius is not establishing a "correlation" between, say, life and bear's paws, or between death and fish. He is illustrating a general rule: when a choice is necessarily to be made, a hierarchization of preferences is to be ascertained and acted upon. Note that what is at stake here is to achieve what "study" (*xue*) is meant for: matching deed with words. The ordinariness of the example may help Mencius' listeners to prepare themselves for the practical jump potentially to be made when one sincerely declares to prefer righteousness over life. Here, comparison is a pedagogical device that does not refers to an analogical grid. Mencius relies on deduction while choosing his example within the ones provided by everyday life.

We need to make our refutation even stronger. Asserting that Chinese thought is indifferent to logical analysis means to put aside the development of Chinese mathematics from an early period onwards.³⁶ This art was subordinated to "procedures" or "algorithms" (*shu* 術 and, in later periods, *lü* 律) which (a) needed to be followed step by step; (b) started with conditions specified by a "let us suppose that…" (*jin you shu* 今有術); (c) were describing operations such as homogenization (*tong* 同); and (d) were comparable among themselves. The term *doushu* 都術 was designating an "universal procedure" upon which subordinate ways of proceeding depended.³⁷

> Proofs relied on algorithms, which had already been established as correct, and […] articulated these algorithms as a basis for establishing the correctness of other procedures. […] The evidence provided by the commentaries seems to manifest a link – perhaps specific to ancient China – between the way in which the proof of the correctness of algorithms was conducted and a systematic interest in the dimension of generality of the situations and concepts encountered.
>
> (Chemla 2012, 481)

Much more could be said about early developments of Chinese logical thinking but these indications might be enough to avoid associating the ancient Chinese worldview with "ambiguity, vagueness and incoherence".

Dialectic and Vagueness

In several places, *Anticipating China* also insists upon the following thesis: Western philosophical options are in general *mutually exclusive*, based on dialectical oppositions, on argument rather than on experience. Conversely, Chinese thought is *accommodating* (a scholar can refer to several systems and traditions), the more so because it makes ample use of data provided by concrete examples and experiences.

> Openness was maintained by the tacit insistence upon connotative 'vagueness' which permits the copresence in a single term of a variety of important meaning. The lack of emphasis upon connotative definition precluded the dependance upon rational systems or theories as the primary vehicles of ideas.
>
> (Hall and Ames 1995, 74–75)

---

36 Rošker (2021, 73–99) offers a good analysis of Chinese logical theories, though very much anchored in the concept of analogy and linguistic considerations.
37 I refer here to the glossary offered by Chemla and Guo (2004). Part of this material can also be found in Guo, Dauben and Xu (2017). As to the (partial) relevance for the pre-Qin period of these observations on Chinese algorithms, see Cullen (2007).

If a single term allows for a variety of important meanings, one wonders why our authors (as we will see in Chapter 2) insist upon reforming the lexicon currently used for translating Chinese notions. In any case, I think that Hall and Ames are right to underline the lexical flexibility of sinograms, but such flexibility requires further elaboration. Theodore de Bary has an insightful remark: "The idea is not so much to analyze and define concepts precisely as to expand them, to make them suggestive of the widest possible range of meaning. Generally, the more crucial or central the concept, the greater the ambiguity" (De Bary 1970, ix). Concepts, if central for the thinking process, need to be made suggestive, so as to show how the "thing" they point towards encompasses all aspects of reality. The most striking example of such propensity is the development of the notion of Ritual (*li* 禮) in the *Analects:* "See nothing outside Ritual, hear nothing outside Ritual, say nothing outside Ritual, do nothing outside Ritual 非禮 勿 視。非禮 勿 聽，非禮 勿 言。非禮 勿 動" (*Analects* 12.1). Though the translation of this passage remains a bit controversial and its overall meaning debated, the meaning that emerges from this sentence is unmistakable: the notion of Ritual hints at something that underlies social phenomena to such extent, that it needs to inform the totality of our ways of perceiving and behaving.

The thesis according to which Chinese philosophical constructions spontaneously "accommodate" each other could be similarly challenged, but the way one constructs oppositions and possible rapprochements among systems partly depends upon the subjectivity of the commentator, and the point is not central for the issues debated here. Still, we should not overlook the seriousness of the disagreements that were opposing thinkers in ancient China. Mozi is ferocious in his attacks against the *Ru* 儒 (the "Confucians"). The opening sentence of the canonical version of the *Laozi*, which claims that "a name that can be named is not the constant name" is a direct attack against the premises of the Confucians' gnoseological and political worldview. Xunzi's stress on artifice as well as on the way the ruler must govern through fear puts him in a kind of isolation – till the Legists challenge even more radically Confucius' and Mencius' reliance on education and virtue. In many respects, "accommodation" is a latter-day phenomenon, fostered by the constraints imposed by state orthodoxy.

As to the "vagueness" attributed to ancient Chinese thought: although the notion is now used as a kind of compliment, I find it misleading. The fact of privileging "ordinary language" in philosophical debates, the reliance on experience, or yet the role given to notions such as *xuan* 玄 (dark, obscure) are in no way akin to "vagueness" in thinking. The ultimate objective of Daoist thinkers remains to reach "illumination", "enlightenment" (*ming* 明). I have quoted already Stanza 16 of *Laozi*. One could refer also to Laozi 33: "Who knows the Other is a sage;

who knows himself is enlightened知人者智，自知者明." Let us listen to what Zhuangzi similarly declares:

> Great knowledge remains at leisure; little knowledge is kept busy. Great words burst forth in flame; little words chatter, chatter. [...]
>
> To speak is not to breathe: he who speaks owns the words, and the words he possesses are not fixed [in their place]. So, are there still words? The words that have not been tried [literally: tasted], are they still words? If [speaking] is considered to be different from the chirping of chicks, it is because through speaking one can argue – is not that indisputable? Has the Way therefore become so obscured that there is both the authentic and the inauthentic? Have the words become so obscured that there is true and false in them? Has the Way gone to the point that it no longer exists? Would speech exist and be capable of nothing? The Way is masked for those who aim little; the words are masked by pomp and arts. Hence the judgments made by Confucians and Moists, some affirming what others refute, others refuting what some affirm. If one wants to navigate assertions and rebuttals, then nothing beats [proceeding by] enlightenment [*ming*]."
>
> 大知閑閑，小知閒閒；大言炎炎，小言詹詹。[...] 夫言非吹也。言者有言，其所言者特未定也。果有言邪？其未嘗有言邪？其以為異於鷇音，亦有辯乎？其無辯乎？道惡乎隱而有真偽？言惡乎隱而有是非？道惡乎往而不存？言惡乎存而不可？道隱於小成，言隱於榮華。故有儒、墨之是非，以是其所非，而非其所是。欲是其所非而非其所是，則莫若以明。
>
> (*Zhuangzi* 2.2 and 2.4)

Four terms are worth considering here: (1) Speech (or words) *yan* 言. The character originally designates the upper part of the throat, and means "to speak, to express". In the *Shuowen jiezi* 說文解字,[38] the term is applied specifically to the fact of speaking in a straightforward way. (2) The character for "flame, blaze, burning" (*yan* 炎) is a homonym of the one used for "speech". (3) The *chang* 嘗 character (taste, savor, and, by extension, experience) finds its roots in the sacrificial repertory: the tasting the meats offered to the ancestors opens up the ritual banquet. 4) Finally, the passage ends with the term "light, illumination" (*ming* 明). Formed by the association of the characters for the sun and the moon, *ming* initially designates the light of dawn, before meaning clarity, manifestation, and, in the context of the *Laozi* and *Zhuangzi*, inner light. In the case of the doublet used here (*yi ming* 以明) the term can also mean: "that which is by itself manifest".

There are, says Zhuangzi, "great words" or "great speech", a "perfect way of speaking" (*da yan* 大言). Speech can be "great", "perfect", "achieved", and therefore partake of the "One", of what is indivisible. Great speech and great knowledge

---

[38] *Shuowen jiezi*: A Chinese "dictionary", the first of its kind, that gives the general meaning of the basic characters upon which other depend (*wen*) and offers explanations for compound graphs (*zi*).

do not proceed by distinctions, additions, subtractions, they go beyond the "true" and the "false", they are experienced as being fire and light. – the light that comes from knowing the constant (*Laozi* 16). Baffling irony can reveal both the strength and the futility of speaking, as when Zhuangzi remarks that it is *indisputable* that speaking allows men to *dispute*. It is when words open the eyes upon what escapes categorization that they are "great".

Indeed, the knowledge that thinkers such as Zhuangzi aim to unveil is experiential. However, experiential knowledge does not trade in vagueness. On the contrary: it struggles to find the language that will open up the whole being of the listener to the experience that is proposed. The *ming* in Zhuangzi and Laozi is close from what "intuition" is for Bergson: an integral experience that is "infinitely simple", so simple, adds Bergson, that the philosopher, knowing not how to express it, tries again and again.[39] Perhaps, as suggested by Jankélévitch, "there is only one Simplicity, or rather one single spirit of simplicity. [...] For intuition is the asceticism of the mind; and asceticism, in turn, is nothing but intuition become the diet, catastasis, and permanent exercise of our soul" (Jankélévitch 2015, 165). This is a form of intellectual rigor that Jankélévitch is describing here – certainly not the *rigor mortis*, quite the reverse; the rigor of a thought that finds its setting in life experienced as the locus of its endless deployment. Put otherwise; nothing could be more rigorous than the language that Chinese philosophy strived to carve during the formative period in which it experienced with a variety of methods and styles, as it endeavored to espouse the movement of life itself.

Does Transcendence Matter?

Wandering further along the Western bank, the next enclosure introduces the visitor to a cluster of interrelated notions and phenomena. As described by Ames and Hall, they include the Roman concept of *humanitas* (unity beyond ethnic and political boundaries); the quasi-synonym *imperium*; the representation of human beings as *imago dei*, itself rooted in the doctrine of the Trinity; and an overarching concept of "transcendence" that grounded "progressive, moralistic interpretations of history and culture" (Hall and Hames 1995, 90). The boat may seem slightly overloaded, but Hall and Ames justify the length of this historical series (which goes through Cicero, Augustine, Thomas Aquinas, Luther, Hegel, Max Weber, and a few others) on the ground that the Western focus on "transcendence" is arguably

---

[39] See notably the essay "Philosophical Intuition" in *The Creative Mind* (*La pensée et le mouvant*) (Bergson 2010 [1934]).

the most alien to Chinese thought, and that its genealogy needs to be traced. As they use it, the meaning of the term "transcendence" is sometimes encompassing, sometimes more restrictive. Behuniak is right to underline the fact that the most restricted of these meanings is central to our authors' argument:

> As Hall and Ames have argued, "strict transcendence" has had an enormous impact on the development of Western philosophy. They define "strict transcendence" as follows: "A is transcendent with respect to B if the existence, meaning, or import of B cannot be fully accounted for without recourse to A, but the reverse is not true." Such thinking in the Chinese world, they have maintained, "has not been a part of the cultural narrative in its classical tradition."
> (Behuniak 2021, 11)[40]

One could find some Chinese cultural accounts congruent with the conditions defining "strict transcendence" for instance the beginning of the *Liezi* (1.1): "It is what was not born that can give birth, what was not transformed that can trigger transformations [不生者能生生，不化者能化化]." But I prefer to follow the line opened up by the following consideration: this way of building a philosophical narrative, even if it points towards meaningful features, obscures more than helps the access to Chinese ancient texts – and, concurrently, to Western ones. Whatever the definition chosen, the term "transcendence" itself is loaded with difficulties. Sometimes, the notions of "transcendence" and "immanence" (used by commentators more than by primary sources, with maybe the exception of the Kantian distinction between "transcendent" and "transcendental") do not even appear in the indexes of contemporary textbooks of metaphysics.[41] "Transcendence" and "Immanence" are not strictly defined concepts; they are rather "root metaphors", as Chin-Tai Kim suggests, allowing for a variety of speculative developments. The same author adds: "The ideas of transcendence and immanence are not mutually exclusive but mutually determinative" (Kim 1987, 537).

Actually, the definition of "strict transcendence" offered by Hall and Ames and summarized by Behuniak may be misleading: one could imagine strictly unidimensional causal chains operating in a world that would still be conceived on the basis of immanentism. The criterion offered for strict transcendence should have to do with the fact that the factor B without which the very existence of A could not even be imagined is located in another world (in another set of foundational requisites) than the one of which A is part. Another factor would warrant further consideration: if the factor B without which the very existence of A could not even be imagined is located in another world than the one of which A is part, then, the rep-

---
40 See in parallel Ames (2016).
41 Consult for instance the lexicon found in Koons and Pickavance (2015).

resentation of B escapes all representations. In so far as it is "groundless", the first cause cannot be figured on the model of a relationship similar in nature to the one existing within the same phenomenal world. What Hall and Ames have in mind is obviously something similar to the doctrine of the creation *ex nihilo* (see Ames and Hall 2001, 12). However, the latter is more an expression of *religious transcendence* than of *philosophical transcendence,* and the two do not work on the same assumptions (except when one tries to philosophically argue that the creation *ex nihilo* is the only "reasonable" answer to the question "why is there something rather than nothing"), and I will show below the importance of the distinction.

Before proceeding further, let us note that one can "believe" in transcendence without adhering to religious creeds and practices. Conversely, religions are not necessarily based on a belief in transcendence. Among "immanent" religions, Chinese Mahayana Buddhism puts emphasis on enlightenment as the self-realization of one's immanent Buddha nature. However, it is not easy to rigorously maintain such immanent stance: the Mahāsāṃghika (at the origin of Mahayana Buddhism) soon asserted that Buddha, Omnipresent, Omnipotent and Omniscient, was living endlessly and eternally, thus opening the way to the belief in transcendent interventions in this world, and on the importance of faith and ritual practices for benefiting of such interventions.

Let us come back to our first enclosure, in which, among "Western" cosmogonies, was presented the first chapter of *Genesis.* To what extent is the narrative focused on "transcendence" or "immanence"? The question remains disputed. After all, God is said to create from a "stuff" which, if formless, seems to pre-exist the narrative. The idea or the dogma of "creation *ex nihilo*" cannot be immediately extracted from the text. Besides, God is not represented as located in a "sacred space" that would be separated from the world. *He is not separated from the world, he creates by separation,* dividing light from darkness, the waters under the vault from the waters above the vault, and land from sea (and the theme of a "separating God" is close from the one of a god who divides, dismembers himself, as narrated in the Babylonian creation epic *Enuma Elish*). Said otherwise, in *Genesis* I, "Sacredness" does not operate in space but rather in time, by the institution of the "sacred time" of the Sabbath: transcendence lies in rest, and appears teleologically so to speak. Julius Wellhausen (1844–1918) was seeing in the fact that God was "creating" through successive acts of separation the remnant of a topic of "immanent evolution", common to other cosmogonies of the region. Hermann Gunkel (1862–1932), for his part, was thinking that "separation from the chaos [could] just as well be produced by an immanent principle as by a creative word" (Gunkel 1895, 8, n. 3.). Such reading of *Genesis* I opens up a more general insight: "The monotheism of Israel (whose situation has always been subjected to tensions which are moreover fruitful) has been 'preserved' not by *suppressing* opposing forces, but by *displacement*" (Beauchamp 2005 [1969], 339).

As to the verdict of "pure immanence" passed upon the Chinese classics by our authors, it is partly grounded into their denial of the presence of independent, identifiable divine figures within the same texts. I will challenge this assertion in the next chapter, as it will deal with lexical issues. However, a discussion about "transcendence" in Chinese classics can provisionally be led while making abstraction of the question of the Divine. In other words, we first can deal independently with *philosophical transcendence.*

"Transcendence" can be a belief ("the world has been created from nothing by an agency external to it") or as a question ("why is there something rather than nothing?"). In the last case, the question of the "There is" necessarily raises the question of the "There is not", and of the relationship existing between one state of things and the other is at the core of the problem. This is exactly the issue that dominates the first stanza of the *Laozi* in its canonical version, a good part of the rest of the book, and all the writings that it has triggered. Let us remember that variants the *Laozi* are, by far, the most common occurrences in the archeological findings that bear textual evidences for pre-Han or early Han China.

The characters *wu* and *you* appear very frequently as a pair in the *Laozi*, starting from the first stanza. Translating them represents a challenge. Speaking of "Being" and "Non-Being" would be misleading. The best strategy is probably to notice that they fulfill a grammatical function before functioning more or less as "nouns" (this vocabulary should not be used for ancient Chinese, but there are indeed *functions* fulfilled by characters or couples of characters, to be determined according to the context and structure of the sentence). The English language knows how to play with the space that both separates and unites the verbs "to be" and "to have". One writes: "There is" and "There is not". One may say that *wu* and *you* speak respectively of "the 'There is'" and of "the 'There is not'". This includes things that are visible and things that are not, things that are empty (a recipient void of water, the center of a wheel) and things that are filled, things that give birth and things that are birthed. The interplay between appearance and disappearance is a prime object of speculation for Chinese thinkers, and is first grasped in its phenomenality. It is through this contemplative observation that a "light" breaks through, illuminating from within not only the law that governs phenomena but their supra- or infra-phenomenal source: the wonder (*miao* 妙) at the heart of *wu* 無, as stated by *Laozi* 1. In no case should the meaning of *wu* as a negation be erased, as do Ames and Hall when they translate in Laozi *wu zhi* 無知 (not knowing, absence of knowledge) as "unprincipled knowledge" and *wu yu* 無欲 (no desire, absence of desire) as "objectless desire" (Ames and Hall 2001, 5). Let us call this a case of "unprincipled creativity".

Are *wu* and *you* inscribed into an unbreakable circularity? One is allowed to hesitate. For sure, *Laozi* 2 states that "'There is' and 'There is not' take birth one from the other [*wu you xiang sheng* 無有相生]." However, the context of the passage weighs heavily upon the meaning to be given to the sentence: Stanza 2 laments the appearance of opposites, the exit-out from the One that is necessarily produced by judgments, by linguistic discriminations. If the idea of the "Beautiful" would not have appeared, there would not be the idea of the "Ugly" – and the same applies to the idea of *wu* and *you*. So, the correct understanding is probably "the ideas of *wu* and *you* generate each other". In contrast, Stanza 40 states:

> Reverting is the Way's motion; Weakness is how it proceeds. In the world, all beings come from a 'there is', and 'there is' comes from 'there is not'.
> 反者道之動；弱者道之用。天下萬物生於有，有生於無。
>
> (*Daodejing* 40)

Out of caution, my translation "all beings *come from*" is actually a bit weak: I translate here the character *sheng* 生. The omnipresence of the latter in our texts should not diminish the strength of its meaning: to give birth (or, according to the context, to take birth from, as the distinction between passive and active forms in ancient Chinese is often contextual – and, after all, *nascor* in Latin is the clearest possible example of a deponent verb and of the implications attached to it). So, the "There is" would take birth from the "There is not"? The conclusion is not absolutely warranted: the sentence should be probably interpreted in the light of its beginning: *reverting* is the movement of the Way... Circularity is possibly reestablished.

I would suggest that, in a logic that is reminiscent of the one deployed by *Genesis* (though obviously through a very different strategy), the *Laozi* leaves open the option of thinking in terms of generation from the "There is not" to the "There is" or in term of an interrupted cycle between the two. The crucial point is that the text does not dwell upon the mere passage from one state of things to another (correlative thinking does just that) but rather upon the enigma of what a *beginning* is to be. This is "enigma over enigma", as Stanza 1 concludes.

The *Laozi* does not ground a transcendent standpoint. But it lets open the question of the Origin as a "There is not", and its philosophical stature rests on this suspension of judgment. I would even suggest that it refers the idea of Origin to a teleological standpoint, since the characteristics attached to the "There is not" inspire the ideal of the Sage emptied of herself: *wu* is both the origin and the term, in the sense that a "term" is a finality induced by an internal dynamism.

The *Laozi* is not the only text that leaves open such questions. Let me mention an excavated text, admittedly short (13 tablets) but of particular significance, the *Hengxian* 亙先. The spelling, meaning and pronunciation of the first character of the title have been the subject of intense debate after the text was published in 2003. Following Ding Sixin, I see in *heng* 恆 a concept in its own right, which designates the Dao as both immutable and celestial (it therefore does not cover all the meanings of Dao in *Laozi* for example), while *xian* is a determinant here meaning "pivot", "fulcrum", the principle which puts *heng* in action.[42] I therefore dare to translate this title (which testifies to the terminological effort pursued at that time to think "what things are" [a "what" expressed later by the character ji 極]) by: "The pivot of the constant law". The beginning of the text is truly majestic:

> The pivot of the constant law is devoid of all 'having [existence]',[43] is simple [of one piece], calm, empty [of itself]. Its simplicity is extreme, its calm extreme, its emptiness also extreme. It is filled without filling up, and [thus] things are set in motion. With motion came the qi. With the qi came Existence. With Existence came Beginning. With Beginning came Passing away.[44]
> 恆 [亙] 先無有，樸、靜、虛。樸，大樸。靜，大靜。虛，大虛。自厭不自忍，或作。有或焉有氣，有氣焉有有，有有焉有始，有始 焉有往。
>
> (Hengxian 1)

Zhuangzi exclaims: "The 'There is not' as a 'There is', even the divine Yu knows nothing about. So, how could someone like me! [無有為有，雖有神禹，且不能知，吾獨且奈何哉]" (*Zhuangzi* 2.4)[45] Here we can hear the voice of the true philosopher, the one who does not limit the perimeter of his peregrinations by ready-made definitions of what "transcendence" and "immanence" are meant to be, but rather stops at the threshold of the Origin.

Besides, Zhuangzi does not content himself with letting open the door to a "Transcendent Origin". Zhuangzi transfers transcendence from the domain of "metaphysics" ("what is beyond the form" [*xing er shang* 形而上]) to the one of teleology: the mode of transcendence that he propounds is an opening to unlimited, unconditional freedom. Still, the transcendental freedom obtained by the one who fully communes with the Dao speaks of the transcendence of the Dao proper. Zhuangzi's approach of the Dao is transcendental by the very fact that the text

---

[42] Cf. Ding (2016).
[43] David Chai gives *xian* a verbal function, and translates: "*Heng* precedes being and non-being". Chai also reads *huo* 或 as *yu* 域 (space, realm) (Chai 2019, 18 and 180). I find the lexical hypotheses ventured by Ding (2016) more convincing, while recognizing that the text remains open to a number of interpretative translations.
[44] My translation is based on analyses developed by Ding (2019) and Brindley, Goldin and Klein (2013).
[45] Zhuangzi refers here to Yu the Great, the hero of the quasi-cosmogony that the Flood narrative constitutes.

speaks both the unfathomable Origin and of the unconditioned freedom located at its horizon (see Liu 2010).

One may dare to suggest that the realm of transcendence is evoked in the *Zhuangzi* by the mere use of the character "big/great" (*da* 大). In relationship with the use of this character, Yuet Keung Lo speaks even of "maximal transcendence", which he aptly links with the Zhuangzian ideal of "free and easy wandering" (*xiaoyao you* 逍遙遊) (Lo 2022, 455): free and easy wandering is truly boundless only if it takes place in the Limitless (*da*), in That which cannot be measured, divided, counted or yet named. One finds a similar idea in Augustine: the first word of the *Confessions* is "great [magnus]" ("Magnus es, Domine"), immediately clarified by the addition: "Your wisdom has no number [i.e., cannot be numbered]" ("sapientiae tuae non est numerus"). That God is "great" is the first of the series of acknowledgments that will come out of Augustine's mouth, and the meaning of this acknowledgment is unveiled only when we have perceived that "being great" means to escape any attempt at measurement and counting.

The space left open by the *Zhuangzi* and the *Laozi* (and even by Confucius through his refusal to deal with questions bearing on the ultimate – see *Analects* 11, 12, among other relevant passages) will be filled in different ways by successive generations of Chinese thinkers. Wang Bi 王弼 (226–249) operates a passage from the "cosmological" to the "ontological" (whatever the adequacy of the word in the Chinese context[46]): Dao (here considered as a name) brings to fulfillment the myriad things by means of its featurelessness (*mo xing* 未形) and ineffability (*wu ming* 無名), states Wang Bi at the very beginning of his *Commentary on the Laozi*. Dao, he insists, is the *reason* for which things come to existence and take their shape (*shi cheng* 始成). It lies beyond the realm of the phenomenal as approaching it by sense experience does not deliver any kind of knowledge: "as a thing" (*wei wu* 為物), Dao is without discernible features (*hun cheng* 混成). Considered "as an image" (*wei xiang* 為象), it possesses not visual features. "As a sound" (*wei yin* 為音), it is silent. "As a flavor" (*wei wei* 為味), it is tasteless. Dao is "not constrained" (*bu xi* 不繫) by anything.

> Wang Bi argues that if something has every determinable (or general feature) to an infinite degree, then it cannot have any specific feature; any specific feature would become a constraint on its infinity. Dao, according to Wang Bi, is such an entity that has every determinable to an infinite degree: it has an infinite image, an infinite size, an infinite sound, an infinite depth, an infinite flavor, and so on. This infinity is the reason why Dao is featureless. Therefore, Dao is infinite, so it is featureless. It is featureless, so it is the reason why the myriad

---

[46] For the debate about the applicability of the terms "ontology" or *bentilun* 本體論 to Wang Bi's thought, see: Tang (2001); Wagner (2003); Hui (2020), 161–170.

things exist and are the ways they are. Dao, by its infinity, serves as the ontological ground for the myriad things.

(Hong 2019, 239)

In contrast, the perspective taken by Guo Xiang 郭象 (252–312 CE) in his *Zhuangzi Commentary* can be described as strictly immanent.[47] Searching for a "ground" that would pre-exist the existence of things amounts to a meaningless operation. With Guo Xiang we are indeed in the presence of a doctrine of "the world-as-it-is" close to the sketch that Ames and Hall were presenting to us at the beginning of *Anticipating China*. Guo Xiang's approach is at its clearest in his commentary of Chapter 22 of *Zhuangzi*:

> What could possibly exist prior to things [*wu* 物]! I might have it that yin and yang were prior to them, but yin and yang themselves are just what we may call things. So what was there even prior to ying and yang? I might have it that Nature [*ziran* 自然] was prior to them, but Nature means just things functioning spontaneously on their own. I might have it that the perfect Dao was there prior to it, but the perfect Dao consists of just perfect emptiness [*zhiwu* 至無]. As such, it has no existence, so what could have been more prior to that? This being so, what then could have possibly existed prior to things! However, since things still come into existence without ever ending, it is clear that they just happen spontaneously and not because something makes them happen.
> 誰得先物者乎哉？吾以陰陽為先物，而陰陽即所謂物耳，誰又先陰陽者乎？吾以自然為先之，而自然即物之自爾耳。吾以至道為一先之矣。而至道者乃至無也。既以無矣，又奚為先然？則先物者誰乎哉？而猶有物，無已。明物之自然，非有使然也。
>
> (Guo Xiang, *Commentary on Chapter 22 of Zhuangzi*. Translation Lynn 2022, 398)

The fact that Chinese ancient texts were escaping the use of categories such as "transcendence" and "immanence" is precisely what helped them to preserve the ineffable character of the Origin and, at the same time, lean towards a form of "teleological transcendence". Their specific way of articulating foundational questions allowed for the development of a plurality of standpoints once Chinese thought entered the age of "scholasticism", commenting upon its classics while assimilating Buddhist doctrines and Indian modes of thinking.

---

47 Following Tang (2001), Yuk Hui thinks that Wang Bi and Guo Xiang "are essentially in agreement, merely placing emphasis on different phases of recursive thinking" (Hui 2020, 167). I think that the opposition between these two thinkers goes far deeper than a mere difference in emphasis in the description they give of the interaction between *wu* and *you*. Richard Lynn stresses the fact that there existed basic oppositions within the *xuanxue* 玄學 tradition. Contrasting the commentaries on the *Zhuangzi* authored by, respectively, Guo Xiang and Xiang Xiu 向秀 (c. 223 – c. 275), Lynn notes: "Using modern terminology, Xiang may be said to have adopted an 'immanent transcendence' position. Instead, Guo insists that no external generator exists because for him, no existence is possible apart from material reality" (Lynn 2022, xlviiii).

The debate about whether or not the Chinese tradition has known a form of "transcendence" took a new impetus from the 1950s onwards. This time, it was explicitly articulated according to Western notions and ways of reasoning. "Transcendence" was translated as *chaoyue* 超越 or *chaoyuexing* 超越性, "immanence/immanent" being expressed through the lexical pair *neizai* 內在 ("within"). We will evoke this debate towards the end of Chapter 3, when discussing a book of the Shanghainese scholar Li Tiangang 李天綱 that examines Chinese religiosity and ritual expressions.

The Otherness That Lies Within

The plurality of philosophical meanings, continue our authors, was preserved in China by "institutionalized vagueness" (Hall and Ames 1995, 104). One may find this particular assertion dubious: we just saw that the difference among the viewpoints articulated by Wang Bi, on the one hand, and Guo Xiang, on the other hand, was neither "vague" nor so easy to reconcile. Still, Hall and Ames rightly point towards the flexibility exhibited by Chinese philosophy, its capacity to reconcile viewpoints and to crisscross frontiers. Such flexibility, they add, comes from the *subjective, non-objectifiable standpoint* that it has been able to maintain all along:

> At least since Nietzsche, the rational ethos defining Western sensibility has been under serious attack. Today movements such as process philosophy, postmodernism and the new pragmatism, by unearthing the analogical, correlative roots of language, have begun to undermine the notion of objectivity as the principal aim of thinking. [...] If we begin to take our cues from these Western thinkers [...], we shall surely be better prepared to understand the Chinese.
> (Hall and Ames 1995, 109)

Ames also states:

> American philosophy [...] offers an alternative, decidedly positive, vocabulary that takes as its target foundationalist philosophy. American pragmatism further resonates with the traditional Chinese philosophical narrative in respecting the processual nature of experience, and thus can serve as a resource for creative philosophizing.
> (Ames 2007, 33)

Ames has made process philosophy the main purveyor of conceptual tools for the rapprochement he and others endeavor to engineer.[48] Such borrowing remains qualified: "Process philosophy", at least in the person of its figurehead, still remains handicapped by the Western heritage:

---

[48] See the lengthy note 1 in Ames and Hall (2001), 54.

> We might find analogy with Whitehead in his concern to reinstate 'creativity' as an important human value when turning to the *Zhongyong* 中庸 (*Focusing the Familiar*) in which the human being is celebrated as co-creator with the heavens and the earth. At the same time, we might be keenly aware that when Whitehead invokes the primordial nature of God and the Eternal Objects this nature sustains, the long shadow of Aristotelian metaphysics has set a real limit on the relevance of Whitehead for classical Chinese *biantong* 變通[49] (processual) cosmology.
>
> (Ames 2005, 349)

The problem with borrowing from process philosophy may not be the one that Ames has in mind: with due respect to a current of thought that has proven to be both insightful and creative, I am not sure that it naturally fosters a genuine rapprochement with Eastern insights. More exactly: I do not deny that the rapprochement has opened avenues of dialogue, but I suggest that it is built upon a misreading. Seen from the perspective of intellectual history, the focus on "process" is the result of a specifically Western philosophical evolution. In *The Human Condition*, Hannah Arendt has described the shift from the "why" to the "how" that took place in sciences and thought (the shift towards technology) in modern Europe, concluding that, *in consequence of it*, "things" or eternal motions were displaced from the center of investigation, to the benefit of processes: Nature or the universe were not the object of science anymore; it rather was *the story of the coming into being*. Therefore, natural sciences too were considered as historical disciplines:

> Nature, because it could be known only in processes, which human ingenuity, the ingenuity of *homo faber*, could repeat and remake in the experiment, became a process, and all particular natural things derived their significance and meaning solely from their functions in the overall process. In the place of the concept of being we now find the concept of Process.[50]
>
> (Arendt 1998 [1958], 296)

In other words: the focus on "process" might correspond to the ultimate stage of Western thought, just like Imperialism is for Capitalism... One may see in this fact an irony of history. In any case, the observation reminds us that any philosophical grand narrative can be easily counterbalanced by another one.

* * *

---

[49] The expression *biantong* is very rare in the ancient classics. Still, it can be found three times in the Ten Wings Commentary on the *Yijing*. Its use becomes noticeably more frequent after the Han dynasty.

[50] Further in the text, Arendt mentions Whitehead's *Concept of Nature*.

Let me highlight the thread followed till now: I have tried to revive "Otherness" within each of the traditions put to the test by contemporary Chinese-Western comparative philosophy. Not a form of "Otherness" that would be merely a "minority opinion" inside a dominant tradition – a minority opinion conveniently discarded when drawing overarching syntheses – but an "Otherness" that points towards the philosophical impetus of each of the traditions considered, forbidding the system in which it is inserted to close upon itself. Such distancing of each tradition from itself resonates with the way Zhuangzi considers "differences":

> Looking at things from the viewpoint of difference, the liver and the gallbladder look {as distant as the states of} Chu and Yue. But when looking at them from the viewpoint of sameness, then all the myriad things are one. When you consider things this way, you do not know them in the fashion they fit eye and ear, [but rather] you release your heart-mind in the harmony of all manifested potentialities.
> 自其異者視之，肝膽楚越也；自其同者視之，萬物皆一也。夫若然者，且不知耳目之所宜，而游心於德之和。
>
> (Zhuangzi 5.1)

"The harmony of all manifested potentialities [*de zhi he* 德之和]"... One could simply translate: the harmony of potencies, the way through which the manifestations of virtue harmonize. I speak here of "manifested potentialities" in order to introduce a point that I will develop in the course of the next chapter: the term "virtue" (*de* 德) refers to what manifests the creative power of the Dao, as plants manifest the life-power proper to water. The myriad things are one in that they originate from the same source and similarly return to it. Somehow, the variety of their manifestations testifies to the unity of their production and destiny. Philosophical productions are subject to such reversal of perspective. Pascal observes that what is seen at a distance as a township appears, as you get closer and closer, as an agglomerate of houses, trees, tiles, leaves, grasses, ants, ants' legs, *ad infinitum*...[51] Still, once the agglomerate has been considered in its dizzying heterogeneousness, you may want to ponder what makes it an organic whole – what ultimately constitutes its Oneness.

---

51 *Pensées* (Sellier 2000, n. 99).

Chapter 2
"Rectifying Names"

"Rectifying names": such was, for Confucius, the paramount political imperative. It is only towards the end of this chapter that I will ponder over the program sketched by Confucius when he was speaking of rectifying names. We will then be able to better define what we exactly *do* when we draw "equivalences" between terms. I first need to further the critical enquiry conducted in the preceding chapter: the philosophical landscaping that we just summarized and questioned needs to "rectify names" in such a way as to allow for the opposites and parallelisms upon which our mirror gardens are designed. What does such operation entail? A quote by Roger Ames may help us to perceive what is at stake:

> There are numerous examples of grossly inappropriate language having become the standard equivalents in the Chinese/English dictionaries that we use to perpetuate our understanding of Chinese culture: "the Way (*dao*道)," "Heaven (*tian*天)," "benevolence *ren*仁," "rites *li*禮," "virtue *de*德," "righteousness *yi*義," "principle *li* 理," and so on. Is being someone's son or daughter a "rite"?
>
> (Ames 2007, 30)

Let me take here the examples raised by Ames and discuss what makes a translation of such notions appropriate or inappropriate. As we will see, our lexical inquiry has direct repercussions on the understanding of ancient Chinese thought.

Di, Tian, Shen, Guishen, Shenming...

Let me start with a term that Roger Ames deems to be "untranslatable": *tian* 天. In their translation of the *Zhongyong*, Ames and Hall, when they encounter the expression "Heaven and Earth [*tian di* 天地]" chose to translate *di* as "Earth" but they abstain to translate *tian*.[52] Similarly, Peter Wong Yih Jiun, does not endeavor to propose a translation of the term when discussing "the experience of the numinous" (Wong 2021). Such stance creates a difficulty where there should be none.

---

[52] See the criticisms addressed by Lauren F. Pfister to the translation of *Zhongyong* 16 offered by Ames and Hall, and notably to their suggestions that textual interpolations took place (Ames and Hall 2001, 144; Pfister 2021, 119–130; Pfister 2020).

Open Access. © 2023 the author(s), published by De Gruyter. This work is licensed under the Creative Commons Attribution 4.0 International License. https://doi.org/10.1515/9783110799118-004

A Semantic Field

I cannot discuss constructively the character *tian* without associating it with (and contrasting it to) another term, the one of *di* 帝 (and the compound *shangdi* 上帝) which Hall and Ames render by "high ancestors" (Hall and Ames 20021) – which is not, I will try to show, an appropriate translation. Related terms will also enter our discussion.

Shangdi 上帝 is the name of the supreme deity revered by the rulers of the Shang dynasty (c. 1570 – 1045 BCE). The oracular inscriptions simply use the character *di* by which they could designate a Supreme Power alone capable of controlling rain and certain other natural phenomena. The long-held assumption that *di* would correspond to the original Ancestor of the dynasty or to a collective of ancestors is now strongly challenged on the basis of *di*'s recognized ability to bring disaster to the dynasty that he protected. Also, the nature of the sacrifices offered to him, differs from the ones performed in ancestors' worship.[53] It is even possible that the cult of *di* weakened as the Shang rulers started to focus more on the ancestors of their dynasty (Keightley 2000, 252–253 and 261–262). In any event, the "Power [*di*] from above [*shang*]" overlooks the supernatural world. (Note that this world is not a "pantheon", in the sense that one does not find there the individuation of the divinities which one usually associates with this term.) Sacrifices are frequently offered, on the one hand to the *manes* (*gui* 鬼) (those of the royal family in the first place), on the other hand to spirits (*shen* 神) of various origins (celestial spirits, spirits attached to places or natural elements, deified men, cultural heroes).[54] Both categories will continue to be grouped in Chinese under the term *guishen* (鬼神), the first term referring to *manes* (and later often to "demons"), the second to spirits in the broader sense. Even after the fall of the Shang dynasty, monarchs continued to celebrate once every five years the most solemn sacrifice of all, the one for *Shangdi*. This sacrifice is depicted by an associated homonymous character (*di* 禘) about whose meaning Confucius confessed ignorance while asserting that whoever would understand it would in fact control the Empire (*Analects* 3,11). The term *huangdi* (皇帝) will be adopted by the Qin dynasty (221–206 BCE) to designate the Emperor. It thus associated with *di* a character (*huang*) des-

---

[53] Among other scholars, Xu Fuguan 徐復觀 has insisted on the importance of the cult of ancestors in the (agrarian) society developed during the Shang dynasty, which the Zhou dynasty perpetuated. (A good summary of Xu's argument can be found in Rošker 2021, 45–47). The point is probably exact. However, one should not read all ancient rituals as participating in ancestors' worship.
[54] One sometimes distinguishes among heavenly spirits (*tianshen* 天神), terrestrial deities (*diqi* 地祇), and spirits of departed humans (*rengui* 人鬼), though the period when this distinction was first made explicit remains undetermined.

ignating the grandfather or the deceased father, establishing both an echo and a contrast between *Shangdi* and the Emperor, between Heaven and the sovereign reigning on earth.

Here we are meeting with *tian*, i.e., with "Heaven". "Heaven" is contrasted to "Earth" (*di* 地). From this basic, experiential contrast, the term takes a number of associated meanings. The supreme god of the Zhou dynasty (1046 to 256 BCE) is invoked under this name. It is also the one used by the peoples of the steppes with whom the Zhou people maintained cultural and geographical proximity (although the exact origins of the Zhou are still subject to debate). In the oracular inscriptions, the character is hardly distinguished from the one, graphically very close, which means "big" (*da* 大). Heaven gives the sovereign a "mandate" (*ming* 命), which he will lose if his conduct does not meet the moral and ritual standards that he must maintain and enforce. The following proclamation testifies the merging which occurred between the figures of *tian* and *shangdi*, probably towards the beginning of the Zhou dynasty:

> The King said: "All of you, from every region of the land, listen carefully to what I [a straightforward man] am about to say. The Emperor above all Emperors [*weihuangdi*] has endowed every person with a moral sense [*zhong*], and this is their essential, original nature. However, to ensure that they stay true to this essential nature, it is necessary to have rulers. The King of Xia lost sight of virtue and became an oppressive dictator. He even oppressed you, my dear people, from every region. And when you were no longer able to bear his bitter and poisonous ways, wrought to his cruel regime, you united to proclaim your innocence before the spirits of Above and Below [*shangxia shenqi*]. You know it is the way of Heaven [*tian dao*] to bring good fortune to the good and to curse the wicked. This is why it has brought disaster upon the Xia, making their terrible sins apparent to everyone. This is why I, unimportant as I am, like a child have been granted the mandate of Heaven [*tianming*] which lights up the whole world with its authority. I cannot ignore it or stop doing [what is asked of me]."
> 王曰：「嗟！爾萬方有眾，明聽予一人誥。惟皇上帝，降衷于下民。若有恆性，克綏厥猷惟后。夏王滅德作威，以敷虐于爾萬方百姓。爾萬方百姓，罹其凶害，弗忍荼毒，並告無辜于上下神祇。天道福善禍淫，降災于夏，以彰厥罪。肆台小子，將天命明威，不敢赦。」
>
> (*Book of Documents*, "The Declaration of Tang" 湯誥. Translation Palmer 2014, 49, modified)

This supreme, moral and personal character of Heaven is attested in an even clearer fashion by the *Classic of Odes*:

> The admirable, amiable prince / Displayed conspicuously his excellent virtue. / He put his people and his officers in concord. / And he received his emolument from Heaven (*tian*). / It protected him, assisted him and appointed him king. / And Heaven's blessing came again and again.
> 假樂君子，顯顯令德。宜民宜人，受祿于天。保右命之，自天申之。
>
> (Ode 249. Translation Chan et al. 1969, 101)

> *Di* said to King Wen: / I cherish your brilliant virtue, / Which makes no great display in sound or appearance, / Nor is changed with age. / Without any manipulation or deliberation, / you followed the principle of *Di*.
> 帝謂文王：「予懷明德，不大聲以色，不長夏以革。不識不知，順帝之則。」
>
> (Ode 241. Translation Chan et al. 1969, 101)

And yet, as in the case in other religious systems, the Will of Heaven is sometimes indecipherable: there is no exact correspondence between merits and rewards....

> Bright is the milky way, / Brilliantly moving around the sky (*tian*). / The king says: Alas! What sins have the people committed now, / So that Heaven (*tian*) has sent down destruction and disorder, / And there have been famines again and again? / There is no god (*shen*) to whom I have not made sacrifices. / I have never kept to myself the sacrificial animals. / I have exhausted my jades. / Has (Heaven) still not heard me?
> 倬彼雲漢，昭回于天，王曰：「於乎！何辜今之人！天降喪亂，饑饉薦臻、靡神不舉，靡愛斯牲。圭璧既卒，寧莫我聽！」
>
> (Ode 258. Translation Chan et al. 1967, 102)

If the relationship between the prince and Heaven is of special nature, *tian* is also in direct contact with ordinary people:

> Heaven enlightens the people, / As easily as the bamboo flute responds to the porcelain whistle, / As two half maces form a whole one, / As the agreement follows the request.
> 天之牖民。如壎如箎，如璋如圭，如取如攜。
>
> (Ode 254. Translation based on Couvreur 1967, 372–373)

The people as its prince must remain conscious both of Heaven's clairvoyance and of the unfathomable character of His ways:

> August Heaven is vigilant / And follows you in all your goings. / August Heaven is clear-seeing, / And witnesses your wanderings and your licentious behaviors.
> 昊天曰明，及爾出王；昊天曰旦，及爾游衍。
>
> (Ode 254. Translation based on Couvreur 1967, 374)

Always present, ready to protect and to bless, as well as to censor when rulers need to be admonished, at times clear in its injunction and at other times acting (or abstaining to act) in a way that is beyond our understanding, Heaven is and remains *Father and Mother* (*fumu* 父母):

> O Heaven dwelling in inaccessible spaces, / Whom we call Father and Mother / That without crime or offence, / I should suffer from disorder thus great!
> 悠悠昊天，曰父母且，無罪無辜，亂如此憮。
>
> (Ode 198. Translation based on Couvreur 1967, 252)

It is indisputable that this way of picturing Heaven influenced the way in which Matteo Ricci introduced in China the Christian idea of God. In his dialogue, *The True Meaning of the Lord of Heaven* (*Tianzhu shiyi* 天主實義), he made a Chinese scholar state:

> My parents gave me this body, I therefore owe them piety [*xiao* 孝]. The sovereign and his ministers gave me a field for breeding and grazing, which allows me to respect my elders and raise my children, so I owe them homage. How much more should we honour the Lord of Heaven, the Very Great Father-Mother [*dafumu* 大父母] the Very Great Sovereign [*dajun* 大君], the one from whom all ancestors come, who governs all sovereigns, who gives birth and nourishes everything – how could I not recognize it, neglect it?
>
> (Translation based on Meynard 2013, 51)

To which Ricci responds with approval: "The goodness of the Supreme Father (*dafu zhi ci* 大父之慈) will not fail to protect the one who teaches and transmits the true Way as the one who listens to it and receives it." (Translation based on Meynard 2013, 51.)

The expression *dafumu*, a lexical invention of Ricci, met the approval of converted Chinese scholars. Li Zhizao 李之藻 (1565–1630), in his preface to the *True Meaning of the Lord of Heaven*, summarizes the teaching in this way:

> People know how to serve their father and their mother, but they do not know that the Lord of Heaven is the Supreme Father-Mother. They know that the country has a legitimate sovereign and they don't know that the Lord who rules Heaven is the supreme sovereign. Whoever does not serve his kinship cannot be a son, who does not recognize his sovereign cannot have an office, who does not serve the Lord of Heaven cannot be a man.
>
> (Translation based on Meynard 2013, 259)

The two other literati Converts who together with Li Zhizao are commonly called "the three pillars" of Chinese Catholicism, Yang Tingyun 楊廷筠 (1557–1627) and Xu Guangqi 徐光啟 (1562–1633), also endorsed and commented upon the expression *dafumu*. The "Terms Controversy"[55] had the consequence of triggering the greatest caution concerning ways to name God. It therefore caused the expression *dafumu* to be largely ignored, without however making it disappear.

This historical inheritance may explain the repugnance shown by some scholars to take into consideration the religiosity displayed by the *Classic of Documents*

---

[55] Anterior to the Rites Controversy, and largely internal to the Society of Jesus, the Terms Controversy was triggered after Ricci's death by Jesuits from Japan who had taken refuge in Macao and were hostile to the process of lexical accommodation. Ricci's successor at the head of the Chinese mission, Niccolò Longobardi, was inclining in their favor, and took the initiative to organize several missionary conferences on the subject.

and the *Classic of Odes*, even if, obviously, how missionaries were interpreting ancient Confucian classics should not weigh in one sense or another into their present-day lexical rendering. The use of their sources by contemporary secular Confucians sometimes looks like a reverse image of the Figurist endeavor in the 18th century: Figurism was essentially a search for correspondences between the Chinese classics and the Bible. The correspondences they were listing were partly "syntactic" (provided by a similar understanding of cosmic and meta-cosmic patterns), partly historical: identifying "figures" akin to the ones of the biblical narrative within the corpus of Chinese classics occupied a good part of their quest. Joachim Bouvet (1656–1730), the main promoter of Figurist ideas, was led away by his enthusiasm towards the *Yijing:* he had found there a "key applicable to all sciences": theology, philosophy and science were to be unified by the use of a common code or language, the one that the "figures" (*xiang*) of the hexagrams were patterning. These images were "the writing system used by scholars before the Flood".[56] Another Figurist, Joseph de Prémare (1666–1736) had one of his manuscripts (completed in Canton and dated 1724) eventually published in a French translation in 1878. Its title clearly states its intent: *Remains of the Main Christian Dogmas, Taken from the Ancient Chinese Books.* This quest for divine *vestigia*, typical of every enterprise of natural theology, heads back to the source:

> One can say with a very great probability that all the *jing* relate to a holy and divine personage as their only object. His virtues, his merits, the benefaction he brings, his mysteries, his holy law, his reign, his glory, even more his very works are reported in these books in a way that is obscure for the Chinese, but very clear for us who know Jesus Christ.
> (Prémare 1878, 47)

There is a danger today to indulge in reverse Figurism, substituting to biblical figures the ones pointing towards an abstract, immanent "process". The following excerpt testifies to the trend:

> *Tian* seems to have had some religious significance for the [Zhou] people who conquered the Shang at the end of the second millennium B.C. Given that the Zhou was a federation of militant, semi-nomadic border tribes prior to their conquest of the Shang, there is no written basis for determining whether or not, or to what extent, *tian* was held to be a personal deity. The fact that *tian* also means "sky" might suggest that in this pre- historic period it was seen as a non-personal, unifying force of considerable dimensions at some distance from the human world. A further reason to believe that *tian* was perceived as a non-personal force is the fact that somewhere in this period the notion developed that the sum of existence is a unity of tian, earth, and human being, each force having its peculiar characteristics, and each existing correlative to the other two. It is important to recognize that there is no final

---

56 Letter of Bouvet to Leibniz of February 28, 1698, quoted in Mungello (1977), 314.

beginning or end in this process; rather, it has the identifiable rhythm, immanent order and cadence of a cycle.

(Hall and Ames 1987, 202–203)

The above paragraph warrants a full discussion, which the following section will unfold.

Internalizing Tian

Ames' and Hall's account rightly asserts that the understanding of *tian* underwent an evolution. However, the process of internalization I am going to sketch is not automatically analogous to a passage to immanence, and certainly not to "strict immanence". In the *Classic of Odes* and the *Classic of Documents*, *tian* is often preceded by another character, which plays the role of honorary suffix, and which emphasizes the character, as the case may be, personal, merciful, omniscient or omnipotent of Heaven. While maintaining the use of these honorific characters, Confucius insisted on the way Heaven acts in the universe and makes His will carried out as "from within" for the one attentive to its manifold though silent manifestations:

> The Master says: "I would like not to speak." Zigong said, "If you do not speak, what will we humble disciples have to report?" The Master said: "Does Heaven speak? The four seasons take their course, everything comes to existence. Does Heaven speak?"
> 子曰：「予欲無言。」子貢曰：「子如不言，則小子何述焉？」子曰：「天何言哉？四時行焉，百物生焉，天何言哉？」
>
> (*Analects* 17.9)

Actually, the *Analects* testify to a tension between the stress on external and on inner manifestations of Heaven: for a good part of his existence, Confucius was looking for a shining sign of the mission entrusted to him. *Analects* 9.9 provides us with the clearest testimony of this pursuit: "The Master said: 'The phoenix does not surge; the [Yellow] River does not bring forth the Chart. For me, it's all over!'" In contrast, in later years (so we may presume), the Mandate of Heaven is sought after through the motions of one's inner core: "At fifty I knew the Mandate of Heaven; At sixty, my ears were attuned. [Now that I am] seventy, I can follow my heart's wishes without overstepping boundaries" (*Analects* 2.4).

In any case, Confucian classics bear witness to a progressive interiorization of the concept of *tian*. It sometimes ends up designating the moral law within the heart (and *tian* may even be identified virtually – but virtually only – with the heart-mind (*xin* 心), or even with what is natural, unaltered, original). Zhang Dainian 張岱年(1909–2004) introduces his presentation of the concept by pointing out a contradiction which has never been resolved between, on the one hand, an approach that makes *tian* an objective and infinite reality (as is the sky), and, on the other hand, a vision that finds in *tian* "God, or the supreme concept" (Zhang 2002, 3–4). Zhang Dainian also sees the progressive identification of *tian* with the notion of "spirit" and/or with moral law the sign of a transition from "objective idealism" to "subjective idealism" (Zhang 2002, 11).[57]

As for the *shen* 神 character (which we already met in the compound *guishen*), its usage and connotations are remarkably flexible. It is close to its namesake *shen* (伸) which indicates extension, a dynamic of enlargement. The first occurrences seem to contrast the uniqueness of *di* with the multiplicity of spirits. *Shen* applies to luminous spirits, to deities, to ancestral spirits also, insofar as the latter have been deified (Sterckx 2007). But the character gradually designates spiritual capacities, what we cannot grasp, the supernatural potential that is present in human beings and leads, at least potentially, to their full realization (we clearly find this meaning in *Huainanzi*, Chapter 7). This explains the plasticity and extension of the meanings that this character will take on.

It seems to me impossible to conduct philosophical inquiry into Chinese ancient texts if one does not remain alert to the richness of the religious world of the society under study, to the variety of relationships that this society was nurturing with its divine interlocutors. The latter were not reduced to a Supreme Ruler who in later days would have been metamorphosed into an immanent "Principle". Princes, literati and ordinary people were also surrounded by "Lesser Deities", as Justin T. Winslett labels them (Winslett 2014). Early Chinese classics such as the *Zuozhuan* 左傳 and *Guoyu* 國語 were "depict[ing] these Lesser Deities in complex ways, constructing identities for them as active agents in socio-political roles with prescribed duties and responsibilities in the religious systems espoused by these texts" (Winslett 2014, 938). In the *Zuozhuan* and in the *Guoyu*, sometimes a divine spirit (*shen*) "descends" upon the capital of a state, observable, it seems, by all (some texts attribute to such spirits supernatural size and hybrid anatomies), and it stays there for a few months. According to circumstances, this may be because the state is meant to rise or, conversely to fall – and in this case the *shen* first observes the extent of its wickedness (see for instance *Zuozhuan*, Zhuang 32.3). There are also mentions of mytho-historical personages and fantastic creatures appearing – Confucius lives in the regret that none of these has ever materialized in front of him. The role of *shen* as guardians of mountains and rivers is of

---

57 In this work, Zhang Dainian's presentation of Confucianism markedly differs from an earlier one, which I will briefly evoke in Chapter 3 (Zhang 1981).

particular importance, and the imperial sacrificial registers will confirm and systematize the local cults associated to these places. As is the case in ancient Roman religion, a trade-off between the human and the divine worlds is constantly taking place, the spirits receiving proper homage (especially under the form of sacrifices) while also being "kept in their place" through such ritual taming. "*Shen* in particular but also extra-humans in general, are part of the rich fabric of life depicted in pre-Qin texts, and were conceptualized and discussed in a variety of ways" (Winslett 2014, 966). No discussion of the thought system of China (and of Confucianism in particular) can take place if one ignores the importance of the religious practices and speculations that were taking place.

Lexical Disputations: Five Notions

In the quote by which I opened this chapter, Roger Ames also asserts that the translations of *dao*道 as "the Way", of *de*德 as "virtue" and of *yi*義 as "righteousness" are a "grossly inappropriate" use of language. I will argue that; in fact, these well-established lexical equivalences are roughly adequate, even if their use is far from being compulsory. The stakes attached to the debate are not insignificant: when a (scholastic) conflict of interpretations opens up, whoever gets the last word on how to translate such or such character ultimately controls the way Chinese classics are understood with regard to other philosophical traditions.

Way, Virtue and Nature

The first amendment proposed by Ames and Hall consists in translating *dao* "the *proper* way" (Hall and Ames 2001, 5), or, sometimes, "proper way-making" (Hall and Ames 2001, 94). And they comment: "At its most fundamental level, *dao* seems to denote the active project of 'moving ahead in the world', of 'forging a way forward', of 'road building', and, by extension, to connote a pathway that has been made and hence can be travelled" (Hall and Ames 2001, 63). It is indeed correct to say that *dao* seems to first correspond to a verbal form meaning "to walk" or "to lead" (and by extension, "to explain, to unfold"). The nominal form then applied to a path, or to a particular way of proceeding. The term appears more than a hundred times in the *Analects* of Confucius, mainly to designate the usual (or required) behavior, the *manners* of something or someone (the Way of the Gentleman [*junzi* 君子] in particular). However, Sarah Allan has shown that the reflection on the Way is inspired by a meditation on the nature of water, itself suggested by the geographic realities of the regions where the concept is developed.

As a consequence, *dao* does not refer to a road that one builds or on which one forges a way ahead, but rather to a course, to a stream oriented towards the east (as are Chinese rivers), and consequently towards the immensity of the sea (Allan 1997, 67). The properties of *dao* are equivalent to those of water, and to enumerate the ones of the second is to enumerate those of the first: water is the source of life when it follows a course, it becomes source of death when it comes out of it; by nature, it flows downwards; water submits to everything but overcomes all resistance; it takes any form; when calm, it becomes a plane and a mirror; and – last but not least – it is not easy to gauge, to apprehend. *Dao* is also compared to the aquatic environment in which fish take their enjoyment (*Zhuangzi* 17 *et passim*) Such speculative references to water are not found in the *Laozi* and the *Zhuangzi* only, but in Confucius (see notably *Analects* 6.23 and 9.17), in Xunzi, and, more abundantly than in all other works, in Mencius. (The theme of the unfathomable depths of water also occurs in *Zhongyong* 26). *Dao*, for Chinese thinkers, became an all-encompassing principle, a mysterious and universally present reality. Devoid of any fixed place although filling the whole world, writes the *Guanzi* ("*Neiye* 內業", IV,1 and VIII,1), the *dao* is always ready to dwell in the heart-mind of the one who has emptied herself so as to welcome it. Similarly, water fills any place left vacant. Additionally, and as shown by the fact that water cannot be divided into discrete parts, one begins to identify with the Way when one gives up making distinctions among phenomena (*Zhuangzi* 6; Graham 1989, 188–190).

At the same time, Ames and Hall translate *de* 德 as "particular focus, excellence" (Ames and Hall 2001, 5 and 64–65), predominantly referring to Confucian texts. In the *Daodejing*, they continue, *de* would correspond to "any particular disposition of the unsummed reality", while the ideas of excellence and efficacy would predominate in the Confucian literature. This interpretation understates the intrinsic connection between *dao* and *de*, which crisscrosses the (often artificial) distinctions among schools. In a nutshell, *de* corresponds to the innate capacity to act according to the *dao*, as plants manifest the vital power of water. *De* is indeed "virtue", as it is customary to translate it, but in the sense that one speaks of the virtue (Latin *virtus*) of a medicine (which explains the alternative translation "potency", which has been privileged of late). Brook Ziporyn's translation of *de* as "virtuosity" makes sense also:[58] water is the domain of hidden "virtuality", the milieu out of which the properties virtually present in vegetal life (and in the other expressions of life) will express themselves. It is through the same analogical line that a third character can be rightly understood: the "nature" (*xing* 性) of a thing – of a human being notably – corresponds to the virtual power contained in a seed, which

---

[58] See translation of the *Zhuangzi* by Ziporyn (2009) and (2020).

develops in a given plant. It is therefore not a "quality", as whiteness would be (cf. *Mencius* VIA, 3, 6 and 7) but one cannot define *xing*, as do Ames and Hall, as "a continuous process that is continuously altered though changing patterns of growth and extension" (Ames and Hall 2001, 83). *Xing* is not a process but rather a pattern – or a software if one prefers: some of the qualities it is comprised of will be developed by the some of the individuals who have been endowed with them, the same individuals leaving others unexploited. We will meet the issue again when discussing Ames and Hall's translation of the *Zhongyong*.

Humaneness and Righteousness

Another pair of characters correspond to key-notions of the Confucian text, while being treated with much distance, if not with irony, by Daoist thinkers. According to our authors, *yi* 義 is to be understood as "appropriateness" (Ames and Hall 2001, 5), while *ren* 仁, generally translated as "benevolence" or "humanity", would be best translated as "authoritative person/conduct": "It is one's posture and comportment, gestures and bodily communication" (Ames and Hall 2001, 75). These equivalences have been disputed and have provoked disarray even among scholars close to Hall's positions, Steve Coutinho for instance:

> While I think that the best term to translate *ren* 仁 is "humanity" (divested of all essentialist implications), for example, Ames rejects this in favor of the unexpected phrase, "authoritative conduct"; while I would urge that "noble" lies among the closest matches for *junzi* 君子, Ames coins the phrase "exemplary personhood" to capture the significances of the term. This difference is not just a matter of personal preferences among translation possibilities but, I suspect, arises from a more fundamental divergence. [...] My tentative hypothesis is that Ames sees meanings as constituted by clusters of significances, equally juicy and ripe for the picking – or if not clusters, then holographic images viewable from multiple perspectives. Since meanings are not defined by an essential core, all aspects of meaning – semantic, pragmatic, aesthetic, etymological, historical, sociological, practical, cultural, metaphorical – can be appealed to when identifying candidates for translation.
>
> (Coutinho 2021, 77)

Now, let me venture my own translation of the following passage of the *Mencius*:

> Humaneness is the heart of the human being, and Righteousness is the path of the human being. Pity the one who abandons the path and does not follow it, who has lost his heart and does not know how to recover it. When people's dogs and fowls are lost, they go to look for them. Yet, when they have lost their hearts, they do not go to look for them. The path to learning is none other than finding one's lost heart, and nothing else!
> 仁, 人心也, 義, 人路也。舍其路而弗由, 放其心而不知求, 哀哉! 人有雞犬放, 則知求之。有放心, 而不知求。學問之道無他, 求其放心而已矣。

(*Mencius* 6 A.11)

Translate the above by: "Authoritative conduct is the heart-mind of the human being, and Appropriateness is the path of the human being". You lose the directness, the immediacy that Mencius is trying to impact upon you. You may also lose the meaning of what is asserted here: *ren* is a capacity for empathy, a way of entering into communication that is first rooted in the heart (or the heart-mind, if one prefers). "Only the *ren* enables us to [truly] love and hate others [唯仁者能好人，能惡人]", says Confucius (*Analects* 4.3). However, such propensity is to be educated and channeled through the *yi*. Here, the translation of *yi* by "appropriateness" is interesting, for the idea is indeed to do what is "appropriate" to the expression of the *ren*, and this is where the appreciation of a concrete situation (say, of the kind of relationships you have with a given person) needs to enter into play. Ritual properties are dispositions that allow one person to enter appropriately into contact with another. (Once again, *ren* comes before properties and rituals: "If one is devoid of *ren*, what is the use of ritual? [人而不仁，如禮何]"; *Analects* 3.3.) But "appropriateness" is nurtured by the idea that you do "what it is right to do": you are not playing a social game that would make you constantly adapt and revise the way you behave. Acting *appropriately* means to behave *rightly, justly*. Let us consider another sentence of Mencius, which I have already quoted.

> I have a liking for fish, and I also have a liking for bear's paws. If I cannot have the two, I will let the fish go, and choose the bear's paws. I have a liking for life, and I also have a liking for righteousness. If I cannot have the two, I will let life go, and choose righteousness (*yi*). I like life indeed, but there is that which I like more than life, and therefore, I will not seek to possess it at any price. I loathe death indeed, but there is that which I loathe more than death, and therefore there are risks that I will not avoid to take.
>
> (*Mencius* 6 A.10)

Again, translate the beginning of the paragraph as: "I have a liking for life, and I also have a liking for appropriateness. If I cannot have the two, I will let life go, and choose appropriateness." You are entitled to think that what the author points towards irrevocably escapes you – and that it is better to let the matter rest with licensed sinologists.

Exercises in Creativity

Let me now go beyond the issues raised by individual lexical choices and look at the insertion of notions into philosophical texts. Here, I will focus on Ames' and Hall's translation of the *Zhongyong* 中庸. The title of this work is notoriously difficult to translate. *The Doctrine of the Mean* is outdated and slightly misleading, *The Constant Mean* or *The Middle Way* are often suggested. Tu Wei-ming has opted for *Centrality and Commonality* (Tu 1989). Ames and Hall prefer *Focusing the Familiar*. I have no issue with that (and even think that "focusing" translates excellently one of the possible meanings – probably the most plausible meaning – of *zhong* in this text), even if, in ancient texts, the character *yong* is principally associated with the idea of a constant capacity to serve, before taking the connotation of "ordinariness". The only mention of the expression in the *Analects* (6.29) associates it with "virtue" (*de*), suggesting that a reasoned, regulated use of one's potentialities carries the latter to their best. There always has been a debate among Chinese commentators as to whether *yong* should be understood as meaning "ordinary [*pingchang* 平常]" or rather "unchanging [*bu yi* 不易]". Zhu Xi, who opts for "ordinary", remarks that what is "ordinary" is also "unchanging" (see *Zhongyong Huowen* 中庸或問1). As we will see below, Zhu Xi's option for "ordinariness" had a moral objective; self-realization starts from the attention given and the sincerity brought to ordinary duties and occupations.

Let me first examine Ames' and Hall's translation of the first sentence of this seminal work:

> What *tian* commands is called natural tendencies; drawing out these natural tendencies is called the proper way; improving upon this way is called education.
> 天命之謂性，率性之謂道，修道之謂教。
>
> (*Zhongyong* 1. Translation Ames and Hall 2001, 89)

This rendering may impede the access to the *sound*, the music proper to the original: the *Zhongyong* starts with some definitions that should be experienced by the reader as coming directly from the "natural light" found in the human understanding. The consequences of these definitions will then be progressively elaborated, so that meditation and practice may be merged into lived wisdom. Translating *xing* by "natural tendencies" aims at avoiding the substantification induced by the term "nature" (which Legge's translation capitalizes), and it keeps the gist of the meaning, but it loses the immediacy of the term so striking in Mencius when the latter establishes a continuum from the heart-mind to nature to Heaven.[59]

---

[59] Note also that several commentators of the *Zhongyong* will identify nature with "goodness" (*shan* 善).

> The ones who exert their heart to the utmost know their nature. Knowing their nature, they know Heaven. Safeguarding one's heart and nurturing one's nature, this is akin to serving Heaven.
> 盡其心者，知其性也。知其性，則知天矣。存其心，養其性，所以事天也。
>
> (*Mencius* 7 A.1)

Compare with the translation of the same passage offered by Peter Wong Yih Jiun, in line with Ames' and Hall's rendering of the *Zhongyong*:

> Mencius said, "Those who engage wholeheartedly (*jinxin* 盡心) realize their human tendencies. In realizing their human tendencies, they thus realize *tian* (*zhitian* 知天). It is in nurturing their human tendencies that *tian* is served."
>
> (*Mencius* 7 A.1. Translation Wong 2021, 114)

The fact of omitting *xin* altogether, of not translating *tian* and of diluting *xing* in the ambiguous expression "human tendencies" (actually, humans are not the only ones to possess a *xing*) completely distorts the dynamic of the passage, grounded on the ascension from *xin* to *xing* and then to *tian*. And translating *zhi* 知 not as "knowing" but rather as "realizing" (even with the double-entendre of "realizing" in English) might be confusing. One loses here the strength of a continuum that is both gnoseological and moral: the path leads from one's individual heart-mind to the characteristics that are shared with the species to which I belong and are actualized in me, and, from there, to Heaven (*tian*) that endows each individual with some of the attributes proper to her species. If I recognize myself to be endowed with heavenly-given attributes I will thus serve Heaven by the fact of nurturing and activating the qualities that have been imparted upon me as a human being. The beginning of the *Zhongyong* is extraordinarily close to this vision.

The translation of *dao* by "proper way" (which I have already commented upon) reminds one of how Legge, in the same opening paragraph of the *Zhongyong*, feels the need to render the term by "The Path of duty". Translators, past and modern, seem to feel anxious that *their dao* may be confused with another, "improper" *dao*. Additionally, the translation of *shuai* 率, as "drawing out" is a strange one when all ancient occurrences point towards the meaning of "directing", "guiding", "establishing a rule". The same observation stands for *xiu* 修: if "improving upon" is indeed an acceptable approximation, the pervasive connotation of "correcting", "repairing", and, by extension, "cultivating" is weakened. As a matter of fact, "improving upon this way" is probably misleading: the issue at stake is not to "improve upon" the fact of directing, guiding our nature (or our natural tendencies), but rather to recognize that such "guiding" goes along a path, and that this path is education, understood as a "civilizing" process": what Heaven has imparted upon us will be made fully human through our effort. Put otherwise, and opening my own translation to criticisms:

> What Heaven imparts to us is called nature. Guiding our nature is called following the Way. Rectifying one's way is called education. [*The last part of the sentence could privilege the collective and read: "Rectifying the way [that people follow] is called Civilizing."*[60]]
>
> (Zhongyong 1)

A major characteristic of the *Zhongyong* – and Ames and Hall are right to stress the fact – lies in its central and innovative use of the character *cheng* 誠 (Zhu Xi, among others, had asserted that *cheng* was indeed the crux [*shuniu* 樞紐: lit., pivot] of the *Zhongyong*). The character does not enter the scene before paragraph 16 (for a total of 33) but it directs the developments of the second part of the work. *Cheng*, argue our authors, besides the meaning of "sincerity" or "integrity" traditionally imparted to it, possesses the one of "creativity" in the sense that Whitehead and thinkers referring to process philosophy in general attribute to the term: creativity, a process leading to wholeness (Ames and Hall 2001, 62), is "transactional and multi-dimensional", while "power" (as manifested in the idea of *creatio ex nihilo* for instance) is always "unilateral". So, "creativity" is not to be seen as "unbounded" (Ames and Hall 2001, 12–14). It is the human way of participating in cosmic co-creativity. Therefore, "the parsing of *cheng* principally as 'creativity' rather than 'sincerity' or 'integrity' brings attention to the centrality of cosmic creativity as the main theme of the *Zhongyong*" (Ames and Hall 2001, 61–63).

While such commentarial translation does unveil specific aspects of the text, it prioritizes a Western lexicon over the attentive consideration of the use of the character in its original context. The graph of *cheng* 誠 refers to the completion, the wholeness of one's speech. It awakens an idea of sincerity, of moral rectitude that is manifested throughout the utterance of words made "wholesome".[61] "Integrity" is not a footnote to be added to the idea of "creativity" but rather is at the root

---

[60] The ambiguity has remained throughout the history of the Chinese interpretations of this passage: the *Zhongyong* may focus on "civilizing" others (*jiaohua* 教化) – a perspective that will be fully developed during the Song period, when the reading of the *Zhongyong* will privilege political implications – or else on self-cultivation proper. Wang and Han (2021) translate *jiaohua* by "shaping the mind through education".

[61] Note that the series of volumes *Key Concepts in Chinese Thought and Culture* translates *cheng* as "sincerity" (Wang and Han 2021) and establishes the meaning of the character mainly through the definition given of the expression *cheng'yi* 誠意 (sincerity in thought): "'Sincerity in thought' has as its preceding stage the 'extension of knowledge'. One can only identify and follow the principle of 'sincerity in thought' on the basis of understanding the moral principles in daily life" (Wang and Han 2021, vol. "Philosophy", entry "Cheng'yi").

of what the character attempts to express. Translators and commentators such as Wing-tsit Chan, Tu Wei-ming and D.C. Lau locate the term somewhere between "sincerity" and "reality". Opting for "integrity" seems to me an appropriate way of balancing the "moral" and "substantial" dimensions of *cheng*. The translation by "creativity", even if surrounded by oratory precautions, is certainly interesting but reverts to the attitude that Ames and Hall rightly criticize in their predecessors: the borrowing of a technical Western concept for expressing a Chinese notion. There is an immediacy in the terms "sincerity" or "integrity" that has the advantage of escaping specialized vocabulary and thus getting direct access to what Chinese philosophy wants us to enter into: a specific and widely shared human experience – the one of the perfect congruence of deeds and words. *Zhongyong* 21 tells us that "rectitude is light [the light brought by understanding of enlightenment], light is rectitude [誠則明矣，明則誠矣]". The whole paragraph is actually a gloss over *Zhongyong* 1: the light that comes from our born rectitude is "nature". And the accrued rectitude that comes from the light that we receive from the fact of immersing into study is a product of education.

In other words, *cheng* can first be seen as a root, an aptitude present in everyone from the time of birth. Undifferentiated at its start, "rectitude" (if one chooses to translate *cheng* in this fashion) is activated in various degrees, is obscured or not, depending on the moral advancement or downfall of the individual. Even when *cheng* is not cultivated it normally remains latent, which encourages every human being to work towards becoming "whole". When a human being makes such propensity more visible and active, not only does she fulfill herself but she acquires the capacity to help all other forms of reality to reach fulfillment.

As one may see, I am far from denying the idea that the *Zhongyong* deals with the notions of growth and fulfillment in its use of the character *cheng* (and here is certainly the theoretical contribution brought by this Classic). I simply insist on the fact that such idea is dependent upon the notion that "clarity" and "rectitude" are twin virtues. "Growth" and "creativity" can appear only in such context. This is actually what Zhu Xi stresses when he comments on *Zhongyong* 16 (the paragraph where *cheng* first appears) and tries to define the notion: "What *cheng* means: true reality, no erring [誠者, 真實無妄之謂]." By the expression *wu wang* 無妄, Zhu Xi refers to the 25th hexagrams of *the Yijing*, the meaning of which is: the moment where the sincerity, the faithfulness of [human] beings (one could also say: the way they are anchored in reality) allows them to proceed with full confidence.[62] This "anchorage into reality [*zai yu shi* 在於實]", adds Zhu Xi in various

---

62 Or, for Zhu Xi: "the mental state of being free from any personal wishes" (無私意期望之心). See Lee (2012), 205.

places,⁶³ is what characterizes *cheng*. At the same time, reality, it seems, is equated by Zhu Xi with *attentiveness*; if I do not pay attention to what I read, then what I have read is not *truly real*.⁶⁴ Things access to reality by the very fact that one's mind is sincerely focusing on them. If the *Zhongyong* remains an open text, Zhu Xi seems to me to have inserted its interpretation into a system that is both highly plausible and very convincing:

> According to the moral vision articulated in Zhu's interpretation of the *Zhongyong*, the supreme value that a moral agent ought to strive to embody is not associated with the social and political status of the agent or the significance of affairs in a conventional value system. [...] [Zhu Xi] encouraged [the literati] to turn their attention to ordinary affairs in their ordinary courses of lives and discover the true value in the middle of carrying out such apparently trivial things in their ordinary spaces.
>
> (Lee 2012, 212)

The focus on "cosmic co-creativity" that Ames' and Hall privilege constitutes a possible reading of the *Zhongyong*. However, it seems to me to constitute neither the most plausible reading nor the one that best unveils the philosophical insights that the text contains.

What's in a Name?

The difficulties that Ames, Hall and like-minded scholars introduce into their revised lexicon are largely due to a constant worry of theirs: avoiding any suspicion of "substantialism", as the latter is supposed to be totally foreign to Chinese thought. This hinders them to confront directly the question of what "naming" may philosophically imply in Chinese thinking. And yet, such questioning opens up a path for a constructive, comparative engagement. This is the path I will explore in this section.

I have alluded at the beginning of this chapter to a famous passage of the *Analects*:⁶⁵

> Zilu asked, "If the Lord of Wei were to let you administer his government, what would be your priority?" The Master said, "It must be to rectify names [*zhengming* 正名]." "Is that so?" said Zilu. "Are you rambling Master? What is the point of rectifying names?" The Master

---

63 Notably *Zhongyong huowen*, 87.
64 References in Lee (2012), 211.
65 For an account of the importance given to this passage in the modern period, which weighs upon the way we read the *Analects* today, see Defoort (2021).

said, "Boorish indeed are you Zilu! A gentleman keeps silent when he does not know the matter at stake! If names are incorrect, speech cannot be adequate [*shun* 順]. If speech is not adequate, affairs cannot be accomplished. If affairs cannot be accomplished, Ritual and music will not flourish. If Ritual and music do not flourish, verdicts and punishments will not hit the mark. If verdicts and punishments do not hit the mark, people will not know how to move their hands and feet. Hence, what the gentleman confers a name upon needs to be possibly put into discourses; and what is put into discourses must be possibly put into action. The gentleman, in the way he speaks, wants to avoid carelessness, and that's it."

子路曰：「衛君待子而為政，子將奚先？」子曰：「必也正名乎！」子路曰：「有是哉，子之迂也！奚其正？」子曰：「野哉由也！君子於其所不知，蓋闕如也。名不正，則言不順；言不順，則事不成；事不成，則禮樂不興；禮樂不興，則刑罰不中；刑罰不中，則民無所措手足。故君子名之必可言也，言之必可行也。君子於其言，無所苟而已矣。」

(*Analects* 13.3)

For Confucius, naming is a matter of adequation. The names (*ming* 名) must accurately translate the relations inscribed into the natural order: "The prince, [let him be a] prince, the subject, subject, the father, father, the son, son! 「*jun jun, chen chen, fu fu, zi zi*君君，臣 臣，父 父，子 子」" (*Analects* 12.11) What this statement suggests is that the names echo a pre-existing reality. At the same time, due to the characteristics of the Chinese writing system, the fact that any name is associated with a specific graph provides it with an additional aura, a kind of magical force. The name has its *mana*. When the names are correct, so are the relationships between people and things, each recognized for what they are, and interactions take place according to the fairness induced by the correctness of language. Political order requires mastery of language. But one should not infer from this that Confucius was paving the way towards the introduction of newspeak. On the contrary, it is *an ethic of political language* that Confucius intends to establish here: the ruler (and anyone who possesses self-respect) must speak as she acts, and act as she speaks. A principle of reality leads to rectifying all the occurrences in which language breaks free from reality.

When names are correct, words, language, speeches are adequate, conform to what they are aiming at (*shun* 順). Taken as a whole, ritual propriety and linguistic conformity help to fluidify social relations. Going one step further: words and rituals are performative: they exert an influence over the cosmic and social order. To think is to name rightly – and this also means to name *justly*, since naming (as we just saw) has political consequences. Names qualify realities, facts and behavior, and, by determining how these realities are considered and judged, they contribute to shaping the course followed by all phenomena.

Here, emerges the picture of an overall epistemological attitude. For Confucius, Mencius or Xunzi (each with his own accents), *thinking* is a travel along the meaning(s) opened up by the fact of naming basic realities. The question is less about defining, enlarging or restricting the meaning of a term, than about *thinking with the terms we are provided with*, going through their implications, the way one also observes geological patterns and heavenly signs: "[The Sage] looking up, contemplates the heavenly signs [*tianwen* 天文], and, looking down, scrutinizes the earthly patterns [*dili* 地理]" (*Xici* 繫辭 I.4). The same character *wen* 文 applies to basic characters (and notions) as well as to heavenly signs.

Incidentally, the Mohists were giving even more importance to the fact of "naming rightly":

> What speaking means: [it is] the capacity of the mouth to utter names. A name is like the drawing of a tiger. To speak means also: speech attains perfection in proportion [to that] of the names [which it uses].
> 言也者, 謂口能之, 出名者也。名若畫虎也。言也謂, 言猶 [由] 名致也。
> (*Mozi* 40.32)[66]

One can discern a hesitation in the early Confucian tradition insofar as it deals with "naming": the operation is seen as being, at the same time, nominalist and realist, conventional and performative. The creative ambiguity attached to the act of naming calls for further analysis:

In many ways, the fact of naming creates the reality that is designated, or rather, "the names give rise to the real" (Granet 1999 [1934], 365). The same Granet goes even further when he writes: "At the origin of the theory of naming [...] lies a kind of magical realism" (Granet 1999 [1934], 366). Beneath its apparent simplicity, what a complex operation it is to name things! Kinship relations (qualified in China with scrupulous detail) illustrate the interweaving of four dimensions that are at stake in the affixing of a name: realism (one needs adequacy between the term and the reality that it is designates); normativity (the designation functions as an implicit injunction); performativity (the emergence of a new reality); and finally, conventionality. Let us specify further: (1) To distinguish the father from the son or the husband from the wife is to honor the dispositions inscribed by Heaven in nature (realism). (2) Naming is made necessary by the fact that the proper functioning family and society can be ensured only through strict distinctions between positions (normativity). The fact that brother-in-law and sister-in-law are prohibited from "naming" each other emerges from the same concern: being of the same generation, they would be brought to use the appellations required between spouses, and that would mean the death of the extended family unit. (3) From the complex interweaving of kinship names and the precision of their detail arises and

---

[66] The reading of this passage is complicated by editorial difficulties, but there is general agreement on some substitutions to be made, and it is therefore the Chinese text as it is commonly corrected that I insert and translate here.

continues the patriarchal family organization (performativity). (4) Finally, the name is indeed convention: whatever the way in which they are conferred, the names are posited so to ensure the continuation of a social organization, and anyone who would dare to alter the proper way of naming would pervert this organization.

The complexity of the issues linked to the proper use of names can be seen in Chapter 22 of the *Xunzi*, *Zhengming* 正名 ("Correct Naming"). Xunzi starts from the later stage of the long process by which names were appended to things: the stage when names were sanctioned by the "later kings". These kings followed Shang customs when it came to naming punishments, Zhou customs for official dignities and titles, the *Book of Rites* for qualifying cultural forms and institutions, and they reiterated the common names imposed by the Xia dynasty in order to harmonize the names of things and beings that were used in the different regions of the Empire. By starting from this later stage, Xunzi undoubtedly intends to underline that the process of "putting names right" initiated by the political authorities is now completed, that it marked the end of a cultural evolution, and that there is no question of going back on the conventions thus fixed.

Yet this opening paragraph is immediately followed by the following statement:

> As for the names concerning human beings: what they naturally possess at birth, we call it "nature" [*xing* 性]; what arises from the harmonies produced by nature, when the essence is in harmony with external stimuli, everything that is effortless and spontaneous, this is also called "nature" [*xing* 性] [...] When upon the awakening of a disposition [an emotion: *qing* 情] the heart makes a choice, this is called "deliberation" [*lü* 慮].
> 散名之在人者： 生之所以然者謂之性 ； 性之和所生 ， 精合感應 ， 不事而自然 謂之性。 [...] 情然而心為之擇謂之慮。
>
> (*Xunzi* 22.2)

This paragraph (of which I am only giving an extract) starts from the "natural", understood both as the "capital" with which every newborn is endowed and as the impetus from which the moral and civilizational process will get started. Natural dispositions constitute the material upon which *xin*, the heart-mind (which receives no definition) will be at work, choosing, correcting, animating, guiding the acquisition of knowledge and skills. Xunzi, here, does not seem to be speaking about "conventional" appellations: he is hinting at the fact that the foundational realities that he brings to light could not bear another name than the one they already possess. To name is to bring to light. Names that speak of "human nature" – names by which human beings learn to tame their nature – seem to constitute a special category, over which Xunzi himself exercises control. However, the manner in which these names are imposed reveals one important fact: the definitions proposed by Xunzi are worded in such a way that they cannot fail to elicit our approval. That is, even when they seem to be decreed by kings, names belong to the domain of *agreement*, even of *alliance or contract* (*yue* 約): they arise from a consensus which, once formed, becomes intangible. Linguistic conventions work beyond the "conventional":

> Names do not have a fixed match [in advance]. Agreement [*yue* 約] on them is what is decisive. What the agreement fixes and is achieved by custom, this is what makes them adequate. What deviates from the agreement, this is what is called inadequacy. Names are not charged with a fixed reality [in advance]. What we agree upon decides of their reality. What the agreement fixes is achieved by custom, this is what is said to make the name real. [However,] the goodness of names is fixed [in advance]: a straightforward, easy name that doesn't go against [its purpose], that's called a "good name".
> 名無固宜， 約之以命， 約定俗成謂之宜， 異於約則謂之不宜。 名無固實， 約之以命實， 約定俗成， 謂之實名。 名有固善， 徑易而不拂， 謂之善名。
>
> (*Xunzi* 22.2 g)

If words are indeed rooted in a *convention*, they are nonetheless bearer of something "magical", and this in three ways: by the fact that a consensus has been achieved around the use of each of these words; by the fact that this maintained consensus is the very guarantor of the social contract; finally, by the fact that, even if a given sound is not attached *a priori* to any given object, we feel, we sense what name is called by such object, what name for a given object is indeed "the right name". If smooth social interactions maintained on the long term constitute a kind of magic (magic operated, for the Confucian tradition, by the respect and activation of ritual proprieties), it cannot be separated from another magic, another mystery: the fact that, while knowing nothing about the origins of the language we share, linguistic conventions remain outside the scope of our disagreements.

Disordering Language

The opening lines of the *Laozi* regain the flavor they have lost with repetition when read as a deliberate attack on the Confucian language order:

> A path that can be unfolded is not a constant path.
> A name that can be uttered is not a constant name.
> What is nameless: the origin of Heaven-Earth.
> What is named: the mother of all things.
> 道可道， 非常道。 名可名， 非常名。 無名天地之始； 有名萬物 之母。
>
> (*Laozi* 1)

The name that is constant, no language can express it properly, because it would be the name of the Way located as the origin (the two propositions which open the chapter are not juxtaposed – rather, they are mutually explanatory). *Dao*, when the term is used as a verb, speaks of a journey that is both effective and discursive: "to travel", and "to discourse". Hence my translation, "to unfold", so as to associate both meanings. From this discursive journey, Laozi intends to turn us away. What is worth thinking about is what escapes all "naming" and what overflows all discourse. The Constant Way cannot be methodically deployed. There is "constant non-desire", whereby one contemplates the imperceptible (*miao* 妙) of the Way; there is "constant desire" by which one contemplates its manifestations, its outer outline (*jiao* 徼). These manifestations "come from the same [place], although named differently [*tong chu er yi ming* 同出而異名]" (*Laozi* 1). Once it has been recognized that the Origin is without a name, then, the name conferred on everything that arises from it is a matter of simple convention, not a return to the "Natural", which can be approached, suggests Laozi, only through linguistic choices that admit to be provisional, approximative.[67] There are many passages in the *Laozi* which assert the provisional, approximate character of naming:

> There is a thing that has been completed in indistinction, and born before Heaven and Earth. Obscure! Trouble! Holding on to itself, affected by nothing, it turns without ever weakening; we can say that it is the mother of all things. I do not know its name, I call it *dao*, and, if I am forced to name it, I declare it "The Great".[68] Greatness implies extent, extent implies distance, distance implies return. Great is the Way, great is Heaven, great is the Earth, great is the King. In all, there are four magnitudes, and the King occupies [one of these positions]. Man is patterned on Earth, Earth is patterned on Heaven, Heaven is patterned on the Way, the Way is patterned on itself. "
> 有物混成， 先天地 生。 寂兮寥兮， 獨立不改， 周行而不殆， 可以為 天下 母。 吾不知其名， 字之曰道， 強為之名曰大。 大曰逝， 逝曰遠， 遠曰反。 故道大， 天大， 地大， 王亦 大。 域中有四大， 而王居。 人法地， 地法天， 天法道， 道法自然。
>
> (*Daodejing* 25)

---

[67] Variations on this theme, sometimes advocating for more moderate positions than the ones found in the *Laozi* and the *Zhuangzi*, abound in the Daoist tradition. For instance, Wang Bi distinguishes between the name (*ming* 名) and the designation (*cheng* 稱), the first one born from the object, the second being inferred by a subject. (See *Laozi weizhi lilüe* 老子微指例略4, as translated and commented in Wagner 2003, 95–96.)

[68] In his commentary of *Laozi* 25, Wang Bi writes: "By the *ming*, the shape [of a thing] is determined; by the *zi* 字, is determined what one can speak about (*ming yi ding xing, zi yi cheng ke yan* 名以定形, 字以稱可言). (Wang Bi *Commentary on the Laozi*, 25. Translation Wagner 2003, 201 [modified].)

Because it cannot be named (at least not in the way that Xunzi wants things to be named), the Way highlights the irreducible artificiality of both language and rites. If language and ritual conventions are recognized (in very varying degrees) by Confucian thinkers as an "artifice", they justify such artifice by two considerations: it is modeled on a pre-existing "naturalness"; and its implementation allows for social mechanisms to function "naturally", so to speak. It is such a system (by which, in the same movement, we name and we assess) that the *Daodejing* is questioning:

> Everyone knows what marks the beautiful as beautiful – and here comes ugliness! Everyone knows what marks the good as good – and here comes the no-good! Thus, the "There is" and the "There is not" are born from each other, the difficult and the easy are formed from each other, the long and the short are assessed one by the other, the top is built upon the bottom, sounds with other sounds harmonize, and "After" follows "Before".
> 天下皆知美之為美，斯惡已。皆知善之為善，斯不善已。故有無相生，難易相成，長短相較，高下相傾，音聲相和，前後相隨。
>
> (*Daodejing* 2)

I already underlined the fact in our first chapter: the simple distinction between what is called "beautiful" and what is not so brings into existence ugliness: all at once, the lack that characterized the "unbeautiful" takes a consistency of its own! Naming "makes reality arise", but not the reality we wanted.

Names in the Abyss

To the first sentences of the *Laozi* let me now juxtapose the beginning of the *Zhuangzi*. This is one of the most beautiful book openings ever written:

> In the abyss [*ming* 冥] of the north is a fish; its name [*ming* 名] is Kun. Kun is "big" [*da* 大], I don't know by how many *li*. It metamorphoses [*hua* 化] and becomes a bird. Its name [*ming* 名] is Peng. Peng's back, I don't know how many *li* it covers. [Peng] shakes, it soars, its wings spread like clouds draping the sky. Such is this bird! The sea is agitated, and as it rises, moves towards the abyss [*ming* 冥] of the south. The southern abyss is the celestial basin.
> 北冥有魚，其名為鯤。鯤之大，不知其幾千里也。化而為鳥，其名為鵬。鵬之背，不知其幾千里也；怒而飛，其翼若垂天之雲。是鳥也，海運則將徙於南冥。南冥者，天池也。
>
> (*Zhuangzi* 1.1)

As already suggested in the preceding chapter, here there is very probably the echo of a cosmogonic myth, which becomes material for philosophical speculation. It all begins in the abyss of the north. The *ming* of "the abyss" is clearly contrasted with the *ming* of "the name". The names are lost in the abyss... The rhetorical effect is reinforced by the very name of the fish, Kun 鯤, the graph of which associates "multitude" and "fish". Kun seems to be made up of a whole bunch of little fry... And Kun is "big", disproportionate. We can neither name it nor measure it. It transforms and becomes a bird. The bird is named Peng. The transformation reinforces the absurdity of the "naming": the thing is one another. It was a fish and now it is a bird – but is it not the same creature that we name twice? They "come from the same [reality], although named differently 同 出 而 異 名" (*Laozi* 1). Both beasts are "mysterious" (*xuan* 玄) (*Laozi* 1), *xuan* being the color of the abyss. The bird swings towards the southern end of the sky. We travel from north to south by a path that speech cannot unfold. If the text had its origin in a myth, the latter was certainly speaking of the seasonal movement, from the heart of winter until the hottest of summer – before the movement reverses. The mention of the "lake (or basin) of the sky" reinforces the idea: germination is taking place (several Chinese medical texts confirm that a "basin" [*chi* 池] is first and foremost a place of germination.). From the most secret point of the sky, life is being sown. Both being basins of germination, North and South join together... And indeed, a little further in our text (*Zhuangzi* 1.2), without concern for possible contradictions, the narrator identifies the celestial basin with the abyss of the north... After all, the bird will probably become a fish again, before it again transforms into a bird... But – and this is the strength of the text – no reverse transformation is explicitly evoked. Zhuangzi is not narrating the myth of the eternal return. The return of the Way is a breakthrough: greatness (*da* 大) does not consist in expanding unceasingly, but rather in making a return (*Laozi* 40). To retrace one's step is to grow. In the last instance, the first sentences of the *Laozi* and the *Zhuangzi* say exactly the same thing: the Way can neither be measured nor unfolded. As the Name of the Way – the Original Name, so to speak –, radically escapes us, all names are mere artifice, an artifice that contributes much more to a process of alienation than of harmonization and order. Harmony (social harmony, cosmic harmony) cannot be ensured by a strategy of regulation, by naming and ritualizing. Conversely, entering into harmony with my own self requires from me to revert to the Way that has neither name nor measure and that operates in me and in all things. At the end of the first chapter, Zhuangzi meets Huizi, the indefatigable debater, who declares: "I possess a tree which is exactly like your words: immense, knotty, twisted, and hard... so, nothing can be made out of it." And Zhuangzi replies "So, go and root your tree into the place where there is nothing. Lie down under its shadow, close your eyes, and then travel freely (*xiaoyao* 逍遙) in the immeasurable" (*Zhuangzi* 1.7). If only he stopped to manufacture names, definitions and arguments, then, Huizi, closing his eyes under the giant tree, would join the immeasurable course of that which flows from one abyss to the other. As long as we remain immersed in lexical debates, we share in Huizi's restiveness.

Chapter 3
Philosophical Narratives in (and about) China

How is the dominant narrative of Sino-Western comparative philosophy interpreted on the Chinese side? Is there a counter-narrative to be found? Understandably, Chinese academics are prone to assert the radical singularity of their tradition, to claim arbitral power as to the interpretation of said tradition, and to coopt the interlocutors allowed to interact with them on the issues at stake. Mutual co-opting on the basis of the uniqueness of the tradition under study allows Chinese philosophers and Western sinologists to regroup, while providing for some measure of disagreement and diversity. The weight induced by political considerations and interventions, as well as the prevalent idea of an "orthodox transmission" (*daotong* 道統) of Confucianism (and, more largely, of Chinese philosophy) also contribute to prevent the surge of strong intellectual dissidence. The above applies in particular to Chinese academics working within Mainland China, with somewhat more diversity spotted outside. For instance, the historian and Confucian scholar Yu Yingshi 余英時 (1932–2021), who was developing his work from the United States, distinguished himself by his rejection of the idea of "orthodox transmission", as already his teacher Qian Mu 錢穆 (1895–1990) was doing. For Qian Mu, the idea of "orthodox transmission" had been borrowed from Buddhism by Confucians. There was without doubt some truth in this statement. However, the social pervasiveness of professional and intellectual *lineages* in Chinese culture and society had made the idea of *daotong* an extremely easy one to adopt.

Putting aside the quarrels engineered by professional rivalries, the field of "Chinese philosophy" is relatively unified, even though "philosophy" in Chinese academic institutions exhibits much diversity: aesthetics, logic or philosophy of language have all carved their protected territories, as have continental, phenomenological or analytical trends of thought... Marxists as well as admirers of Leo Strauss or Alasdair McIntyre, followers of Heidegger, Habermas and Gadamer, disciples of Merleau-Ponty and Foucault, Liberals or Confucians of all shades ... All species are represented.

Let us first listen to the narrative broadly sketched by Tang Yijie 汤一介 (1927–2014) as to the contrasts and relationships between Western and Chinese philosophy. The first two moments of the said encounter are summarized as follows:

> Western philosophy was imported into China at the end of 19th century. Its earliest and most influential introducer, Yan Fu (嚴複), had translated a great deal of western philosophical works, especially those on Darwin's evolutionism. Afterwards, Kant, Descartes, Schopenhauer, Nietzsche, and so forth, were all introduced into China in succession, which provided a point

> of reference to the problem of "whether there is Philosophy in China". [...] We have to admit that, before the importation of western philosophy, Philosophy was not separated from Canon studies (經學) and non-Confucian Masters studies (子學) as an independent discipline. [...] From 1930s on, Chinese philosophers had employed traditional Chinese intellectual resources to construct several important modern types of 'Chinese philosophy' on the basis of the absorptions and adaptations of western philosophy. First, Xiong Shili (熊十力) and Zhang Dongsun (張東蓀), and then Feng Youlan and Jin Yuelin (金岳霖). After 1949, however, this trend of constructing a modern 'Chinese philosophy', as well as further study of western philosophy, was interrupted. It was not until in the 1980s that western philosophy began to flow once again into China [...], broadening not only the horizon of Chinese philosophers, but also the referential system for the poly-perspective study of Chinese philosophy.
>
> (Tang 2007, 21–22)

Act 1 of the play is thus about "importation" (happening in successive waves), and Act 2 about "synthesis". Act 3 confronts the challenge brought by the "synthesis" crafted from the 1930s onwards, as the latter seems to necessarily entail a construction on which the Western model serves as normative reference. The very idea of a possible synthesis is complicated by the following characteristics of what "Chinese philosophy" is about:

> In my opinion, from ancient Greeks on, especially from Descartes on, Western philosophy has focused more on the systematic construction of philosophic knowledge; while in the Chinese tradition, our sages put more emphasis on the pursuit of a *jing-jie* (境界), a philosophical realm of virtues or latencies to be realized) of life. A quotation of Confucius may embody this feature: "Better to like it than merely know it; better to take delight in it than merely like it." The ultimate pursuit of life is not to achieve knowledge (or skills), but to seek a place where one can "settle one's body and life" (安身立命), i.e., a *jing-jie* where body and mind, the exterior and the interior, are in harmony. This was pursued also by Sung and Ming Confucian philosophers as "where Confucius and Yan Hui took delight". The Taoist philosopher Zhuangzi pursued all the more a *jing-jie* of Free Roaming (逍遙遊) above the ego and the mundane world, which was called by him the selfless (無我) realm. Zen Buddhism in China makes a point of seeing Tao in daily life, as naturally as "Clouds are in heaven and water in vase".
>
> (Tang 2007, 24)

Tang Yijie leaves open the question of what ought to be a Chinese philosophy truly liberated from the Western model (faithful to its original inspiration) while aiming at being global. Simply, such philosophy "must take up the standpoint of its proper tradition, and appropriately absorb and adapt contemporary western philosophy" (Tang 2007, 26). Some of his proposals may look slightly counter-intuitive, for instance when he writes: "certain special notions in Chinese philosophy should not be adapted to Western terminologies at all, but be transliterated with annotations, in order to keep the pregnant particularity of Chinese philosophy. Only when this is kept, could Chinese philosophy make special contributions to World Philosophy" (Tang 2007, 26).

Based on this initial narrative, which can be found in many variants, I intend to proceed in four steps. I will start by recalling a historical stage that is not explicitly mentioned in Tang's narrative, i.e., the rebellion against the Confucian tradition. I deem such a step necessary because taking into account this episode influences our understanding of the evolutions that followed. Second, I will attempt to assess what were exactly the project, presuppositions and methodology of the Chinese philosophers who, from the 1920s to the 1980s, attempted to develop a style of Chinese philosophy largely constructed on a Western model (that is at least the description offered by Tang Yijie) – an attempt nowadays submitted to serious criticisms, as we already perceived. I will then distinguish two narratives propounded by present-days Chinese scholars when marketing their own philosophizing. The first one, I will call "the Beijing Model" (third section), and the second (the fourth and final section of this chapter), "The Shanghai Variant".

The May Fourth Movement as a Philosophical Event

On May 4, 1919, three thousand students gathered in central Beijing in order to protest against the preliminary provisions of the Treaty of Versailles which ceded the German possessions of the province of Shandong to Japan. A nationwide boycott of Japanese goods followed, as well as a general strike in Shanghai, then the country's industrial capital. Very quickly, the movement broadened its demands: young intellectuals and students challenged the legal, familial and social provisions that were determining women's fate; they sang the praises of "Mr. Science" and "Mr. Democracy" in opposition to the Confucian worldview and the ritualism associated with it; they endeavored to have modern Chinese replace literary Chinese as the language of instruction. The May Fourth Movement was in fact inseparable from the New Culture Movement (*xin wenhua yundong* 新文化運動) epitomized by the literary magazine *La Jeunesse* (*Xin qingnian* 新青年), active from 1915 till 1926.

The conviction that culture plays a decisive role in the destiny of peoples had been prepared by the success of translations of works by Darwin, Spencer, J.S. Mill, Adam Smith or yet Montesquieu. Universities organized on the Western model were beginning to shape the Chinese intellectual landscape. The founders of the New Culture Movement were grouped around Peking University, founded in 1898. Their natural leader was Cai Yuanpei 蔡元培 (1868–1940), president of this university and eclectic reformer. Chen Duxiu 陳獨秀 (1879–1942) taught from 1916 onwards at the same university. It was Chen who had launched *La Jeunesse*; the magazine published in 1917 the Manifesto of Hu Shi 胡適 (1891–1962 – a disciple of the American philosopher John Dewey) calling for the establishment of a modern standardized language, then, in 1918, the first work in vernacular Chinese of modern literature, *A Madman's Diary* by Lu Xun 鲁迅 (1881–1936). Chen Duxiu founded with others the Chinese Communist Party in 1921 and was its first secretary general. Because of his Trotskyist tendencies, he was expelled from it in 1929. Other future luminaries of the Chinese intelligentsia – the philosopher Liang Shuming 梁漱溟 (1893–1988), the historian Gu Jiegang 顧頡剛 (1893–1980) – also participated in the movement.

The social and political aspirations proper to the May Fourth Movement were thus depending upon an intellectual current characterized by a strong philosophical and literary component:

> Political reform – this is the originality of the Movement – requires above all a literary reform and the rejection of old literature, supposedly [merely] dedicated to the tribulations of the powerful or to ghost stories that only serve to divert the attention of readers from the problems of ordinary people and of the existing society.
> (Veg 2010, 350)

Echoing Confucian orthodoxy, the movement aimed at making literature and knowledge a moral force, but this force had to work *against* traditional Confucian values. The alternative values promoted by the May Fourth Movement were deeply influenced by the anarchist tradition, notably when it came to reforming the family, ethics, and the individual himself (Gasster 1969).

The May Fourth Movement was combining a fierce desire to fundamentally reform Chinese ethos and culture – "mired in shameful filth", declares Chen Duxiu – with an equally assertive nationalist surge (uneasily mixed, as we will see, with internationalist ideals), which developed into an ever-reaffirmed imperative: "Save the Nation!". The junction that it operated between these two requirements was necessarily fragile. Some of the May Fourth actors quickly returned to substantive cultural work: this was the case with Gu Jiegang, who engaged into textual criticism in order to systematically deconstruct traditional Chinese historiography.[69] Other actors chose instead to favor political action over cultural combat.

---

[69] For the critical importance of historiography in the debate around the "Chinese tradition" in the first half of the 20th century, and beyond: Wang (2001); Brown (2011).

The Invention of a Language

The May Fourth Movement was first and foremost a language and a style – the very language and style that would define journalism and publishing in China, as they triumphed during the 1920s. To be a journalist, a columnist, a newspaper or magazine editor was then to become a man of sizable influence, to accumulate intellectual and social prestige. Newspapers become profitable enterprises, as advertising greatly helped finance them. A publishing house like the Commercial Press (*Shangwu yinshuguan* 商務印書館), created in 1897 in Shanghai, became a company managed as a modern for-profit enterprise around 1921. It was able to found and finance a large library open to all (the library was eventually destroyed in a Japanese bombardment in 1932).

Lu Xun published *The True Story of Ah Q* in weekly installments from December 1921 to February 1922. The novella was speaking, with a sort of despair, of the (im-)possibility of giving birth within Chinese society to an *individual* worthy of the name. This quest for individuality was theorized by the writer Zhou Zuoren 周作人 (1885–1967), Lu Xun's brother. In December 1918, Zhou published in *La Jeunesse* a founding text, "The Literature of Humanity [*Ren de wenxue* 人的文學]". Zhou Zuoren promoted a humanistic thinking that stressed healthy self-appreciation. Quoting the commandment "Thou shalt love thy neighbor as thyself" (which he attributed directly to Jesus, apparently ignoring its roots in *Leviticus* 19,18), Zhou noted that loving others without first loving oneself represents an impossible task (Zhou (1996 [1918]), vol. 2, 85–93). The "modern humanism" he was aspiring to build was not borrowing from Confucianism (which he rejected as radically as Chen Duxiu did). Rather, besides explicit references to Christianity, Zhou found inspiration in the works and life of Leo Tolstoy for instance. Rival conceptions of what "Humanism" was meant to be would soon see the light of the day. Through the prism of this new concept they would reinterpret the Confucian tradition in various ways and criticize Zhou's and Chen's borrowing of Christianity and "universal values" as vehicles for Western expansionism in China. Therefore, at first glance, the promotion of the Confucian "Middle Way" for grounding an alternative "Humanism" could be read as a reaction against the Christian and European versions of this concept. However, the fact that well-known Christians such as Zhao Zichen 趙紫宸 (C.T. Chao, 1888–1979) were among the promoters of a "Chinese Humanism" (contrasted to the blueprint that the early articles of *La Jeunesse* had sketched) shows that the intellectual and political debate of Republican China was shrouded in innumerable contrasts and nuances. Individual parameters make the matter even more intricate. The convoluted travels of Lin Yutang 林語堂 between Chinese culture and Christianity, as well as the influence that such travail entailed on Lin's ever-evolving political views, is a case in point (see esp. Lin 1959).

The relationship between the May Fourth Movement and Christianity was a complex one. The Bible, made available in vernacular from 1919 onwards, was providing thinkers with an alternative resource in the face of the deadlock met by Chinese culture (at least in the view of the promoters of the movement). Indeed, many Chinese intellectuals saw Christianity and biblical texts as indispensable assets to "save the nation". This idea extends beyond the borders of the May Fourth Movement. Among other warlords, Feng Yuxiang 馮玉祥 (1882–1948), converted to Methodism and built a "Christian army" where military exercises were combined with religious songs. Chang Kai-shek supported and guided the translation of the Psalms by the Catholic scholar John Wu Jingxiong 吳經熊 (1899–1986). As for Sun Yat-sen, he compared the unrest following the revolution of 1911 to the wandering of the Israelites in the desert, and, more generally, found in the story of Moses, the narrative scheme of the liberation of the Chinese people.[70] The biblical reference was also found within the foremost political representatives of the May Fourth Movement: Jesus is first of all "the friend of the poor", declared Chen Duxiu: "Crossing through the door of Jesus himself, we should internalize, make our own, the great characteristics of Jesus and his profound concern for humanity" (Chen 1920, 19). And several Protestant theologians of the 1920s and 1930s echoed such assertions (see Vermander 2021c).

At the same time, as I already underlined, the inspiration of the movement was heavily drawing on an anarchist tradition that was extolling liberation from traditional moral prescriptions, exalting the individual, and challenging any power relationship. It was sometimes referring to Nietzsche (in the case of Lu Xun notably). Fittingly, anarchist influence was combined with frequent statements of internationalism, even if, as we have seen, it is on a nationalist agenda that the May Fourth Movement crystallized. A witness to the anarchist current underlying the Movement was the writer Ba Jin 巴金 (1904–2005), even though he was born too late to participate directly in it. Sometimes in petto, sometimes publicly, Ba Jin would remain faithful all his life to the anarchist convictions he had discovered before he was even 20 when reading *An Appeal to the Young* by Kropotkin and *Le Grand Soir* by Leopold Kampf.

Some of the actors of the movement shifted to political action: the drama into which China was sinking ultimately required from them to gather into strong organizations, or so they felt. The founding of the Chinese Communist Party proved decisive. Other figures of the New Culture Movement – notably Hu Shi – refused to make such a turn: they had not freed China from the slavery of Confucius to fall into that imposed by the Soviet Union, would declare the latter.

---

70 Sun (1986 [1924]), 537–538; Chen (2008).

Thinking about May Fourth

In 1939, the Communist Party found its own way of co-opting the movement while keeping it at bay: it made the anniversary of May Fourth China's Youth Day (as it remains to this day). The fact remarkably summarizes the constant attitude of the Party towards the Movement: May Fourth constitutes only one stage on the road that begins with the revolution of 1911, undergoes a decisive advance with the formation of the Communist Party, and takes on its full significance with the founding of New China in 1949. The party passes an overall positive judgment on the movement, but also asserts its lack of political maturity.

On two occasions at least, the reference to May Fourth took on special significance. The first time was in 1979. China had just entered the era of Reforms and Openness. This time, the call to "free the mind" was not directed at Confucius, but at Mao, and was central to the aborted students' democratic movement of 1978–1979. The significance of the event was renewed in 1989. Many of the students' aspirations of that year coincided with those of their predecessors, even if the events in Tiananmen Square could not be seen as a mere repetition of those that took place in the same place 70 years earlier. But the failure of the April–June 1989 movement echoed that of May 1919, which subsequently experienced only official "embalming", including at the time of its one hundredth anniversary.

While the strictly political significance of May Fourth has been neutralized by subsequent events, the movement's long-term cultural impact remains a subject of debate. During the past 20 or so years, some Chinese intellectuals have launched strong attacks against it. Such criticism of Confucianism, they say, was unwarranted; it could only weaken China by deconstructing "the essence" of Chinese culture. Love of the nation requires not to attack its history. As stressed by Chen Lai 陳來 (b. 1952), a philosopher we are soon going to meet again:

> Culture is the soul of a nation. Over five millennia, Chinese culture has informed the nation's spiritual pursuits and this is the spiritual mark that sets us apart from other nations. Its central notions have structured the spiritual world of the Chinese, its core values have sedimented like the cultural genes of the nation and over a very long historical development have become the nation's spiritual lifeline. To transmit Chinese culture is precisely to maintain this line of life. Nation and culture are one thing: no Chinese culture without a Chinese nation, and vice versa.
>
> (Chen 2017)

The link between Chinese culture and Chinese classics is organic. The May Fourth Movement and its aftermath brought a radical challenge to the authority of the latter. In 1934, for example, Cai Yuanpei strongly protested against a plan to reintroduce Confucian state-sanctioned Classics into basic education, and this because they were conveying counter-productive values, such as asymmetry between the sexes or between the sovereign and his subjects. Presently, the intellectual class generally takes distance from the hypercritical spirit of the May Fourth Movement. However, some of its members recognize the danger arising from too radical a distancing. For instance, meant as a reaction against the May Fourth spirit, attempts at re-sacralizing the Classics lead to legitimize anew the social ethos that the May Fourth Movement aspired to overcome: primacy of the group over the individual; instrumentalization of obedience and "filial piety"; ritualization of social life against unconstrained creativity. The writings of Lu Xun or Cai Yuanpei retain their critical power when read against the backdrop provided by today's China.

Moreover, it may be less the Classics than the interpretations by which they had been codified that raise questions. Since 1919, the development of hermeneutical resources has made it possible to re-read Confucius or Mencius in a different way, to put these authors in dialogue and tension with their protagonists, to understand them as testimonies of a living experience and not as fossilized authorities. In the end, the impertinence and extraordinary creativity that characterized Chinese intellectual life from the 1910s to the 1940s did not rid China of its heritage. Today, with a century of distance, the May Fourth intellectuals allow us to rediscover the Classics equipped with new interpretative tools, and the upheaval of consciousness they fostered has been crucial in the forging of these tools. Paradoxically, we need to accept and assess the heritage of the May Fourth Movement in order to give Confucius new relevance.

Recreating Philosophy

Stressing the historical significance of the May Fourth Movement opens up the only counter-narrative to the one sketched by Tang Yijie. If only latent, this counter-narrative remains relevant: till today, for some Chinese, the impact of the "traditional culture" that the Classics are meant to encapsulate remains subject to interrogation, or even to strong skepticism. In the 1990s and at the beginning of the 2000s, "liberal" thinkers expressed distaste for the traditional Chinese ethos (experienced as oppressive, embedded into social forms now defunct). Such critical distance was after all a defining feature of Chinese Marxism, this until the (very recent) time when "sinicizing Marxism" became an imperative that imposed upon intellectuals the duty to find ways of reconciling the classics of the two traditions.[71]

---

71 The depth and the nature of the Marxism absorbed by Zhang Dainian 张岱年 (1909–2004) and

As rightly stressed by Tang Yijie, the shock of the encounter between the translated Western "classics" (notably philosophical and historical works of the 19th century) and the Chinese canon led thinkers to attempt intellectual syntheses, and this from around 1930 onwards. For a long time, these syntheses were equated with modern (or contemporary) "Chinese philosophy". The situation is much more complex now that well-established academics question whether syntheses between Chinese and Western modes of thinking may be cogent, sustainable, even if these academics generally express such opinion with the reverence to be shown to elders whose memory is still alive. Still, in the view that today prevails, basic notional incompatibilities would make it impossible to associate concepts and approaches across cultures.

These criticisms target the first two generations of Chinese "professional" philosophers – I use the term "professional" because the scholars we are now going to meet with have been closely associated to the establishment of departments of philosophy throughout the Chinese world: the mainland, Hong Kong and Taiwan. There is no doubt that, nowadays, the syntheses they attempted appear to many disconcerting, somehow clumsy, far too encompassing in their design. However, they may still offer an alternative to the present way of doing comparative philosophy as described in our first two chapters – proceeding through couples of opposites so as to engineer a "typical" way of doing Chinese or else Western philosophy. If the first Chinese professional philosophers were largely concerned with identity issues – as Chinese philosophers still are today – if they wanted their philosophy to be decidedly "Chinese", they were also tackling questions not primarily defined by these same identity issues: they were attempting to think *along* philosophers coming from different traditions, and to pursue the line of questioning endeavored by these philosophers. In this respect, the marked interest for Indian thinkers exhibited by many of the New Confucians shows an ability to think beyond binary lines. Referring to India was a way to ensure ecological diversity in the philosophical gardens, so to speak. As a matter of fact, in India, for the tradition initiated by Dignāga (c. 480–540), universals have no ontological footing whatsoever, whereas Udayana (c. 975–1050) tries to root the very idea of substance in pure logical reasoning. And yet, in the course of their development, throughout their very oppositions, Dignāga's and Udayana's traditions have constantly learned from each other.[72]

Li Zehou 李泽厚 (1930–2021) remain a debated topic. Makeham (2008) provides examples of Marxian Confucians active in the recent decades.
72 Cf. Siderits (2021), 220 ff.; Ganeri (2009), 72 ff.

Feng Youlan and Philosophical Cross-fertilization

Along with Liang Shuming (already mentioned), Xiong Shili 熊十力 (1885–1968), Ma Yifu 馬一浮 (1883–1967) and Zhang Junmai 張君勱 [Carsun Chang] (1886–1969), Feng Youlan 馮友蘭 (1895–1990) is one of the founding members of the New Confucianism School (very much inchoative in its structure and evolution), which forged an alternative to the overthrowing of Chinese tradition propounded by the Fourth May movement. However, if most New Confucians refer primarily to Lu Jiuyuan and Wang Yangming 王陽明 (1472–1528), figureheads of the School of the Heart-Mind, Feng is solidly inscribed into the more "rationalist" tradition of Cheng Yi 程頤 (1033–1107) and Zhu Xi.

Feng is not at the origin of the New Confucian School, the beginning of which may be dated from the publication, in 1921, of Liang Shuming's *Eastern and Western Cultures and Their Philosophies* (Liang 1987 [1921]), a book that pleaded for the Chinese "Middle Way" in contrast to the Western focus on the satisfaction of desires and India's intent to destroy them to the root.[73] Afterwards, Zhang Junmai, adept of a "metaphysical" approach to existence, centered on existential values and self-cultivation and engaged in a debate with followers of the May Fourth Movement who had adopted the Western ideal of science as a basis not only for exploring the physical world but also for approaching and transforming the mental and social universe. The perspective of Zhang Junmai was furthered by Xiong Shili, who expounded an intuitionist approach to knowledge, and revived an already well-established distinction/complementarity between Chinese learning seen as "substance" (*ben* 本) and Western learning used as "function" (*yong* 用). The development brought up by Feng Youlan (who had studied at Columbia University from 1920 to 1923 and had received his PhD there) is double: (1) through his *History of Chinese Philosophy*, written between 1930 and 1934 and translated early on into English, he put the parallel between Chinese and Western thoughts into a chronological and developmental framework (Fung [Feng] 1955; see also Fung [Feng] 1962). (2) Feng's series of six books – a series to which he gave the general title *The Purity Descends, Primacy Ascends: Six Books* (*Zhenyuan liu shu* 貞元六書) -, written between 1938 and 1946, offers the first systematic presentation of what could be a philosophy anchored in an "amalgamation" between Chinese and Western traditions. This presentation was also aiming at overcoming both the "science or metaphysic" opposition and too facile a divide between East and West, which Feng complemented with a contrast between "ancient" and "modern" soci-

---

[73] For a global history of the movement, see Bresciani (2001).

eties and cultures. Around 1934, Feng was introducing his project in the following fashion:

> Our comparisons between Chinese and Western thought are not meant to judge which is right or wrong, but rather to clarify one with the other. We hope that in the not-so-distant future, European philosophy will be supplemented by Chinese philosophy with regard to intuition and experience, and Chinese philosophy by Western logic and clear arguments.
>
> (Feng Youlan, quoted in Lin 2013, 5)

The work was also anchored in a dramatic political context: "Feng borrowed from *The Book of Changes'* description of the cycle of change, from low ebb (*zhen* 貞) to high tide (*yuan* 元), to describe his hope for China in its war against Japan" (Lin 2013, 3).

Feng's philosophical style is probably the one that is now subject to the clearest rejection, and, indeed, its frailties are glaring. At the same time, seen at a distance, Feng's ambition epitomizes both the risks and opportunities associated with the fact of engaging into a global philosophical enterprise with a variety of resources intended at fostering cross-fertilization. Let us examine the "Six Books" through the prism provided by the most important of them, the *New Treatise on Man* (*Xin yuan ren* 新原人), first published in 1943 (Feng 2006; Feng 2014).[74]

So as to give new ground to the Neo-Confucianist tradition, Feng worked to "re-found it logically" (as he used to write), guided by the method of analytical philosophy, while subverting the goal that analytical philosophy was assigning to itself. Whereas the thinkers of the Circle of Vienna thought to have demonstrated that metaphysical propositions are devoid of meaning, Feng Youlan intended to logically establish the truth of Neo-Confucianist metaphysics by going beyond analytical negativism, an enterprise that he compared to that of Kant, who, awakened from his dogmatic sleep by Hume's skepticism, discovered critical thinking as the path leading to the refutation of skepticism without falling back into dogmatism. Feng was thus roughly following the path established by Bertrand Russell and other "New Realists" but adding to it a distinctive Chinese touch: Alongside analytical knowledge (purely formal) and empirical knowledge (purely hypothetical), Feng asserted the existence of a knowledge of the third type, capable of metaphysi-

---

[74] One can also grasp Feng Youlan's overall project by reading the translation of the last book of the series: *The Spirit of Chinese Philosophy* (Feng 1962). The *New Treatise of Man* benefits from an excellent annotated translation in a Western language: *Nouveau traité sur l'homme. Introduction, traduction et notes par Michel Masson* (Feng 2006). For the summary that follows, besides direct reference to Feng's works, I have referred to Lin (2013) and to an extended, groundbreaking book review by Léon Vandermeersch that discusses Feng from the viewpoint of Masson's translation (Vandermeersch 2007).

cally establishing Neo-Confucianism, a formal knowledge of empirical data: that of what the Chinese tradition includes under the term of *li* 理.

The concept of *li* points towards the intrinsic *reasons* that account for the specific nature of each discrete reality: the fact that a mountain is a mountain, a horse a horse, a square a square. Applying to things the knowledge obtained by the analysis of their forms does not produce any scientific knowledge; it rather opens the mind to a kind of metaphysical intuition, which will deepen until it leads to self-realization. With Zhu Xi, such metaphysics remained insufficiently theorized due to a lack of suitable methodology. To ground it in all rigor, Feng Youlan resorts to a method defined as "the analysis of the reasons [intrinsic to things] [*li*] starting from the critique of names" (*bianming xili* 辨明析理).

Such analysis relies upon abstracting common characters from the observation of concrete realities, characters that our language designates. If all realities were signaled by proper names, the discourse would be so loaded with details that it would explode in profusion. Common names denote the outlines of reality. The critique of names allows us to analyze the forms taken by ordinary experience. Feng refers here to Guo Xiang 郭象 (252–312), who himself referred to Huizi 惠子, Zhuangzi's interlocutor and the promoter of the doctrine of "names and forms" (*xingming* 形名), i.e., of the analysis of reality through language criticism.

As they are abstract forms, the *li* of the things are not within these things. They act upon them a bit like formal causes do in Aristotle, but they arise from a transcendent order (*xingshang* 形上) as is the case with ideas in Plato. The transcendent order, Feng Youlan calls it the order of truths (*zhenji* 真際), as opposed to the order of realities, that of immanence (*xingxia* 形下). When it comes to the grounding of the order of realities, matter or "material" (*liao* 料) must be understood as a relative notion: bricks are the material of the house but themselves have clay as material, which in turn comes from various minerals, and so on, up to an absolute designated by the character *qi* 氣 (often translated as matter-energy). *Qi* itself is *li*-free – its name is a proper name. The name *taiji* 太極, often mistakenly taken as pointing towards the concept of an absolute *li*, corresponds only to the aggregate of all *li* that act upon the myriad things. Processual emergence (*daoti* 道體) makes the world evolve from chaos (*hundun*, 混沌) or ultimateless (*wuji* 無極), to the supreme ultimate (*cong li zhi quan* 眾理之全 or *taiji* 太極), when all things had developed to the maximum allowed by their *li*.

What understanding of human nature does Feng's metaphysics imply? Confucianism defines as "feelings" (*qing* 情) that which, in human nature, comes from the heart, and gives the name of "desires" (*yu* 欲) to the other components of the human psyche. The thesis of Mencius, that of the innate goodness of human nature, amounts to recognizing that every human being comes into the world with the seeds of good feelings inscribed in her nature through the *li* proper to this one, and that these seeds, properly cultivated, lead to discipline one's desires and attain self-realization. The standpoint expounded by Xunzi recognizes on the contrary that every human being comes into the world with dominant egoistic desires which need to be corrected. Neo-Confucianism, both in Zhu Xi and in Wang Yangming, takes up the doctrine of Mencius. However, for Feng Youlan, the question of the goodness of human nature cannot arise in the *order of truths*, which transcends the opposition of good and bad, but in the *order of realities* (that of the existential nature of individuals). What distinguishes individuals from one another is that, in the existential nature of each, the proportions of the various determinations by which existence takes shape vary from one individual to another, leading to differences in the dynamics of feelings, desires and projects which underlie behavior.

Feng Youlan thus starts from the concreteness of human nature to answer the question of what kind of meaning existence may possess for the conditioned human beings that we are. Meaning is only felt and discovered through a kind of intuitive knowledge that Feng Youlan calls *juejie* 覺解. He relates it to "awakening" in the Buddhist sense of the term, the fact of integrating into self-awareness the understanding of the world specific to a given consciousness. The *New Treatise on Man* characterizes different forms of self-awareness by differentiating among the worldviews attached to them. To that effect, Feng develops the concept of *jingjie* 境界, that is to say of the world in the sense that it takes for our consciousness of being-in-the-world (said otherwise, for the consciousness of living in a specific existential environment). Accordingly, Léon Vandermeersch interprets the *New Treatise on Man* as a "phenomenology of consciousness" (Vandermeersch 2007), a phenomenology that describes the movement by which consciousness rises in the world through four stages: *natural consciousness* sticks to the world without distance; the *interested conscience* distances itself from the world by the utilitarian viewpoint it constructs; *moral conscience* inscribes itself into a social universe; eventually, in *cosmic consciousness*, the vision transcends the order of realities by locating itself within the order of truths (Feng Youlan compares such vision to that described by Spinoza as taking place *sub specie aeternitatis*).[75] Once communing with the Dao of Heaven, human nature is realized in bliss.

There are logical inconsistencies in Feng's vision.[76] The discrepancy that exists between his pre- and post-1949 writings further eroded his influence. This should not lessen the respect to be felt towards a bold attempt at doing philosophy

---

75 For an analysis of the reference to Spinoza in Feng, see Masson (1985), 203–204.
76 See the second part of the article by Lin (2013).

through the criss-crossing of resources, the complementary or uniqueness of which are meant to reveal something about the structure of the world and the way human experience relates to it. Here, the variety of philosophical resources is not merely *made use of*. It is rather *conceived of* as a path towards the elucidation of the relationships existing between language, logic and the ultimate structure of reality. Song Kuanfeng writes: "[Feng Youlan] constructed his own philosophical system by interpreting and reconstructing the history of Chinese philosophy; and his own philosophical system, in turn, actualized the inheritance and development of previous Chinese philosophical systems" (Song 2021, 39). Song's overall reconstruction of Feng's methodology is insightful, even if we need to introduce an important amendment: it is rather by locating himself at the point of tension between the histories of Chinese and Western thoughts that Feng was ultimately able to articulate his own contribution.

Before focusing on present-day Chinese paradigms (what I have called the Beijing Model and the Shanghai Variant) I will briefly sketch two other attempts at grounding New Confucianism, attempts that have exercised a direct impact upon the present state of philosophical engagement.

The 1958 Manifesto

The year 1958 saw the publication of a "Manifesto for Chinese Culture Respectfully Addressed to World People [為中國文化敬告世界人士宣言]" written by Mou Zongsan 牟宗三 (1909–1995), Xu Fuguan 徐復觀 (1902–1982), Zhang Junmai, and Tang Junyi 唐君毅 (1909–1978). The text was translated into English in successive versions (extended and abridged), with the name of Xie Youwei 謝幼偉 (1905~1976), who had been consulted during the draft of the original version, being added to these versions.[77] The signatories (notably Tang Junyi, Mou Zongsan, and Xu Fuguan) are considered to be the leaders of the second generation of the New Confucian ideals, even if the term "New Confucianism" does not appear in the Manifesto. From the viewpoint of our discussion, the main interest of the text lies in the way our thinkers envision the relationship between Chinese and Western thoughts. I will thus limit myself to a reading of some of the topics discussed in the Manifesto, complemented afterwards by a few remarks on Tang Junyi's philosophical enterprise.

---

[77] On the convoluted textual history of the Chinese and English versions of the Manifesto, see Solé-Farràs (2014), 172–180 and Simionato (2019).

The title of the Manifesto's Part I-4, is remarkable: "The position of Chinese philosophical thought in Chinese culture and its difference from Western culture [中國哲學思想在中國文化中之地位，及其與西方文化之不同]". The point here is not a difference in *content* but rather in *positioning*. The expression "philosophical thought [*zhexue sixiang* 哲學思想]" is also worth noting, as if, even as the signatories were betting on the existence of a Chinese *philosophy*, they were keeping open the possibility to escape a term-by-term comparison with what defines "philosophy" in Western context and then to speak simply of "Chinese thought". These terminological issues would endure for decades to come.

> Thus, when investigating Chinese cultural history, we must consider it as *an objective expression of the spiritual life of the Chinese people* [中國民族之客觀的精神生命之表現]. But where do we find the core of this spiritual life? We may say that it lies in Chinese thought or philosophy [中國人之思想或哲學]. This does not mean that Chinese thought determines the history of Chinese culture; it means that only if we start from Chinese thought can we throw light on the spiritual life of Chinese cultural history.
>
> (*Manifesto for Chinese Culture* 1.4)[78]

Our authors contrast the "single-rootedness" (*yibenxing* 一本性) of Chinese worldview to the diversity of sources – Greek, Hebrew and Roman – characteristic of Western thought. Whatever the limitations it induces, such continuity is seen as a strength, the one provided for by the "orthodox transmission [*daotong*]" or orthodox cultural lineage that extends from Confucius to Mencius to the Cheng Brothers, Zhu Xi and their continuators. Such single-rootedness lies in the notion that

> [Chinese culture] stresses the moral relationship [literally: the ethical morality 倫理道德] between man and man, but not the religious relationship [literally: the religious faith 宗教信仰] between man and God. [And yet, continue the authors, Western observers] have not perceived that, behind moral relationships there was an inner spiritual life that included transcendental feelings of a religious nature.
>
> (*Manifesto* 1.5).

---

[78] There have been a number of slightly different versions of both the Chinese and the English texts of the Manifesto. The English version provided by Chang (1962) has been often used, though it is a slightly abridged one. See also "Manifesto for a Reappraisal of Sinology and the Reconstruction of Chinese Culture," in De Bary and Lufrano (2000), 550–555. Other translations are available. I refer here to the Chinese version published in Mou et al (1989 [1958]). Working from the Chinese text, I have introduced some minor changes in the English translations usually quoted, for instance when the word "objective" in "objective manifestations" had been omitted.

The expression "transcendental feelings of a religious nature [宗教性之超越感情]" is repeated in other parts of the Manifesto. The direct reference is to Mencius and to the way exercising one's heart to the utmost leads to know one's nature, and ultimately to know Heaven, as well as to the reiteration of this axiom at the beginning of the *Zhongyong* (see Chapter 2 of this book).

> Chinese culture arose out of the extension of primordial religious passion to ethico-moral principles and to daily living. For this reason, although its religious aspects have not been developed it is yet pervaded by such sentiments, and hence is quite different from occidental atheism. To comprehend this, it is necessary to discuss the doctrine of *xin-xing* 心性 (concentration of mind on an exhaustive study of the nature of the universe), which is a study of the basis of ethics and is the source of all theories of the "conformity of heaven and man in virtue." Yet, this is precisely what is most neglected and misunderstood by Sinologists.
>
> (*Manifesto* 1.5)

The Manifesto thus contrasts the objectivation of phenomena typical of Western investigation with the improvement in human subjectivity which, for Chinese thinkers, takes place by the very fact of meaningfully investigating the world. The contrast, as sketched in the text, is less cosmological or gnoseological than moral and existential. What Western thought can learn from the Chinese tradition is an *attitude*, rooted in humility, gentleness, compassion, attention to the present, and, when needed, non-action (I gather here a number of traits mentioned in the course of the Manifesto). Such an attitude is, indissolubly, ethical, spiritual and intellectual. It has to do with both knowing the world and acting (or non-acting) upon it. Still, the Manifesto calls for mutual learning and appreciation. In the following generation, and with different accents and methods, Tu Wei-ming [Du Weiming 杜維明] will repeat the call:

> Confucianism can benefit from the dialogues with the Jewish, Christian and Islamic theologians, with the Buddhists, Marxists, Freud and the post-Freud psychologists. Confucianism has achieved a great deal by being subjected to the analysis with the categories of Kant's philosophy and Hegel's philosophy. Such efforts must be expanded to absorb new philosophical insights of the 20th century.
>
> (Tu 1993, 59)

There is no doubt that the Manifesto shows a propensity to "essentialize" the traditions it discusses. Still, it does not envision them as being incommunicable: it recognizes their sharing of common objectives, such as knowing the world and grounding a form of virtue ethics,[79] while stressing the contrasts observed in methods and attitudes. At the same time, the Manifesto does not call for grand synthesis

---

[79] On this point, see Yu and Lei (2008).

but rather for transformative dialogue, which would allow each tradition to overcome some of its limitations and to gain in universality. Yet, if the Manifesto has represented a decisive moment in the affirmation of Neo-Confucianism as a current of thought active in the intellectual rejuvenation of the Chinese world, for a long time its role has been extremely limited when it comes to the way world philosophy is shaped and developed. Even today, accrued references to the Confucian tradition may have more to do with the prominent role played by China on the global scene than to any wholehearted and dialogic engagement with the mode of thinking developed by the same tradition.

The Worlds of Tang Junyi

A glance at Tang Junyi's philosophical endeavor will complement our narrative of 20th-century Chinese philosophers' engagement with both the Western tradition and their own. This historical background will help us to better assess the way current debates are shaped when it comes to what comparative philosophy is (or ought to be).

As stressed by Bresciani and Solé-Farràs, there might be three "Tang Junyi" to be looked for when perusing the over-abundant production of this author (Bresciani 2001, 301–329; Solé-Farràs 2014, 1271–1228). The first one is a traditional Confucian philosopher: moral issues and the cultivation of the Self are paramount in works such *The Building of the Moral Self* (道德自我之建立) (1944) (Tang 1989, vol.1). The second one is the historian and commentator of Chinese philosophy whose contribution culminates in the six-volume strong *Origin and Development of the Basic Concepts of Chinese Philosophy* (中國哲學原論) published between 1966 and 1975 (Tang 1989, vol.14–16). This second Tang Junyi has justly attracted the attention of Roger Ames, who finds in him analyses congruent with his own understanding of natural cosmology, human nature, and role ethics (see Ames 2011). Ames' reading relies upon the one propounded by Tang, though grounded into a lexicon that sometimes risks to distort Tang's intention: whereas Tang speaks of human beings' "free nature" or "nature marked by freedom [自由之性]", Ames translates by "spontaneity" (Ames 2010, 147). Whereas Tang speaks of the "life patterns [or principles] *shengli* 生理" that define "nature *xing* 性", Ames speaks of "life force", a distortion that allows him to translate *xing* by "natural tendencies" (Ames 2010, 146).[80] And if Ames is right to point out the "infinite

---

80 In the course of one sentence, Ames translates the same character *li* 理 once by "pattern" and twice by "force".

changeability" of human nature in Tang's view, one should stress that such radical changeability is a consequence of the infinite aspirations proper to human beings, which distinguishes them fundamentally from other sentient beings. In last analysis, the human Self as described by Tang is much less "transactional", as Ames defines it, than transcendental.

It is the third Tang Junyi who retains here mostly our attention, the one whose thought culminates in his last book, *The Existence of Life and the World of the Spirit* (生命存在與心靈境界) (Tang 1989, vol. 23 and 24; Tang 2006 [1977]). I keep here the usual English translation of the title though it may not adequately describe the purpose of the book, which links and contrasts the *phenomenon* of Life with the *world* of the Spirit. Its construction consciously parallels the most systematic attempts of 19th-century Western philosophers. Tang's book explores the activity of the human spirit in all spheres of existence and knowledge. As conceptualized by Tang, there are nine spheres in all. Three have to do with the world as collection of objects. Three are centered upon the Self or Subject. And the three last ones constitute the world of transcendence. Not only is there a hierarchy among these three categories, but there is also one within each of them. Basic knowledge is the sphere through which the subject perceives objects as separate entities; the same subject distributes objects and entities into species or categories (second sphere); and then realizes that there are causal connections between them (third sphere). We then ascend into the spheres of the subjective: the mind first reflexively examines its own sense perceptions; this leads it to reflect on its own reflecting activity; and it thus makes it access towards the sphere of moral conduct. A new ascent leads the subject to the three spheres of transcendence. The sphere of the Return to the One coincides with the accession to the idea of monotheism. The approach to Absolute Void, as epitomized by Buddhism, gets beyond desires and illusions. The ninth and final sphere is the transcendent realm as conceived of by the Chinese tradition: the virtue (*de* 德) of Heaven at work. It goes further than the "positivity" found in monotheism and the "negativity" propounded by Buddhism do: from heart to nature and from nature to Heaven, it brings the whole of humaneness (and, potentially, of humankind) to the world of the Transcendent.

Tang Junyi is not the only one to have engaged into this style of synthesis. In the perspective developed by Fang Dongmei 方東美 (1899–1977), Chinese philosophy is primarily concerned with the universe seen as a moral territory where life can circulate and expand (see notably Fang 1980). Fang Dongmei expresses his conception of life dynamics by means of a pyramid ordering the various levels of existence and experience. Within this system, the spheres of elemental life, art, ethics, and religion offer a path through which humankind has to realize and accomplish itself, pointing in the process towards the hidden firmament of the Godhead.

The philosophical reconstruction led by Neo-Confucianism throughout the 20th century cannot be equated to a term-by-term opposition between Chinese and Western systems. The representative figures of this current were sensitive to the variety of resources and alternative modes of thought offered by the latter. One may deplore that their reading of the Chinese tradition was, in many ways, more unilateral than was their understanding of the Western tradition: the Confucian prism may have impeded them to perceive the exegetical richness that Zhuangzi, Laozi or Mozi provide thinkers with once they are considered outside the canon that locates them into their (subordinate) positions. At the same time, most of these philosophers undertook an endeavor surprisingly "Western" in style: systematizing their insights into the building of "intellectual monuments" probably meant to compete with the Kantian, Hegelian or Marxian cathedrals within which they were taught to find the apex of Western thinking. In any case, both their avowed ambition to erect philosophical *systems* and the stress they put on the transcendental dimension proper to the Chinese tradition distinguish them from the paradigm of Chinese thought that many Western sinologists have in mind and that was at the center of our first chapter.

The Beijing Model

Today's re-reading of their classics by Chinese intellectuals often goes along with an enterprise of identity reconstruction. The promotion of "National Studies" (*guoxue* 國學), which has been taking place from the 1990s onwards, with variations in the scope and significance of the phenomenon, testifies to the task at hand.[81] The term "National Studies" applies first to the traditional cursus of study (followed almost until the end of the Qing dynasty), and second to the revitalization of the study of these same texts, often in reaction to a modern curriculum based on the Western grid of divisions among the sectors of thought, experience and knowledge (Liu 2008). Sébastien Billioud and Joël Thoraval have studied this endeavor throughout the strategies it follows: changes in curricula within contemporary academic institutions; attempts to define or redefine a normative canon; initiatives meant to encourage the reading of classics by children; and the rebuilding of traditional educational structures cautiously engineered by private actors (Billioud and Thoraval 2015). If certain nomenclatures of the "National Studies" literary corpus strictly follow that of the *Complete Library in Four Sections*

---

[81] For an historical account of the *guoxue* phenomenon, especially in its initial phase, see various contributions by Chen Lai gathered in Chen (2009).

(*siku quanshu* 四庫全書),[82] the use of the term "classics" (*jing* 經) is often loosened, and a very selective set of texts is often found to be at the basis of the "National Studies" enterprise.

Chen Lai, between History and Ontology

We already met philosopher Chen Lai, who epitomizes present-day mainstream academic Confucianism, a position confirmed by his successive appointments at Peking and Tsinghua University. His research into the history of Chinese philosophy – Confucianism mainly – is marked by a certain "evolutionism" that leads him to see a line of progressive intellectual refinement running from Zhang Zai 張載 (1020–1077) and Shao Yong 邵雍 (1011–1077) to Cheng Yi and Zhu Xi, before we reach the time of Wang Yangming. The trend goes from the establishment of cosmological principles to the internalization of ethical rules that can be universalized.

What does such historical recapturing of Chinese philosophy entail when deployed into the framework of a comparative or cross-frontiers endeavor? At the dawn of the International Congress of Philosophy held in Beijing in August 2018, Chen Lai gave a lengthy interview to his colleague Fang Xudong 方旭東.[83] The talk starts with a double assertion: (a) "philosophy" is universal in scope; (b) and yet, questions discussed in the West and in China were of a different nature.

> Western philosophy is only a particular aspect of philosophy, an example of it, not its standard. Therefore, philosophy as a name should not be defined in the sense given to it by Western tradition, but should be an inclusive universal concept in a multicultural world. The study of moral principles [*yili* 義理] in ancient China was a theoretical system allowing Chinese philosophers to think about the universe, life, and the human mind, and the issues discussed in it were not the same as those discussed in Western philosophy. For instance, Song-Ming Confucians were unceasingly debating and minutely analyzing the "before and after the passions arise [已發與未發]", the "four seeds of virtue and the seven feelings [四端與七情]", "the innate and the acquired [本體與功夫]", or yet "the innate knowledge of goodness and its maximal extension [良知與致知]". These are all issues different from those of Western philosophy. In other words, although both China and the West think theoretically on life and the universe, the issues that structure their respective systems are different.
>
> (Chen 2018)

---

[82] See for instance Chen (2008). (The *Siku quanshu* is a 18th-century encyclopedia/collection of books, containing an annotated catalogue of more than ten thousand titles along with a compendium of 3,593 of them.)
[83] In Chen (2018). The following quotes are translated from this interview.

The broadening and reformulation of the issues being recognized as object of thought and debate is thus the most urgent philosophical task, with broad implications for the future of humankind:

> As far as Mainland China is concerned, the academic circles have not conducted in-depth discussions on whether there are common issues in the history of Eastern and Western philosophy, let alone reached a consensus. Western philosophical circles have long refused to treat Chinese philosophy as philosophy, studying it only as a thought and a religion, precisely because they found no Western philosophical issues in Chinese philosophy. This prejudice has a long history – see how Hegel doubts Confucius' status as a philosopher. If our standard is whether or not Western philosophical issues are discussed, I am afraid that a large number of ancient Chinese thinkers will not be ranked among philosophers. This is obviously absurd. Making Western philosophical questioning "philosophy", and judging on this basis whether there is philosophy in non-Western cultures is a manifestation of Western cultural centrism. Today, one of the important tasks for non-Western philosophers is to develop a broader sense of what "philosophy" is about, to spread it around the world, to deconstruct the Western-centered position on "philosophy", and then can we truly promote a cross-cultural philosophical dialogue and develop a human philosophical wisdom for the 21st century.
> (Chen 2018)

Such task also implies to introduce some shifts in one's argumentative style, with more emphasis brought to textual commentary and historical introspection:

> Whitehead introduced the notion of "creative synthesis". A philosophical creative synthesis is not merely a synthesis of different theories, but should also emphasize the synthesis of the historical dimensions of philosophy. In this regard, Hegel and Feng Youlan provide us with good examples. Of course, how one chooses a style of philosophical writing and a specific discourse strategy depends upon our specific writing goals. This cannot be generalized. Today, it may not be appropriate to completely model oneself on the writing methods of the ancient Chinese philosophers. Still, these philosophers were emphasizing interpretation and transmission, a fact reflected in the fact that their writing were comprising a large number of historical narratives. This approach is not outdated. McIntyre's *After Virtue* also uses numerous historical narratives and his analyses progresses through them.
> (Chen 2018)

In the perspective developed by Chen Lai, one specific contribution that present-day Chinese philosophers may offer would consists in articulating a specific "ontology" (*bentilun* 本體論) – an ontology grounded in the relationality of the Self (*renxue bentilun* 仁學本體論), as the notion of *ren* 仁 allows for such endeavor. (Chen Lai argues that nothing exactly corresponds to the field covered by the term "ontology" in ancient Chinese philosophy. However, he also says that the way we today interpret ancient discussions about the origin, reality and ultimate end of existence enables us to speak of a "Chinese ontology".[84])

> From the point of view of an ontology of *ren*, core social values should be separated from individual basic morality. The former focuses on the country's social and political values. The latter [is divided in two parts]. One part is individual ethic (*basic individual morality*), another part is social ethics (*basic individual social morality*). The *basic individual morality* as requested by contemporary society should include: benevolence, righteousness, honesty, trustworthiness, filial piety and harmony. The next level includes self-reliance, perseverance, courage, integrity, loyalty, and integrity. The *basic individual social morality* includes: patriotism, benefiting the community, respecting ritual propriety, abiding by the law, promoting justice, and professional dedication. According to the Confucian understanding, the most important core values should be: benevolence [仁爱], freedom [自由], equality [平等], justice [公正], and harmony [和諧]. One can call them the "New Five Virtues". Benevolence, freedom, equality, and justice can be called the "new four virtues" to distinguish them from the traditional four virtues of "benevolence, justice, ritual propriety and wisdom [仁義禮智]". [...] Song Confucianism used to say "*ren* envelops the four virtues". Accordingly, we may say that the relationship between *ren* and the new four virtues is that "*ren* unifies the four virtues." [...] Benevolence is the spring of *ren*, freedom is the summer of *ren*, equality is the autumn of *ren*, and justice its winter of benevolence. This because freedom can be regarded as *ren*'s unhindered activity, equality is looking at the community in the optic of *ren*, justice is about fair dispositions [in the spirit of] *ren*, and harmony is the overall requirement that flows from the essence of *ren*. Some people might say that the formulation of the principle "*ren* unifies the four virtues." shows a propensity towards monism. We do not deny that our understanding of values under the ontology of *ren* is monist. But this kind of monism can accommodate pluralism. And this because we do not reject freedom, equality, and justice. On the contrary, we hope to incorporate these values into the Confucian value system so as to form a multicultural structure in which each part complements the other. Of course, elucidating social values such as freedom, equality, and justice is not the main focus of Confucianism. The main focus of Confucianism has always been in the field of morality and ethics, in the task of establishing value rationality and moral direction. It would be unreasonable to ask Confucianism to change its normal focus and to advocate for relatively unfamiliar values.
>
> (Chen 2018)

Under the "core social values [*shehui hexin jiazhi* 社會核心價值]", as Chen Lai says, can of course be found the official definition of "the core socialist values [*shehuizhuyi hexin jiazhi* 社會主義核心價值]" enshrined by the Party in 2012, and divided into four national, four social and four individual values. Thinkers meet here with a kind of Party monopoly, and Chen takes refuge in the "individual" realm – though "individual values", he adds immediately, comprise both "private" (*si* 私) and "public" (*gong* 公) dimensions. The basic idea is to offer a helping hand to

---

[84] If I chose here to translate Chen Lai's own summarized expression of his philosophical project, the latter's full development can be found in Chen (2014).

the authorities when it comes to the task of grounding morality in both private and public behavior. *Ren* constitutes the essence of the individual, and other subordinate values can flourish from this seed, as long as the *ren* is cultivated. This ontology, Chen suggests, is an anthropology that the Confucian tradition contributes to world thought and not only to today's China, an ontology/anthropology shaped by a multiplicity of trends and influences. According to times and places, *ren* may unify an (evolving) set of (relative) values, and thus accommodate a number of values now deemed to be "universal". However, if Confucianism can *accommodate* freedom or justice, one should not ask it to *promote* such values. Besides, in the present Chinese context, Confucianism limits itself to nurture *value rationality* within the individual realm, avoiding to make the attitudes and options it nurtures criteria for social or political discernment. Eventually, Chen's enterprise is a work in *distanced accommodation*, vis-à-vis (a) the Party, (b) contemporary culture and society seen from the viewpoint of (Confucian) tradition, and (c) philosophical currents wholly external to China. A number of equilibriums need to be carefully preserved.

Zhao Tingyang and the Quest for Universalism with Chinese Characteristics

The work of Zhao Tingyang 趙汀陽 (b. 1961) represents another expression of the "Beijing Model" I am here attempting to describe – a model for which "thinking philosophically" means first and foremost "rethinking China", i.e., recovering China's own ability to think, reconstructing its worldviews, values and methodologies, and thinking about China's future, its specific vision of the future and its world responsibilities.[85] And Zhao specifies:

> Philosophically speaking, "rethinking China" as a movement means to be thinking about the "future", the possibilities and various aspects it presents. This entails completely different attitudes and aspiration from previous movements that were thinking about China. They were aiming at the "past", so were anchored into historical and social criticism, while the "Rethinking China" movement has a more philosophical and analytical temperament.
>
> (Zhao 2011, 7)

---

[85] Introduction to *The Tianxia System* (Zhao 2011, 1–22). I base myself on the second Chinese edition of *Tianxia tixi* [天下体系], published in 2011 at People's University Press (the first edition was published in 2005 in another publishing house – see Zhao 2005). I prefer here to closely follow the Chinese original text so as to better communicate the feeling that emanates from it. The introduction is the best part of the book, rather repetitive in its further developments. See also Zhao (2016a) and Zhao (2021).

A professor in the Institute of Philosophy at the Chinese Academy of Sciences and a senior fellow in one of Peking University's research institutes, Zhao, though younger than Chen Lai, is almost as much an institutional figurehead as is the latter, very much present on the national scene but also active in international circles, with books and articles published in foreign languages and with semi-official endorsement. He defines himself as a philosopher for whom political philosophy, and especially philosophy of international relations, is "first philosophy" (*philosophia prima*).[86] The political turn of philosophy is expressed by Zhao in the following way:

> The "Rethinking China" thought movement is not a school, but an inevitable step in the overall development of Chinese thought. The various viewpoints that seem to belong to this thought movement are not unified, they may even seem contradictory. These are not important. The important thing is to think, speak, and act on the basis of China. [...] If [this movement] fails to form cautious and rigorous thinking, it will not enter into real theoretical analysis, but will only be satisfied with writing another kind of narrative. [...] Narrative scholarship detached from real thinking has produced irresponsible discourses, such as the ones inspired by radical and nationalist discourses or yet postcolonialism and cultural criticism. The Chinese discourse of activism expresses emerging patriotic feelings, but it also adopts the logic of Western Darwinism. [...] Similarly, the post-colonial/cultural critical discourse also falls into a kind of Western routine. It is used to re-narrate China's own history. [...] Everything is still narrated within the framework given by the West. Therefore, this way of regarding China as the "Other", of rewriting Chinese society and Chinese history through Western methods while saying that this constitutes a new narrative about China, is very similar, one may say, to the narrative deployed by Western Sinologists about China.
>
> (Zhao 2011, 8)

I do not intend here to enter into the minutiae of Zhao's system. It is merely its relationship with "philosophical engagement" that is of interest for us. Therefore, the following constitutes only a selective summary:

Western theories of international relations and of the nation-state within the global system have created a "non-world" or "failed world". In response, *tianxia* 天下 (All Under Heaven), a concept anchored in Chinese ancient thought, refers at the same time to the earth, to a latency, a choice in which all people may share, and to a global system. Thus, material, psychological and institutional dimensions must concur in apprehending what "the world" ought to be. Also, the Chinese conceptualization places "the world" in a natural continuum (*yiguan* 一貫) together with "the family" (*jia* 家) and "the state" (*guo* 國) (Zhao 2011, 16). Therefore, "the central idea of 'all-under-heaven' is to reconstitute the world along the lines of the family, thereby transforming the world into a home for all peoples, as it should

---

86 *The Axis of Philosophia Prima* 第一哲学的支点 (Zhao 2013).

be" (Zhao 2009, 11). Fairness and inclusiveness are other characteristics of the concept. Harmony is another one, as the balance between the different parts of the system (and therefore the absence of any hegemonic power) ensures its sustainability. Its constant improvement is ensured by a strategy of "imitation", in which the different players borrow the strategies used by the most successful ones (what Zhao calls "Confucian improvement"). The interlocking of interests is thus only one aspect of the order being ensured. Though Zhao does not insist upon this, harmony is also a product of "imitation" – an approach, one should note, which does not seem to ensure genuine diversity.[87]

The references made by Zhao to the (ideal) political model of the Zhou dynasty rather than to latter-days imperial tributary system testifies to its anchorage into the Confucian tradition. At the same time, his project consists less in "returning" to a pre-existing reality than in "constructing" a new model, making use of resources that an exegesis of ancient texts makes possible. Still, this goes with certain presuppositions, such as the ones contained in the following passage:

> The Western framework of thinking is that [...] there are only two kinds of things that [...] are absolutely heterogeneous: God and the Other. Therefore, God is designated as the source of all things, and Others, especially infidels [*yijiaotu* 異教徒], are regarded as mortal enemies (if a person is of one mind and with me, he is indeed "himself" but an "Other"). Recognizing that the theoretical consequences of recognizing the reality of a "transcendence" are [found in] religions and in political theories that establish Others as enemies constitutes the trump card of Western thought. Concepts such as "individualism", "paganism", "law of the jungle" as well as political theories based on dividing between the "national" and the "international" are all related to the recognition of the concept of transcendence. China does not recognize transcendence as an absolute otherness, and therefore has opened up another world of thinking. Chinese thinking assumes that there are ways to integrate any Other in harmony; in other words, any discordant relationship can be transformed into a harmonious relationship. [...] Western thought can think about conflict, but only Chinese thought can think about harmony.
> (Zhao 2011, 10)

Zhao's system has been polemically characterized by Chishen Zhang as produced by "the urge to make *chinoiserie* theories at the expense of theoretical coherence and logical consistency" (Chang 2011). The same Chishen Chang has also pointed out that Zhao's *tianxia* concept is more a theoretical elaboration guided by contem-

---

[87] Fabian Heubel provides the reader with a more sympathetic account of Zhao's thought than the one I offer here. He writes: "To prematurely suspect Zhao Tingyang of justifying a new Chinese imperialism and authoritarianism seems to me to be based on a misjudgment of the relationship between Marxism and Confucianism in contemporary China" (Heubel 2021, 25). Still, Heubel sees the conceptual apparatus engineered by Zhao as lacking the focal point that the Confucian tradition provides for, namely, self-cultivation (*xiu ji* 修己).

porary, global characteristics than the result of a reading of the classical texts referring to the expression.

We still need to take seriously Zhao's construction, and this for three reasons at least: first, it has partly nurtured the official presentation of China's role (or putative role) in the world, and the understanding of the latter by part of the Chinese people. Second, this political representation is anchored in a cosmological (and metaphysical, or anti-metaphysical) system. Implicitly, the same line of thought can be found in the way Xi Jinping makes use of the following quote of *Zhongyong* 30: "All living things can coexist without jeopardizing one another, just as the different laws of the universe can apply without contradicting each other [萬物並育而不相害，道並行而不相悖]".[88] Third, in Zhao's presentation, the political consequences of the term-by-term comparison between the "essences" of Western and Chinese traditions (immanence/transcendence, analogies/logical reasoning, correlative thinking/dialectic) are clearly drawn and expressed. This last point deserves a few developments:

In an English-language article, Zhao states:

> My emphasis on the fundamental position of the *facio* and heart in philosophy could be understood as a renewal of Confucianism as a radical humanism that insists on the autotelicity of the human world, hence a refusal of any religion or theology, and as a philosophy of relationalism that is the opposite of individualism. The difference between the approaches of the *cogito* and the *facio* now becomes clear. The *facio* creates relationships that provide a validity for values and norms through their recursive reciprocal reconfirmation by those others who are joined by those relationships, so much so that it avoids self-reference, whereas the *cogito* resorts to reflexive consciousness that fails to escape from self-referential egoism.[89]
>
> (Zhao 2012, 32)

As could be expected, the denial of any kind of transcendence within the Chinese tradition goes along the construction by Zhao of a "political transcendence". First, in a 2016 book, *Blessing China* (*Huici zhongguo* 惠此中國),[90] Zhao asserts that the

---

[88] I select here the translation offered by the English-language site that promotes Xi's reading of the Classics: http://chinaplus.cri.cn/classics-quoted-by-xi/index.html (Xi n.d.).

[89] There are notable stylistic differences according to the language used by Zhao. English-languages contributions strive towards academic respectability, while Chinese-language essays use a more direct rhetoric.

[90] This is a tentative translation of a Chinese expression that comes directly from the *Min lao* 民勞 Ode, in which it means "Bring grace [benefit] to the capital of this state". The meaning of *zhongguo* as "the country at the center" will come later on. Here, *zhongguo* refers to "the center of the country". The English title affixed to Zhao's book runs: *The Making and Becoming of China: Its Way of Historicity.*

tianxia model was already announced by the spirit and internal structure of China, "a land [where] a multicultural and multiethnic unified state was formed. The so-called great unity is essentially 'a country with *tianxia* as its inner structure' [所谓大一统，实质就是以天下为内在结构的国家]" (Zhao 2016b, 16). The next step in Zhao's argument is crucial:

> Precisely because China's internal structure has always maintained a world pattern of "conforming to [the will of] Heaven [*pei tian* 配天]",[91] China has therefore become a being invested with divinity and an [object of] faith. This can explain the problem raised by spiritual faith in China. Any civilization needs some kind of spiritual faith so as to ground its status and its destiny as well as to give an absolute basis to its self-assertion. It is generally believed that China lacks religion in the strict sense, and therefore lacks spiritual faith, but this understanding is problematic. In the absence of faith, how can we explain that the Chinese spirit had remained intact and stable? This is an enigma that has never been effectively explained. An expedient explanation is to understand Confucianism as a quasi-religion. [...] However, if [the existence of] Confucianism can roughly explain the social structure and way of life in ancient China, it cannot give an account of its faith, since Confucianism is based upon ethical principles. [...] There is no covenant model between humankind and a god in Chinese culture, so no religion in the Western sense, but there is another form of faith, that is, the mutual conforming of the Way of Humanity and of the Way of Heaven. Every existence that conforms to Heaven becomes a sacred existence – and here is the [object of] faith. The reason for which China's spiritual faith is hidden is that it is tacitly understood. In fact, [the object of] spiritual faith in China is China itself. Put otherwise: China is what Chinese people believe in. The China whose principle of existence is to act in accordance with Heaven is the sacred [object of] belief.
>
> (Zhao 2016b, 16–17)

A monopoly on sacredness is here asserted, to the benefit of a "divine being", China, which is so defined because, alone of all communities, it has always known what it means to live according to the *tianxia* ideal, i.e., to "conform to Heaven" so that Heaven may conform to Humanity. It is also asserted that a *tianxia*-shaped world will eventually arise through the very "centripetal whirlpool" (*xiangxin xuanwo* 向心漩涡) process (i.e., attraction rather than expansion) by which China itself was constituted. Summing up, Zhao articulates three successive theses: (a) China is a divine being. (b) Like a whirlpool, China attracts everything located in its orbit rather than enlarging its sphere through expansionism. (c) The *tianxia* model will take its universal expression in a way similar to the one through

---

[91] Bronze inscriptions indeed offer the expression *pei ming* 配命: being in conformity with the Mandate of Heaven, or *pei huang tian* 配皇天: being in conformity with August Heaven. *Pei tian* (or *pei tiandi* 配天地) occurs notably in the *Book of Rites*, the *Zhongyong* and the *Xunzi*.

which it created China. And these three propositions need to be understood as a whole.

Radical immanence becomes a form of "political transcendence", or, to say it otherwise, an extreme form of political religion.

On Civil Religion, East and West

As a matter of fact, the debate on civil religion is to be integrated into the framework of the Sino-Western intellectual engagement that constitutes our focus (see Vermander 2019). The term "civil religion" (*gongmin zongjiao* 公民宗教) remains a specialized one, as it is in other languages after all, but is just as solidly attested as it is in English or French. The first complete Chinese translation of Rousseau's *Social Contract* was published in 1902. Several other translations succeeded, the one by He Zhaowu 何兆武 (1958) being regularly reprinted (Chen 2007). Generally, attempts made at applying the concept to China find in Confucianism a ground similar to the *religio* of ancient Rome: Chinese and Roman traditions both stress ritual orthopraxis rather than doctrinal orthodoxy, and make ritual communion a vector of political religiosity. The debate has antecedents in Late Qing and Republican China:

> While Liang [Qichao] rejected Confucianism as a model, others tried to develop a modern understanding of history as a sign of the nation by referring to Confucian social ethics as the "spirit of the nation" (*minzu jingshen*, 民族精神). This form of neo-Confucianism as a kind of spiritual nationalism ultimately failed to take root in China, since it turned out to be too difficult to unmoor Confucianism from the now defunct imperial system and turn it into the civil religion of the modern nation-state.
>
> (Van der Veer 2014, 56)

Towards the end of the period when the issue was most actively debated (2000–2015, more or less, as at some point new directives on religious sinicization closed the discussion), an article by Professor Sun Shangyang 孙尚扬 (b. 1965) of Peking University answered negatively the question as to whether Confucianism can be constructed as the civil religion of contemporary China. The arguments Sun develops ground a position that is probably shared today by the majority of Chinese scholars: (a) The lack of a tradition that confers the ultimate sovereignty to the people makes it hard to establish Confucianism as a civil religion, at least in the Western understanding of the term. (b) The approach to "Heaven" that Confucianism develops inspires neither love nor fear, two elements that makes traditional civil religions effective. (c) Today's Confucianism lacks the organizational elements typical of the "Church" model that makes a religion socially functional. (d) Some scholars have interpreted American civil religion as an ideological system that maintains and justifies oppression of minorities. Similarly, Confucianism could be read as a system of oppression of the Han majority against national minorities, especially the ones with a monotheistic tradition. In other words, the concept comes with a few pitfalls (Sun 2015).

Similar conclusions were probably reached by the team that set up the ideological basis of Xi Jinping's "New Era" policies. Official discourses and policies make it clear: these political advisers concluded that, during the Reform and Opening era, China had erred in not consistently building a system of civil beliefs and worship that would substitute for Maoism. And the same team finds it obvious that the Party is best equipped for managing symbols of legitimacy and sacredness, as it does inspire both love and fear, functions as a Church, and unites under the same ideology Han people and minorities. The Party is the sole basis on which to construct and nurture both orthodoxy and orthopraxis. Religions should be seen not as concurrent but rather as subordinate channels of orthodoxy and orthopraxis, which the Party oversees through the sinicization policy. And, if consistently followed, religious sinicization may contribute additional resources for developing the dogmas and the expressions of an all-encompassing "civil religion" that, "making the country the object of the citizens' adoration, teaches them that service done to the State is service done to its tutelary god" (Rousseau, *Social Contract*, IV-8, in Rousseau 1990–2009, vol.4, 219).

Zhao's reading of Chinese tradition presents a few differences with other "political Confucians" (insofar Zhao may be considered a Confucian). Referring to Ames' understanding of the same tradition, Sarah A. Mattice discusses the stance of Jiang Qing 蔣慶 (b. 1953) in the following way:

> Ames […] consistently argues that early Confucianism had no place for a Creator Deity (God) and no significant role for predetermined, external principles. His account of Confucianism tends to focus on self-cultivation through roles and relationships, and the importance of family as the concrete source for not only ethical development but also political and cosmic order. […] On the other hand, in *A Confucian Constitutional Order*, contemporary public figure Jiang Qing argues against a secular reading of Confucianism, advocating not only that Confucianism be adopted as China's state religion but also that the Chinese government reorganize itself as a Confucian constitutional government, with Confucianism explicitly understood as a transcendent religion: "Confucianism is a comprehensive traditional system of thought, in which there is a transcendent, sacred metaphysics of the way of heaven." […] He argues that the only true source of political legitimacy stems from Heaven (*tian* 天), or the Way of Heaven (*tiandao* 天道), which he sees as transcendent and sovereign.
>
> (Mattice 2007, 135)

Jiang Qing 蔣慶 (b. 1953, the scholar to whom Mattice alludes) shows more distance than Zhao Tingyang does towards governmental orientations. Today, Jiang's proposal for a Confucian parliament system cannot be openly propounded the way it was when he first exposed it. Also, Jiang exhibits an attention to history that he shares with Chen Lai, and which distinguishes their generation both from earlier Neo-Confucians and from younger scholars such as Zhao Tingyang who turn decidedly (as we have seen) towards the future, thus running the risk of neglecting the lessons of the past.

Our summary may leave us with a certain impression: willingly or not, the Beijing Model contributes to turning Chinese philosophy inwards. Fabian Heubel's diagnosis certainly deserves to be pondered over:

> The field of Chinese contemporary philosophy dealing with classical texts is increasingly turning inward. In the process, an "inner circuit" (*nei xunhuan* 內循環) of ideas and interpretations of these texts is emerging that is largely self-sufficient. The references to the "outside", in particular to the history of the modern reception of European philosophical history in China, are thereby cut or made unrecognizable […]. Thus, important parts of the philosophical discourse disappear behind a veil of allusions and comments, whose meaning must remain incomprehensible without a certain familiarity with the classical texts and their historical context. This tendency, on the other hand, threatens to reinforce a Western discourse about China that also revolves primarily around itself and is cut off from internal Chinese developments.
> (Heubel 2021, 31)

The merit of the "Shanghai Variant" that I am now going to describe is to escape such self-referential circle and to continue to nurture a mutual engagement among traditions. As we will see, this may constitute also its "fragility", but fragility is inseparable from engaging in the act of thinking.

The Shanghai Variant: A "Dual Ontology"

What I call the "Shanghai Variant" of the Beijing-based narrative of the recapturing and reconstruction of Chinese philosophy shares (and sometimes specifies) several traits of the "Chinese ontology" that we have seen being expounded in various shapes by Tang Junyi, Chen Lai and Zhao Tingyang notably. However, it also recognizes that the "Western" (or "modern/contemporary") ontology is here to stay. Chinese intellectuals are thus living in a "dual essence" (*shuang chong benti* 雙重本體) worldview. The term has been coined by Sun Xiangchen 孫向晨 (b. 1968), of Fudan University, and I will soon introduce a book of him that excellently summarizes the factors at play in the "Shanghai Variant".[92]

---

[92] Sometimes, Sun, speaks (in English as in Chinese) of "dual ontologies [*bentilun*]". At other mo-

A (Double) Landscape

Fudan University is Sun Xiangchen's alma mater as well as the place where he teaches, and the fact is not without significance: the curriculum of said university reflects what "dual ontology" may be about. Wenyu Chai lists the reading courses offered by Fudan to its students, and describes the strategy that inspires their organization:

> There were a total of two full-year courses offered; the first (*Guided Reading of Chinese Classics*) focused on a systematic reading of key world classics critical to Chinese civilization, while the second (*Guided Reading of Western Classics*) focused on their Western equivalents. [...] [They] focused on a collection of works rather than one specific classic of either civilization, in order to represent the collective cultural heritage and spirit of both Chinese and Western civilization. In the 2005 syllabi, the first term of the course on Chinese classics focused on selected materials from The Book of Rites (Li Ji), The Analects of Confucius, The Mencius, and other Confucian classics and small classics from Daoism and Buddhism; the second term focused on the selected works of Confucian scholars from the Song, Ming and Qing Dynasties, as well as the ROC period. In particular, the course incorporated the works of Zhang Zhidong and Liang Shuming, Confucian scholars of the late-Qing Dynasty and late-20th century China, respectively, to show Confucian scholars' thoughts on and responses to China's "drastic changes" in each period. The first term of the course on Western classics, in 2005 and 2006, focused on selected materials ranging from Ancient Greece and Rome to the Renaissance, such as The Odyssey, The History of the Peloponnesian War, the works of Plato and Aristotle and The Bible, among others. The second term focused on selected works from the Renaissance to the end of the 19th century, including works by Descartes, Newton, Rousseau, Kant, Hegel and Karl Marx.
>
> (Chai 2013, 110–112)

One may assess the curriculum described here in several ways. One of them will positively appreciate the diversity of sources with which students are confronted, especially since Western students are generally not exposed to such diversity, certainly not to the cultural and intellectual thread that runs from the *Book of Rites* to Liang Shuming. Alternatively, one is entitled to adopt a more skeptical attitude, observing that such format allows for the reading of a few pages, while being selective in scope (consider the gap that runs from ancient Rome to Descartes). A rapid perusal of a succession of excerpts leads the student to come up with a formatted view of intellectual history and even of what "philosophical thinking" is about. Such skepticism is reinforced by an insider knowledge of what "teaching philosophy" means in a large number of cases (not all of them): presenting the "main

---

ments, he stresses the fact that the term *benti* should not be equated with either *ousia* or the Kantian noumenon (Sun 2019, 33).

ideas" of a given thinker as located into a genealogical (and often evolutionist) succession. Still, the aforesaid curriculum certainly indicates a characteristic of the "Shanghai Variant": the fact of taking multiculturalism (and its impact on contemporary China) seriously, both as an object of thought and as a vector of study.

Home, Sweet Home

Multiculturalism is indeed a departure point for Sun Xiangchen when he reflects upon the way "dual ontology" may define the ethos of present-day China: *On Family/Home. Individual and Family Ties* (*Lun jia. Geti yu qinqin*論家 – 個體與親親), published in 2019.[93] We could also translate the term *qinqin* 親親 as "mutual feelings among kinfolks", or simply as "relationships", as some scholars do. Although the issue of "family/home/household [*jia* 家]" has progressively mobilized Chinese academic circles, confronted as they are to the eroding of traditional structures, it has been difficult, notes Sun, to find a way to insert their concerns into a discourse on modernity. The radical stance of the May Fourth/New Culture Movement has had a profound impact: *jia* was regarded as the greatest obstacle of the entry of China into modernity (here Ba Jin's novel, *Family*, comes to mind). Sun intends to adopt an approach that adheres to the freedom of modern individuals and still respects the fundamental, *essential* Chinese value of kinship. In the West, as can be observed in philosophers such as Hobbes or Kant, "individuals" had prevailed over "family", while the Chinese cultural tradition organizes all its important insights (from "unceasing generation [*sheng sheng* 生生]" to "family ties", from "filial piety" to "benevolence", and from *jia* to *guojia* [country] and *tianxia*) in a way that goes far beyond the unearthing of an ethical norm but rather gives to *jia* an ontological status.

Before going further in the reading of Sun's essay, let me here articulate two preliminary observations. First, Sun's concept of *jia* is anchored in philosophical speculations rather than anthropological observations. The way Stevan Harrell re-

---

[93] I follow here the current habit of translating *jia* 家 by family/home. In my view, the translation by "household" would suffice. I am also very skeptical in front of the claims for a radical singularity of the Chinese concept of *jia*. I find it strikingly similar to the nexus of concepts indicated in Latin by *domus, dominus, domesticus*, while agreeing with the approach of Fei Xiaotong summarized below. I see in *jia* an anthropological reality symptomatic of humankind's self-domestication through a process that James C. Scott suggestively summarizes (Scott 2017), even if Scott's book suffers from over-generalization, the discussion of which would go far beyond the topic of this book.

fers to the findings of the celebrated anthropologist Fei Xiaotong 費孝通 (1910–2005) will help us to perceive what is at stake:

> China's greatest anthropologist, Fei Xiaotong, very early saw through the misleading stereotype, perpetrated by Chinese and Sinologists alike, that China was a group- or family-centered society in contrast to the individual-centered societies of the West. In his most valuable and original work, *Xiangtu Zhongguo* [鄉土中國], first published in 1947 and translated by Gary G. Hamilton and Wang Zheng as *From the Soil*, he took issue with the whole notion of family as applied to Chinese society. Both the English term "family" and the Sino-Japanese neologism usually used to translate it, *jiating* 家庭, said Fei, were terms for groups, terms that fit well into a group-model of society (*tuanti geju* 團體格局) derived from the social structure of Western countries. But China, he said, was not organized on a group model, but rather on a model he called *chaxu geju* 差序格局, or "a mode of organization based on differences and orderings." Fei foreshadowed by almost a decade the invention of network analysis in Western anthropology of the family. We should immediately make it clear to the puzzled reader that Fei was not denying the importance of kin relations in Chinese society. Like just about every other analyst before and since, he considered kinship to be of central importance. But kinship was not about groups; it was about networks of relationships organized around status differences and status orderings. If there was a name for some kind of unit that embodied these relationships in Chinese society, it was not *jiating* but *jiazu* 家族, the patrilineal kinship cluster of relationships whose strengths fade out from any particular individual who is a node in the network.
>
> (Harrell 2013, 72–73)

These correctives relativize Sun's analysis but do not invalidate it: as a community that links together the departed and the living, a community that needs to be ritualistically preserved and nurtured whatever the adaptations that changing times and material circumstances call for, *jia* possesses indeed a kind of ontological status. Still, *jia* used to be incarnated, rooted in a parcel of land symbolically related to the lineage (whatever its mode of ownership and of insertion into a given settlement). When this material anchorage altogether disappears, the fluidity and multilayered character of the "home" reference extends to the extreme, causing the representations of *jia* to become virtual or "imagined". At the same time, the sacredness of "home" is progressively transferred to other settings, first and foremost the (public) ones in which ancestor rituals take place. By the very fact of loading public places of worship with some of the "home" characteristics, the new model of urban religiosity also gives accrued importance to official religious expressions over popular ones.[94] Therefore, the current sociological and anthropological shift observed in urban China is not about the fact that temples located outside the communal territory now often host the ancestral tablets, or that "family",

---

[94] Chen and Vermander (2019); Faure (1986); Fei (1992 [1947]); Freedman (1958).

"home" and "household" are realities that are lived and expressed at various territorial and psychological levels. It rather bears on the radicalness of the dispossession felt by family actors in search of landmarks and of ritual agency. This may imply that the "ontological status" that was conferred to *jia* has been fractured beyond repair.

My second observation on Sun's attempt bears on the way he approaches *qinqin* (family ties, affection among kinfolks; see Sun 2019, 235–239). As could be expected, he stresses the *harmony* from which such feelings flow and that they nurture. If Sun quotes one relevant passage of the *Mencius*, he omits the first and probably most important mention: Mencius is engaged into a dispute over the meaning of the Ode 197 (*Xiao bian* 小弁), which describes the sadness and resentment of a ruler's son that his father has disinherited, and he justifies such "resentment":

> Suppose that a man from Yue drew his bow for shooting me, I might plead with him in a relaxed way, and this for no other reason that the man is not related to me. But if my own brother draws his bow in order to shoot me, then I will implore him by weeping and crying; and this for no other reason than that he is so close to me. The "resentment" [*yuan* 怨] felt in the Ode [we are disputing about] [originates from] "feeling among kinfolks" [*qinqin* 親親].[95] Feelings among kinfolks, this is the *ren* 仁.
> 越人關弓而射之，則己談笑而道之；無他，疏之也。其兄關弓而射之，則己垂涕泣而道之；無他，戚之也。小弁之怨，親親也。親親，仁也。
>
> (*Mencius* 6B.23)

The same passage of the *Mencius* includes a reference to Shun 舜. The story of Shun, related by the *Shujing*, has always struck the imaginations: at the instigation of his mother-in-law and his half-brother, Shun's father treated him as badly as he could during all his adult life, whatever the testimonies of filial piety Shun could provide him with. Shun's father had obviously irremediably lost the nature imparted to him by Heaven. A *denatured father:* an extreme case, a case for textbook discussion. In such extremity, nothing causes Shun to deviate from his duties or alter the ardor of his family feelings. It was his filial piety as much as his ability to rule that led Emperor Yao 堯 to choose him as his successor rather than to appoint his own son. Following the example of Yao, Shun did not allow his son to succeed him on the throne, and his choice fell on Yu (Yu the Great). With the latter, the imperial succession became hereditary. While warmly approving the feelings shown by Shun (*Mencius* 5 A.1), Mencius also recognizes that true filial piety even recognizes

---

[95] The directness of my translation may surprise the reader. But I closely follow the original: 小弁之怨，親親也。親親，仁也。Let me recall here *Analects* 4.3, already quoted: "Only the *ren* enables us to [truly] love *and* hate others [唯仁者能好人，能惡人]" (my emphasis).

the duty of disobedience: Shun decides not to inform his father of his marriage, fearing that the latter, if he were to forbid it, would sin against himself by breaking the principle of generational continuity. Mencius' interlocutors ask him how it is that Shun, who knowingly neglected to inform his parents of his nuptials, can be considered as a paragon of filial piety. Mencius retorts that the biggest offense against filial piety is letting them without descendants. By not informing his parents, Shun was adhering to the greater good dictated by filial piety proper (*Mencius* 4 A.26). True obedience is therefore distinguished from formal docility. Sometimes it even turns disobedience into a duty. In Mencius, as can already be felt in Confucius, though to a lesser extent,[96] there is a complexity in "family feelings" that comes from the potential conflict between them and moral duties. *Ren* arises from family feelings but shows a propensity to go beyond them in a way that is not necessarily as smooth and harmonious as latter commentators would like it to be.

These two reservations having been made, we can now come back to our reading of Sun's *On Family*. One of the interests of the work is to clearly acknowledge the complexity that links together two pairs of opposites: China and the West on the one hand; tradition and modernity (i.e., a kind of "universalization of the West") on the other (we have seen that this distinction was already directing Feng Youlan's way of locating his philosophical endeavor). If modernity is characterized by "rationalization [*lixinghua* 理性化]" it is important to give Chinese tradition, and its focus on *jia*, a "reasonable mode of expression [*heli de xingshi* 合理的形式]" (Sun 2019, 3).

The equilibrium to be found between the two competing ontologies is reached when alternating focuses on the individual and on the family group. Actually, the stress put on the individual dimension by the May Fourth Movement has not been sufficient for anchoring said value within the workings of Chinese society: the focus on the individual has weakened the traditional value system without crafting an alternative to it. A new focus on "family" will give relevance to both the individual and the communal dimensions of existence (Sun 2019, 112).

Jia must also be understood as meaning "home" (and indeed, as we have seen the notions of family, extended group, household and home, are all present in the uses of the character). This is why it provides those who refer to it "a basic way to understand the world. [...] Without 'home', the world as allowed by the understanding it provides for will also be overthrown. [...] [And yet,] 'Family', the most usual unit of existence and value-building in Chinese cultural traditions, has been absent from the categories used in modern philosophy" (Sun 2019, 115).

---

96 Confucius criticizes the attitude of an official emissary who, out of state funds, provides his mother with a generous portion of millet (*Analects* 6.4).

The introduction of the *jia* concept leads Sun to examine the balance found between the individual and the family in some core works of Western philosophy. If Sun's readings of Aristotle and Hegel deliver few surprises, one notes with interest the reliance on Emmanuel Levinas' *Totality and Infinity*: "Levinas constructs a 'continuous' view of time, a view of time that is constantly 'renewed' throughout ruptures and continuation" (Sun 2019, 212). Sun refers the "renewals" conceptualized by Levinas to the developments attempted by the latter on desire/eroticism or yet the relationship between father and son. In such exchanges – and others similar to them – "appropriation" and pleasure are not akin to "possession" and destruction.

> Levinas' analysis is extremely creative, revealing many dimensions long forgotten by the Western philosophical tradition. Levinas does not deny that his analysis has a certain biological imprint, but, within the framework of ontology and time, Levinas shows that this biological imprint is not a structure. [...] These relationships possess an ontological status.
> (Sun 2019, 212–213)

Levinas' insights on the "infinity" opened by the fact of not reducing the Other to the Same is thus seen by Sun as providing China with resources that help to maintain the *qinqin* relationship as an ontological basis while allowing for greater individual fulfillment, this by modifying the way *qinqin* is understood and nurtured.

Towards the end of the book, Sun comes back to an approach of the Chinese traditional ontology in terms of continuum, notably the one that goes from the family to the country, and from the country to *tianxia*, citing with approval the work of Zhao Tingyang: "The *tianxia* consciousness focuses on a concept of diversified civilizations, not on a 'world' under the same civilization" (Sun 2019, 341). This is more or less the conclusion of the book, which reveals some of its limitations, probably determined by a concern for political conformity. Still, Sun's attempt offers a nuanced view of the parts of Western tradition that he mobilizes – a view more nuanced in fact than the presentation he makes of Chinese classics, the diversity of which is overlooked: Daoist's "free wandering" is certainly independent from the *jia* ontology, as is, very early on, the Buddhist focus on "leaving one's home" (*chujia* 出家). Let me quote here the very beginning of the *Sutra of Forty-Two Sections* (*Sishi'er zhang jing* 四十二章經), supposedly the first Buddhist treatise that would have been, if not directly written in Chinese, at least freely adapted from a Sanskrit source:

> The Buddha said: the one who has left his home, the śramaud (the monk) cuts off selfish desires and gets rid of his affections. He knows the source of his own mind. He understands the profound principle of the Buddha and intuits the uncreated elements of existence (*dharma*). Internally, he clings to nothing, and externally he seeks for nothing. His mind is not bound by

any way (*dao*), nor is it wrapped up by action-influences (*karma*). He does not rehash and does not [deliberately] engage into action. He does not correct himself or others. He does not progress through stages but he naturally reaches the pinnacle. This is called the Way [*dao*].

佛言：「出家沙門者，斷欲、去愛，識自心源；達佛深理，悟無為法；內無所得，外無所求，心不繫道，亦不結業；無念無作，非修非證，不歷諸位而自崇最，名之為『道』」。

(*Sutra of Forty-Two Sections* 2)

This work is certainly very far away from the *jia* ontology described by Sun Xiangchen, and yet it exercised a tremendous influence throughout China. As to the *Settling of Doubts* (or: *Settling of Confusion* [*Lihuo* 理惑]) of Mouzi 牟子 (end of the 2nd century CE), a book that attempts to refute Confucian objections made against Buddhism, it makes generational continuity understood as the apex of filial piety "the mediocre scholar's way of doing things" and considers the attainment of virtue and illumination though abstinence and celibacy the most exalted spiritual path (*Mouzi* 9 and 10).

Global Questions in Local Context

If Shanghai thinkers are often more prone than their Beijing counterparts to make a genuine effort at cross-fertilization, the approach found in Sun Xiangchen' *Family* does not encapsulate the diversity of their endeavors. We will be meeting with Bai Tongdong 白彤東 (b. 1970), who also teaches at Fudan's School of Philosophy, in the course of our sixth chapter. Earlier in this book, I have mentioned the name of Sun's and Bai's Fudan-based colleague, the historian Li Tiangang 李天綱 (b. 1957). Li Tiangang has devoted much research to the encounter between Confucians and Jesuits in the Late Ming/Early Qing period. He has presented the insights generated by the exchange as a kind of "Chinese Renaissance" (Li 2001), contributing to foster the persistent interest that some sectors of the academia express in the textual products of this encounter (early translations from Aristotelian treatises, Chinese apologetic or polemical pamphlets...). Another research focus of Li Tiangang has been on popular Chinese religion, in the Jiangnan region mainly, stressing the fact that a positive approach of popular rituals and religiosity leads to a healthier appreciation of China's cultural diversity and religious inventiveness. For Li, Chinese religion is the result of both an unyielding tradition that extends over three thousand years (the uninterrupted continuation of blood sacrifices is one sign of it; Li 2017, 368–369)⁹⁷ and of a series of ruptures that has continuously redefined its boundaries. Notably, growing separation among different "confessions" is not a mere consequence of the surge of "foreign religions" but a characteristic of modernity (which triggers the division of work among different organizations and the subsequent shaping of "churches"). Nowadays, the features defining "religious modernity" also affect Buddhism's and Daoism's self-understanding (Li 2017, 516–517). The well-avowed fact remains that, historically, "the organizational model of Chinese religion is not Church-like but is the one of the soil altar and of the [voluntary] society" (Li 2017, 415).

Li Tiangang keeps mostly silent on the "sinicization of religions" rhetoric engineered by the state from around 2015 onwards, and such silence constitutes a telling fact by itself. In many ways, the description he offers of Chinese religion can be read as a deconstruction of the background against which such rhetoric has developed. For him, (a) Chinese religion is not defined by an essence, but rather by a combination of opposites that together construct a solid though ever-evolving system; (b) Chinese religion is less a set of "functions" than a dynamic that puts into motion the overall process of social exchange and circulation; (c) communal agency possesses a resilience of its own, which makes Chinese religion "muddle through" the interventions by which the state attempts to define its essence and its uses; (d) and finally, the fact that the basic features of religious life take their origin from the ones governing grassroots society constitutes the unifying factor of Chinese religion. Consequently, when it comes to religions of foreign origin, "localization" or "sinicization" simply means to integrate religious forms with social structures. In other words, the integration of religious devotions and organizational forms into the social fabric of the society in which the new faith inserts itself is sinicization proper (Li 2017, 369).⁹⁸

I just stressed the fact that Li Tiangang considers "Chinese religion" as defined by pairs of opposites. One of these pairs contrasts what Li calls the "Zhou 周 tradition" (referring to the culture hero Duke Wen of Zhou, 11th century BCE) to the "Kong 孔 [Confucius] tradition". The "Zhou tradition" is based on rituals that were allowing the participants to "feel" the approach of manes and spirits (gan guishen 感鬼神) and has consistently relied upon an interpretation of the classics that perpetuated the ritual ethos. The "Kong tradition" asserts itself from the Song dynasty onwards, cultivating the moral way (dao 道) instituted by Confucius and

---

97 Li Tiangang has drawn general conclusions on the religiosity proper to the Jiangnan religion from extended fieldwork conducted in the township of Jinze.
98 See also Vermander (2019).

by Mencius, and instilling in the elites a sense of the primacy of the "inner" over the "outer" (Li 2017, 163–180 and 517–521).

At this point, Li Tiangang offers fresh perspectives on the question of Chinese "transcendence" or lack thereof, which we have cursorily discussed in Chapter 1. For understanding the context of Li's contribution, we need to operate a return to the New Confucian movement. The authors of the *Manifesto* in general, and Mou Zongsan in particular, had pioneered the concept of "immanent transcendence" (*neizai chaoyue* 內在超越), contrasting such approach not only to the "external transcendence" (*waizai chaoyue* 外在超越), supposedly characteristic of the Western tradition, but also to representations of the Chinese tradition that deny the presence of any transcendent dimension within it.[99] For Modern Confucian philosophers, "human innate qualities or humanness (*ren xing* 人性) became that potential that not only formed the moral or spiritual Self, but also transcended the individual's empirical and physiological characteristics" (Rošker 2021, 40). Li Zehou 李泽厚 (1930–2021) was one of the thinkers who opposed such a description, stressing the link between Chinese immanentism and holism: Chinese thought, says Li Zehou, sees the universe as unique ("One-World-View") and self-sufficient. Li Zehou's perspective leads him to describe the Chinese approach to human condition and action as shaped by "pragmatic rationality" and certainly not by "immanent transcendence" (see Rošker 2021, 36–40). Likewise, the philosopher Zhang Dainian, already mentioned, was denying any transcendental character to the Confucian and Neo-Confucian traditions, and was speaking of a "Confucian rationalism" (Zhang 1981), even if his presentation of Chinese intellectual history evolved with time.[100]

Li Tiangang distinguishes between immanent and outer transcendence. However, he explicitly borrows the distinction from Paul Tillich (*Theology of Culture* [Tillich 1959] was translated into Chinese in 1988) rather than from Chinese scholars. Li further relies on the theologian's conceptualization of an "Ultimate Concern" as well as on the way Tillich sketches two types of religious approaches, the ontological and the cosmological. Following Tillich, Li notes that, most of the time, these two approaches interact within the same philosophical/religious system, such or such variant emphasizing either the ontological dimension (which nurtures "immanent transcendence") or the cosmological one (vector of "outer

---

[99] "The Way of Heaven, as something 'high above', connotes transcendence. When the Way of Heaven is installed in the individual and resides within them in the form of human nature, it is then immanent" (Mou Zongsan, translated by Rošker [2021, 40]).
[100] At the time of publication (1981), if Zhang Dainian's influential article presented Song-Ming Confucianism as an objectivist, rationalist philosophical devoid of any religious spiritual character, it was largely for the purpose of rehabilitating its academic study.

transcendence", and, as such, more turned towards rituals and symbols). To contrast a Confucian "immanent transcendence" to a Western "outer transcendence" is not justified, Li asserts. First, such a distinction operates in the midst of Western religious traditions. Second, the Chinese religious system is a totality, shaped by contrasts that can be found elsewhere. "Immanent transcendence" is preferentially found in the "Kong tradition", while "outer transcendence" is characteristic of the "Zhou tradition" (Li 2017, 178–180). In the Zhou tradition, sacrifices to Heaven, the communication between Heaven and Man, the intervention of the spirits and the existence of a "soul" (*hunpo* 魂魄)[101] are all prominent factors. The tension between the heart-mind (*xin* 心) and the universe (*yuzhou* 宇宙) triggers the one existing between the ontological and cosmological dimensions of Chinese religiosity, and, therefore, between the "immanent" and "outer" understanding of "transcendence" (Li 2017, 180). While agreeing with the New Confucians in their understanding of the Confucian tradition proper to the literati, Li Tiangang offers an overall picture of both Chinese religiosity and approach to transcendence that is thoroughly dissimilar to the one offered by New Confucians, on the one hand, and the promoters of "Chinese pragmatic rationalism", on the other hand.

* * *

Towards the beginning of this chapter, our reading of Tang Yijie was highlighting a "philosophical narrative" articulated as a play in three acts. Having tried to enrich and, at times, correct this narrative, we may now divide the last hundred years or so of Chinese intellectual and philosophical history into four sequences that are not merely chronological: even if the determination of these sequences depends upon historical events, their impact remains very perceptible in the way debates are still shaped, and many are the thinkers who refer to currents that have become "subterranean" but certainly not "outdated".[102]

The first sequence is of course the May Fourth/New Culture Movement: its criticism of the Chinese/Confucian tradition has been so radical that all subsequent trends of thought necessarily referred to it, endorsing it with qualifications or often rejecting it almost entirely. It gave relevance to authors such as Rousseau, Darwin, Nietzsche or Spengler, whose perspectives became entangled with the issues facing China. However, the movement's reverence for "Science" sometimes

---

[101] At various places of his book, Li Tiangang studies the characteristics and historical evolution of this latter concept.
[102] An alternative account of the developments of Chinese modern/contemporary Chinese philosophy can be found in a (well-informed but rather scholastic) article by Peng (2018). It quotes several important names not mentioned here, as I have chosen to select a few figureheads who best illustrate the sequences I distinguish. See also Bartsch (2023).

evolved into scientism. And its call for "Democracy" rapidly gave rise to four extremely different strategic choices: Communism, Anarchism, nationalistic authoritarianism, and, for a small minority, liberal democracy. In other words, as a political philosophy the movement never stabilized.

The second sequence has as main actors the Confucian intellectuals who, from 1930 to the end of the 1980s, attempted ambitious syntheses aimed at integrating the Chinese philosophical tradition into questions and systems shaped by Western philosophy. They were hoping to give new relevance to the national tradition (both at the world level and for China proper) while rising above its logical or conceptual shortcomings. Many of these thinkers worked outside China from 1950 to 1980, but found an audience in the mainland afterwards. While their attempts have often fallen out of favor, their willingness to tackle shared philosophical issues and to risk innovating rapprochements explains why their work remains both influential and debated. The biggest limitation I personally sense in many of them is a reading of the Chinese corpus exceedingly influenced by the concept of *daotong* (orthodox transmission), which often leads to surprisingly limited perspectives as to what the greater Chinese tradition may offer if read outside the prism of orthodoxy.

From the beginning of the 1990s onwards, the "Beijing Model" took distance from the New Confucianist Movement (although the "Beijing" thinkers certainly learnt a lot from their Confucian elders) by rebelling against the Western-inspired formatting of philosophical issues. How to develop a philosophy that proves to be genuinely Chinese not only in its concepts and language but also in the way it selects and discusses the issues at its core? This general question was generating two additional interrogations: is there a way to make such an enterprise relevant in the disputed field of world philosophy? How can such philosophy contribute to the task of national rejuvenation? These aspirations were and remain legitimate. Still, they are meeting with a number of severe limitations: the view of the Chinese tradition on which they rely remains influenced by an (often implicit) reliance on the "orthodox transmission"; philosophical positions have been far too dependent from political winds; philosophical "wonderment" has been substituted by identity issues; and, finally, the marketization of intellectual life has led to extreme formulations of theses that would deserve to be expressed in more nuanced ways.

Located vis-à-vis the Beijing Model, the "Shanghai Variant" gathers these attempts that stick to a broader understanding of what cosmopolitism is about. They mobilize a greater variety of resources, and they hope to suggest an innovative, supple reading of the most revered Chinese texts and concepts. They also try to offer interpretations of contemporary Western philosophers that meet the expectations of their Chinese public. However, they often depend upon trends and debates about which they offer no more than correctives or alternative interpretations: being "variants", they present themselves in a position of subordination.

When it comes to political theory and standpoints, they are also remarkably adaptable, oscillating at times between the latest ideological prescription and (alternatively) meritocratic, liberal or "New Left" inflections. The "Shanghai Variant" versatility is both its strength and its weakness.

Is there a way to assess and formalize the relationship between these intellectual sequences and Western sinology's approach of the Chinese tradition? First, the latter has borrowed from the reconstructions of Chinese philosophy offered by some of the New Confucianists – probably assimilating more from Tang Junyi or Mou Zongsan than from Qian Mu or Feng Youlan, even when taking into consideration the popularity of the English translation of Feng's *History of Chinese Philosophy* (Fung 1955). However, Western sinologists have considered such works more as *cultural reconstructions* than as the *creative cross-cultural syntheses* that they were meant to be. Second, whereas the promoters of the Beijing Model display only moderate interest towards American pragmatism or process philosophy, they find in the affirmation that Chinese and Western systems work upon dissimilar basic questions and opposite sets of assumptions a justification for an enterprise that propounds a "world philosophy" essentially based on Chinese concepts and issues rather than through attempts at cross-cultural syntheses. Our third and final consideration will be slightly dispirited. In general, these philosophical rapprochements trigger polite conversations rather than the new, exciting dialogues and collaborations one could hope for. Till now, most philosophical attempts remain enclosed in the prison house of their respective mother tongues and specialized idioms.

Part II: **Reimagining the Engagement**

Chapter 4
Encoding the Way

The first part of our "critique" has examined the conditions under which the Chinese-Western philosophical encounter generally takes place under present circumstances. I have described its historical and conceptual formalization, the lexical operations authorized by the said formalization, and the thought systems emerging on the Chinese side, the nature of which is largely determined by the way the genesis and effects of past philosophical syntheses and confrontations are represented. The second part of this book will also be divided into three chapters. The present one offers a general understanding of Chinese thought (restricted here to the period anterior to the Eastern Han dynasty). It is meant to offer an alternative to the perspective that we dissected in our first two chapters, which was driven by conceptual oppositions. The approach that I pragmatically develop in the course of this chapter prepares the theoretical developments of Chapter 5, focused on a dialogic and experiential apprehension of the tasks proper to comparative philosophy. Chapter 6 illustrates the relevance of such tasks – and the potential fecundity attached to the dialogic/experiential approach – by sketching four ongoing debates concerned with topics having to do with social, political and moral philosophy.

As I will describe it throughout the course of this chapter, the "drive" that led to the development of ancient Chinese philosophy (a guiding force that also ensures its continued relevance) came, on the one hand, from a focus on the performative nature of both rituals and signs/graphs/texts, and, on the other hand, from a conviction that approaching the mystery of the Way helped to ensure the smooth continuation of the cosmic and social workings. The focus on *proper performance* was fostering *attentiveness* (attentive observation: *guan* 觀), a virtue required from readers as well as from ritual performers. Attentiveness was seen as constituting the most paradoxical and yet most basic of all "arts" (*shu* 術). Reading the *Classic of Documents* (*Shujing* 書經), the *Classic of Odes* (*Shijing* 詩經) and the *Classic of Changes* (*Yijing* 易經) according to the connections that unite them into a gnoseological tripod sheds light upon the *decoding and the subsequent re-encoding of the Way* that Chinese classics endeavored to operate.[103]

---

[103] A first version of this chapter has appeared under the title: "Encoding the Way: Ritual Ethos and Textual Patterns in China" (Vermander 2022c). Several modifications have been introduced in the text after its first publication, notably in order to conform to the focus of the present book.

Ritual, Language, and Text

Ancient Chinese thinkers had clearly recognized the performative nature of ritual. They had made the efficacy of ritual performances part of an overall understanding of both cosmic and social realities. Such understanding was in turn governing the one of the nature and function of *wen* 文 – a character referring both to *graphs* (of divinatory origin) and *texts* (organizing graphs into patterns, and put into motion during ritual occasions). One of the consequences of the linkage between ritual ethos and textual composition was that literary arrangements came to be crafted in such a fashion as to manifest the workings of the natural and/or human universes that rituals were sustaining. I do not focus on the "structural rhetoric" principles through which compositional patterns were aligned with cosmological and social motives.[104] I rather aim at ascertaining how the Way that governs all phenomena was evoked, celebrated, and, to some extent, activated throughout the modeling of a formal language – a code of which classics were offering the standard. At the same time, as they were pointing towards underlying patterns and processes to be scrutinized and somehow interiorized, classics were fostering *attentiveness*, the core faculty that readers and ritual practitioners needed to nurture and display.

Among other approaches and definitions, the term "rituals" refers to these collective behaviors that sustain a community's cohesiveness while sometimes challenging or reshaping power relationships within the same community, regardless the size of the latter.[105] Often, the social efficacy attached to rituals is related to the fact that they function as a language, a syntactic form.[106] Like linguistic interchange, ritual makes things, people and meaning circulate. It generates a circle of exchange and communication. Analyzing rituals on the model of a language has led researchers to consider their successive *sequences* (for instance: prepara-

---

104 In Vermander (2021a), I have attempted to detail how the formal composition of one specific Chinese Classic conforms to the political and cosmic patterns it unveils. I have expanded the analysis in the fifth and sixth chapters of Vermander (2022b). Pelkey's (2021) detailed reading of the second chapter of the *Zhuangzi* as a ring composition goes in the same direction.
105 How can ritual be both sustaining and challenging? Working on the Ndembu, a Bantu population, the anthropologist Victor Turner considered the rituals as dramas, which operate a "symbolic condensation", contributing to conflict resolution. Turner's studies were focusing on healing sessions and rites of passage. They were highlighting the role of divination, by which latent tensions appear in the open and the resolution process is set in motion. By reshaping the distinctions that organize daily life, the ritual allows for reworking the social bond, acting on a knot of difficulties. At the time of its publication, Turner's vision was contrasting with the view that considers the ritual simply as a force that preserves established order and tradition (Turner 1968).
106 See for instance Ferro-Luzzi (1977).

tions, invocations, the killing of an animal, the communal meal that follows) as the equivalence of *sentences*. These are not to be firstly approached in term of what they mean. Rather, analysts ponder over the "grammatical rules that generate and structure ritual as a form of communication" (Bell 1997, 68). Such a research trend has been reinforced by the parallel realization that some ritual sequences/sentences possess an efficacy of their own. For making use of the paradigmatic Austinian example, an "I do" (or another law-sanctioned formula) that is (twice) uttered in the context of a valid marriage ceremony and is answered in the proper way by the officiant receiving the vows creates legal, reciprocal obligations (Austin 1962, 5). Ritual is a *performance*, not only in the sense of a theatrical performance but also in that a state of affairs is changed by an action having been "performed". For taking another example: at the end of an atonement ceremony the culprit is effectively reintegrated into the community: the reconciliation has been both *acted out* and *effected*.

Ritual: The Chinese Paradigm

Xunzi 荀子 (c. 310/314 – c. 235/217 BCE) has brought to the extreme the Confucian stress on *li* 禮, considered as permeating all aspects of human interactions and making them sustainable. Such a claim is not as radical as it may sound to us today. Besides (or below) large-scale celebrations, "interaction rituals" (Erwing Goffman) permeate everyday life (Goffman 1967). Often overlooked, interaction rituals enable our daily social contacts, and their non-respect quickly turns out to be a major cause of deterioration of social ties. Ignoring the proper way of shaking hands or of bowing, of giving thanks, of letting someone go through the door can still be forgiven when coming from someone foreign to the group culture, but its infringement by an insider needs to be compensated by a restorative rite, of which the simple act of quickly apologizing is the most basic expression.

For Xunzi, ritual, when properly performed, not only expresses and fosters virtue, it also manifests social distinctions and redistributes resources accordingly. It nourishes human life, which it ornaments and refines. It progressively transforms humans mind and contributes to nurture vital breath. It leads one on the path to Sagehood. Additionally, by the mere fact of observing the attitude adopted by commensals during ceremonies, formal functions, the sovereign will discern who among them are most proper to higher offices.[107]

---

[107] See the detailed summary of the overarching conception of Ritual developed by Xunzi in Sato (2010), 419–423.

Ritual also plays a cosmic function, as heavenly order and social harmony go hand in hand:

> Ritual serves Heaven above and Earth below, it honors forefathers and ancestors, and it exalts lords and teachers. [...]
> Ritual always starts with the release [of emotions], develops into proper form, and is accomplished in contentment. At its most perfect, [emotions and forms are both] completely fulfilled.
> 禮、上事天，下事地，尊先祖，而隆君師。[...] 凡禮，始乎梲，成乎文，終乎悅校。故至備。
>
> (Xunzi, On Ritual. Translation Hutton 2014, 202 and 204, modified.)

The step-by-step performance of ritual allows participants to symbolically perform a return to the One, asserts Xunzi: "By ritual, Heaven and Earth harmoniously combine" (Xunzi, On Ritual). Particularly solemn in its expression, the reverence shown by Xunzi towards ritual forms and observances is far from being an exception: Confucian thinkers always emphasized that rituals were a privileged way to educate both the personal and collective body, to institutionalize ethical care and the sharing of resources, to make human society coordinate with cosmic order, and to govern without relying first and foremost on law and punishment. To that effect, rituals were to be conducted according to strict rhythms and patterns. Rhythms had to do with seasonal observances and musical performance, and patterns were determined by the order of sequences in ceremonies as well as by conventions governing the chanting/reciting of formulas, songs and texts. Whatever the criticism that Daoist thinkers were aiming at such a perspective, both the *Daodejing* and the *Zhuangzi* show a deep knowledge of ritual practices.[108] In many cases, Zhuangzi's stories can be read as the representation of *counter-rituals:* Butcher Ding is an officer who fulfills the traditional role of preparing meat for sacrifice (*Zhuangzi* 3.2). His way of carving a beef without ever blunting his knife is both a celebration of freedom and a kind of ritual dance. Likewise, when Zhuangzi crouches down and sings, knocking on a pot, after the death of his wife (*Zhuangzi* 18.2), he releases emotions according to patterns not congruent with social norms, but this counter-ritual remains a rite, even if it calls to question the meaning of the performance.

If state power has been prone to instrumentalize Ritual (the alliance between the King [*wang* 王] and the Shaman [*wu* 巫], which marks a departure from a stateless society, based on hunting or at least on pastoralism, towards agriculture-based states, testifies to the trend), Chinese authors have tried to limit and to frame such instrumentalization by describing sacrifices and ceremonies as a

---

[108] See for instance Boileau (2013).

channel of humanization: state rituals were supposed to exercise a function of regulation, appeasing and controlling appetites, operating spiritual transformation, and inserting people into an ever-widening horizon. They were based upon a conception of harmony (*he* 和) first based on cultural practices – musical or culinary – and later on enlarged into a cosmic vision: The *Book of Rites* (*Liji* 禮記) makes the exchange of energies (*qi* 氣) between Earth and Heaven an operation that is both musical and ritual. Since music is the "motor" of the cosmos,[109] ritual musical performance was seen as contributing to the proper functioning of the latter. Far from seeing its symbolic importance diminish over time, ritual performance and its musical dimension received an increasingly central place in Chinese thought.[110]

Mental, Ritual and Textual Threads

The above points towards a fact that is both manifest and elusive: in all societies, mental structures (which allow for ways of reasoning and specific representations), social patterns (such as hierarchies, decision-making processes, or yet procedures followed for exchanging things) and cultural end-products (rituals, texts, clothing or architectural designs) are intricately interrelated and – what is more – obey similar formal dispositions.

This may naturally lead one to study ancient texts as "patterns", the way we do for rituals: we can approach a classic as a *totality* – a self-sufficient, self-organized whole – the way Claude Levi-Strauss was doing when looking at the structure of a Latin-American indigenous villages. Maybe classics are structured as a Bororo village apparently is.[111] Or, for staying closer to our initial comparison, they could be organized like a group of ritual dancers.[112] Or yet, their patterns are possibly similar to geometrical designs adorning clothing. After all, at the time they were composed and edited, Chinese classics were being *woven* into patterns from a given

---

[109] One finds also such conception in the chapter "On Music" of the *Xunzi*.
[110] Brindley (2012) shows that, if the discourse on music seems first limited to its social function, it progressively stresses the cosmic dimension of musical performance. The *Guanzi* 管子 and the *Huainanzi* 淮南子, encyclopedic writings edited during the early Han period, both insist very much on this aspect.
[111] Lévi-Strauss (2012 [1955]), Fig. 43. I write "apparently", for Lévi-Strauss insists on the fact that, behind this circular organization, a Bororo village is actually divided into three hierarchized subgroups, each of which intermarries within itself.
[112] See in Amiot (1779) the various figures representing the arrangement of a group of dancers during an ancestor worship ceremony. Amiot's work is based on the work of Zhu Zaiyu 朱載堉 1536–1611 (see Lenoir, and Standaert 2005).

combination of threads, as one does with a loom.¹¹³ The same imagery has been brought up by Nicolas Standaert when researching the transformation of Christian funerals in Late Ming/Early Qing China: at that time, Standaert writes, Christian and Confucian threads, were somehow woven together into new ritual expressions (cf. Standaert 2008).

In the same line, the British anthropologist Mary Douglas has unearthed in classics originating from different civilizations circular patterns that organize texts and mental schemes in similar fashion:

> A ring is a framing device. The linking up of starting point and end creates an envelope that contains everything between the opening phrases and the conclusion. [...] There has to be a well-marked point at which the ring turns, [...] and the whole series of stanzas going from the beginning to the middle should be in parallel with the other series going from the middle back to the start.
>
> (Douglas 2007, 1–2)

Such a description recalls ritual and social *figurations*, as Norbert Elias would have it,¹¹⁴ while delineating mental schemes different from the ones fostered by linear reasoning and exposition.

There are of course other reasons that encourage the analyst to circulate between ritual patterns and textual ones. Among these reasons: stories and stipulations found in classics partially determine the way rites are performed (till now, Korean Confucian rituals of ancestor worship take the *Analects* and the *Book of Rites* as their normative and often practical reference). At the same time, rites do not merely *replicate* classics, they rather provide an *interpretation* of them; they deliver a living, embodied performance of the way the text has been passed on and is nowadays understood. In fact, the understanding of the classics proper to a civilization or another is prone to be deeply altered when rituals are not passed down alongside classics, when the two go separate ways. In the past, ancient classics were not textbook materials. Rather, they were lived and performed. The recitation of the classics, as was also the case for a ritual dance, was going through a series of sequences to be enacted in order. As long as they were read ritualistically, it was easier to consider their patterns as an unveiling of the social and/or cosmic order of which they were speaking. Probably, it was even felt that this overall order was subsiding partly thanks to their ritualized reading.

---

113 Among recent contributions, see Zürn (2020).
114 Elias sees figurations or configurations as ever-evolving networks of relationships from which the individual grows and that concurrently she helps to shape. Among other comparisons Elias makes use of, he invites us to imagine a group of dancers, their gestures being meshed and synchronized with those of other dancers (Elias 1991, 19–20).

How Can the Way Be Decoded?

In classical China, both cosmic and social orders were seen as being triggered and sustained by the *dao* 道, a term now acclimatized in Western languages. As I argued in Chapter 2, translating *dao* simply by "the way" (or "the Way") is perfectly acceptable. The popularization of the term in the West has been accompanied by representations that are vague in their detail but coherent as a whole: *dao* would refer to an original and universally active principle that cannot be described either as "divine" or as "creator-like" but that does not absolutely preclude these significations. Dao is to be understood in reference to *de* (virtue, potency), but also to other concepts already discussed in Chapter 2.

A code, as all dictionaries tell us, is a system of signals or symbols for communication. Such a system is sometimes designed so as to convey secret meanings. A "coded language" plays on the ambiguity between the explicit and the implicit, using a word or expression in place of another so as to communicate a message without stating it explicitly. Additionally, the genetic code is the biochemical basis of heredity, and its sequences appear to be uniform for nearly all known forms of life. Nowadays, "code" also refers to a system of instructions given to a computer, which should not make us forget that, in more ancient usages, "code" is a body of law, or yet a system of principles or rules (moral, ethical code). This constitutes a useful reminder since it draws our attention towards the Latin *codex*: a writing tablet; hence: a piece of writing – and then: a systematized set of writings, the legal corpus constituting the model of the latter in Rome. Let us note in passing that the word *codex* suggests the idea of a certain "efficacy" in the very act of writing since the genre first covered by the term is, behind the juridical corpus, the one of the Last Will, of dispositions that one's death will make effective.

Considered as the source, the movement or yet the influx from which life arises and decays, the Way is its own code and pattern (*fa* 法), on which everything is in turn modeled ("the Way is patterned on itself [*dao fa ziran* 道法自然]", *Daodejing* 25). As we have seen, observing water – its nature, its way of proceeding – already allows the observer to "decode" the rules that determine the emergence and succession of all phenomena. More broadly, the potency of the Way – its manifestations, similar to the surge and growth of the plants alongside the river – furthers the decoding operation. Processes of divination, progressively mathematized, constitute a further stage of the decoding of the Way. However, there is no decoding that does not require an encoding operation, namely the writing down of the rules deciphered through a specific language and support. What the Sage decodes, the Text will encode.

Three Characteristics of Early Chinese *Wen*

In oracular and bronze inscriptions, *wen* 文 means "distinguished", "enlightened", with special reference to the person of a king, and then of deceased family members or of ancestors more distant in time. In the *Classic of Documents* it forms a pair with the character *wu* 武, *wen* referring to everything that is civil, civilized, soft, accomplished (related texts associate this notion to the one of variegated clothing, or yet, of tattoos), while *wu* speaks of physical strength and of military matters. The *Analects* associate *wen* with civility and refinement and also with texts and written documents, the one seemingly indissociable from the other. Yan Hui 顏回, the favorite disciple of Confucius reflecting on the latter's educational strategy, exclaims: "He enlarges me by the Letters, and he restrains me by the Rites [*bo wo yi wen, yue wo yi li*博我以文, 約我以禮]" (*Analects* 9.11). Note the polarity/complementarity of Ritual and Letters in the training process through which potentialities contained into one's nature are brought into fruition.

Texts and documents are made of *signs*, and this last notion determines the use of the character *wen* in the *Zuozhuan* as well as in the *Classic of Changes*: birthmark, ideogram, written style, heavenly manifestation, symbolic figure or drawing.... Stars and cosmic manifestations are "heavenly signs" (*tianwen* 天文). Applied to literacy, *wen* will take two different meanings: on the one hand, it designates the sinograms composed of a single graph (as opposed to *zi* 字, made of an association of elements, semantic and/or phonetic); on the other hand, it refers to all written compositions. The above should help us to better grasp the three following characteristics of the notion:

- *Wen* was a privileged channel of communication between Heaven and Earth.
- *Wen* was performative: what it was speaking about, at the same time it was making it happen.
- *Wen* was thought of as a matrix, a source-code, rather than as what we call today a "text".

A Privileged Channel of Communication between Heaven and Earth

The written sources that precede and shape the formation of our classics are not as ancient as in the case for other civilizations. The system of signs that grounds Chinese writing appears only towards 1250 BCE, much later than the writing systems conceived in the Near and Middle East. (Writing – or, at least, a system of signs that can be described as writing – appears for the first time in human history around 3400 BCE, in Sumer.) Initially, this system fulfills two functions: accounting (counting the king's properties); and notations of astronomical observations, which are the basis of the Sumerian divinatory system. From there, the graphic systems of the Near and Middle East, then the West, will develop into scripts, either alphabetic or syllabic. These systems were primarily based on a way of "recording" speech, which Chinese writing most probably was not.[115]

The Chinese writing system was developed to record the procedures and results of divinations performed on the shoulder blades of oxen and the shells of large turtles. A burning wooden rod was applied to the recesses, one part of which was tangential to the other. On the other side, the resulting cracking took a 卜 (*bu*) shape. The result of divination was considered auspicious when the latitudinal part was ascending, negative when it descended, doubtful when it formed a right angle with the longitudinal part. The divinatory documents thus obtained (on which inscriptions, engraved next to the result of the divination, specify the date of the operation, the name of the person who carried out it and the prediction to be validated such as "the king must not go hunting") were archived, and it is this archiving process that led to the development of a system of signs correlating to cracks. It is worth noting that the statements that the diviners were submitting to divination were not exactly framed as questions. We are dealing here with predictions of assertive value (Djamouri 1999). Divination in ancient China first seeks confirmation of a planned action. Unfavorable prognoses could lead to sacrifices intended to alter the predicted outcome.

If the Mediterranean civilizations also practiced divination on a large scale, the material used (observation of the flight of birds, examination of the viscera of animals) obviously made it impossible to constitute divinatory archives. The *wen* is perceived from the start as being a *double sign:* the sign inscribed in Heaven, and that inscribed on the divinatory document. This jointly celestial and terrestrial character of the *wen* then gives it a *third value:* that of being the sign of the alliance between the one and the other. We have met already with a foundational assertion of *Xici* 繫辭 commentary: "[The Sage] looking up, contemplates the heavenly signs [*tianwen* 天文], and, looking down, scrutinizes the earthly patterns [*dili*

---

[115] Vandermeersch (2013, 87) describes Chinese writing as a "semantic grid". He notes the paucity of results obtained by approaches that, shaped by European linguistic, focus on oral etymologies, such as the one systematized by Wang Li (Wang 1982). Debates on this subject can be acrimonious (Hansen 1993; Unger and Hansen 1993), mainly because, behind them, opposite theories bearing upon the nature of perception and language are at stake. One may want to approach the topic in a more pragmatic and evolutionist fashion, taking as a given that the Chinese writing system took shape in the collation of data obtained through divinatory practice, while its development complexified its structure, its resources and the way readers related to it. In other words, the origins of the Chinese language may have very little influence, if any, on the way a reader, today, approaches and assimilates a text written in Chinese characters.

地理]" (*Xici* I.4). The *wen* then occupies a position identical to that which the *Classic of Documents* gives to the Son of Heaven (*Tianzi*天子). His position, both privileged and solitary between Heaven and Earth is what allows him to sustain the "moral standard [*zhong* 衷]":

> The King said: "All of you, from every region of the land, listen carefully to what I [a straightforward man], am about to say. The Emperor above all Emperors has endowed every person with a moral sense [*zhong*], and this is their essential, original nature. However, to ensure that they stay true to this essential nature, it is necessary to have rulers."
>
> (*Book of Documents*, "The Declaration of Tang" 湯誥)

A displacement thus takes place: initially, its divinatory nature allows the *wen* to connect the Earth with the Sky. Without losing this character, later on the stress shifts towards its ability to preserve and transmit the moral standard. More generally, the thought process that takes place can be described as follows: originally, the divination process leads to the discernment of the *forms* (*xing* 形) taken by observable phenomena. What is revealed of the order of the cosmos through the process of divination will gradually be brought closer to the form of the body (*xing-ti* 形體),[116] then to the principle that animates any living body, and then to the moral order which governs beings and events. On the basis of the graphic language, an analogical thought will gradually take shape: elaborate ramifications (between the main viscera of the human body and climatic states – hot, cold, dry, humid – emotions, musical notes, colors, seasons, all this transcribed in a "base five" arithmetic) allow the ones who master the *wen* to observe pragmatically a set of correspondences. At the same time, these analogies become morally significant (in Chinese medicine, the state of the body is associated with a combination of emotions about which a moral judgment as to their balance and intensity is enacted.). An evolution has occurred, which leads from the divinatory to the ethico-political dimension.

The Performativity of *Wen*

Let us further the previous analysis through some considerations on the *Classic of Odes*. I will start with a statement of Confucius that is much more significant, at least in my view, than is generally thought:

---

[116] This expression appears in the *Xunzi*, but the concept it refers to precedes this work.

> The Odes number three hundred. One expression may summarize them: "No perversity in his thoughts."
> 詩三百，一言以蔽之，曰「思無邪」。
>
> *(Analects* 2.2)

The verse quoted by Confucius comes from Ode 297 (*Jiong* 駉), which features a prince whose thought is rightly directed towards the breeding of his horses. It is the inflexible direction of the prince's thoughts that leads the horses to – literally – walk straight.

> These carriage horses are robust. / In the thoughts [of the prince], no perversity. / He thinks of his horses, and thus they go forward.
> 以車祛祛。思無邪、思馬斯徂。
>
> (*Classic of Odes*, Ode 297)

The thread chosen by Confucius speaks of rectitude aimed at a goal. The connection that the poem establishes between the disciplined gallop of the horses and the rectitude of the prince's thoughts expresses the ideal of *performativity* detected by Marcel Granet in the *Odes*, as we will see below. If so, the interpretive key suggested by Confucius says more about the *Odes* than is usually recognized; it establishes a firm relationship between the rectitude of a desire put into motion (exemplified by the course of thought of the prince) and the progress of social and cosmic affairs (illustrated by the conduct of the horses). What is more, it implies that performativity arises from analogy – the one between the single-mindedness of the Prince and the straightness of the horses' gallop in this case.

We must handle this hypothesis with caution: other passages from the *Analects* approach the *Odes* in terms of moral teaching reduced to a few elementary principles (*Analects* 1.15; 3.8; 13.5). Such an interpretive moral thread was of course systematized by the commented edition that Mao Heng 毛亨 and Mao Chang 毛萇 edited during the Western Han dynasty, from which the *Odes* has been studied and understood for a very long time. Marcel Granet gave an explanation of the operation by which literate officials have moralized to the extreme the popular songs that were sung at the two annual gatherings of peasant communities which, for most of the year, were living dispersed from one another: these gatherings had quite naturally a ritual character, and, therefore, the latter-day moralization of the *Odes* was part of the moralization of the ritual as a whole (Granet 1919, 6–7). For his part, Granet chooses to treat the *Odes* as "a document specific to the study of the beliefs which inspired the ancient Chinese seasonal ritual" (Granet

1919, 7).[117] In the spring, through the joust between the sexes, the alliance which united different local groups into a traditional community was restored. A close reading of these poems shows that the participants were seeing the rites of which the chanting of the *Odes* were a part as being endowed with effectiveness. "[These gatherings] possess the entire efficiency and the ever-reborn youth of games and rituals. [...] It is the dance and it is the singing which, making the partridges mate and the seasonal flood swell to its appropriate level, will succeed in making all the signs of spring appear" (Granet 1999 [1934]), 57–58). To make use of a vocabulary that was not the one of Granet, the ritual, by what it does and what it sings, is *performative*.

In examining the terminology and the images displayed by poems that sinologists read too quickly like sketches of mere drunkenness, Granet was able to rediscover the momentum and the sequences of the sacred game: turning over the vases and the pots is part of the liturgical feasts offered to the ancestors; the wild dancing evoked in certain poems as well as in the *Book of Rites* describes exactly the behavior expected from people preparing for the arrival of the spirits; the fall of the official bonnets prepares the obligatory swirling of the hair let loose when these same spirits have arrived; and the portrayal of an endless whirlwind dance evokes the movements of the dancer as he mimics the fact of being driven away by the wind. Drunkenness, here, is, by essence, ritual acting. These poetic formulas offer the reduced model of that other reduced model which the festive rite constitutes: as with Russian dolls, *the poem is the reduced model of the celebration, which itself is a reduced model of the social and natural reality.* The community conforms to the laws that govern society and the cosmos. At the same time, it must put into motion these same laws through the performativity of the ritual, and this performativity presupposes the one contained in the poem. (The mere recitation of the poem is not performative, and becomes so only within a ritual context, the same way the Austinian "I do" has no performative effect if the marriage ceremony is not properly conducted.)

In the description offered by Granet, it is in the nature of reality to call upon itself human intervention. And indeed, ancient texts hint at the fact that without the rites the stars could not turn nor the harvests reach maturity. This is made explicit in the "On Ritual" chapter of the *Xunzi*, which distinguishes the *general role* of "cosmic regulator" played by the rite from its (very dubious) effectiveness in a *particular circumstance*, such as persistent drought for example. For Xunzi, ritual

---

[117] We should not confuse this thesis with that of an essentially oral transmission of the *Odes*. Shaughnessy (2015) rightly emphasizes the importance of the writing in the process by which the Odes have come down to us.

performance constitutes the human task *par excellence*, the one that defines humankind's status and role vis-à-vis nature.

A Source-Code

For a very long period, the *Classic of Changes* constituted less a text properly speaking than the formatting of a system of divination that was based on the count of yarrow stems drawn by lot (the choice of yarrow explained by the structure of the plant, unfolding its many ramifications from a single stem, as the One gives birth to the multitude of phenomena). Derivatives of trigrams, the hexagrams constructed by drawing lots were fulfilling the role previously played by divinatory cracks. Both methods were meant to reflect the play of the cosmic forces that bring about the advent of such and such a situation. However, in contrast to the use of divinatory cracks, basing predictions upon hexagrams meant to proceed through a kind of algebra whose theoretical principles were developed in the "Ten Wings" (*Shiyi*十翼) Commentary. This algebra reduced the base numbers used in divination to the binary of even and odd numbers, itself equated to the polarity of *yin* 陰 and *yang* 陽. (Note that the *Yijng* itself, as merely composed of hexagrams and short explanations, does not yet mention the terms *yin* and *yang*, which appear in latter-day commentaries.)

Such device implies that the *Yijing* had to be read with reference to a diagram structure, and not as a linear text. In fact, the evolution that the *Yijing* underwent until it was canonized under the Han remains controversial though it may probably be summarized as follows: for a long time, as illustrated by several anecdotes from the *Zuozhuan*, the way of referring to the *Yijing* (to draw "knowledge" from it) was an object of competition between diviners (*wu* 巫) and scholars (*shi* 士). The *Xunzi* does not yet make the *Yijing* a "Classic" (*jing*). Towards the end of the Warring States period, the *Yijing* is still considered as a mere manual of divination, a practical guide so to speak. The commentaries deployed around the *Yijing* will eventually make it a "textual object". Grouped into the "Ten Wings", these commentaries organize a system of interpretation by which each hexagram (*gua* 卦) calls for a weighing (*tuan* 彖) and a figurative reading as an image (*xiang* 象), any hexagram being taken successively in its entirety and in its components. The *Xici* Commentary in particular presents a cosmological interpretation of the whole.

At the same time, reading the *Yijing* through the "Ten Wings" (especially through their last three parts) ensures that each hexagram is considered within the process of transformation that alone gives meaning to it. If the *Yijing* delivers the images (*xiang*) upon which the forms (*xing*) are modeled, a dynamic of continuous transformation perpetually erases these manifestations. I have already quoted the initial statement of the *Xici:* "Images take shape in Heaven. Forms take shape on Earth. Thus, transformations and evolutions are made visible" (*Xici* 1.1).

In this worldview, individuals as well as communities need to ensure both vital growth and social balance. This entails that they must strive to recognize (through the consultation of the *Yijing*) the opportunities offered at a given moment of time (and solely at this moment). This is why the *Yijing* is less a text than a *source-code*, the knowledge of which is essential for anyone who wants to decipher the game of incessant phenomenal transformations in order to find one's (constantly evolving) setting into it. Additionally, the idea of a *correspondence* between macrocosm and microcosm present in the *Yijing* has made the Chinese tradition inclined to recognize in it *less and more than a text: the matrix of all texts.*[118]

Mutations of the *Wen*

The characteristics described above constitute the premises of the conception which, from the Warring States period (453–221 BCE) onwards (or maybe even earlier), animates the production of the written text: the latter needs to be the *form*, the *recipient* or the *body* through which the movement of constant transformation of the images that make up the universe manifests itself. The characters (*zi* 字) derive from the trigrams (themselves born from the traces – *ji* 跡 or *ji* 迹 – left by birds and game), affirms Xu Shen 許慎 (58–147) in the preface to the *Shuowen jiezi* 說文解字. "To write is to create a simile[書者, 如也]", asserts the same preface.[119]

Mark E. Lewis expresses with force – but with some systematism – the political extensions of such ambition:

> The culminating role of writing in the period, and the key to its importance in imperial China, was the creation of parallel realities within texts that claimed to depict the entire world. Such worlds created in writing provided models for the unprecedented enterprise of founding a world empire, and they underwrote the claims of authority of those who composed, sponsored, or interpreted them. One version of these texts ultimately became the first state canon of imperial China, and in this capacity it served to perpetuate the dream and the reality of the imperial system across the centuries.
>
> (Lewis 1999, 4)

---

[118] Besides the *Yijing*, another seminal text opens up perspectives on how the *wen* was approached as a source-code, and therefore read within a diagram structure. I am speaking here of the *Hongfan* 洪範 chapter of the *Classic of Documents*, already evoked in the course of Chapter 1.

[119] A similar formulation can be found in *Mozi* 40.32.

A more cautious reading would spare ancient classics the reproach of being engulfed into the dream of *mastery*, be it virtual or real, which Lewis intends to denounce. The classics' gnoseological premises could also work secretly against the systematization of the imperial enterprise – in other words: their textual principles could also prevent these "parallel worlds" from entirely closing in on themselves: "The great perfection has something of a flaw [*da cheng ruo que* 大成若缺]", asserts *Laozi* 45, and the axiom can be applied to the text itself. Still, Lewis' position furthers the understanding of the principles we have just unearthed.

The divinatory "text" standardizes the predictive procedures to the point of producing hexagrams, it then passes from hexagrams to numbers (*shu* 數), and, through the latter, organizes into coherent propositions the multiple realities of the world, the images of which are suggested by characters – as already indicated, these characters can be simple, expressing primordial realities (and are in this case called *wen*文) or they can be compounds, and are then called *zi* 字. Deciphering a text (and a "text" at its most general level is composed of figures and/or numbers), we are made able to perceive the incessant transformation of things, the passage from one phenomenal and numerical state to another. So, divinatory knowledge reveals to us the "Constant" (*heng* 恆 or *chang* 常), precisely because it makes us perceive a constant flow, the continuous transformation and return of all things. Any text *is* what it speaks of, and, at the same time, constitutes its parallel: it provides the model by which to see the interior of the phenomenon it describes, and, therefore, it is a tool by which to get a grasp on reality – a grasp that comes from an internalization of the laws discovered when reading the text.

Summing up, the fact of reading synoptically *Documents*, *Odes* and *Change* leads us to draw three conclusions:

a) Humankind was tasked with the mission of ensuring the perpetuation of the natural and social order by binding language (*yan*言), Ritual (*li* 禮) and knowledge (*zhi* 知) into a unified system of principles and duties.

b) Knowledge (be it mantic, moral, historical or experiential) was expressed and organized in texts (*wen*) loaded with some kind of performative efficacy, at least when associated with ritual utterances/performances. Image of the Way (*dao*), bearer of its Virtue (or Potency [*de*]), the *wen* unfolds the mystery of cosmic workings to the point that it eventually merges into it. I am tempted here to go further than Mark Lewis does: not only is the text a "parallel world", but also it ends up underpinning and carrying the "real world".

c) Knowledge, however, does not stand alone: one enlarges the mind by the text, and one restrains behavior by the rites (*Analects* 9.11). One makes assessment through mantic principles, and one ultimately takes decisions according to the

Word (*yan*) that unveils the moral principle (*zhong*) implanted in each one by Heaven. Of course, perfect knowledge easily discerns that mantic teaching and moral prescription ultimately coincide.

From "Texts" to "Classics"

At the time here considered (5th to 1st centuries BCE), texts could be written on wooden tablets (*du* 牘) or slats of wood or bamboo (*ce* 冊, *ce* 策, or *pian* 篇). In its original script, the character *ce* 冊 represents two tablets connected by two cords. The homonymous *ce* 策 describes bamboo tablets that were strung and gathered into a "file". *Pian* refers to a writing tablet, to the divisions of a work, or even to any literary composition. The character *du* is less frequent than the others. Later on, the use of silk made it possible to collect these relatively short units of text into longer scrolls (*juan* 卷).[120] Personal or state collections organized the same material in different orders. Possibly, a specific order of composition tended to stabilize when silk rolls were preferentially used. However, as noted by Sarah Allan, there were texts of appreciable length already in circulation during the Warring States period, even if most of the pre-Qin transmitted texts did not reach their final form until they were rewritten on long rolls of silk in the Han dynasty (Allan 2015, 321). In any event, the *physical fragmentation* of the material induced by the original supports does not imply that this same material could not have been the subject of an *ideal grouping* into continuous "texts" – even more so in the hypothesis of an essentially combinatorial textual structure, on the model opened up by the *Yijing*. As to the term *jing* 經 that, later on, will refer to texts that the state has canonized as "Classics" and made the subjects of state-sponsored examinations, James Legge is arguably the first to note (in 1883) that both the Latin term *textum /textus* (let us think here of "textile" and "texture") and the character *jing* contain the image of "thoughts woven into writing" (Girardot 1999, 1110). At the same time,

---

[120] "The increasing use of silk as a writing surface in the third and second centuries BCE contributed to the parallel construction of writing and weaving. During the pre-Han period, writers began to utilize silk fabrics to produce texts. However, it seems as if the production of silk was still so expensive up until the late Warring States period that fabrics were reserved for sacred image-texts. […] This rare use of silk for texts, however, might have changed during the late Warring States period in the third and second centuries BCE when the Middle Kingdoms possibly developed advanced weaving technologies such as complex looms. […] These developments might have led to a wider dissemination of silk as a medium for writings. […] Texts from the Warring States and early imperial period clearly construed writing and weaving as homological processes beyond their shared utilization as writing materials and vertical orientation" (Zürn 2020, 378–380).

jing will always evoke more than a textual, state-sponsored selection: a standard, a model that applies virtually to any writing.

How does one proceed from *wen* to *jing*? In order to understand what *jing* eventually refers to, it is necessary to track its evolving meanings throughout early writings. The *Classic of Documents* designates by the term a rule, a constant law or phenomenon, or yet, when treating it as a verb, refers to the act of drawing the blueprint of a city. The *Classic of Odes* similarly implies that *jing* refers to the action of measuring and drawing a map. The *Classic of Changes* sees it mainly as a noun that designates a direction, and specifically the roads that go from north to south. The *Mencius* attributes to it a verbal value ("to take as a rule"). Later on, a variety of texts gives to *jing* an array of related meanings: the meridians recognized by Chinese medicine; monthly periods; the warp of a fabric; or yet texts or prayers that are ritualistically recited. As to the *Shuowen jiezi*, it simply indicates: "*jing*: weaving [*jing: zhi ye* 經：織也]".

The above helps us to make sense of the first appearance of the character in its meaning as "reference writings". This happens in the *Xunzi*, probably around 250 BCE or slightly later:

> Where does learning begin? Where does learning end? I say: Its order begins with reciting the classics (*jing*), and ends with studying ritual.
> 學惡乎始？惡乎終？曰：其數則始乎誦經，終乎讀禮。
> (*Xunzi*, "Exhortation to Learning" 勸學. Translation Hutton 2014, 5)

The rest of this fragment makes clear that, when speaking of *jing*, Xunzi is referring to the *Classic of Documents*, the *Classic of Odes*, the *Spring and Autumn Annals* (*Chunqiu* 春秋) and probably the lost *Classic of Music* (*Yuejing* 樂經). Still, the *Xunzi* continues to give preferentially to *jing* the meaning of "a rule, to rule, constant law". Probably around the same time or a bit later, the semi-comical character that the *Zhuangzi* names "Confucius" enumerates a slightly longer list of classics (*jing*). Marc Lewis has rightly noted that this passage associates "classics" and "footprints/traces/vestiges" (*ji* 跡). It reads as follows:

> Confucius said to Laozi, "I have studied the six classics – the Odes, the Documents, the Rites, the Music, the Changes, and the Spring and Autumn Annals – for what seems to me to be a long time. I thoroughly know their contents. With them I have confronted seventy-two rulers. I have discussed the Ways of the Former Kings and made clear the path [*ji*, literally "footprints", "traces"] of the Duke of Zhou and Duke Shao. Yet not one of them has ever employed me. How difficult it is to persuade people! How difficult it is to make clear the Way!"
> 孔子謂老聃曰：「丘治《詩》、《書》、《禮》、《樂》、《易》、《春秋》六經，自以為久矣，孰知其故矣，以奸者七十二君，論先王之道而明周、召之跡，一君無所鉤用。甚矣夫！人之難說也，道之難明邪！」
> (*Zhuangzi* 14, "The Turnings of Heaven" 天運. Translation Lewis 1999, 276)

In his answer to "Confucius", the similarly theatrical "Laozi" describes indeed the six classics as the vestiges of the ancient kings, but immediately contrasts them with the way some birds supposedly operate fertilization by simple eye contact. "Laozi", notes Lewis, "uses [the term 'vestige'] specifically to suggest the lifeless remains of what was once vital and moving. [...] The natural generation of living things [...] contrasts with the dead Confucian texts, which singularly fail to do so" (Lewis 1999, 277). If the *jing* is a further elaboration from the traces of the cosmos already found in the footpaths of birds and tigers (these footpaths that have inspired the graphs of the *wen*), such process can be seen as testifying either to a moral and civilizational journey or to growing alienation from original spontaneity.

The character *ji* (trace) thus starts the long career it will undergo throughout the developments of Daoist thought, a career that is far from being affected by mere negative connotations: the *jishen* (迹身 or 跡身), usually translated as "trace-body", corresponds to the appearance taken by the Ultimate in function of the characteristics and specific situation of the mind that receives it. Though each trace is particular, it still speaks of an over-encompassing reality. Traces take on added significance as other traces appear along the way, as other layers are discerned over the surface of reality, combining into a symphony of meanings.[121]

The primary notion associated to *jing* remains the one of regularity, constant rule, unchangeable patterns. It applies to a far larger array of operations and domains. In other words, weaving is only one expression of the way the universe – cosmic, social and material – is designed and is kept constant. If a Classic is indeed *woven*, it does not always present itself as a *weaving*. A whole range of metaphors speaks of the way a text may embody what it is discoursing about, and, ultimately, organic metaphors prove more pregnant than mechanical ones.

Summing up, the *wen* testifies to the process through which humankind decodes the cosmos and its source, and it points towards its underlying principles. It also attempts to formalize insights and findings through the creation of a language that expresses such principles to human ears and makes them applicable within the social, educational or political realms – the *wen* starts to operate an encoding. However, not every *wen* can translate the code of the Way (should we say "the Code that is the Way"?) into a consistent, complete and user-friendly language. This is the privilege in theory attached to *jing*. To put it otherwise: *wen* are elements, section, trial versions of a code, while a *jing* comes up with a fully complet-

---

[121] For illustrations of this trend of thought in contemporary settings, notably in discourses on Chinese painting, see Vermander (2021b).

ed version. The models privileged by different *jing* may diverge, leading them to organize and represent the "writing body" that they constitute under varying metaphors.

Attentiveness: The Reader as Ritual Practitioner

In *Small World*, David Lodge's campus novel (Lodge 1985),[122] Morris Zapp is a prominent American professor who, as he goes from one academic conference to another, keeps repeating that "every decoding is another encoding". The comical nature of Zapp's appearances does not hide the mixture of complicity and distance felt by Lodge (himself a foremost literary critic) towards the views that the character he created holds so dear. "So dear", indeed, since Zapp knows the craft of converting academic brilliance into (substantial) financial rewards. Zapp's theorizing will compete with others – structuralism, reception theory, feminist Marxism, traditional humanism... – in a forum that should decide upon the name of the luminary who will obtain a richly endowed UNESCO Chair of Literary Criticism. However, the young Persse McGarrigle (the Percival of the academic romance that *Small World* endeavors to be) will put Zapp and his competitors off balance by asking the simple question: "What follows if everyone agrees with you?" A question that the Patriarch of literary criticism, Arthur Kingfisher, interprets in his own fashion by concluding that "to win is to lose the game".

Persse's challenge is a reminder that the coding metaphor needs to be taken with a grain of salt: the decoding/encoding operation is not an endless game that would be pursued for itself. For the one who endeavors to approach Ultimate Reality through the study of its *vestigia* (*vestigium:* footprint [as Augustine chose to express it, with an image almost identical to the one attached to the character *ji* 跡]),[123] these *vestigia*, once discovered, need to be translated into a language that a community is able to appropriate. While the encoding operation is necessitated by humankind's inscription into nature as by its distance from its origins, it is ultimately directed towards fellow-human beings.

In this regard, the language or the code used by Chinese classics is only a medium through which to foster an art of living and studying, an existential attitude:

---

122 The readers of *Small World* will remember that speaking of it as of a "campus novel" is rather paradoxical since the novel takes place at the time of the nascent "global campus", and its protagonists unceasingly move from one location to another.
123 In *De Trinitate*, Augustine's quest for the *vestigia Trinitatis* focuses both on external objects in their multidimensionality (water as source, stream and lake) and on human inner constitution (memory, understanding and will).

the way of perceiving and describing reality they develop is characterized by the *attentiveness* that they require and display. The attentiveness towards the inner and the phenomenal world shown by our classics is meant to become our own *attentiveness* towards them.

Observing for Being Transformed

Often, Chinese classics break up into tiny paragraphs that connect with each other through cross-references and resonances rather than through linear expansions. And, just as often, these paragraphs revolve around extremely condensed formulas. Let us stop on an example taken from the Mencius, which I already briefly made use of in the Introduction. For the clarity of what will follow I divide it into three parts:

a) Confucius climbed the Eastern Mountain, and [the State of] Lu became small; he climbed Taishan, and the world became small. Thus, for those who have contemplated the sea, it is difficult to make case of rivers; for those who have traveled to study under a Sage, it is difficult to give importance to speeches.
b) There is an art [*shu* 術] in observing water; we must observe its undulations: when the sun and the moon shine, the rays that [these undulations] necessarily receive penetrate them.
c) When flowing, water is made in such a way that it cannot move forward without first filling the pits. As for the path [the way] on which a gentleman has set his mind, if it is not fulfilled at each stage, it cannot attain completion.
a) 子登東山而小魯，登太山而小天下。故觀於海者難為水，遊於聖人之門者難為言。
b) 觀水有術，必觀其瀾。日月有明，容光必照焉。
c) 流水之為物也，不盈科不行；君子之志於道也，不成章不達。

(Mencius 7 A.24[124])

There are three propositions in this paragraph: (a) the one who has had access to an "eminence" (a high mountain or an eminent Sage) no longer cares about what is of lesser height; (b) one can "see" and probe water only by paying attention to its movement; (c) in the movement of their progression, the water and the Way fill all things.

---

[124] The division of this paragraph in three sections is of course introduced by me.

Before even asking ourselves what logically links these propositions, let us note the images and pairs of opposites that make the paragraph a whole. (1) Metaphors related to water link together the successive statements. (2) The height of the mountains and the depth of the sea trenches respond to each other. (3) Each part of the whole deals with phenomena that are difficult to observe, either because, usually hidden, they have to come to light, or because, usually visible, they disappear from a distance. (4) Finally, in the first and third clauses the focus is on the person who is immersed into study – and we will see that the intermediate clause is not unrelated to this topic.

It is indeed in this second, central proposition that the enigma lies. Let us first notice the nature of the link between the first and the third assertions: in the first one, the fact of embarking on the path of study leads the student to travel, to climb, and thus to learn to appreciate true greatness, judging the rest from the broadest possible viewpoint. In the final proposition, it is said that entering into the path of study means to engage into underground work, a work that leaves nothing behind, that pays attention to each step rather than trying to advance too quickly, a work that enters into the depths – and then, when everything has been filled and probed, the Way arises for each to see. In the process, a transformation has taken place. To avoid any misunderstanding, it should be specified that the work here described is not about trying to make one's knowledge universal but rather about entering more deeply into what one chooses to study. Mencius notes that, for knowledge as for anything else, it is necessary to respond to priorities without seeking exhaustivity for itself: "Though a learned man may know everything, he applies himself to what is of first concern [*zhizhe wu bu zhi ye, dang wu zhi wei ji* 知者無不知也，當務之為急]" (*Mencius* 7 A.46).

At the center of our paragraph: the art of observing water. Water reveals itself to us through its manifestations, its movements. The commentaries specify that, in this context, "to observe water" means first to gauge its depth (gauging water's depth may be useful for irrigation work, crossing over, or yet navigation…). Mencius' idea appears to be that the play of ripples and rays stealthily reveals the objects that water conceals, thus allowing the observer to gauge the bottom, while still water remains impenetrable. One may infer that studying under a Sage is akin to interact with him and that the Sage's inner depth will be revealed from his reactions, his moves, the sudden glimpses he offers. The third proposition then explains both how water proceeds, and why the person who engages fully in study resembles the one who observes water. One learns how to gauge depth – that which, in essence, is barely discernible, imperceptible (*wei* 微) – through the play of transformations. One learns from water the way one learns from the Sage: one learns to "dive" as deep as it is possible. The "height" referred to in the first proposition is literally reversed: it is none other than that of the pit where one has to descend, rather than spreading oneself over the surface. Considered in this light – considered in its undulations – the paragraph is admirably coherent by the way in which, through the interplay of three propositions (the one located in its middle functioning both as a key and as a principle of reversal), it introduces us to *a way of seeing, an art of scrutinizing.*

Located at the center of Mencius' paragraph, the character *guan* 觀 is defined by the *Shuowen jiezi* as "looking attentively" (*dishi* 諦視). Though accurate, the translation I give of *dishi* remains weak: as the graph of the character *di* 諦 suggests (it evokes the words proffered by the Supreme God), *guan* 觀 has a ritual origin: it corresponds to the twentieth hexagram of the *Yijing*, representing the attitude of the celebrant at a precise moment in the ritual process: "*Guan:* he has washed his hands, but not yet presented the offering, [he shows] sincerity and a serious demeanor [*Guan: guan er bu jian, you fu yong ruo* 觀：盥而不薦，有孚顒若]" (*Yijing, Guan* 1). The moment in question is the one when the officiant, having completed the preparations, is going to perform the sacrifice. His concentration, focused on the coming of the spirits, corresponds to the decisive moment of the ritual: it is when the celebrant does nothing, when he is simply attentive, that the essential happens. "From below, all observe him and are transformed [by this] [*xia guan er hua ye* 下觀而化也]", says the synthetic explanation (*tuan* 彖) of the hexagram (*Yijing, Guan* 1). The ones looking at the officiant are transformed by his way of behaving as well as by the very fact of observing him. The transformation happening in the participants shows that the attitude displayed by the officiant is already performative.

Performativity goes even further: attentiveness provokes not only the transformation of the participants but also the advent of the divine beings for whom the sacrifice is offered.

> He was sacrificing [to the *manes*] as if they were there; he was sacrificing to the spirits as if the spirits were there. Confucius was saying: "If I am not present at the sacrifice, it is as I am not sacrificing".
> 祭如在，祭神如神在。子曰：「吾不與祭，如不祭。」
>
> (*Analects* 3.12)

It is not a skepticism about the existence of *manes* and spirits (*guishen* 鬼神) that the sentence signals, but rather the conviction that their actual presence depends upon the participants. As already noted in Chapters 1 and 3, "feeling" the presence of *manes* and spirits (*gan guishen* 感鬼神) in the course of the ritual is a dominant feature of ancient Chinese religion, still perceptible today in the ethos of popular religion (see Li 2017, 163–180 and 517–521). However, the process of religious normalization undertaken by the literati, especially from the period of the Song dynasty onwards, has tended to make ritual observance a path favoring "interior transcendence" at the expense of any sensitive manifestation.

The Art beyond All Arts

The ritual origin of the term *guan* does not exhaust its meaning. The character occurs in the first chapter of the canonical version of the *Laozi:* "Rooted in the absence of desire, one contemplates (*guan*) the mystery of the Constant; rooted in desire, one contemplates its manifestations [*chang wu yu yi guan qi miao chang you yu yi guan qi jiao* 常無欲, 以觀其妙; 常有欲, 以觀其徼]." Whatever the difficulties raised by the conciseness of the expression (my translation is tentative), it hints at the fact that *guan* applies just as well to what is deep, subtle, hidden (*miao* 妙) as it does to things manifest, located at the outermost (*jiao*徼). Said otherwise: the art of contemplation can focus both on the center and on the borders. One contemplates the same mystery by one or the other of its faces: the marvel of the "there is not" which gives birth to the "there is", the latter manifested by the multiplicity of beings, all of them being animated by desire (*yu* 欲) and all of them eventually returning to their origin.

This return to the origin is the subject of the second significant appearance of the *guan* character in the *Laozi:*

> Reaching the extreme of vacuity, I firmly hold quietness. All beings are activated, and I contemplate their return. Every living being flourishes, each of them returns to its roots. Returning to one's roots, this is called quietness, which means turning towards one's fate. Turning towards one's fate is called Constancy. Knowing Constancy is called Illumination.
> 致虛極, 守靜篤。萬物並作, 吾以觀復。夫物芸芸, 各復歸其根。歸根曰靜, 是謂復命。復命曰常, 知常曰明。
>
> (Daodejing 16)

Contemplating an *object* (or even the absence of it) is not the spiritual practice undertaken by Laozi. The paragraph focuses on a *cycle* and, specifically, on the return (*fu* 復). This may indicate an additional degree of interiorization compared to Mencius' contemplation of water.[125] The character *fu* speaks of the movement specific to the Way, manifested by the cycle of water, or yet the cycle of the seasons, the return of the leaves to the soil and the roots, forming the humus. It is through this contemplative observation that a "light" (*ming* 明) breaks through, illuminating from within not only the laws that govern all phenomena but also their source.

---

[125] The point is debatable: after all, Mencius says that we observe water *by looking at its waves*.

The way classics nurture in us the art (*shu* 術) of contemplation (*guan*) does not apply only to our way of looking at the world, but also at our way of reading these same classics. It notably invites us to look beyond the apparent meaning so as to pay more attention to the hidden dynamic that allows for the deployment of the meaning throughout the text.

Attentive observation (contemplation) is an *art*. Let us note two other occurrences of the character *shu* 術 in the *Mencius*:

> Is the arrow-maker less humane than the breastplate-maker? The arrow maker only fears that arrows won't hurt; the other only fears that they will hurt. The same goes for the healer and the coffin maker. Thus, one could not be too careful in the choice of one's art [profession] [*shu*].
> 矢人豈不仁於函人哉？矢人唯恐不傷人，函人唯恐傷人。巫匠亦然，故術不可不慎也。
> (*Mencius* 2 A.7)

> There are many techniques [*shu*] in teaching. [So,] he whom I do not deign to teach, that is how I teach him – and that is all.
> 教亦多術矣，予不屑之教誨也者，是亦教誨之而已矣。
> (*Mencius* 6B.16)

Shu 術 is both what constitutes your livelihood and a way of proceeding that you have incorporated. It defines who you are – how you see yourself, how others see you. But the way you relate to what you are and what you know can differ greatly from individual to individual, and it is this difference that the last chapter of the *Zhuangzi* (*Tianxia*) will thematize and systematize:

> How many are the experts at governing the world! And all of them think that nothing is lacking [with respect to their expertise]. What was called of old the Art of the Way [*daoshu*], where can it be found? Let us respond; 'No place where it would not be there!'
> 天下之治方術者多矣，皆以其有為不可加矣。古之所謂道術者，果惡乎在？曰：「無乎不在」。
> (*Zhuangzi* 33.1)

The prince's advisers, like the makers of arrows or coffins, are merely the bearers of a given method. Simply, less modest than the craftsmen, they believe that their method has universal application and value. However, in this passage, the *shu* that they master is qualified by the character *fang* 方. *Fang* originally refers to a tillage implement; then, to a territory – probably initially to the farming plot, but, little by little, *fang* will designate large and small territories, and even the directions towards which the territories are ordered. It is probably the fact that the character designates both an *anchoring* and a *direction* that confers to it the meaning of "method". The art of government – any art – is therefore a *local* method, but the myopia of all those who are rooted in a territory, in a "field" or a "discipline" prevents them from perceiving how restricted is the field of application of the technique they master.

In contrast, the Art of the Way (*daoshu* 道術) has no fixed place – it is found everywhere and nowhere – because it is rooted neither in a domain nor in a technique. The other chapter of the *Zhuangzi* where the term *daoshu* occurs features a pond that sustains a colony of fish:

> The appearance of fish is shaped in water, and the human appearance is shaped in the Dao. Whatever takes shape in water knows all about the pond [in which it resides] and takes its subsistence from it. Whoever takes shape in the Dao does not worry about how to ensure one's living. Thus, it is said: the appearance of fish disappears in lakes and rivers, and the human appearance disappears in the Art of the Way [*daoshu*].
> 魚相造乎水，人相造乎道。相造乎水者，穿池而養給；相造乎道者，無事而生定。故曰：魚相忘乎江湖，人相忘乎道術。
>
> (Zhuangzi 6.6)

In other words: in due time, one no longer distinguishes a person who has melted into her vital environment from her environment itself. The way in which the Dao proceeds becomes the motion that propels those who live in its "atmosphere". The vital environment which gives us a specific shape ends up innervating us into its own form. And it so happens that the process of the Dao is that of a "formless form": "The great [i.e., perfect] image has no shape" (*Daodejing* 41). The *Tianxia* chapter of the *Zhuangzi* quotes the words of Guan Yin 關尹, whom it makes the contemporary or close disciple of Laozi:

> [For the one] who lets nothing settle within herself [who lets nothing take possession of her innermost], the forms of all things are made manifest. Her motions are like water, her stillness like a mirror, her responses like an echo.
> 在己無居，形物自著，其動若水，其靜若鏡，其應若響。
>
> (Zhuangzi 33.5)

Ultimately, the observance of ritual ethos and the deciphering of textual dispositions will lead both readers and practitioners beyond figures, motives and codes. In stillness as well as in motion, followers of the Way enter its innermost: the province of the Formless, out of which all forms and all patterns originate.

Chapter 5
Comparative Classics, Comparative Philosophy

The preceding chapter has attempted a general reading of ancient Chinese classics, and has done so by focusing on some features which, in my view, need to be kept in mind when "comparing" Chinese philosophy with other thought systems and worldview. I have insisted upon the fact (a) that by fostering attentiveness, Chinese classics nurture an experiential form of thinking; (b) that they mean to *achieve* something, endowing signs, graphs and texts with a special, performative status; (c) that they focus less on notions than on patterns; and also (this point would deserve further developments) (d) that they do not absolutize these patterns but rather work towards their assumption: "The perfect image has no shape" (*Daodejng* 41) – a sentence that also applies to the encoding of the Way that classics operate. The combination of these features creates a given *style*, a style that any comparative endeavor needs to appreciate and respect. At the same time, identifying such features may help us to highlight characteristics present in other thought systems, as rhetorical features bear upon our understanding of their authors' ways of proceeding and ultimate motives. This chapter will keep in mind the Chinese style of thinking as it starts to articulate more general, more theoretical propositions.

From Notions to Motions

Throughout the course of the first three chapters, I have at times directed criticisms towards current attempts at doing philosophy comparatively. This should not hinder us from recognizing their merits: they put into relationship traditions of thought that, for centuries, were following parallel trajectories. They show much creativity in their way of rethinking and re-interpreting concepts and categories that their positioning into specific languages and systems had sometimes stultified. They renew the issues that world philosophy can and should confront. Actually, the difficulties with which several of these attempts are meeting may be summarized by one question: what does it mean to "compare" philosophical traditions? Can it be truly equated with the fact of establishing sets of contrasts? Let us risk a tentative definition of the method and purpose associated with a renewed understanding of what "comparative philosophy" is about:

Doing comparative philosophy means to think and operate dialogically, i.e., to unceasingly circulate from one's original tradition to the thought and corpus with which a privileged and transformative relationship is taking shape. And when several thinkers starting from different standpoints are consciously engaged into the same task, then this dialogical relationship becomes *mutually transformative* of the traditions being considered.

I now explore the consequences of the definition I have just formulated. I will start by some quick remarks about the first period of the Sino-Western philosophical encounter (c. 1600–1730), remarks that do not aim at drawing an historical picture of the events it triggered but rather at anchoring what will follow into a point of departure. Afterwards, I will address two questions: (1) What does "thinking dialogically" entail? (2) How can we read and interpret texts (classics) interculturally? The developments authorized by these two questions will help us to suggest, not exactly a method, but rather a *style* congruent with the approach to comparative philosophy I suggest here.

The process through which Aristotelian and scholastic vocabulary and logic were introduced into China has aroused great interest in recent years.[126] The conclusions to be drawn from these studies remain uncertain: the first attempts to translate Aristotle into Chinese were very partial and still embarrassed by problems of terminology that would take much time to unravel. Missionaries themselves were not in agreement as to the importance to be given to the introduction of Western philosophy, or to which system to favor. Moreover, they were relying on the philosophy and logic textbooks they had used during their studies in Europe (first and foremost those used at the Jesuit college of Coimbra, Portugal) rather than on Greek originals. Their thought was permeated by scholasticism and Aristotelianism, even if Jesuit training was far from being influenced solely by Thomism. It is therefore less in a particular text or translation than in the way they argued and organized their works that one can discern how Western philosophy entered China. This is especially true during the 17th century. From the 1680s onwards, the arrival of French missionaries went hand in hand with a less Aristotelian and more Cartesian tone. More importantly, missionary culture began to be shaped by the in-depth assimilation of Chinese texts, notably of the *Four Books*, which were translated, studied, commented upon, which quite naturally changed the style of argumentation. Some Jesuits – François Noël (1651–1729) for instance – even apprehended and appreciated the logic and concepts proper to Neo-Confucianism, whereas Ricci and his immediate successors were referring only to "original" Confucianism, latter-day expressions being in their view contaminated with Buddhism (Meynard 2018). We must therefore avoid a narrow focus on how such or such a notion was (mis-)translated into Chinese, which would privilege an analysis too philological or conceptual in scope. It is better to take the texts produced throughout a given period of exchange as a constantly evolving whole, and to evaluate their circulation and practical impact. In this overall process, the Aristoteli-

---

126 Han (2000); Meynard (2015); Witek (1997).

an and scholastic concepts did not represent an isolated continent, and the misunderstandings that occurred around words or characters used in treatises and discussions did not make a meeting of thought and mind impossible. As is the case for all social processes, the one that guides intellectual encounters is messy. And it continuously evolves and develops.

It remains true that polemics bearing specifically on terms on characters and notions to be used, did occur, notably when it came to the Aristotelian concept of "cause" and that, fundamental in all ancient Chinese philosophy, of "transformation" (*hua* 化). In the first chapter I have shown that, when related to the entirety of their respective systems, the opposition between the two is less absolute than generally thought to be. Still, the writings of Matteo Ricci and Giulio Aleni (1582–1649) are already marked by this clash between two logics, which reverberates on the understanding of the Christian concept of creation. Charles Jones aptly sums up the philosophical nature of the confrontation:

> The Jesuits learned from their [textbook commentaries] the Aristotelian view that things do indeed transform from one thing into another, but there is one crucial difference. While the Chinese saw the process of transformation as smooth and seamless, the Jesuits posited a hiatus between a thing and its derivatives: Air does not turn into fire; it returns to subtle being and emerges from that state into fire. This insistence on a hiatus between that which transforms and that which becomes ensured that causes would remain separate from effects.
> (Jones 2016, 1265)

It remains that the stress should be on the fact that such a debate has been *mutually transformative:* Today, while the study of "logic" as a discipline in China basically follows the model of causation and effects, Aristotelian argumentation no longer appears as a necessary component of Christian theological reasoning. Among other potential pitfalls, it is recognized that it risks distorting the meaning given by the authors of *Genesis* to the creation narrative. If the conceptual debates were probably, and for all parties concerned, the most frustrating of those that engaged Christian missionaries with Chinese literati, they retrospectively relativize the debates that merely center around notions, encouraging one to focus upon the way a sharing of experience among protagonists may produce durable effects. This is the process that Xu Guangqi was inciting Niccolò Longobardo (1565–1655) to delve into when the latter was working on a memoir on Chinese religious worldview – but Longobardo, gathering arguments meant to prove the atheistic nature of Chinese thought, was far too engrossed with scholastic logic and concepts for paying attention to the inner spiritual life of the Converts, who were suggesting to him that a given term could easily be substituted by another one.[127] Still, the thought process and encounter became progressively, almost naturally *experiential*, for example when the Jesuits began to read the *Zhongyong* through certain categories of the *Spiritual Exercises* of Ignatius of Loyola, which describe the *movements* that stir the conscience during self-examination (Mei 2013). This attempt at interpretation – inseparable from an attempt at translation – was incomplete, no doubt partly unconscious, and it possibly produced other kinds of misunderstanding (does one ever progress in understanding other than by dissipating one misunderstanding after another?). But such an interpretative engagement was not only creative but also faithful in spirit to an authentic Confucian intuition: one that refuses to separate meditation from action, and vice versa. On this ground, Jesuit and Confucian conceptions relating to the mutually reinforcing relationship between the discernment of inner motions and engagement into the world were able to come together, this beyond conceptual differences. We will come back to some of these points in the next chapter.

Models of Dialogue

The above already specifies one of the two questions raised at the beginning of this chapter: practically speaking, what does the fact of *meeting and thinking dialogically* mean? Roger Ames presents us with a pessimistic understanding of what "dialogue" entails in the Western tradition:

> In the early days of the Western philosophical narrative, "dialogue" as a form of conversation comes to be understood rather explicitly as "talking through"[128] an issue with the purpose of arriving at truth through the dialectical exchange of logical arguments. For Plato, dialectic is a rational, synoptic ascent in search of "unhypothezied principle (eidos)," while for Aristotle, dialectic entails an analytical descent in the process of taxonomic categorization. I would suggest that it is this understanding of "dialogue" [...] that has allowed philosophy as a professional discipline with its univocal method of "rational argument" and its impatience with any other putative approaches to acquiring knowledge, to become a monologue in its relationship to alternative philosophical traditions. Philosophy understood in such terms can speak, but it

---

127 On this episode, central for the understanding of the "Term Controversy", see notably Longobardo (1701); Maître (1949); Standaert (1988), 83 ff.; Gernet (1982), 45–58.
128 Let me note that translating *dia-logos* by "talking through" is debatable. I prefer the commentary made by Raimon Pannikar: "Dialogue does not seek primarily to be *duo-logue*, a duet of two *logoi*, which would still be dialectical; but a dia-logos, a piercing of the logos to attain a truth that transcends it" (Pannikar 1979, 243).

cannot listen. A dialogical understanding of philosophy that in its very definition assumes such a monopoly on knowledge might not be open to conversation.

(Ames 2007, 36)

Let me here attempt to *think about dialogue dialogically*, i.e., to mobilize the variety of resources through which dialogue, conversation, exchange or yet *disputatio* are considered, so as to distinguish among the *models of dialogue* that influence the way cross-fertilization – including philosophical cross-fertilization – actually takes place.

Is dialogue the object of a specific field of knowledge? The answer is a qualified "no". For sure, the study of dialogue (the study of the strategies that allow for its unfolding as well as of its social and epistemological implications) aims at constituting itself into an autonomous discipline (sometimes labeled "dialogism" or "dialogic"). However, "dialogue" is less an *object* than a *locus*, a knot, a place of confluence, the examination of which requires that it be broken down into questions relating to disciplines and traditions that are not so easily reduced to each other. The study of dialogue (its conditions, its styles and its implications) is subordinated to the issues that mark out specific fields such as "communication sciences", interreligious dialogue, or yet social sciences when they focus upon the dynamics of labor disputes or international relations for instance.

The difficulty of carrying out an autonomous study of "dialogue" stems in large part from the fact that the word belongs to a class of terms called upon to constantly enlarge their meaning(s) and references – for dialogue happens everywhere. At the same time, the widening of the term goes hand in hand with a specification of the "style" of the activity it refers to. To put it otherwise: the term "dialogue" today preferentially designates a set of attitudes and practices likely to govern the norms of communication to be found in the family, at school, at the office, in therapy, or in exchanges between peoples and cultures. It is the word *style* that matters here – style of communication and style of life inseparably – a *dialogical style* capable of extending to all areas of human activity. However, the generalization of the dialogical style is first of all that of a mode of communication governed by rules, norms and values inscribed in (Western-inspired) modernity. If this is the case, we can understand the reluctance that can be aroused in other cultures by extending dialogical style to all areas of social activity, for example to family relations, to political sociability or to the spiritual and religious field. (Obviously, a "dialogue" between humankind and the godhead constitutes a meaningless proposition for some religious traditions.) The interest in dialogue cannot be "neutral": the description of the rules governing the functioning of dialogue (and the explanation of its possible dysfunctions) does not easily separate cultural, logical, epistemological and ethical registers. "Dialogue" seems to be far too much anchored in the axioms that govern Western modernity for constituting a neutral, objective methodology.

Our questioning of its apparent neutrality is redoubled by the fact that the term dialogue, in its current meanings, is embedded in a network of notions that it is often difficult to untangle. At a first level, "communication", "exchange", "conversation" or "interaction" act as quasi-synonymous or referential notions. At a second level, terms like "empathy" or "tolerance" suggest the programmatic nature of any dialogical style. The polysemy of the concept cannot be eliminated by a simple terminological "cleaning". Its ambivalences are linked to its history, to its most recent developments, to the cultural baggage that it necessarily carries with it.

We thus need to approach "comparative philosophy" in its dialogical dimension by reflecting upon the cultural depth of the term dialogue and the practices it covers and/or uncovers, sketching out a path: one that starts from the *fragility* of dialogue (notional fragility, fragility of the exercise) in order to think about the universality that constitutes its horizon – and, conversely, to think about "universality" as necessarily sharing the fragility that characterizes dialogue.

There remains a preamble to formulate: there is a constitutive difference between a "conversation" – an oral exchange carried out in a context that defines its rules[129] – and a "written" dialogue (exchange of philosophical letters and arguments for instance), which often seems to be constituted by a series of alternated monologues. Yet, we are dealing here with dialogue as a whole, in the totality of its oral and written expressions, and this because of the circularity that brings them together: not only will a dialogue held orally receive later on a canonical embodiment (this is the case of the Socratic dialogue, or of the conversations recorded in the *Analects*), but also written, canonical dialogues will give way to renewed oral exchanges. Therefore, oral and written dialogues develop over time as in chain. It is precisely their propensity to continue and spread further that will retain our attention.

"Exchanging" Words

The very term dialogue introduces us to the realm of the *exchange of words*. "Exchanging words" enables the interlocutors to test whether or not they share some basic assumptions about the fields of knowledge on which the exchange will

---

[129] For instance, the rules of dialogue in a classroom are not the same as in a United Nations forum.

bear.[130] Knowledge can be of two types – either it relates to a science, for example physics, or it relates to the human being in her nature and her being in society. In the first case, the exchanges take place at the same level of reality as the practical experiments and theoretical formulations through the dialectical sequence of which knowledge of reality progresses: they verify facts and consistency. In the second case, the truth is not mathematical. Its *locus* is that of histories and cultures, to which, in a privileged way, dialogue gives access. It is no longer a question of *verifying* but of *establishing* a relationship, and, in the dialogical exercise, the bringing into relation is reflected in the fact that speaking is coupled with listening. The very mention of the term dialogue and the attention to its contexts therefore makes one distinguish among *orders of truth*. Put otherwise, the determination of different "orders of truth" is linked to the establishing of (logical) relations and of (human) relationships, each of the modes of these connections qualifying as "dialogic style". Let me specify how the joint determination of orders of truth and dialogic styles operates:

- Dialogue understood as a *mere logical exercise* intends to identify propositions that are universally valid and included in a system based on non-contradiction. It is not fundamentally different from what would be the soliloquy of a scientist establishing the validity of a scientific proof. Yet even in the Aristotelian dialectic, the presence (sometimes implicit) of an interlocutor is required in order (a) to ground the principle of non-contradiction (*Met.* Γ4, 1006a); (b) to found propositions which do not belong to the strict domain of science but rather to that of opinion (*doxa*). In other words, in Aristotle, styles of discourse are differentiated according to the nature and hierarchy of truths one is trying to establish (*Met.* B1). More generally, the soliloquy – philosophical or deliberative – is already a *dia-logical* exercise.
- Socratic dialogues are written in a dramatic fashion, the tension being provided by the fact that the very possibility of reaching an agreement will be tested in different ways. They are sort of short dramas culminating in success or failure, with the trial of Socrates illustrating the intensity that dialogical confrontation can ultimately achieve. Livio Rossetti has shown that the formulation of the rules governing Socratic dialogues coincided with the sudden generalization of the term "philosophers" at the very end of the 5th century BCE: the "coding" of the dialogical exercise and the invention of the figure of "the lover of wisdom" were parts of the same enterprise. Besides, the birth of philosophical dialogue as a literary genre coincided with a marked decline in the production of new tragedies (Rossetti 2011, 216–217). At a second level, the literary format-

---

[130] For a history of Western-style disputations, see Weijers (2013).

ting of the Socratic dialogues corresponded to an epistemic posture developed by their writer – Plato: Truth is the discovery of unity in and through the multiple, and it is realized and represented by the progressive unity achieved between the protagonists of the dialogue – or else it remains veiled by disagreements and rhetorical loopholes (see Cossuta and Narcy 2001). The dialogical form works as a device for operating *emplotment*.
- In a scholastic-type dialogue, the reference to the principles of "natural light" (i.e., to the shared exercise of reason) is strictly regulated by a textual reference: the texts recognized by the doctrine in question (the canon) define the order of principles and references accepted. The principle of non-contradiction is then exercised within the reading of these texts.
- In contrast, a dialogue of sapiential and educational type, of which the *Analects* of Confucius provides a prime example, is first of all a "dialogue of life" which aims at ensuring that acts and convictions coincide. Dialogue is the gateway through which to make Truth, Path (*dao*) and Life coincide, pointing out the gap that still separates them.[131] Dialogues found in the gospels are very close to this model, but are less *sapiential* in scope than based on a *discernment* to be exercised in the here and now: the emphasis is usually placed on the decision which must come out of the exchange (cf. the dialogue between Jesus and the rich young man in Mark 10, 17–31).
- We could then distinguish different models of "enlightenment" dialogue, in which the *Zhuangzi* or (much later) the Zen Buddhist tradition participate: the dialogue is pushed to a point that precisely breaks the principle of non-contradiction and brings one of the participants to a sudden transformation. In the *Zhuangzi*, in one instance the questioner's "enlightenment" is even expressed by the fact that he falls asleep before the "master" has finished answering (this to the latter's great pleasure: sleep is a sign that the interlocutor has "seen" the inanity of his questioning). The questioner's entry into sleep also avoids the "master" (who did not want to become one) the embarrass-

---

[131] Donald Holzman has given an insightful account of the Chinese "conversational tradition": "It is in the discussion of particular facts of human existence that Confucius, and after him the philosophers in the conversational tradition, produce their particular insights, short, incisive stabs, into the human condition. To organize his insights into a system would be to devitalize them; therefore, his disciples have tried to keep them as close to their original, particular, concrete form as possible and have preserved these Conversations or sayings on different particular occasions. The same can be said for all the later philosophers in the conversational tradition. And the fact that this can be said for later philosophers is important: it shows that the form of the Conversations is not an archaism, the fumbling attempt of the first Chinese philosophers to put their ideas, pell-mell, into some sort of order, but is an integral part of Confucius' thought, and, indeed, an important clue to the character of Chinese thought in general" (Holzman 1956, 226).

ment that would have been the forced acquisition of a disciple (cf. Defoort 2012). In this dialogic style, an exchange conducted in truth always implies the reluctance of one of the interlocutors to engage in the exercise. Dialogue then arises on the verge of an "in spite of myself", on the basis that (as Confucius famously puts it) "I would prefer not to speak [*yu yu wu yan* 予欲無言]" (*Analects* 17.19).

- Finally, there is what one might call the "democratic" style of dialogue, the inspiration for which is not only valid for political exercise but also applies to certain models of interreligious dialogue for example. Its principle is that *reciprocal listening must be transformative for all partners who enter into an empathic understanding of the other's positions and experiences.* Such reciprocity is triggered by the necessity of finding a "third term" position which allows decision, coexistence, or (at the very least) continuation of the exchange, as the case may be. Dialogue is then a *producer of truth* in ways other than those provided by the logical confrontation of possibly contradictory or reconcilable assertions: it is the reciprocity of transformations that founds the truth that it establishes. One may here refer to Habermas: "[With the development of democratic societies], the authority of the holy is gradually replaced by the authority of an achieved consensus" (Habermas 1987, 77). And elsewhere: "Only those norms can claim to be valid that meet (or could meet) with the approval of all affected in their capacity as participants in a practical discourse" (Habermas 1990, 93).

More generally, we could label *performative dialogues* all those in which the trust placed in the interlocutor and in the transformative character of the dialogic experience is engaged, and *constative dialogues* those that mean to verify a conformity of fact or opinion, or an adequacy of the theory to the facts. Ordinarily, dialogues do not entirely fall into one or the other of these categories, which rather constitute poles to which a lived dialogue (or its written expression) comes more or less close. It is possible to consider dialogic styles as so many *language games*, the rules of which are associated to different styles of life.[132] In this

---

[132] Wittgenstein uses the term "language games" more flexibly than his commentators sometimes acknowledge. I understand and use the term as he defines it very simply as soon as it appears in his lexicon: "Ways of using signs simpler than those in which we use the signs of our highly complicated everyday language" (Wittgenstein 1969, 17). The fact of using the operational concept of "language game" in order to approach a phenomenon as fluid as the multiplicity of dialogues experience obviously poses a problem. Only the creative openings that such usage allows for can justify it, and it is therefore for the reader to judge.

approach, each dialogic style is a system defined by rules, and these rules allow for a set of "thought experiments".[133]

There is however a major difference between the Wittgensteinian "language game" and the actual practice of dialogue: if the rules governing the former are intangible, the characteristic of a lived dialogue is precisely that *the rules governing the interlocution will constantly change over the course of the exchange*. Actually, Wittgenstein himself offers a vivid example of everyday adaptiveness:

> We can easily imagine people amusing themselves in a field by playing with a ball like this: starting various existing games, but playing several without finishing them, and in between throwing the ball aimlessly into the air, chasing one another with the ball, throwing it at one another for a joke, and so on. And now someone says: The whole time they are playing a ball-game and therefore are following definite rules at every throw. [...] And is there not also the case where we play, and make up the rules as we go along? And even where we alter them as we go along.
>
> (*PI* 83; Wittgenstein 1972 [1953], 39)

We experience the ever-changing character of everyday dialogue on a daily basis: the exchange with a stranger requires avoiding at the start certain subjects (money, family) and certain ways of expressing oneself (cracking a joke may be risky). The way the exchange evolves will modify the rules in question, in general to make them more flexible, but also sometimes to make them stricter if certain sensitive subjects or ways of speaking have been spotted. While generally obeying a much slower tempo, intellectual exchanges obey comparable evolutions: the few simple instructions that govern a debate at its beginning will be complexified over the course of the interaction, as the interlocutors negotiate not only on the substance of their exchange but also on the terms governing its rules and dynamic: Chinese and Western philosophers discuss less about "the nature of reality" than on the legitimacy and communicability of the logic and approaches that enter the discussion. Of course, certain styles of dialogue (legal debate, for example) leave very little room for the negotiation or renegotiation of rules, while others (interreligious dialogue as well as comparative philosophy) seem primarily concerned with achieving an agreement on the rules which govern them. The attention we pay to the ongoing transformations in the rules of exchange leads us to go beyond an understanding of dialogic styles as so many "closed systems".

At first glance, the more strongly the formal rules of exchange are codified (as they are, for example, in the scholastic *disputatio*), the "purer" may look the insights allowed by the dialogue. However, one may wonder whether insights do

---

[133] For an example of a Socratic dialogue that presents itself at its beginning as governed by rules similar to the ones governing a "language game", see *Gorgias*, 449c–d.

not surge in the freedom that a "side step" away from the rules may allow rather than in striving for perfect formal expression. It is less the *formalism* of the rule that makes possible the vigor and rigor of an intellectual and spiritual experience than the *radicality* of this same rule, radicality manifested by the extent of the displacement that each of the interlocutors needs to take – displacement from a specialized lexicon, from the academic stage, or yet from one's ordinary life setting.

What precedes can be summarized as follows: (a) different dialogic styles function as so many language games, (b) the rules of which can be negotiated and updated as the exchange progresses, (c) thus blurring the operation of closure of such games, (d) and such language games are all the more "real" as the radicality of the rules which govern the exchange provokes a thought experience transformative of one's life-style.

A Mode of Inhabitation

The constitutive relationship which unites the notions of dialogue and culture is made evident by the sole fact that the place where the passage from "nature" to "culture" takes place is *language*. The arbitrariness of language means that it cannot result from human nature, even if it is inscribed in it. A given language, associated to a collective memory and history, configures a human group. At the same time, human corporeality (nature) is at stake in language (one speaks with the totality of one's body), and thereby in culture. Corporeality continues to be expressed in particular in the privileged place that art holds in any culture and, more generally, in the way in which each culture defines a way of *inhabiting the world*. It is by defining how it relates to the corporeality that founds it that a culture specifies its (artistic, relational, or yet culinary) "styles" – and "dialogical styles" are parts of this cultural set.

The above seems to hint at the *a priori* impossibility of intercultural dialogue, or even of any dialogue between members of different communities, if it was a question of wanting to put in relation mutually unintelligible languages: "We bring numerous only loosely connected languages from the loosely connected communities that we inhabit" (Hacking 1986, 458). However, as we will now see, dialogic styles, as rooted as they are in the particularities of the cultures in which they find form, are also the vectors by which these same cultures are permeable to others, and thus contribute to forge forms of universality.

As already noted, "speaking" is the locus where the incessant (and reciprocal) passage from nature to culture (from corporeality to arbitrariness) takes place. So much so that one can wonder if (as Rousseau wanted it to be) *singing* does not precede *speaking*, if the full deployment of one's voice – progressively detached from the cry so as to become a controlled mode of expression – is not what leads ultimately to articulate speech. However, one can consider in the fact of "speaking" not the act but rather the capacity that authorizes it: the capacity of human organs to emit articulate sounds. The phonatory apparatus is to singing what the foot is to dancing: an immediate bodily anchoring, the use of which can gradually be freed from the constraints imposed by both the subject's primary awkwardness and the requirements associated with survival. It is on this basis that a "social capacity" of singing and dancing develops, which codifies and enriches its cultural expressions.

If song and dance can legitimately appear to be present in any culture and society, the ability to draw lines (to draw figures, design symbols, paint) seems to be just as important for linking nature (here, manifested in the potential shown by the human hand) to symbolic arbitrariness. When the hand is not used for activities directly useful to the subject (grasping or making an object), it explores by drawing the animality from which it proceeds: as shown by parietal paintings, natural forms, animals and even abstract and symbolic forms refer to the "naturalness", which it is now imparted to human gestures to control, as song and dance also do through the symbolic figuration that they perform in space and time. The solidarity of song, dance and drawing stems from their joint symbolic framing of the space-time where walking, speaking and gesturing can then meaningfully take place.

Here, Merleau-Ponty goes a long way: "The first drawings on cave walls were confronting the world as [a reality] 'to paint' or 'to draw', and were thus calling for an indefinite future of painting. This is why they 'speak' to us and why we respond to them with metamorphoses through which they collaborate with us" (Merleau-Ponty 1960, 75 [my translation]).[134] The observation is of primary importance: While they do rely upon the natural capacities of the man to draw, prehistoric paintings nevertheless ground a type of universality which, from the start, is not of the order of our "natural capacities" but rather of "cultural dialogue". First, they are already "dialogical" because they place humankind and the world in a relationship that the entire history of painting will develop – they are the basis of a first "dialogue", that of humankind and its environment, precisely because drawing defines the world as an "environment" to inhabit. Second, they are "dialogical" *a posteriori*, insofar as the gesture of the first painters has called for our task to continue *to inhabit the world by representing it*.

---

[134] The original French reads: "Les premiers dessins aux murs des cavernes posaient le monde comme 'à peindre' ou 'à dessiner', appelaient un avenir indéfini de la peinture, et c'est ce qu'il fait qu'ils nous parlent et que nous leur répondons par des métamorphoses où ils collaborent avec nous."

In each case considered, the passage from walking to dancing, from speaking to singing, and from grasping to tracing includes both a caesura and a continuation. The caesura that takes place is, one might say, a *dialogical rupture:* human representations reveal the anchoring of humankind in its "nature" by simultaneously uncovering the fragility of a symbolic order that no gesture can close and that remains alive by the very fact that it continuously evolves throughout dialogue and exchange.

A Fragile Access to Universality

Dialogic styles produced by various cultural matrices entertain among them relationships marked with the seal of universality. Paradoxically, such an imprint comes from the fact that these relationships need to be constantly reworked and continued. There is by nature an *incompleteness* of all dialogues. They can be taken up, pursued, amplified, distorted by other dialogic styles as they travel through space and history. Even today, the *Analects* of Confucius, Socratic or Gospel dialogues as well as scholastic controversies are being continued to the exact extent that their overtures allow them to be reopened. The vulnerability of dialogue is what makes its continuation possible, because particular dialogues can be interrupted and started again, their rules can be negotiated, and their expressions indefinitely transformed.

Dialogic styles are called to be continued and reshaped both by the dialogical experience itself and by the concomitant evolution of the styles of life that first founded them (the ones of the communities gathered around Confucius or Jesus, or the University of Paris at the time of Thomas Aquinas...). We dialogue with because *we live with*. Sometimes, we "live together" without belonging to the same group (this is the case in all multicultural contexts), a situation in which dialogue becomes a necessity: *dialogue or death* – this is often the alternative. The advent of the world *oikumene* illuminates and directs the interconnection of dialogic styles as well as the transformations in the lifestyles associated with them.

Dialogue should then be made a regulating idea, animated by three principles which turn out to be both constative and programmatic: (a) The historical and cultural variety of dialogic styles prohibits any of them from being established as a norm. (b) The current strength of the idea of "dialogical style" (with the Western sources that shape and limit it, as suggested earlier) comes from the way dialogic styles developed in different contexts throughout history are now brought together and transformed. (c) However, the fact that these dialogic styles meet and are transformed also modifies, in a very progressive way, the very modalities of the meeting: a "common habitation" of the *oikumene* virtually leads to the emergence of a "meta-dialogic style", this from the confluence of dialogic styles that enter in contact. To put it otherwise, dialogic styles are universalized (and become factor of universalization) through the fluidity which they exhibit or progressively develop. Fluidity makes a third party enter the game in turn, share the rules of the language game that is played, and, by sharing them, expand and transform them little by little. The more a dialogic style is anchored in living relationships, the more it is inscribed in a given time and an environment, the more it is marked by sinuosity, fluidity – and the more it deploys its own charge of universality, because it lends itself to being creatively continued. Intellectual history could be seen as the fabric of an unfinished conversation, admittedly often cut off but always expecting to be furthered.

Modes of Reading

It is from such a perspective that we can now fruitfully tackle the second question raised at the end of the introduction to this chapter: How can we read and interpret texts (classics) interculturally?[135] I will start again from a statement by Roger Ames. As we will see, the thesis, though accurate in its core, may be weakened by a propensity to systematicity that weakens its relevance:

> There is a failure of interpreters to be conscious of and to take fair account of their own Gadamerian "prejudices." They offer the excuse that they are relying on some "objective" lexicon when the truth of the matter is that this lexicon is itself heavily colored with cultural biases, thereby betraying their readers not once, but twice.
>
> (Ames 2001, 22)

Gadamer actually offers a defense of "prejudice" (*Vorurteil*), described as the necessary path through which "understanding" can gradually take shape. Whereas "prejudice", in English as in German, first designates a judgment passed before all facts have been examined (which may sometimes be justified), the Enlightenment period gives the word the meaning of "ungrounded judgment", ungrounded insofar it refers to the tribunal of "tradition" rather than to the one of "reason". A critical systematization that leads Gadamer to famously declare: "there is a prejudice against prejudices in general" (Gadamer 1990 [1960], 291 – my translation from the original German). For Gadamer, philosophical hermeneutics needs to go through a deconstruction of the anti-prejudices prejudice... We need to recog-

---

[135] I provide in this section a modified, shortened version of theses first published in Vermander (2022c), 87–125.

nize and elucidate our prejudices, even sometimes to critically confirm the validity of some of them, rather than to endeavor to eradicate them as a matter of principle. Let me acknowledge at this stage that the criticisms directed towards the Gadamerian hermeneutics are many: it runs the risk of dissolving the specificity of a given text into an ontology of language; it gives a normative role to the tradition as shaping our sense of aesthetic appreciation; it makes "prejudices" constitutive of our reading. Denis Thouard (Thouard 2002) and others have tried to sketch out the model of a (post-Gadamerian) "critical hermeneutics", which among other features, rehabilitates the philological dimension of the hermeneutical endeavor. I appreciate the fact that these attempts give their full importance to textual criticism as well as to the study of the context and conditions of production of the corpus. I still think that Gadamer's approach (a) can be understood and practiced without falling into the traps highlighted by critical hermeneutics; (b) that it remains central to a *philosophical* thinking on what hermeneutic entails. This being said, I will soon point out some limitations of the Gadamerian project when it comes to the setting-up of a dialogic reading of texts coming from different traditions.

Let us now walk the road that opens up in front of us once we renounce the idea that we could be radically freed from "prejudices" when entering a given cultural corpus – ours or another. "Understanding", for Gadamer, is more than the subjective operation of a "I": "understanding" entails to recognize that we are inserted into an uninterrupted process of transmission where the past and the present constantly meet (Gadamer 1990 [1960], 295). Such an approach does not teach us how to read Chinese (or Western) classics but it certainly speaks to us of what is at stake in the very act of reading and "understanding".

What does it mean to refer to "my" tradition? It is clear that such an act of appropriation is often akin to a claim for identity mixed with intellectual fantasies: one may refer to one's tradition and yet never take the time to read its foundational texts and appreciate its basic tenets. Actually, people who like most to refer to their cultural roots are often the same who develop a stultified version of what such tradition corresponds to. The fact remains that I necessarily come from a tradition that guided me throughout my psychic, intellectual and spiritual development. And this tradition has determined the set of my "prejudices". This is where we meet with Gadamer's reflection on "prejudice" and the debates which resulted from it:

Protesting against the negative connotation of the term, Gadamer finds in prejudices the concrete conditions which shape our experiences, as prejudices function as *anticipations* by which access to the world opens up. At the same time Gadamer recognizes the need to discriminate between prejudices that need to be overcome by critical reason and those in which an embodied human experience is rooted. Still, the criteria for such discrimination have been the subject of many of the criticisms leveled at Gadamer, which do not need to be detailed here. Gadamer offers a general response to these criticisms by locating the horizon of understanding in an "in-between" (*Zwischen*): "understanding" supposes a distance, but a distance which is not insuperable. "Understanding" also supposes belonging to a community, but through a mode of belonging that remains flexible and open. The very act of understanding starts from presuppositions rooted in a given tradition, presuppositions that lead me to discern within a text the "strangeness" which challenges my tradition and allows it to be enriched – a strangeness that the objectivity of historical knowledge cannot point out and that a total closure on my tradition makes me unable to accept. Interpretation and understanding are located in-between tradition (rooted in "prejudices") and objectified knowledge (Gadamer 1990 [1960], 317).

Understanding itself as a reflexive return upon one's tradition, the Gadamerian hermeneutics has not been devised in order to reflect about the experience of dialogically reading the classics of *another tradition* – and reading them in their strangeness which, as in a mirror, speaks of the "strangeness" of the texts to which I am used to refer as being "mine". Still, Gadamer allows for such opening: hermeneutics, he writes, is "participation in a common meaning" (Gadamer 1990 [1960], 297). Now – and the point is of great importance for the journey outlined here – a "common meaning" is constructed in a dialogical way by checking whether my understanding meets that of the other (without necessarily identifying with it). We generally progress in our understanding of an artwork or of a written text – whether this work belongs to our own cultural continent or to that of another community – by deepening our distance from the "pre-understanding" of the work which was obscuring its access. Even in the case of a work that belongs to my own cultural world, a taking of distance (akin to the fact of submitting oneself to the gaze of someone else) turns out to renew my understanding of the cultural expression that I approach. In this respect, all hermeneutics is potentially transcultural, because it needs to carry me beyond my original sphere. Gadamer sums it up by saying that distance (and first of all temporal distance between the work and me) is constitutive of meaning: "As soon as one understands, one understands *differently*" (Gadamer 1990 [1960], 302). This stress on "in-betweeness", on the distance through which meaning is produced, on the inner transformation that takes place as one understands the Other (be the Other a text, an artwork or a person) is what leads Gadamer to consider hermeneutics as a necessarily dialogical endeavor. Entering into dialogue means to think *with* others, and then to consider in return "Oneself as Another" (as Paul Ricoeur puts it). This thread of thought will be dominant in Gadamer's works after the publication of *Truth and Method*.

"Strategic", Naïve" and "Symptomatic" Readings

Keeping in mind the framework developed above, I now intend to formalize models through which to identify the variety of reading operations of which the (Chinese) classics were and still are the subject. Recognizing that the act of reading is characterized by a ductility, an inventiveness of which no modeling can capture the flow, I draw here the outline of seven modes of reading, and I will try at the same time to show how the limits specific to each of these modes allow and sometimes require the passage from the one to the other.

A classic text is usually not discussed "for itself". Its inclusion in an officially sanctioned cultural and/or educational corpus inscribes it within the strategy of the one who places it there: the text becomes a point of anchorage for a given cultural and national community; it transmits a vision, the acquisition of which conditions the mode of reading. It is gathered among other texts, their totality defining the boundaries of cultural and behavioral options considered acceptable by a collective. In other words, the determination of the corpus as the well as the mode of reading the classics determine who holds power and what legitimates it. In Han China, the shaping of state ideology is linked to the determination of a "system of the Classics". They offer the pattern of the cosmological system within which the Emperor plays an ordering role, a role both justified and tempered by the literati, the only ones able to remonstrate with him. Any conflict around the interpretation of the texts becomes of itself a political conflict. It is this observation that leads Anne Cheng to write: "The question of the truth of the Classics has never been asked systematically. [...] Rather, it was the way of understanding and interpreting them that was the problem" (Cheng 1984, 24).

Identifying the strategy that determines a given "mode of reading" does not in any way invalidate the latter. It is merely a way to attempt at "reading the reading" underwent by other readers. It becomes an enterprise of self-elucidation if I consider my own way of engaging with the text, discovering for myself that "reading is [always] at the service of an intention" (*intentioni enim servit lectio*).[136] However, when a reading strategy becomes conscious of its own premises, the reader is faced with a choice: either she pursues her path as if self-awakening had not happened, and then reading dries up, as the text has become consciously instrumentalized. Or, perhaps, the self-elucidation that the reader has reached leads her to engage into another reading mode.

In a way, any reading of the classics can only begin by obeying a given strategy: whoever studies them from within the cultural system that has canonized them

---

136 Guillaume de Saint-Thierry, *Lettre aux frères du Mont-Dieu*, quoted in De Certeau (2013), 205.

does so on the basis of the logic that justified their insertion. Conversely, whoever discovers them from outside necessarily confronts them with the logic of the corpus in which she has grown up, in a way that will be refined as the knowledge of the new textual continent deepens. In any case, the elucidation of my prejudices leads me to want to reach an opposite kind of reading, to approach the text "as it is given", entering a form of "second naivety". The more we discover our presuppositions and our cultural baggage, the more we wish to read with an "empty mind" (*xu xin* 虛心), as Zhu Xi invites us to do, as this would be the only way to capture "the meaning of the Sages [of the authors]" (*The Art of Reading* II 讀書法下). Taking into account the rich philosophical history of the character *xu* 虛, it is necessary to read Zhu Xi's proposition in all rigor: an emptied mind is one which, in its interior, brings to their *realization* (which makes actual, real) the potentialities present in the text that is read.[137]

The desire to enter into a text "as it is given" probably constitutes a mere utopia. When, for example, one studies Chinese texts dealing with Ritual, a careful reading necessarily raises questions that make the reader swiftly take distance from the text: what is actually at stake behind the question of etiquette? How and why is such topic located at the center of philosophical and political elaborations? What other issues does it correlate with? In other words: the "second naivety" (i.e., the wish to forsake any "strategic" intention in reading) does not of itself tell the reader *how to read*. It can even reify a question originally destined to remain in flux: how do we take into account the fact that, when reading *Laozi* or the *Analects*, it is often difficult to determine "what the text is talking about?" To borrow from Northrop Frye's famous saying: "The axiom of criticism must be, not that the poet does not know what he is talking about, but that he cannot talk about what he knows" (Frye 1957, 5). The sentence is illuminating when applied to ancient Chinese texts in which the subject matter appears ever-shifting, evanescent, elusive. This is the case, of course, for the *Laozi*, of which we cannot say whether it is a political, mystical, bodily techniques-oriented, cosmological or yet military treatise (all of the above at the same time, and none of it), but the same observation applies in many ways to the *Mencius* or to encyclopedic treatises such as *Huainanzi* and *Guanzi*. If we widen its field of application, Frye's axiom undermines the dream of an original transparency of the text to which the reading could reach by dint of making himself "innocent" by going beyond successive strata of interests and prejudices. Any text undermines the innocence of anyone who claims to read it "as it is given", if only because the author always provides us with some-

---

137 On the hermeneutic of Zhu Xi, see Berthrong (1991).

thing other than what she was intending to offer: the act of reception changes the nature of the gift.

What I call here "symptomatic reading" corresponds to the search throughout the text for a reality other than the one it seems to speak of – like the therapist who, in the patient's words, listens to the symptoms of what is not said and perhaps not "known" by the patient (at the very least, "she cannot talk about what she knows", as Frye's quote was stating). For example, reading the *Odes*, Marcel Granet finds in them the structure of the seasonal renewal festivals held in the peasant society of ancient China. In *Danses and Légendes de la Chine ancienne*, a work subsequent to *Fêtes et chansons anciennes de la Chine*, the symptomatic reading undertaken by Granet is further theorized upon in Chinese historical accounts, Granet does not find a source of facts to be verified. Rather, he seeks to rediscover the *mental schemas* which organize the selection and the writing of facts presented as "historical", without worrying whether these facts are historical or legendary. The work performed by the imagination on the stories transmitted by tradition, which eventually results in the fixation of the canonical texts, is not primarily of an individual nature: it reveals to us collective representations that we would not reach otherwise.

Confronting the Text as a Text

The reading methods mentioned so far (strategic, "immediate", and "symptomatic") have a common premise, that of taking the text as a *given*. It is against this premise that the "history of forms and sources" works. Taken to the extreme, this mode of reading questions the existence of the very object – the text – it is working upon. The history of forms and sources constitutes the model for the "scholarly" reading of the classics, the one that has dominated the academic field since the second half of the 19th century. Beyond the subdivisions that could be introduced into it, the history of forms and sources approaches the text as a collation of small units corresponding to a micro-form (for example, the proverb). First theorized and implemented in the context of biblical research, this approach greatly influenced how translators and commentators still measure up to Chinese classics today. It leads the critical reader to see all the levels above the micro-unit as the result of an editorial collation, on the whole not very significant: the text, basically, is always "poorly composed"...

In its beginnings, such a line of research started from the idea that the comprehension of texts could only be achieved by retracing the course of their formation and by going back to their source, ridding them of the successive layers added by the tradition. Such an effort involved identifying the *forms* taken by the texts. A *form* is the set of elements that make up the same type of conventional literary unit. Since a form arises in a given situation (a death occurring in a family generates the use of the literary genre of the funeral notice, a harvest festival triggers the genre of songs found in the Hebrew Psalms or in the *Classic of Odes*. *Formgeschichte* (Form criticism) first seeks to identify the *Sitz im* Leben (setting in life) which produces such and such a type of form. However, after World War II, a current often referred to as *Redaktionsgeschichte* (Redaction criticism) partly reoriented the field of research, pointing out that the evangelists did original work determined by the theology they intended to develop; hence the renewed importance to be given to the study of the editorial framework that they had constructed – while nevertheless keeping a historicist perspective: the project of locating the authors and their editorial intentions always implies concentrating on the "anomalies", the "inconsistencies", "contradictions", traces of modifications that the text would have undergone during its development. Today, whatever their differences, *Formgeschichte* and *Redaktionsgeschichte* have combined into what one might call the modern historical-critical method. The historical-critical method is now a prerequisite for any attempt to read the classics. This does not mean that it is unsurpassable. The logic that it deploys cannot amount to the ultimate erasure of the text (and therefore of the very possibility of reading) but rather to the diversification of the text considered into its successive or competing states. The question then becomes to know by which means to relaunch the act of reading.

The realization that a text takes shape through the editorial transformations that it undergoes unveils continuous "textual chains" in place of texts clearly distinguished from one another. In the context of our subject matter, the highlighting of such textual chains triggered renewed interest in the Chinese commentarial tradition (see Henderson 1991). For cultures that see themselves as based on a canon, the approach to the latter was framed by the work of commentators who canonized works that in the process became "Classics". This *modus lectionis* is particularly characteristic of China. As a consequence, Chinese thought and science has been shaped through commentaries on these Classics. At the same time, the question of the distinction to be made between Classics and commentaries is both difficult and stimulating. Challenging a chronological schema which would make the commentaries (*zhuan* 傳) follow the Classics (*jing* 經), Anne Cheng notes that "the texts which we now qualify as canonical only became so when they were the subject of commentaries" (Cheng 1984, 14). So crucial was the importance of the commentarial genre that it has been said that there are as many versions of a given Classic as there are commentaries on it.[138] The perpetuation and the influence of Classics (in particular of Confucian texts) would then be directly related to the elasticity conferred on them by the commentarial enterprise.

Some sinologists now claim that one needs to read Chinese classics "by and with the commentators". They rebel against the tendency, long dominant, to return to the "original text" against the barriers that the Chinese commentators would have erected to prevent its access. The detour through a commentary, or through the history of the reception of the text, is today rediscovered as an exegetical path in its own right. Among these attempts is the one led by Rudolf Wagner, for whom the famous commentary by Wang Bi (226–249) effectively discovers the structure of the *Laozi*. This commentary, writes Wagner, accomplishes three tasks: "the construction of the text into an understandable utterance; the explanation of the philosophic logic behind the text's statement; and the deconstruction of previous constructs enshrined in the mind of the reader" (Wagner 2000, 299). Wang Bi's personal genius led him to develop a highly original hermeneutical strategy while strictly adhering, from start to finish, to the need for internal consistency within the text. Wang Bi was particularly interested in the formal and structural processes of the *Laozi* as well as in its approach of language: the text of the *Laozi* provides us with the very principles that allow for its interpretation.

The genre and hermeneutical enterprise of the classical commentary are arguably not repeatable today. At its apex, its limitations were pointed out already. These limitations may have been triggered by the very success of the genre; essential turned out to be the interiorization allowed by the commentary, an interiorization equivalent to subjectivation. The most striking expression of what such interiorization eventually entails is that offered by Lu Jiuyuan 陸九淵 (1139–1192): "Classics comment upon me, and [by this very fact] I comment upon Classics [*liujing zhu wo wo zhu liujing* 六 經 注 我, 我 注 六 經]" (*Record of Words* I, Lu 1980, 399). This sentence is found in a "record of word" (an oral statement *yulu* 語錄), in which Lu responds to a disciple asking why the Master has not written any commentary of the Classics… Though strikingly short, Lu's answer is clear: a real commentary on Classics is that offered by an existence shaped by their content. From the Song dynasty onwards, the genre of the record taken on the basis of oral teaching, revelatory to a trend towards orality, created new exegetical paths. At the same time, the framework of the interlinear commentary continued to protect the canonical edifice until the beginning of the 20th century when the methodology

---

[138] See Gardner (1990). See also Richard Lynn's introduction to his translation of *The Classic of Changes* (Lynn 1994).

propounded by the history of forms and sources brought together Chinese and Western philologists in a common critical project.[139]

Besides a renewed focus on the commentarial tradition, as described above, another hermeneutical project aims to overcome the dead ends where the historical-critical method engages the reader. This project, which directly challenges the *Formgeschichte* tradition, is centered on "structural rhetoric": the latter method would make it possible to understand the organization of our texts, and therefore to consider them again as "texts" in their own right. What is meant by "structural rhetoric"? In the tradition of the history of sources and forms, one of the reasons that explains the uneasiness felt when reading texts seen as a collation of independent units undoubtedly stems from the primacy that its Western promoters gave (without even discussing it) to Greco-Latin rhetoric – the descriptive and normative model of the composition of a text. Any text that did not fit these rhetorical rules, could not be really "organized", and therefore had to be dissected in order to trace the history of the (awkward) collage of which it was necessarily the result.

That the text can and should be read, understood and appreciated according to the rhetorical processes that structure it is in no way a new assertion. Nevertheless, if from Aristotle to Cicero and Quintilian, Greco-Latin rhetoric was the object of an early theorization, it was much later that it was recognized that different cultures organize the structure and logic of the texts they produce in different ways (argumentative and/or narrative). The identification of the laws specific to Semitic rhetoric began to take place from the 17th century onwards, but these laws have been systematically explored only in recent times.[140] When it comes to Chinese rhetoric, its rules were somehow already theorized in the *Wenxin diaolong* (文心雕龍 – a title tentatively translated as *The Literary Mind and the Carving of Dragons*), a work by Liu Xie 劉勰 (465–522) that focuses not only on stylistic issues (with the *Zhuangzi* as a model) but also on compositional ones – and applies these same rules to itself. Much later on, some writers, including Japanese and Korean ones, turned towards the genre of "rhetorical commentaries", focusing not only on stylistics but also on textual structures. "Readers today do not comprehend the fundamental features of texts (*wenyi* 文義) they read", writes the Korean scholar Wi Paekkyu 魏伯珪 (1727–1798), before noting in a given passage of the *Mencius* the symmetry between its beginning and its end, a ring composition being thus established: "At the beginning of this paragraph, Mencius referred to the use of profit by the King. At the end, he referred to benevolence and rightfulness based on what

---

139 On the encounter between Western and Chinese philologists during the first decades of the 20th century, see Chang (2016).
140 See notably Douglas (2007); Meynet (2012); and my discussion of the debates awakened by the application of the methods of structural rhetoric to ancient Chinese Classics (Vermander 2021a).

was said before, and suddenly dismissed the King's opinion, saying 'Why must Your Majesty use that word profit?'"[141]

Leaving aside a focus on the text as a completed structure, framed for instance as a circle divided into a series of symmetrical fragments,[142] some recent works explore classical Chinese rhetoric as a device aimed at modifying the *habitus* (the usual way of behaving) of the one who enrolls under a given teacher.[143] In the Confucian universe, this perspective helps to strengthen the connection between ritual practices and ethos, on the one hand, and the texts that establish and comment on them, on the other. The *Analects* in particular would constitute a *rhetoric of ritualization:* intended effects on pupils were produced not by words alone but through a combination of discourse and ritualized conducts. Nevertheless, these approaches often fail to offer the sketch of a coherent textual frame, failing to show how the principles they enunciate practically apply. In contrast, the strength of the historical-critical approach remains to function on the hypothesis that the unveiling of such a frame, if it exists, matters less than that of the temporal process which led to the final editing of the text as we know it today.

The Text as Experience

The reading experience can be transfigured into a "garden of affects", writes Michel de Certeau: "The 'savors', the 'taste', the 'fervors' that punctuate it presuppose a reading made up of movements: *motions* and emotions are combined; the *affectus* involves and stimulates a *motus*. *Lectio* is therefore considered an *actio*" (De Certeau 2013, 208). Here, let us borrow an example taken from the ancient Chinese corpus. Asked to explain why Ritual is more important than food or the satisfaction of the sexual appetite, Mencius responds in the following way:

> By twisting your older brother's arm to take what he is eating, you could get food; you can't if you don't – will you twist his arm? By scaling the wall to the east of your property and kidnapping your neighbor's virgin daughter you could acquire a wife; you can't if you don't – will you go and take her away?

---

141 See You (2018), notably 506 and 510.
142 See Vermander (2021a); Pelkey (2021).
143 See Lu (1998); Mao (2007). Xioaye You asserts: "I would like to define rhetoric broadly as the art of modifying human minds and behaviors through symbols. I would argue that the *Analects* is a rhetoric on the multimodality of ritual symbols, dealing with the rhetorical process of symbolic identification and transformation in ritualistic performance" (You 2006, 429). For a different and most refreshing approach to Chinese rhetoric, based on its usage of humor: Harbsmeier (1989) and (1990).

紾兄之臂而奪之食，則得食；不紾，則不得食，則將紾之乎？踰東家牆而摟其處子，則得妻；不摟，則不得妻，則將摟之乎？

(Mencius 6B.1.)

The emphasis of the text is on the twisted arm and the climbing of the wall: representing himself engaged in such an action, the listener or the reader realizes that the ritual is a question of life or death, as Mencius already had said about justice (*yi* 義), comparing life to fish and justice to bear's paw: the gourmet summoned to choose will not hesitate to sacrifice the first to keep the second (*Mencius* 4 A.10.). The saying it intended not only to inculcate a moral teaching but also to make one enter an experiential mode of knowledge.

Stanza 15 of the *Laozi* allows us to go one step further in our understanding of the way such "conceptual metaphors" work:[144] it describes the Sages "cautious as when crossing a river in winter [豫兮若冬涉川]", and "evanescent as ice that begins to melt [渙兮若冰之將釋]". The character *huan* 渙 (melting) corresponds to the 59th hexagram of the *Yijing:* the moment when the weak, through its dissemination, acts in accordance with the strong.[145] In *Laozi*, and beyond, metaphors often speak of a certain type of experiences: the ones that seem to happen in the same time as they are erased (hastening when crossing a river that at any time may start to melt). For there are experiences that require from us a special quality of attentiveness. They come and go throughout the flux of life: the wise traveler threads quickly and lightly on a surface where it is better not to stop. Likewise, the reader must focus not upon a state of things but rather upon a *movement.* If her mode of reading makes her enter into the very center of the text, it also prompts her not to dwell too long on the same text, not to substitute the text for lived experience.

It is likely that ancient Chinese texts were originally composed so as to engage the bodily act of memorizing and reading them aloud into the experience of what they were speaking about. In the context of the *Suwen* 素問 (*Basic Questions*), a medical text, Claude Larre rightly detects an almost therapeutic exercise of the breaths that is offered to the reciter: a Classic is first

---

144 On the notion of "conceptual metaphor": Slingerland (2011).
145 A note from the *Oxford World's Classics* translation of *Laozi* illustrates how an essentially historical-critical reading orients and may distort the interpretation given to the text: noting that the incise of Laozi 15 mentioning the ice which is beginning to melt is not in the *Guodian* version, the translator treats it as a "footnote" and not as an integral part of the text. He therefore sees in it an almost superfluous addition, which describes the Sage remaining isolated (as when the melting ice isolates individuals on separate blocks of ice). The experience suggested by the text is seen in a different light when considering the received version on its own merit and giving its full importance to the mention of the melting ice (cf. Ryden 2008, 33 and 172).

an expression of the vital breath. [...] The breath sustains the continuous flow of the discourse, at the same time as it deforms itself so as to allow the elementary articulation of the characters that organize the sentence into an intelligible whole. This is how one clears the ground for the hand [of the medical practitioner] that will abolish the anomaly and operate the cure.

(Larre 1987, 17)

The thing is facilitated by the structure of the Chinese language, notes Claude Larre, because of the alternation between "full words" (loaded with semantic content) and "empty [or: hollow/function] words [*xuci* 虚词]" which articulate the sentence. The text then becomes "a kind of vertebrate whose movement is carried by function words", and the text thus appropriated by the body of the reader expresses the vital breath which organizes it and passes through it (Larre 1987, 17).

Reading the (Chinese) classics is an operation that can legitimately be carried out through each of the modes considered above, and which, perhaps, invites us to mobilize them in succession. However, in the dialogic perspective studied throughout this chapter, I put special emphasis on the two last modes of reading: structural and experiential.

The first mode focuses on the weft, the invisible weaving of the text, and on the way it articulates details into a whole. A given textual web structures the way of thinking of an era and/or of a cultural sphere. At the same time, its analysis unveils constants, structures of thought, that escape cultural and historical determinism. A linear structure (the one that goes "from A to Z", so to speak) better accommodates causal reasoning and logical progression. A circular structure (which links together the beginning of the text with its end) hints at the completion of a wholly ordered system of thought. Other ways of "composing" a text could certainly be deciphered. One should not attribute too easily such or such rhetorical genre to a culture or another. If some modes of writing indeed predominate at a given period of time, in a given environment, these same modes generally succeed each other, to the extent that their articulations become unintelligible at latter times. Mary Douglas has contrasted historical moments when "repleteness", closure, was preferred, and others privileging open-endedness. "Civilizations may rest on different principles of organization", Douglas was stating. At the same time, within each civilization, there is regular alternance between the stress on "cognitive coherence" and "cognitive opportunism", cognitive coherence showing affinities with ring composition, cognitive opportunism with open-ended (mostly linear) textual structures (Douglas 2007, 146–147).

A dual focus (focus on the way the subject's body is affected by the text, focus on rhetorical composition as revelatory of the mode of thinking that underlies a given textual production) helps us to enter into a cross-cultural, comparative reading of our respective canons. A text – a philosophical text – is not simply an arrangement of notions. As far as it reflects a lived experience and a system of thought that remains alive, it is a living organism: it needs to be apprehended as a whole, as a space where breath circulates. The text is both skeleton and living flesh. Meetings among classics is as such akin to a meeting among persons, not to a comparative evaluation of the respective workings of two mechanics. This is why working with full texts – rather than selected excerpts and catalogues of concepts and definitions – is crucial: you need to meet with the entirety of the text – including its inconsistencies, hesitations and aporias. You need also to evaluate the *effects*, the *affects* that the text exercises upon you.

Some questions will help the reader to enter into dialogue with, say, Chinese classics, and then to reflexively return to the tradition she comes from: listening to the voice that pierces throughout the text, what seems to have been the experience proper to the author (the one triggered by a constant state of warfare for instance, as during the Warring States period in China), the experience that he tries to communicate to disciples and readers? What rhetorical means does the author use in his attempt to make disciples and readers share in the same experience and make it a "thought experience"? Again, let us think about the way Mencius makes all issues discussed become questions of life or death when drawn to their ultimate consequences. This is a rhetorical device; at the same time, it helps us to understand that "rhetoric" is not about empty words or mere "tricks": the rhetorical radicalization of the issues at stake does say a lot about the way Mencius understands humaneness and proper way of behavior. An additional question might be: what are the effects of the text upon myself, and how does its rhetoric influence the way I re-read my own experience, which the text may have reawakened?

The Text as Garden and Body

Let us go back to our "gardening" imagery, imagining textual productions as Chinese gardens. Chinese gardens are "texts" in their own way: you enter into them through an opening, an initial viewpoint (for instance, some gardens in Suzhou have doors shaped in the form of a pear). Such initial viewpoint displaces perspectives, it encourages us to look anew at what surrounds us. Besides, a garden obeys a specific structure, which conveys meaning, it leads us along pathways, and it inserts us into a microcosm, which may help us to think about our setting in the macrocosm. This is akin to what happens when we "stroll" throughout a text without hastening, letting the text lead us where it intends to.

Also, the dreams and worldviews that were embodied into the Chinese literati's psyche could be represented through the garden metaphor. Chinese gardens were often created by scholar-officials aspiring to escape the worries of their offices or who had fallen into disgrace. Accordingly, they could be seen as a dream land, a utopia, a labyrinth of hidden thought ... As peaceful and serene as they remain today, they were built over a sea of worries and sufferings – hence the Buddhist undertones they so often possess.

However, first and foremost, a garden is a living body, complete with orifices, vessels and limbs. Orifices, first ... The garden, a small and secluded place, endlessly increases its size through its internal divisions – mounds that break the perspective, walls running along the walkways, partitions all around its pavilions. But these partitions are pierced by openwork windows, round doors, and numerous small openings through which the walker can appropriate space and sight. The openings suggest the paths to be followed. Windows and doors gradually reveal the garden to our senses, as the painter's hand unfolds with pride and caution the scroll on which he made the roaring waterfall, the trail on the side of the mountain, the grove pines and the sea of clouds come to life... The garden indeed is a scroll, a miniature world opened up and enlarged by our walks and our whims. Pierced with orifices, the garden is irrigated by vessels through which life, breath and seasons circulate... Water animates a garden – water collected in a pond and divided into channels that flow in its interior, water that makes small garden rocks the mimes of formidable mountains. Then, irrigated by the vessels that transform it into a living body, the garden can deploy its limbs, taking the form of a lying dragon, a unicorn, or perhaps one of these Taoist immortals of whom we are not sure whether they are humans or gods. Its limbs are made of its eminences, these modest mountains that transform the pond into a sea, the channels into giant rivers, and the courtyards into continents.

Additionally, a garden can work as a metaphor for not only a text but also a system of thought that continues to grow and evolve, or yet for a community or any kind of living organism – and, ultimately, for the cosmos in its totality. The garden metaphor thus inserts the text (the Classic) into practices and representations from which it is in fact unbreakable.

Entering the garden has also led us to cross the threshold of "comparative philosophy" without having ever noticed it. For the use of the same metaphor helps us to envision the categories of "sameness" and "difference" by associating (rather than by opposing) them. *Sameness:* we are entitled to use the garden metaphor for speaking of all texts that help us to "experience" what it means to think – and therefore to think by ourselves – the way Kant was implying when propounding the *conceptus cosmicus* of philosophy. Gardens as a living space of organic growth speak of all processes of thought organized into a textual construction destined to be appropriated and continued by the reader. *Difference:* we are similarly entitled to contrast Chinese gardens with their French or English counterparts, thus underlining dissimilarities in atmosphere and arrangements. Leisurely pacing gardens that all testify to the same life (and thought) process and yet that differ in the experience they convey does not mean to follow pre-ordained circuits. Wandering about, strolling back and forth, shifting from one path, one perspective to another – this is also part of the philosophical experience.

Beyond Comparative Classics

One may wonder whether the mode of entering into philosophical engagement through the structure/experiential reading of the classics I am suggesting here is not akin to a return to the *modus scholasticus* of "philosophizing" that Kant challenged in the lines evoked at the very beginning of this book. I rather think that this mode of comparatively reading our respective classics triggers two results that ultimately facilitate an understanding of philosophy that is "teleological", in the sense it fosters concerns (as well as a style of interaction) that are activated by a dynamic of continuous universalization.

The first result obtained by the comparative mode of reading described above is to develop a sense of empathy that roots itself into attentiveness – attentiveness to the *experience* and the *intention* that animate a given text, make it a whole, a living body. Let us come back to Gadamer: a "Classic", says Gadamer, is indeed a historical reality (*geschichtlich*) but a reality to which the historical consciousness (*historisch*) is subject insofar as what is "classic" is withdrawn from the fluctuations of time and from the variations of taste registered at a given time. We qualify a work as "classic" because we are aware of something permanent in it, independent of the circumstances. But since a classical work represents the fulfillment of a genre, the culmination of a given style at a given time, the concept also acquires historical significance. (Gadamer 1990 [1960], 292–294) "What in history asserts itself alive in the present is the Classic" (Zarader 2016, 216). Texts are not only objects of objectified knowledge, they continue to be carriers of a word addressed to us in the present. This also means that the empathy through which we are able to discern the present within the past extends to the one and the other tradition we are comparatively investigating. We do not need to "denigrate" or belittle our own tradition in order to discover the strength and novelty of another one, no more that the appreciation of our roots would signify a lesser interest for alternative ways to engage into the act of thinking. Even if his system may not allow for an explicit assertion of what follows, what Kant calls reflective teleological judgments (judgments informed by ends that are both necessary and universal) need to be informed by such empathy, reciprocally displayed and nurtured, and this precisely because they are directed by ends that are *necessary* (thus inscribed into the human condition) and discovered as *universal* (the human condition being inscribed into our common *oikumene*).

Another result is induced by our comparative mode of reading: it allows us to proceed behind and beyond the texts that are read. The stress I have consistently put on the *intentio lectionis* and on the author's ground experience speaks of the fact that hermeneutical attentiveness first proceeds "below" the textual level: it unearths its source, what makes it alive. For the same reason, attentiveness, as displayed throughout the textual journey, projects itself into what the text from the beginning tends towards, the *ends* that it assigns to its readers. Our way of reading enables us to recognize that the text is not an end to itself. A Classic is not a "closed world". It is a vector that aims at drawing us back into the world, transformed by our reading experience. It is outside the classics, and mutually transformed by their reading, that people coming from various traditions are called to meet.

Interpretation and Inventiveness

We thus read *teleologically*, and this is what enables us now to speak of "comparative philosophy" as being carried by the text and yet liberated from the act of reading. The last section of this chapter sketches the task that reading comparatively allows us to engage in, freed from endless debates on texts and commentaries.

We all wish to experience "meaningful" encounters. What we aim at when expressing such a wish refers to an array of feelings and perceptions: some kind of *taste* developing throughout the exchange (the pleasure that arises from conversation, mixing of languages, exoticism, discovery, friendship perhaps); also, a mutual acknowledgment that reciprocal displacements are taking place in the process (broadening of views, change in opinions and prejudices, sharing of emotions and memories, be they collective or personal). Relationships transform, create, carry forward *meanings*, experienced as crystallized perceptions, evaluations and interpretations of facts, people, places, texts or events. Eventually, a "meaningful" relationship develops from or evolves into shared projects and practical cooperation in order to fulfill common objectives.

The first glimpse of "meaning" that appears in a transcultural exchange has to do with the discovery of some *commonality*. However, ordinarily such commonality is not of a positive nature but *rather of a negative one: it is about the sharing of crises and challenges*. This might be true within the framework of metaphysical or religious exchange (the sharing of the fact that we are all mortal beings), but also of cultural and social dialogue. Globalization is first and foremost the globalization of crises and challenges. Global warming, deforestation, waste of natural resources, migrations, crisis in the educational model represent challenges common to all of us, though with varying degrees of intensity and sometimes with stakes that may seem to (provisionally) differ (migration is a case in point), though their solutioning is wished for by all. The feeling of commonality might also arise from the collapse of traditional ways to understand one's world, identity and culture, from the spreading of a culture of violence at school or in society at large, or from the difficulty to implement mechanisms of harmony and reconciliation. What we first share is a feeling of urgency and disarray.

The second stage of the process is to realize anew the *variety of the cultural resources we mobilize or could mobilize for answering such challenges.* If we do confront common problems and crises, it is true also that there remain tremendous differences among worldviews rooted in Taoism, Buddhism, Islam, Christianity or among the core values found in Confucian, African or European societies. On life itself, on authority structures, on relationships with nature or with the Other, on processes of discussion and evaluation, our ground intuitions, logical approaches, canonical texts and ingrained norms of behavior are varied, divergent or contradictory. Furthermore, our cultural traditions are embedded into historical memories that conflagrate one with another. Discovering the wide array of our differences might be, at the same time, exhilarating and extremely puzzling. Thus, our perception of what might well be "meaningful" springs from the crux of "difference", as we ponder over what both unites and separates us.

This is where a strategic choice is to be made. Let me suggest that "meaning" continues to flow and to circulate when we decide to make this tremendous variety of cultural resources the toolbox that enables us to interpret anew our own tradition and culture. Our cultures, worldviews and creeds are being reformulated through the interpretative resources offered by the other cultures, worldviews and creeds – and this operation happens simultaneously for all participants in the exchange. Such interpretative process can become a sophisticated intellectual endeavor when, for instance, it aims at re-interpreting Christian theological categories through the concepts and vocabulary of Mahayana Buddhism – or at reading Chinese philosophical tradition through the conceptual arrangements found in the West, as were attempting to do some of the New Confucianists we encountered in the course of our third chapter. At times, the attempt to reinterpret one's tradition through the resources offered by another cultural corpus can be pretty straightforward. I remember a Chinese friend, expert in Daoist scriptures and history, whom I was asking what his projects were now that he had completed a major publication. He answered me that, for some time, his contacts with Christianity had convinced him that the success met by this particular religious form throughout the world had to do with its capacity to confront the challenges of modernity, making its thought and vocabulary evolve and develop with the modernization process. He wanted, he told me, to comparatively explore the ways through which Daoism could similarly become a truly "contemporary" religious form. Similar reflections and intellectual endeavors have taken and are taking shape in innumerable minds and circles. Each time, the evolving relationship with the Other makes this very relationship the set of interpretative resources, through which I assess and reformulate my own identity. In this perspective, all cultures, creeds and worldviews are perpetually reshaped, are ever-evolving, and what defines them is never taken for granted but rather is being discovered *and* challenged throughout the process of exchange and interpretation. Thus, the core of our identity is never "behind" us, it is always "beyond"; it is related to the Other whose identity is similarly challenged and reshaped.

We enter into dialogue so as to cross-interpret our own tradition through the wisdom, sensitivity and tradition that belong to an Other by birthright, so to speak: we borrow our tools from another toolbox. Through this process, we invent "localized solutions" that have gone through a "globalized" interpretative process. At the same time, this ever-evolving reshaping of one's culture, creeds and worldviews does not lead to a confusion or a mix, it defines and sometimes sharpen one's sense of belonging and core values. Though identities are mobile and changeable, they are still discrete entities, and the solutions to our common challenges will remain localized, different in the way they are conceived of and implemented. However, throughout the interpretative process, these particular solutions will considerably vary from the ones suggested by the traditional understanding of one's culture and identity, and the array of solutions devised from one's culture or group to another will then be legitimately understood as a correlated set of attitudes, choices and decisions.

Translation, Memory and Imagination

Two points here deserve qualifications. First, the standpoints that define people's and cultures' sense of crisis and identity take place in the diversity of their languages – verbal and non-verbal. Furthermore, within a given society, endeavoring to mutually "translate" the various sets of symbolic and rational languages that coexist within the social and political field is also a requisite. For instance, marginal groups are confronted with a discourse originating from power centers, such discourse being also legitimized by the style and vocabulary of globalized, technocratic English. In this perspective, intercultural exchange is about allowing a group of people to express itself in its mother tongue while giving them the means to understand other participants' mother tongues and being understood by them. This is a highly sophisticated process – and yet, a task that requires much more than the setting-up of sophisticated technical procedures. In this respect, the "global ethics" that the world community is insistently looking for is inseparable from the translation process itself. In many ways, it is the fact of sticking to the interpretative process that constitutes the global ethics. To put it another way, a global ethics *is* a language ethic.

Another point bears upon the model of interaction sketched above: in the process I am sketching, particular importance is to be given to "memory" and "imagination". Here, another metaphor may be of help: in Renaissance Europe, the construction of a "Memory Palace" (part of the *ars memorativa*) was a way to remember a store of knowledge, the material repository of which you could not easily access. By walking through the rooms of a building that you had built in your mind, you were able to find the image associated with a set of data at the place where you had stored it. The striking character of the images involved was a determining factor for memorizing them easily. A second principle was equally important: "To everything that we wish to remember, wrote Matteo Ricci introducing the method to the Chinese, we should give an image, and to every one of these images we should assign a position where it can rest peacefully until we are ready to reclaim it through an act of memory" (Spence 1984, 92, referring to Ricci 1596).

Due to his Jesuit background Ricci may have been especially sensitive to the role played by memory for educating people who would be skilled both at self-knowledge and at successful communication: Ignatius of Loyola' *Spiritual Exercises* put the stress on "memory and imagination": during the course of a spiritual retreat, one's time of prayer starts with "a composition, seeing the place": one focuses on a "corporeal place, as for instance a temple or mountain" or else on representing "with the sight of the imagination" an invisible reality.[146] Imagination works together with memory. *Remembering* is a struggle against forgetting, a struggle that requires from you to mobilize some means to that effect. Ricci speaks of letting an image you have stored "in a position where it can rest peacefully until we are ready to reclaim it", but this involves having first arranged the respective positions of your troves of images through reflective attempts at optimal architectural disposition, to be repeated each time you enlarge the Memory Palace.

Interestingly enough, Ricci recommends to build up *fictive* Palaces of Memory – or at least "half-fictive (*ban shi ban xu* 半實半虛)" (Ricci 1596) – rather than following an existing model. This way, he says, the Palace can be expanded at will, whereas relying on something one knows too well limits the future expansion of the Palace and the subsequent storage space. The Memory Palace stores the stories and figures that we gather in the course of our quests, *but it does so within a struc-*

---

[146] Cf. Ignatius of Loyola, *Spiritual Exercises*, n. 47 (Fleming 1996, 42).

ture, a form, a space that is called to perpetually expand. This might be an apt metaphor for speaking about the continuous enlarging of our sensitivity and intellectual empathy called for by the very fact of entering a new model of intercultural dialogue. Understood this way, "comparative philosophy" requires from us to perpetually broaden the space in which we meet in truth with the Other, so we may be mutually transformed, evolving and growing in ways that we could never have foreseen.

Chapter 6
Exploring New Gardens

Are there philosophical conversations that currently develop in accordance with the dialogic spirit of comparative philosophy suggested in the course of the preceding chapter? This question guides the selection of the four topics that I will soon introduce, as I intend to outline ways to crisscross Chinese and Western resources in ways akin to the experiential-teleological model I have tried to describe. These four topics differ in their degree of formalization as well as in the interlocutors participating in the debates they generate. Whatever their limitations, and notwithstanding the aporias with which they sometimes meet, these same debates constitute suggestive attempts at crafting modes of reading and arguments that exhibit multicultural sensitivity.

I will first examine what Western thinkers have learnt from the Chinese traditional focus on "Ritual", and how such concern about a given *topic* has generated, or is starting to generate, some shifts in the *style* of exchange. In a second part, I will reflect upon the attempt by the philosopher Bai Tongdong (mentioned towards the end of our third chapter) to confront global political issues equipped with the resources proper to ancient Chinese thought. As in a mirror, this will be succeeded by a study of the way Chinese thinkers today read and interpret Hannah Arendt, an author who decidedly anchored her thinking into the core of the Western canon. Finally, I will revisit the encounter between Jesuits and Chinese literati around the *Zhongyong* with respect to the art of self-examination and discernment, asking myself whether and how the criss-crossing of Confucian and Ignatian resources brings light upon the process through which one reaches decisions anchored in both conscience and reason. These four cases are merely illustrations of what the Chinese-Western engagement may look like, and of the fruits one can expect from it. They are meant to show that there is a multiplicity of paths that can be followed, provided that (at least some of) the principles developed in our previous chapter inspire the hermeneutical strategies put into motion.

Ritual: Terms, Issues and Styles

I will discuss the progressive entry of the Chinese notion of Ritual (*li* 禮) into the mainstream of social philosophy in a way that will allow me to illustrate three successive theses: (a) A Chinese notion that was central for ancient thinkers has become a source of renewal for global social philosophy. (b) The plasticity of the notion is by itself a source of inspiration, introducing new perspectives for looking at our social conducts. (c) Even if it remains tentative, the dialogue between Confucianism and the Christian approach to Ritual and Liturgy culminates into a *style of life and thought* – that of "ritual hospitality" – which subverts a mere "notional" approach to what dialogue is about.

Has the notion of Ritual become as central as I assert here? Below, I will mention such recognized figures as Erving Goffman (1922–1982) and Herbert Fingarette (1921–2018), scholars who have done much for popularizing "ritual studies" in the context of contemporary societies, and who were both aware of the Chinese roots of the approach. Romans and Greeks certainly knew how to carry out a distanced reflection on the rituals which organized their collective life. We can think of Cicero's *De divinatione*, which probes the legitimacy and effectiveness of divinatory procedures, or of the way Livy relates the ceremony surrounding what he calls "the first contract concluded in history" (*Ab Urbe condita*, I, 24, 3–9), which is based on sacrifices and oaths made by each of the parties involved. Similarly, the biblical texts that relate the refoundation of the community from 538 BCE onwards, after the Exile in Babylon, provide us with a description that is both normative and ethnographic of the rituals that accompany it. Nevertheless, it is the ancient Chinese texts, and in particular the Confucian ones, that offer the most systematic and reflexive insights on our subject – it is no coincidence that one of the initiators of the field of ritual studies as conceived of today, Catherine Bell (1953–2008), was a sinologist by training.

Among present-days thinkers, let me mention Byung-Chul Han (b. 1959), a South Korean-born Swiss-German: *The Disappearance of Rituals: A Topology of the Present* (Han 2021) starts by presenting rituals, performed in time, on the model of the house: the latter helps us to locate our existence in space, ordering other landmarks around a central point. Similarly, rituals introduce cognitive discontinuities in our relationship to time that allows for a temporal mapping. This is to say that, as Han sees it, the "disappearance of rituals" deeply disrupts foundational social phenomena and relationships. Somehow, when rituals disappear, we are left homeless...

Let us turn back towards some considerations first developed in Chapter 3: Ritual (*li* 禮), wrote Xunzi

> serves Heaven above and Earth below, it honors forefathers and ancestors, and it exalts lords and teachers. [...] With ritual, all things can change yet not bring chaos. [...] High indeed is the pattern of ritual! Those who take violent arrogance, haughty indulgence, and contempt of custom for loftiness fall when they try to enter it.
>
> *Xunzi, On Ritual.* Translation Hunton 2014, 202, 205.

For Xunzi, the invention of Ritual allowed humankind to proceed from savagery to civilization, and only proper ritual observance could ensure correct social functioning. Particularly solemn in its expression, the reverence shown by Xunzi towards ritual forms and observances is far from being an exception: throughout history, Confucianism developed as a system of thought and practices that has given to *li* overarching importance. Its main thinkers emphasized that rituals were a privileged way to educate both the personal and collective body, to institutionalize ethical care and the sharing of resources, to make human society harmonize with the cosmic order, and to go beyond a way of governing that would have been based merely on law and punishment. At the same time, the understanding of and importance given to *li* has varied according to authors and historical circumstances.

When turning towards Christianity, the landscape is somewhat different. Even if human existence is meant to be infused with a sense of continuous worship (1 Th 5:18), life forms shaped by Christian beliefs are generally less ritualized than in traditional Confucian settings, except for some particularly close-knit fellowships, such as monastic communities. Besides, from one Christian church to another the forms given to divine worship and rituals differ greatly. However, all churches share in the same biblical inheritance and the insights provided by the New Testament as to the reinterpretation of the former. "Worship" constitutes a basic attitude and duty, which must be directed towards the One from whom comes "every good and perfect gift" (James 1:17). And all Christian churches consider divine worship and the shaping of brotherly communities as being closely interrelated missions.

There are "family resemblances" among the various human practices gathered under lexical categories such as *li*, "rituals", "ceremonies", "observances", and the like. Coming back to Wittgenstein (the thought of whom we already mobilized in our analysis of dialogic forms), the notion of "language games" is introduced so as to engage into the study of "languages" and utterances as a set of "relationships" (*Verwandtschaft*).

> Consider for example the proceedings that we call "games". I mean board-games, card-games, ball-games, Olympic games, and so on. What is common to them all? – Don't say: "There must be something common, or they would not be called 'games'" – but look and see whether there is anything common to all. – For if you look at them you will not see something that is common to all, but similarities, relationships, and a whole series of them at that. [...] And the result of this examination is: we see a complicated network of similarities overlapping and crisscrossing: sometimes overall similarities, sometimes similarities of detail. I can think of no better expression to characterize these similarities than 'family resemblances'; for the various resemblances between members of a family: build, features, color of eyes, gait, temperament, etc. etc. overlap and crisscross in the same way. – And I shall say: "games" form a family.
>
> (*PI* 66, 67; Wittgenstein 1972 [1953], 51–52)

In other words, to know what a game is (and similarly, to know what a *ritual* is) amounts to the fact of recognizing the range of meanings of the term, not to narrow it down. We play a game with the word "game", says Wittgenstein, in that its use is partly regulated and partly cannot be, in the same way that there is no rule which determines how high or with what force a tennis ball can be thrown. My knowledge of what is a game cannot be expressed in the formulation of a general definition. It is given in the differentiated description that I will give of a set of games, through which I will account for the possibility of constructing games analogous to the ones I describe. Paradoxically, the hesitation I show when asked whether such or such activity is a game or not also testifies to my intimate knowledge of what the word "game" practically means. Knowing "what is a game" can be only partly expressed. It constitutes a kind of knowledge that lies somewhere between what it means "to know the height of Mont Blanc" (fully expressible) and (at the other extreme) what can mean "knowing how a clarinet sounds" (a form of ineffable knowledge) (*PI* 68, 75, 78). The same thing can be said about "rituals" – and this is not mere coincidence, as games, play, and ritual are interconnected activities.

Magic and Music

All ritual forms and behaviors, large or small, are potentially covered by the Chinese character *li*. *Li* also covers certain codes of conduct: if a prince happens to die at the time an enemy state is attacking its territory, the invader is supposed to halt the military campaign and to retreat, so the long and solemn funerary rituals may take place: this is acting "according to the ritual [*li ye* 禮也]" (cf. *Zuozhuan, Xiang* 4, 2 and 19, 7), Among other ritual manifestations, the term encompasses the blood sacrifices (*ji* 祭) performed in honor of the dead, the ancestors, and the spirits. As a matter of fact, the *li* character represents a husk of cereals deposited in a ritual vase. In contrast, the *ji* character, represents a hand grabbing a piece of meat presented to the spirits. Still, *li* possesses a much broader meaning than *ji*, as it refers to the rules governing everyday behavior, observances attached to specific circumstances, blood sacrifices and bloodless offerings, and the ethic attached to this array of conducts.

In 1972, the American philosopher Herbert Fingarette decisively introduced the discussion on *li* into the context of Western social philosophy. In *Confucius: The Secular as Sacred*, Fingarette argued that Confucius had perceived that all forms of rituals carry into effect the *magic of the social*, through which, as if by a natural mechanism, society "works". We can then understand why Confucius was discerning a continuum between the everyday politeness and the most solemn ceremonies: "The explicitly sacred rites can be seen as a deliberate, intensified and highly elaborate extension of everyday civilized intercommunication" (Fingarette 1972, 11). Confucius (continues Fingarette) identifies in ritual practice the lineaments of a social ideal: "Human life in its totality ultimately appears as a ritual, at once vast, spontaneous and holy: the community of men" (Fingarette 1972, 17). The flaws that we occasionally perceive in the functioning of Ritual thus reveal more substantial social flaws. Goffman illustrates this point by universalizing the Chinese conception of "giving face": the "face" obtained through the fact of behaving adequately in a given social context sacralizes the individual as a recognized and competent social actor (Bonicco-Donato 2022). When face recognition is not duly granted, social dysfunctions necessarily worsen, threatening the social fabric.

In the Confucian optic, conforming to ritual observances amounts to educating the Self (and, first of all, the body[147]), which fosters personal realization. At the same time, Ritual shapes society by nurturing mutual respect, humanity and justice. *Li* is not only a practice, it is a virtue, that of relational effort, which fully civilizes both the person and the group. This virtue is destined to become innate, to manifest spontaneously in all circumstances. As presented by Confucius and some later texts, ritual practice both *orders* and *liberates* the subject. Similar to musical performance, its excellence reveals the degree of sincerity and inner freedom of the performer. The person who lives according to humaneness and ritual observance can be compared to one of the sacred vessels in which the ritual offerings are offered; such person is in a way sanctified by her practice. The one who follows the Way is a "Holy Vessel" (Fingarette 1972, 79).

Beyond (or rather behind) such lofty ideal, and throughout Chinese history, rituals have largely become part of the state's power apparatus. This was not their original setting: as described in canonical writings, rituals were meant to bring to such perfection interpersonal interactions that one could almost do without rulers. Who rules must be "motionless like the North Star" (*Analects* 2.1).

By the late 19th century, the spread of Western epistemic categories (science, religion, politics), and social institutions (universities, churches, the press, and parties) challenged Confucianism's self-image as a cosmologically, ritually, and educationally perfected system. Attempts to save the encompassing character of the Confucian teaching (*jiao* 教) led to its reformulations, either as religion (conceived in relation to and contrasting with Christianity) or as philosophy. After the Maoist period and notably the Cultural Revolution (1966–1976), Confucian reconstruction

---

[147] Even simple rituals imply bodily postures such as standing still, shaking hands, or bowing down. Some bodily requirements can be much more strenuous.

passed through different stages and strategies. Researchers have found evidence of the vitality of a "popular Confucianism" organized around lineage temples (*citing* 祠堂) aimed at ensuring communal harmony. Or yet, various academics and educators have advocated widespread reading if the classics, and pleaded for a much greater focus throughout the educational cursus on practices such as calligraphy, painting, and meditation (see Vermander, Hingley and Zhang 2018, 156–157).

In some East Asian countries – Korea principally, but also Vietnam – and in Chinese overseas communities, Confucianism probably permeates everyday life in a much more tangible way than in Mainland China proper. In these various contexts, several of the inner attitudes and insights summarized above remain valid, though sometimes in a barely recognizable fashion, as Confucian national traditions are challenged and reshaped by modernity as well as by other local praxes. At the same time, Confucianism remains alive as long as it remains reinterpreted – as was the case throughout most of its existence.

Dialogue as Ritual

The resilience of Confucian ritual is intrinsically linked to that for ancestral veneration. In Korea especially, creeds and practices inspired by filial piety towards the deceased have been instrumental in maintaining Confucianism as a relevant cultural and religious expression. They have also been the source of tensions between Confucianism and Christianity, the first expressions of which had appeared during the Rites Controversy that almost annihilated the Catholic Church in China in the 17th and 18th centuries (Min 2016).

Admittedly, Confucianism and Christianity are both in constant danger of making the observance of Ritual mere "Ritualism". Christian scriptures abound in warnings as to such a temptation: worship is to be given to God "in spirit and in truth" (John 4:23). And the letter of the Law – like that of the Rite – carries death if the Spirit does not enliven it (2 Cor 3:6.). Both the Rite and the Law are paths of education, till the time comes when the heart instinctively elects the conduct that pleases Heaven. The Confucian expression of this principle is well-known:

> The Master said, "At fifteen, I had my mind bent on learning. At thirty, I stood firm. At forty, I had no doubts. At fifty, I knew the decrees of Heaven. At sixty, my ear was an obedient organ for the reception of truth. At seventy, I could follow what my heart desired, without transgressing what was right."
>
> (*Analects* 2.4)

Similarly, in Christian context, practicing rituals in a regular and reflexive fashion can be seen as creating a *habitus*, an arrangement of qualities that disposes human actions towards a certain direction (cf. Thomas Aquinas, *ST* Ia IIae, q. 49–54). When some "habits of the heart" are firmly established, then free decisions can truly be made – including decisions to depart from customs and habits if the situation requires it. At the same time, the common recognition of the dangers associated with "ritualism" can ground, at least virtually, a cross-cultural hermeneutic.

Another factor gives rise to the cross-hermeneutic endeavor: rituals are less "spoken about" than "lived" and performed – and performed side by side when different traditions share a common social space. Their parallel performances often bring to each of them almost unobserved alterations: they become woven together. The transformation of Christian funerals in Late Ming/Early Qing China provides an excellent example of the process (Standaert 2008). Actually, rituals are always evolving, even within a unified cultural sphere, even when presented as "traditional", supposedly transmitted without any alteration from one generation to another.

There is yet another way to enter "cross-ritual hermeneutic". While the literature on interreligious dialogue often underscores the importance of everyday interactions, gathered under the expression "dialogue of life", the encounter of Confucianism and Christianity may bring a renewed attention to the *forms* taken by dialogue. The forms such encounter has taken reminds the observer that dialogue is an activity directed by *rules*, be they implicit or explicit. In other words, historical as well as ethnographic observation leads us to approach dialogue as a *Ritual*, and, consequently, as a *transformative practice.*

Misunderstandings in dialogue usually happen when the rules governing the use of language are unilaterally changed by one of the players, overconfident as to the degree of mutual comprehension already reached. The *ritualization of dialogue* operated through strict respect of its initial rules will allow for its progressive enrichment, as the understanding developing among the interlocutors fosters the enrichment of the "syntax" governing the exchange. Both Confucianism and Christianity consider rites as a vector of respect and sharing, as a way of growing forms of life that need to be protected and nurtured. This suggests that paying attention to the *forms* taken by rituals, exchanges and lifestyles is a privileged vector for entering into their *substance.*

As already noted, both Confucian and Christian traditions have approached Ritual in a way that allows them to proceed from their letter to their spirit: rituals are ultimately a path towards full humanization that is based on social sharing, inner refinement, and gratitude towards previous generations. Most importantly, the latter characteristic (i.e., gratitude) points towards an Origin that our ceremonies are unable to grasp and control. This commonality of meaning is of such importance that, once recognized, it certainly allows for inventing new forms of "ritual sharing" that may culminate in joint worship and celebration.[148] Yang Huilin 杨慧林, professor at People's University (Beijing), takes up the main hermeneutical proposals of the "Scriptural Reasoning" movement: present in various countries, the groups belonging to the movement, which gather participants coming from different scriptural traditions, strive to preserve an ethic of mutual hospitality, each participant hosting also alternating in the task of and leading the meetings.[149] Yang Huilin and other Chinese scholars explore the applicability of such an approach to China as well as the possibility of inserting a shared reading of the Chinese classics into it. After all, the central role given to texts and to the confrontation of their interpretations is, in China, the foundation of the study and production of knowledge. By highlighting the fluidity of interpretations that characterizes the Chinese hermeneutical tradition, Yang hopes to enrich global Scriptural Reasoning (Yang 2012).

Rituals transform our inner world as far as we acknowledge our essential relationality. At the same time, they contribute to shape the forms it takes in time and space. Sharing in ritual conviviality translates into a new dialogical style, and, reciprocally, dialogues constitute one of the ritualized expressions through which our social and spiritual space becomes progressively enlarged.

Confucian Meritocracy: Between Authoritarianism and Democracy

Let us now shift to our second example. As described by China's leaders and part of its intellectual community, the Covid pandemic has shown to what extent the Chinese mode of "scientific" social management positively contrasts with the irrationality of the decision-making process followed by the West today. This would prove that multi-party elections associated with uncontrolled freedom of discussion and information irreparably disrupt the quality of governance in an era when the complexity of the problems requires first and foremost expertise and long-term vision. At the same time, the technocratic dullness attached to the Chinese mode of management is meant to find its antidote in the construction of a civil religion as well as in the inspiration provided by the guiding figure of Xi Jinping.

The "meritocratic solution" is obviously rooted in Chinese tradition: outlined by the Han dynasty (206 BCE–220 CE) which adopted Confucianism as the official

---

[148] Among other works on this topic, one may want to refer here to Moyaert (2019).
[149] On the "Scriptural Reasoning" movement, see for instance: Ochs (2002).

doctrine of the Empire, it finds its expression in the system of imperial examinations instituted in 605 and abolished only in 1905. Sun Yat-sen tried to give it a new expression. From the 1980s onwards, the current regime has offered a flexible and modernized version of it, combining the mechanisms of promotions and training dispensed within the Party with the importance accorded to university degrees.

Initially, the Confucian revival that took place from the last two decades of the 20th century (some aspects of which I evoked in the third chapter) did not focus on governance issues. The "Boston Confucians" (with Tu Wei-ming as their figurehead) were mostly interested in moral and metaphysical considerations. Other interpretations gradually took shape, which stressed the pragmatism of the Confucian tradition and the links forged in history between its intellectual developments and the solutioning of the political crises faced by the country. The Canadian political scientist Daniel A. Bell, professor at the universities of Qinghua and Shandong, has made himself the eloquent advocate of a new political Confucianism based on meritocracy and the refusal of the elective system applied to the selection of leaders, praising his potential for reforming Western political systems (Bell 2015). A book published in early 2020 by Bai Tongdong will serve us as a guide for framing our discussion: *Against Political Equality* (Bai 2020) is partly based on an earlier work published in Chinese by the same author, *New Mission for an Old Country* (Bai 2009), while clarifying and radicalizing theses that the context of the first publication did not allow to bring to fruition.

For a Hybrid Confucianism

The failure of the current liberal democratic model does not mean, insists Bai Tongdong, that the Chinese model is a success. All contemporary frameworks and discourses have proven inadequate when it comes to tackle social and political problems. Perhaps, a political model drawing its inspiration from early Confucianism will better address at least some of today's predicaments. The ideal regime would consist of a hybrid of the Confucian model and other political forms. Political theory, continues Bai, tries to respond to some basic issues that each society necessarily faces – among them: (1) each nation must find an identity, a "flag" which will ensure its unity. (2) It must also appoint the people responsible for maintaining order, determine the procedure for their selection, and ensure the legitimacy of the said procedure. (3) Finally, it is necessary to establish the mechanisms regulating the relations between the various nations that divide the international space. In the Springs and Autumns period (771–476 BCE) and even more during the time of the Warring States (475–221 BCE) Chinese thinkers were confronted with problems that were thought of in terms quite similar to those encountered during the European transition from the Middle Ages to Western modernity. Ideas that we usually date from this latter period (freedom, equality, market, secularism) had emerged in other garbs during Chinese Antiquity, this being due to the disappearance of the feudal nobility as it existed in the early days of the Zhou dynasty.

The early Confucians, continues Bai Tongdong, "were revolutionaries with a conservative facade" (Bai 2020, 30): the way they were appealing to tradition was merely a strategy through which new ideas were made acceptable. As they were anxious to rebuild the political order, they were open to the idea of institutional "design". Bai finds mainly his inspiration in Mencius: the latter initially appears "awfully democratic" (Bai 2020, 43). Mencius holds the idea that the government is *for the people:* it is responsible for meeting the needs of the people (and not just its material needs), and the latter is to judge whether or not those needs are being met. However, careful reading proves that, for Mencius, government is in no way exercised *by the people.* Division of labor is in order: if we all share a common humanity, we must nevertheless *learn to become human,* and leaders need to be chosen among the ones who have progressed the furthest on this path – a progression illustrated by a spontaneous focus on the most universal needs. In contrast, people whose time and energy are primarily devoted to daily work are unable to give serious attention to political matters and cannot be given the task of governing the state.

In other words, the state is for the people, and in this respect the people indeed *is* the sovereign. Yet, no matter how much educational effort the state endeavors to deploy, the masses can merely decide whether or not they are satisfied with the government, not what policy best satisfies their needs. Moreover, continues Bai, the fact is amply proven by the evolution of contemporary democracies: climate change signals a "perfect storm" amassed against the principle of "one man, one vote". Not only have voters already largely proven their blindness to this challenge, but those who must suffer the most are those who are not old enough to vote, or even those who are not yet born – who, incidentally, may never know the light of the day because of the inaction of today's voters.

All these reasons argue in favor of a "Confucian hybrid regime": in such a regime, the rule of law and human right is firmly established (Bai 2020, 68). At the same time, the government is in charge of meeting material, social, moral, political and educational needs. In particular, it needs to provides civic education to all, so as to maintain mutual empathy and to propagate principles conducive to a healthy exercise of government. Leaders must be morally and intellectually superior to the governed (morally superior in the sense that they are willing to care for all whom it is in their power to help). Since "meritocrats" are not subject to the popular vote as are the legislators elected by universal suffrage, they are likely to take into account the interests of the minorities as well as the long-term interests of the people at large. It is also likely that they will maintain stable and coherent policies, as such institutional arrangement works towards this end.

However, distinctions are to be made according to the levels of government being considered: all citizens should be authorized to participate in local affairs and to vote on them. For higher levels, the bicameral system could be maintained, with an all-important reversal of the presently prevalent situation: the members of the lower house would be elected by universal suffrage but their powers would be reduced to the role of spokespersons. And the upper house, meritocratic in nature, would deliberate on the content of the policies. The mainspring of meritocracy would of course be a sound examination system, as was the case during much of the period of the Chinese Empire. In summary, the overall structure of the hybrid Confucian regime combines democracy at the local level and meritocracy at the upper ones.

How to ground such arrangement? From Antiquity, the Confucians have insisted on the need to provide for "social cement", to be found in the virtue of humanity, in compassion (*ren*). Mencius' emphasis on *ren* answers a problem typical of all forms of "modernity": the search for a new social bond when the one found in tradition does not play its role anymore. "If this interpretation holds, then, the moral concept of compassion is primarily a political concept, and is an ethical one only in an instrumental sense" (Bai 2020, 123). It is in the work on the Self as well as in family values that the feeling of humanity is first formed, a feeling gradually extended to even broader spheres: taking charge of others is always "graded and hierarchical" (Bai 2020, 133).

It is therefore a question of refusing "the liberal neutrality of values because this does not allow the State to challenge the formidable force of the free market by promoting certain values specific to the Good" (Bai 2020, 169). Bai's discourse becomes noticeably more authoritarian at this stage: the "Good" is obviously known only to the Sages and the Virtuous; also, in contemporary China, "the National Ethnic Affairs Commission should not be an institution that maintains and promotes ethnic identities, as it currently does, but an institution that promotes integration and a common identity of all ethnic groups ethnicities in China" (Bai 2020, 210). Similarly,

> an independent Taiwan would become a pawn of Japan and the United States, and the interests of its people would be sacrificed for the interests of Japan and the United States. [...] Under these circumstances, Confucians would oppose Taiwan independence, and some form of pressure – acceptable measures being based on the principle of humanity – can be applied to prevent Taiwan from becoming independent.
>
> (Bai 2020, 212)

In any case, "we must abandon the taboo that a liberal state cannot promote other virtues than 'thin' virtues like equality and autonomy" (Bai 2020, 284).

Confucius versus the Confucianists

The project sketched out by Bai is obviously a utopia, even if he affirms that this utopia is more realistic than the adjustments to liberal democracy proposed by John Rawls for example (Bai 2020, 109). Bai's utopia goes against both the Western democratic model and the current Chinese system. Bai's sincerity on this last point is obvious. However, when one takes some distance from the vision he propounds, one cannot but be struck by the number of premises it shares with the current regime. Bai could retort that the hybrid Confucian system he proposes includes freedom of information and debate, a major difference with the current system. This would have made it possible, for example, to know from the start (i.e., in December 2019) about the spreading of a new virus in Wuhan.

The fact remains that Bai's proposal frontally clashes with democratic principles: no ethics of discussion is outlined here, no reflection on the fact that voting and debate constitute in themselves factors of moral, political and social education, no reflection on what constitutes a "good" decision beyond its technical efficiency. Moreover, the institutional arrangements remain very vague: what about the separation of powers, for example? On this point, Bai may observe, on the one hand that his project is not to establish a Confucian constitution (Jiang Qing – evoked in our third chapter – details further his own proposal), on the other hand that the distribution of talented persons in institutions, all missioned with well-defined tasks, answers the problem. After all, the imperial government had ensured a division of tasks between administrators and censors.[150] Similarly, the examination procedure and the rules that would surround the exercise of non-elective functions would render the question of alternation between political parties obsolete.

Disconcertingly, Bai (who, like most Chinese scholars, sets up only one counter-model and stooge in front of him, the United States) seems unaware that his proposals have somehow *already been implemented*, and that it was largely the "hybridity" of the democratic systems as it works today that unleashed the populist storm that the West is now weathering: the Jesuits popularized Chinese institutions in Europe to the point of having the "office" system (which was hopelessly

---

[150] The Constitution of the Republic of China adopted in 1946 (still applied to Taiwan, though subject to significant revisions and adaptations) divided powers into five branches, according to a partly meritocratic approach, approaching the question of the separation of powers somewhat differently from the traditional democratic approach.

venal) replaced by that of examinations. In France, the Revolution and then the Empire instituted hybrid systems, in which the people would decide upon the major options while their overall "design" as well as the details of administrative implementation (and the devil, in politics like elsewhere, is in the details!) were (and remain) in the hands of "meritocrats" (labeled "technocrats"). Today, there is no finer example of hybrid Confucianism than the one provided by the functioning of the European Union. It is against the educated, the virtuous, those who know how to make "general interest" triumph (and in the United States against the mythical incarnation of the same stratum: the *deep state*) that the so-called populist movements rise up. At the same time, it cannot be denied that some of the Confucianist criticisms against the classical democratic model are correct. The question of the balances to be (re-)established between technical expertise and popular will, between equality and merit, between formal democracy and substantial values ("thick values"[151]) has not finished haunting us.

To engage further in a debate with meritocratic Confucianism would require going through a hermeneutical operation that would simply consist of *reading Confucius* – and this can present difficulties and surprises on a par with those provided by reading Plato's *Republic*. For stating the obvious: we will not find in Confucius the traces of any examination system as the latter will not take shape until a millennium after his death. The cantor of imperial meritocracy is not Confucius, it is "Confucius" – the "author-function", as Foucault says –[152] to whom a corpus of texts and thesis has been attributed when legitimizing the ideological enterprise of the Han dynasty and the entire imperial system. The freshness of the *Analects* reveals to us a Confucius very different from "Confucius".

One could almost find in Confucius the thinker of *the society against the State* (Clastres 1977): in the vision drawn by the *Analects*, Ritual was not created for legitimizing the government, but rather to bring interpersonal interactions to such perfection that one could almost do without state and state power (see *Analects* 2.1 *et passim*). Besides, deliberation and equality are among the collective virtues that Confucius forcefully propounds: Confucius fosters continual interactions, insisting on the fact that "knowing others" means both to identify the strengths of each person and to cultivate mutual confidence. Among the three pillars of state conservation, i.e., among capabilities for defense, wealth creation and mutual trust, "trust [*xin* 信]" is, for Confucius, the most basic factor of institutional sustainability (*Analects* 12.7): he compares it to the crossbar through which one fastens ox or horses to

---

151 I do not agree with the qualification of "thin values" given by Bai to autonomy and equality. These are clearly "substantial" (thick) values. But they define liberal democracy as a *formal system*, and it is from this point of view that Bai apprehends them.
152 See Foucault's well-known article: "Qu'est-ce qu'un auteur?" (Foucault 2001 [1969]).

a carriage (*Analects* 2.22); without a crossbar, "nothing goes". Trust reigns primarily among equals (*Analects* 1.4 and 2.26) and it is on such basis that communal discernment can meaningfully take place. And trust grows through "conversations" (such as shown by the discussion initiated by Confucius in *Analects* 11.26) rather than through formal process (see Holzman 1956). Moreover, as we saw at the beginning of Chapter 3, and as a political reading of some streaks of the Daoist tradition would further show, an authentically anarchist tendency has persisted throughout Chinese history, nourished by an alternative reading of the classics, and vigorously expressed by the May Fourth Movement, even if, at that time, "Confucius" the author-function had overshadowed Confucius to such an extent that the philosopher was the privileged target of the young revolutionaries.

If we were to engage the debate further, perhaps then we would come back again to Mencius, the thinker whom Bai most likes to quote and whom I already quoted saying: "I have a liking for fish, and I also have a liking for bear's paws. If I cannot have the two, I will let the fish go, and choose the bear's paws. I have a liking for life, and I also have a liking for righteousness. If I cannot have the two, I will let life go, and choose righteousness" (*Mencius* VIIA.10) We then would ask whether there is not, in such assertion a form of rebellion of the "meritocratic" mode of thought against its own premises: will not sometimes justice (righteousness) go against the way "Meritocrats" organize the sustenance of physical life at all cost? We will come back to this question when discussing Arendt's reception in China.

Despite the reservations and criticisms that I have just expressed,[153] I appreciate in the thinkers of Confucian meritocracy their willingness to seize sensitive subjects head-on: the very fact of directly mobilizing Chinese ancient thought for tackling contemporary issues in political philosophy reminds us that the former abounds in intuitions that allow us to approach interrogations on our "living together" in a way that triggers global discussions. This illustrates the fact that Chinese classics – as anchored as they may be in specific historical experiences and rhetorical strategies – remain truly alive today, providing specific insights that pierce throughout the complexity of human relationality and social engineering.

---

[153] When reading Bai, one thinks sometimes of Zhao Tingyang, to whom Bai refers in his Chinese-language publications. However, Bai avoids the kind of idealized reconstruction of the Chinese past that Zhao engages into, and proceeds in a much more pragmatic fashion. He also shows a deeper understanding of the Western tradition and present-day debates.

Thinking about Thoughtlessness

The next "philosophical engagement" we are going to examine differs in several respects from the case discussed above. While Bai Tongdong mobilizes Chinese resources for confronting anew Western institutional structures and – more importantly – global political challenges, Hannah Arendt (1906–1975) was firmly anchored in the Western canon and mode of thought. As underlined by Peter Baehr, "despite being the premier theorist of totalitarian formations, Arendt's interest in China was half-hearted and her analysis often wildly inadequate" (Baehr 2020, 267). However, Arendt's work has benefited from an attentive and generally warm reception within the Chinese intellectual world, likely a sign of its relevance for this cultural and geographical sphere. In order to elucidate the contribution of Arendt's thought to the Chinese debate and to our understanding of China's inscription into global trends, it is necessary to go beyond Arendt's well-known analysis of totalitarian dynamics, and to embrace her moral and political vision as an organic whole. Ultimately, today's China may speak of the deadlocks met by humankind when confronting (or avoiding to confront) the "condition" that defines its cohesiveness and its ends. Said otherwise, reading Arendt enlarges our understanding of China – and this enlarged understanding may bring new light to our apprehension of Arendt as a cogent, global thinker.

China: A State of Its Own

Arendt was 43 when the People's Republic of China was established. She was then completing *The Origins of Totalitarianism* (*OT*), a book published two years later and subsequently amended a number of times (Arendt 1973). The changes introduced by Arendt were not easily assimilated into the structure of the work, as is shown by the way the chapter on the Hungarian rebellion was integrated into and then deleted from the book. *The Human Condition* (*HC*) was published at a time (1958) where few information was available as to the nature of the new regime, the direction of which was still submitted to contradictory currents. And Arendt died a few months before the demise of Mao Zedong unleashed a stream of revelations and political shifts. Between 1958 and 1975, the essays she wrote revisited the past of Europe or dealt with the present of her new country. There was not in Arendt's life a missed appointment with China – rather, no *rendez-vous* at all. The only meeting of sorts may have been the one between *HC* and Malraux' eponymous novel (*La Condition humaine*, improperly translated as *Man's Fate*), in which a Soviet emissary meets with Chinese revolutionaries and laborers in 1927 Shanghai. The intertwining within the two works of the topics of human labor, political action and social bonding makes their sharing of one and the same title something more than a mere coincidence.

Let us come back to Baehr's paradox: Arendt's references to China's momentous political transformations are glaringly insufficient, and yet several of her axioms on the nature and mechanism of totalitarianism closely apply to Mao's regime. As a matter of fact, the idea of a "perpetual motion-mania" (Arendt 1973, 306, 391 *et passim*), which goes with a constant radicalization of the standards of revolutionary or ethnic purity applies to Maoism from a very early stage and finds its climatic expression in the triggering of the Cultural Revolution. Also, as was stressed by Arendt herself, the necessity to perpetually "sacrifice" a large amount of "superfluous" people to such motion-mania starkly increases the chance of establishing totalitarian regimes in hugely populated countries such as China – and India, she adds (Arendt 1973, 310–311).[154] At the same time, Arendt failed to notice the appearance into China of characteristics that were fully congruent with the ideal-type of totalitarianism: reliance on a front groups' strategy; use of clichés and techniques of self-criticism meant to "terminate" independent thought process; a never fully abolished ideal of global dominance; the reduction of targeted "enemies" to subhuman species through a camp system (German *Lager*, Russian *Gulag*, Chinese *laogai*), struggle sessions and psychiatric treatments (Baehr 2010, 276–279).

Most commentators agree that the aftermath of the Cultural Revolution witnessed a progressive transition from "totalitarianism" (in the broader sense of the term) to authoritarianism. Though such authoritarianism remained under the inflexible principle of one-party rule, some of the regime's contradictions during that stage even led some analysts to locate it into the "fragmented authoritarianism" category (Lieberthal 1992). Since then, a counter-transition period (2008 till 2012–2016) has prepared the conscious rebuilding of a formation sometimes dubbed "neo-totalitarianism" (Kang 2018; Béjà 2019), though the applicability to the present stage of some of Arendt's discriminating axioms remains much controverted.

After the global financial crisis (2008) and the Arab Spring (2011), "stability" and "security" became the bedrock of state policies. From the eighteenth congress (November 2012) onwards, the team led by Xi Jinping systematized the struggle against potential disruptive factors. Operating step by step during the first five years of Xi's mandate, it achieved a new ideological synthesis at the nineteenth congress (2017): the proclamation that a "New Era" had started amounted to stipulate that the principles that had guided the era of "Reforms and Opening" were largely outdated.

---

[154] Arendt is alert to the *possibility* of such mass sacrifices taking place but does not seem to have noticed their actual happening in Mao's China.

The current situation can be assessed in two different ways. One way leads to suggest that China is *post-totalitarian* while, in parallel, Western societies are *post-democratic:* challenged by a number of far-reaching factors (the rise of Internet-based services and corporations, interaction between financial and political sources of power, globalization and anti-globalization trends), each system is negotiating in its own fashion its fundamentals, its flexibility and the limits it encounters. The second way follows Roland Boer's assertion according to which the Chinese regime strictly follows Leninist categories. However (and here we depart from Boer's view), the current reinforcement of the (political) Leninist principles within a (social) context that maintains a certain diversity would lead one to conclude that the system obeys "quasi-totalitarian" proclivities: it leans towards a Leninist model, corrected by factors proper to contemporary societies (notably their relative affluence) and by Chinese characteristics. Still, the inscription of the system into the classical Leninist framework cannot be denied:

> The CPC's leadership is predicated on the fact that it represents the vast majority of the people, initially rural and urban workers and now also the middle-income group that has arisen as a result of the thorough poverty alleviation program. But this basis is simply a beginning. To go further, Chinese scholars distinguish between founding and ruling. The initial reference is historical, in the sense that the foundation of the New China was impossible without the CPC, but also that the Communist Party has become responsible for the construction of socialism and thus ruling the country. The technical Marxist term for the latter is the dictatorship of the proletariat and peasantry.
>
> (Boer 2021, 216)[155]

The reading of *The Origins of Totalitarianism* offers only partial lessons when it comes to the understanding of China's political regime and of its evolutions. And yet, Arendt has been warmly received in the Chinese intellectual landscape. The scope and reasons of this reception warrant further examination.

The Reception of Arendt in China and Its Significance

The first Chinese-language article specifically dedicated to Arendt appeared in 1994 under the title "Practice Precedes Theory, Action Precedes Thinking". Published in two parts, it introduces the life and destiny of a "woman philosopher", "who was fortunate enough to meet with some of the greatest philosophers of this century" (Zhang 1994, 53). It continues by providing sympathetic but short and distanced

---

[155] Xi (2018) provides the reader with a particularly authoritative self-assessment of the nature of the Chinese regime.

summaries of *OT* and *HC*. In fact, the very first mention of Arendt in Mainland China seems to appear a very short time before Zhang's article, through the translation of an English-language article that, in the course of its argument, criticizes Arendt's understanding of the Marxist concept of labor (King 1991/1993). The context provided by this indirect introduction may have helped in the "accreditation" of Arendt in China, where she is still sometimes presented as a Marxist thinker, partly criticizing, partly enriching Marx's theory of labor, notably through a new understanding of the process and meaning of alienation in a consumerist society.[156]

The third Part of *OT* was translated into Chinese in 1982. However, at that time the publication was meant for the Taiwanese public (it is probable that the book reached the mainland shortly after, though I found no trace of its possible impact). The first Mainland China translation (integral, this time) appeared in 2008, and a new edition by the same translator followed in 2014.

At first glance, *HC* appears to have been the most successful of Arendt's publications in China. A first edition sees the light of the day in 1999. A new, authoritative translation appears in 2009, revised and republished in 2017 and again in 2021. A concurrent Taiwanese translation appears in 2016 and, in a fully revised version, in 2021. However, the success of *HC* may have been recently equaled by the one of *Eichmann in Jerusalem:* a translation of the latter appeared in 2003 is republished in 2011. Another translation is offered on the market in 2014, and there is also a Taiwanese translation (2013).

As to other available titles: *Between Past and Future* appears in the Chinese Mainland in 2011 and in Taiwan in 2021. *Men in Dark Times* is presented to the Chinese public in two different translations in 2006, one of them benefiting from a second edition in 2016. *On Revolution* appears in 2007 (new editions in 2011 and 2019). *The Correspondence of Hannah Arendt and Mary McCarthy* appears in 2016, *The Promise of Politics* in 2010 and 2017, with another translation offered in 2016. *Lectures on Kant's Political Philosophy* benefits from a translation in 2013. There have been two editions of *Responsibility and Judgment* in the PRC (2011 and 2014), and also two in Taiwan (2008 and 2016). *Within Four Walls* (the correspondence between Hannah Arendt and Heinrich Blucher) is made available in 2004 and again, in a thoroughly revised edition, in 2019. In the year 2006, *The Life of the Mind* appears simultaneously in two different translations in the PRC and Taiwan. Chinese readers have also access to *Karl Marx and the Tradition of Western Political Thought* (2007, 2008 and 2012), the correspondence between Arendt and Heidegger (2019), *Crises of the Republic* (1996 for Taiwan, 2013 for Main-

---

[156] Jiang (2014); Cheng Guangyun (2016); Yang (2020), among others works.

land China), *Love and Saint Augustine* (2019), a thick volume of collected essays, and Arendt's preface to Benjamin's *Illuminations: Essays and Reflections*.

The scope and continuity of this transmission process are striking. Where does Arendt's impact exactly lie? In which ways does her work speak to her Chinese readers? When one refers to the academic articles published about Arendt, one cannot but notice that the joint topics of "evil" and "thoughtlessness" loom large. Guo Fuping 郭福平 and Liu Yaqing 劉雅倩 stress the passage from radical evil (which, in their view, Arendt makes an attribute of *systems*) to ordinary evil (an attribute of *individuals*). Guo's and Liu's thesis is supported by such passages: "Radical evil has emerged in connection with a system in which all men have become equally superfluous" (Arendt 1973, 459). In the Chinese versions of Arendt's works the expression "banal evil" generally stands for the one of "banality of evil". Their privileged reference to Chinese translations makes scholars such as Guo and Liu speak of "mediocre evil" (for "banality of evil") when they translate their Chinese summary into English, which may give an indication as to their interpretation of the original concept (Guo and Liu 2017, 105–108).[157]

Guo and Liu note that "evil" and "thinking" in Arendt's vision refer to two poles. "Thoughtlessness" constitutes the premises under which "ordinary evil" tales shape, and eventually identifies with the human condition as "ordinarily" experienced today: if thoughtlessness, as Arendt understands and develops the concept, has been shaped by totalitarian regimes, it has since become a characteristic of all or most human societies, note our commentators. Thoughtlessness implies the disappearance of the Self and the impossibility of starting any Socratic form of dialogue, the latter being in history the prime educator of moral conscience. Hence the value attached to maintaining dialogic thinking in the mind and practice of at least a few individuals.

> The dialogue with the "Self" is more active than all activities in active life, [which can be explained by the following paradox: such dialogue] is at its most active when it does nothing, and it is least lonely when it proceeds alone. "Thinking" cannot rescue "action", but at least it can proceed even when in solitude. Undoubtedly, the paradox [that links] "thinking" and "action" is inscribed into Arendt's [thought], but even more in our times.
> (Guo and Liu 2017, 108)

Zhou Yi 周毅 – another scholar having contributed a noteworthy study on Arendt – has also echoed the strong connection established by most Chinese commentators between "thoughtlessness" and "ordinary evil", and the fact that, for these

---

[157] For a more thorough discussion of the uneasy relationship between "radical" and "banal" evil in Arendt, see Dege (2021).

same commentators, "thinking" has been understood as the privileged expression of "acting". Zhou considers that this quasi-equivalence established between thought and action erases the political dimension of Arendt's approach, and notably the link she establishes between "thinking" and "civil disobedience". The fact of propounding civil disobedience has turned Arendt's attention away from the background of totalitarianism and made her focus on post-totalitarian democratic societies. However, notes Zhou, in totalitarian contexts "thinking" may indeed be the only form of political disobedience available, even if such disobedience is not "civil" (not made public). And, whatever the context under study, maintaining "value rationality" over "instrumental rationality" is akin to persisting in thinking while making such persistence the hallmark of humaneness (Zhou 2019).

At the beginning of 2022, the issues raised by such discussions suddenly were revived on social medias when harsh measures were imposed on the covid-stricken city of Xi'an, among other places:

> The government has the help of a vast army of community workers who carry out the policy with zeal and hordes of online nationalists who attack anyone raising grievances or concerns. The tragedies in Xi'an have prompted some Chinese people to question how those enforcing the quarantine rules can behave like this and to ask who holds ultimate responsibility. "It's very easy to blame the individuals who committed the banality of evil," a user called @IWillNotResistIt wrote on Weibo, the Chinese social media platform. "If you and I become the screws in this gigantic machine, we might not be able to resist its powerful pull either."
> (Li Yuan 2022)

The mention infuriated Hu Xijin 胡錫進, the editorialist and former editor-in-chief of the nationalist tabloid *Global Times:*

> More than 800,000 Americans died from COVID-19 in the US. Behind these numbers, how many sad and desperate stories are there? How many people died alone without any terminal care? And how policies have been implemented and promoted because they are favorable to capitalists, but ignore the fact they may cause more infections and deaths? These are the real "banality of evil."
> (Hu 2022)[158]

Yet another scholar, Le Xiaojun 樂小軍, puts the stress on the kind of "truth" called for by the very nature of the political realm. He stresses the fact that Arendt reestablishes "plurality" and "action" as the measure of what determines judgment in politics, contrary to traditions for which absoluteness and external certainty define the norms applicable to the political sphere: "Arendt is looking for a truth

---

[158] The change of covid-related policy that China underwent in December 2022 would warrant further discussions, but they would go beyond the scope of the present analysis.

that belongs to the political realm, and not for one that would be external to it" (Le 2019, 119). Le notes also that Arendt finds in some trends of the Western tradition (notably Plato's *Republic* and *Laws*) elements conducive to totalitarianism but certainly not their direct cause: in the cultural sphere associated with the Greek and Latin tradition, lived political experience has always been going against such trends. And it is, he argues, the dynamic of the *political experience* that Arendt tried to unearth and revive (Le 2019, 129.).

At least one observer, the political theorist Hong Tao 洪涛, openly formulates a most sensitive question: is Arendt's thought relevant for today's China? His answer is a bit convoluted. China, one may infer from Hong's developments, shares the same regime of modernity as the West, and, in this respect, both civilizations are equally interested in Arendt's analyses. Besides, China could learn from the way Arendt faces the decline of her own tradition. Can China confront in a similar fashion its own intellectual past? Hong's conclusion suggests an (indirect) answer:

> Technology can create a "new world", but only actions that truly come from human nature can create a truly human world. As information technology can make people find new horizons, real communication in the public arena remains inseparable from the Socratic model of dialogue. Can the classical spirit of engagement, of action – that is, the actions accomplished by real people – experience a new birth under today's material and social conditions? To this, we can only answer: first we must be able to know [what such spirit consists of],[159] and then we must practice it.
>
> (Hong 2015, 194)

A Chinese-Straussian Challenge to Arendt

Arendt's association with Heidegger, whose influence on contemporary Chinese philosophers cannot be overestimated,[160] constitutes another reason for the interest she has triggered in China. Already in 1994, Zhang Shen was offering a rather Heideggerian reading of Arendt (Zhang 1994). At the end of his book on *Heidegger and China* (2017), the very influential (and controversial) philosopher Liu Xiaofeng 刘小枫 also firmly locates Arendt in the position of a (sometimes unfaithful) student of Heidegger, this before launching an attack on her that in some places be-

---

[159] In the original, "what" exactly is to be known and practiced remains elliptical (*ta* 它: "it", "this"), but Hong does seem to refer to the "classical spirit", subject of the preceding sentence.
[160] He is the only Western philosopher, asserts Liu Xiaofeng, whose influence in China has never waned during the last 40 years or so (Liu 2017, 1–2).

comes venomous (Liu 2017, 252–276).[161] The following sentence may give an idea of Liu's acrimony: "After a girl [*nühaizi* 女孩子] as gifted as was Arendt had entered the door of philosophy, she was fortunate to encounter such a philosopher as Heidegger, and she was fortunate also to learn to no longer be surprised by things such as pure beauty and absolute goodness" (Liu 2017, 266). Liu here sardonically targets "the pathos of wonder" as expounded by Arendt. For Liu, such pathos should be awakened only by objects of contemplation that have nothing to do with "plurality", "commonalities", or anything political. A disciple of Leo Strauss,[162] Liu borrows from a way of presenting his argument consciously open to conflicting interpretations. His "esoteric" art of writing probably originates from his judging – as Strauss does – that philosophical truths are intrinsically dangerous to political order and stability.[163] No doubt that the Chinese context has accrued Liu's receptiveness to such reading of Strauss. It also explains why the dialogic approach of politics that is characteristic of Arendt seems a delusion to him. If Liu uses with predilection the style of writing known in Chinese as "subtle words [conveying] important meanings [*weiyan dayi* 微言大義]", the gist of his argument remains clear: notions such as "public philosophy" and "plurality" go against the intrinsic nature of what the philosophic quest is and must be. Under the pretext of giving new relevance to Socrates, Arendt shows herself to be blind to the fundamentally undemocratic character of Socrates' thought and method, sufficiently shown by the fact that it was a democracy, Athens, which condemned him to death. Targeting what he thinks is Arendt's biased or contradictory reading of the classical corpus, Liu directs his strongest sarcasm towards her plea for civil disobedience. More generally (probably being closer to Heidegger than Arendt was, at least in this respect), he denies the very possibility of establishing a "political philosophy", especially if understood as a "public" or "civil" philosophy (Liu 2017, 265).

Paradoxically, Liu's attack against Arendt illustrates the fact that the latter has earned relevance in China. After a stage of progressive assimilation, Arendt's thought is now a participant in the country's intellectual debate, even if, in

---

161 As we have seen, Zhang (1994) had also introduced a misogynistic element in his presentation, but he was at least praising Arendt's intellectual acumen.
162 See Marchal and Shaw (2017); Rong (2020). In his book on Heidegger, Liu Xiaofeng starts his discussion of Arendt by borrowing from the lecture "The Problem of Socrates" (see Strauss 1996 [1958]). In the same book, Liu shows his reliance upon Strauss through frequent references to Xenophon (a favorite of Strauss for apprehending Socrates). See also Bartsch (2023: 127–145).
163 See Drury (1985). I recognize that there are alternative ways to approach Strauss. The point, here, is that the understanding of political writing as "secret" or even "deceptive" in nature does seem to shape Liu Xiaofeng's own strategy (Rong 2020 offers a slightly different approach to Liu's reliance on Strauss).

these last years, arguments on the nature of society and political actions have become more subdued and oblique. One may even say that a country able to translate, read and discuss Arendt cannot be labeled "totalitarian", at least in the strict sense expounded by the same Arendt. The fact remains that Liu's acerbic reading does show that the very principle of open debate remains a contentious one.

One striking feature of Liu's contribution is that, ignoring *OT*, it mostly focuses on the beginning of *HC*, besides some references to various essays and lectures.[164] Let me consider what makes *The Human Condition* a work of special relevance for contemporary China.

China and the Human Condition

Translators meet with a problem specific to the Chinese language: should the word "condition" be translated as *tiaojian* 條件 (logical condition, stipulation, clauses, and, by derivation, state or condition) or as *jingkuang* 景況 (situation, condition, circumstances)? Most Chinese recognize that *jingkuang* "sounds" much better. Yet, not only have the two terms competed from the start for translating the title of *HC*, but also Wang Yinli 王寅麗, who had given in 2009 an authoritative translation based on the term *jingkuang*, revisited it in 2017, keeping *jingkuang* only for the title and changing "condition" for *tiaojian* everywhere else. She explains herself as follows

> In this book, Arendt [...] understands the human "condition" neither as the so-called essential human attributes nor as a transcendental condition that determines human experience, as Kant means, but rather as the ontological characteristics that Humankind is given on earth: the conditions proper to *labor* are the ones that people must live through. The conditions proper to *work* are necessary in order to build a world of things. The conditions [determining] *action* correspond to human "plurality", within which people communicate and make themselves known so as to answer the question "who am I?". Outside such conditions, life is no longer "human" life. In this sense, people are conditioned beings. But their activities create conditions for their survival at a further stage [of development]. For example, the globalization of labor beyond the boundaries of families and countries [...] have fundamentally changed [what will be] the living conditions of mankind in the future. In Arendt's view, these three human activities also have their own constraints (conditions) of space and time. [...] Paul Ricoeur [...] analyzed the way these three activities are shaped by time. As to the spaces corresponding to them, these are Nature, the [human] world, and the public domain. These *forms* taken in space and time together constitute the *conditions* for humans [to engage into] *vita activa*.
>
> (Wang 2017, 303–304)

---

[164] Besides the texts gathered in *Between Past and Future*, Liu also refers to *The Life of the Mind*.

It is thus under the register of *conditionality*, one might say, that *HC* is understood in the Chinese context, and this resonates well with the dizzyingly rapid rhythm of transformation from one dominant regime of production to another undergone by China since 1979. One statistic may summarize the changes experienced in the *conditions* of both life and production: China's urban population accounted for 12 percent of the total in 1950, less than 20 in 1978, 52 percent in 2012, more than 60 percent in 2019, and will reach 70 percent by 2030.[165] "Loneliness" (with its German echo of *Verlassenheit*), "superfluousness" (Arendt 1973, 457, 475) uprootedness – topics developed by Arendt, first at the end of Chapter 12 and in the course of Chapter 13 of *OT*, before she takes them anew in *HC* – are concepts and experiences understood in China throughout such seismic changes in *condition(s)*. A crucial sentence located towards the end of *OT* opens up the Chinese reading of *HC*: "Political, social and economic events everywhere are in a silent conspiracy with totalitarian instruments devised for making men superfluous. [...] *Totalitarian solutions may well survive the fall of totalitarian regimes*" (Arendt 1973, 459; italics are mine).

This may also explain why Chinese readers do not spontaneously read *HC* through the outlook that Paul Ricoeur privileges when he sees in this book an attempt to solve in a radically new fashion the questions raised by totalitarian trends and movements (Ricoeur 2018 [1983], i–vii). In China, a sense of ineluctability makes it difficult, it seems, to listen to the (admittedly feeble) echoes of hope that appear towards the end of *HC* when Arendt introduces the theme of "novelty" and asserts that the human capacity for action remains intact today. There are two reasons at least for such "tragic" line of reading: (a) A continuous process of uprootedness has been experienced from the time of Maoism to that of Reform and Opening Up, and uprootedness begets a sense of helplessness. (b) Contemporary China vividly experiences the circular relation between "laboring" and "consuming" that Arendt describes. For Chinese ears, Arendt's axiom does not speak first of political upheavals but rather refers to the robotic dynamic of unstoppable growth: "All laws have become laws of movement" (Arendt 1973, 463).

Going one step further, one may account for the fact that Chinese readings privilege the category of "ineluctability" over the one of "novelty" through another rationale: if the notions of "labor" and of "work" as Arendt understands them can find equivalents in Chinese classics, the one of "action" raises a number of issues. Its modern equivalent (*xingdong* 行動) is devoid of the connotations that Arendt associates to it. Equivalents of the former can be found in the character *wei* 為, which, in ancient Chinese, refers to "to do", "to effectuate", "to engage into", or

---

[165] World Bank and Development Research Center of the State Council (2014), 3.

yet "to govern". The difficulty lies in the fact that the model of action offered in such semantic context is the one of "non action [*wu wei* 無為]", the limits one fixes to oneself so as to avoid disturbing natural processes, as would be the act to transgress ritual proprieties, or yet of asserting oneself in a way that eventually ruins one's reputation rather than enhance it.[166] Extreme restraint in action is what makes action efficient and commendable. For instance, a general can be remembered and praised not for invading a rival principality but rather for abstaining to do so at the time the overlord of the enemy state had died, as invading it under such conditions would have been to go "against the ritual" (*Zuozhuan, Xiang* 19.7). For sure, such restraint may resonate with the quote of Cato that closes *HC* ("Never is he more active than when he does nothing"), but Arendt's use of the quote is both ambiguous and paradoxical, while a translation in ancient Chinese would make the statement appear as obvious, a point of departure that prepares further developments. This cultural trait accounts for the current Chinese insistence on "thinking" as the only way to provide human beings with a possibility for "acting" in the sense that Arendt gives to the notion. Even Zhou Yi, the solitary voice we heard stressing the political dimension of action, was highlighting civil disobedience, the form of political action that may best be understood as a form of "non action" (*wu wei*).

The most intriguing dimension of Arendt's analysis of the *conditions* that define humankind's destiny today probably lies in her insistence upon the reversal that made individual life gain prominence over the life of the body politic. This part of *HC* is replete with difficulties (Arendt 1998 [1958], 313–322). My own interpretation would stress the fact that the life of the individuals has progressively been amalgamated with that of the species itself, while the "body politic" has been voided of its substance by the triumph of the *animal laborans,* fully reliant on nature and entirely dedicated to the survival of the species and of his family.[167] The common point between the totalitarian experience and that of modern society would lie in a comparable reduction of the human to instinctive animality, human existence being apprehended according to the conditions of the vital processes, of *nature.* The benchmark activity is the same: labor. And once the mechanical maintenance of the vital process turns into a frenzy, the twin value of consumption requires not only the perpetuation of labor but "ideally" its uninterrupted character: labor maintains a cycle that can never be left, making humanity unable to "build a

---

166 For an overall study of the *wu wei* doctrine in Ancient China, see Slingerland (2003a).
167 Besides, nationalist ideologies consider the nation as an extension of the family, a natural entity. This is particularly obvious in the Chinese case, where, as we have seen, the term "nation" (*guojia*) associates the characters for "country" (*guo*) and "household/family" (*jia*).

world" through work and action, as it is entirely focused upon the cyclical process of labor and consumption (see Ménissier 2011).

In the line I privilege, China provides us with the paradigmatic example of a "post-political totalitarianism": after having exalted the sacrifice of the individual during the Maoist period, the state now grounds its legitimacy on the prominence it gives to "biological safety at all cost", except when such priority ends up threatening the labor/consumption cycle. There is a continuum between enforcing biopolitics, managing a nation as if it were an organism to protect, and prioritizing the survival of the Party, which guarantees the primacy given to "preservation at all cost" and the efficacy of the mechanisms that make such preservation effective. As stated by a spokesperson of the Chinese Foreign Ministry:

> No matter when and no matter which country or society we are talking about, the first order in protecting human rights is to ensure every individual's right to life and health and defend the value and dignity of every life. To live a life free from want, with food on the table and a roof over one's head, that is what I call basic human rights. During the recent Spring Festival holiday, the usual mass movement in China was not possible due to COVID-19. However, the Chinese people had a safe and happy holiday strolling in parks, going to the cinema and enjoying the company of loved ones at home. [...] At the same time, a cold spell gripped the southern U.S. state of Texas, causing power outages affecting millions of households. [...] Dozens of lives have been claimed. All this has given us a deeper understanding of what human rights truly mean and how to better protect them.
>
> (Hua 2021)

Ultimately, there are two ways of understanding the shaping of a body politic. The first one sees such body as crafted and perpetually transformed through the interactions of people finding their own voice and their way of acting by the very fact of living a "plurality" of positioning. The second envisions the body politic as a kind of metabolism[168] governed by "laws" that are ultimately natural/historical forces unhindered by human action (Arendt 1998 [1958], 465). Such laws necessarily register a constant oscillation between the necessity to sustain and propagate the species, on the one hand, and the imperative to periodically engage in "creative" destruction, on the other hand. If totalitarian regimes have revealed and engineered such oscillation with particular clarity, the mechanisms that trigger it survive the apex of these regimes, and are rooted in social and intellectual phenomena that precede totalitarianism proper.

Seen under the light provided by its Chinese commentators, the continuity of Arendt's thought along the two poles that *OT* and *HC* constitute hints towards the

---

[168] The application of this word to the social domain is originated by Marx, and Arendt often comments on it.

one experienced by the Chinese regime from 1949 onwards, whatever the shifts and oscillations that the same regime has registered.[169] Today, the continuity of the regime ultimately depends upon making the laboring (and, concurrently, consuming) capacities of humankind its ultimate point of reference, transforming politics into a biological process. In this perspective, the zero Covid policy has become the best available example of what the term "biopolitics" may refer to. From 1980 onwards, China has progressively asserted its place at the very center of the global system, not only because of its astounding economic growth but also because it has made abundantly clear the principle on which the global system had been already living, namely "that life, and not the world, is the highest good of man" (Arendt 1973, 318). It might be that, be it in the West or in China, such a principle has now become prevalent.

Phronesis in the Confucian and Ignatian Traditions

The last part of this chapter will offer a contemporary interpretation of the meeting between Confucian literati and the Jesuits. This way, we will retrieve some of the issues discussed in the course of this book:[170] How should we read and interpret the *Zhongyong*, a text central to the Confucian worldview? In the context of comparative philosophy, what status is to be given to experiential ways of understanding that cut though lexical difficulties? Can philosophical dialogue be seen as a meeting of wisdoms? In the present case, wisdom is to be understood as *phronesis*: "a true and reasoned state of capacity to act with regard to the things that are good or bad for man" (Aristotle, *Nicomachean Ethics*, 1140b5, as translated in Ross 2009), a definition on the basis of which the term is elucidated as "practical wisdom", "moral discernment" or yet "prudence".

Chinese scholars, whose mindset was shaped by the reading of the *Analects*, *Mencius* and the *Zhongyong*, and Jesuits, who had walked the path of the *Spiritual Exercises* (*Exercitia spiritualia*, henceforth *ES*) crafted by Ignatius of Loyola (1491– 1556), were both anxious to develop in their students and disciples a three-fold capacity: (a) to examine themselves in daily life; (b) to exercise sound discernment when confronted with (potentially difficult) decisions to take; (c) and to effectively

---

169 Besides, as we have seen, the displacement that the Chinese commentators operate from "acting" to "thinking" provides them with a way to circulate between the reading of *HC* and the one of *Eichmann in Jerusalem*.
170 This section is based on Vermander (2022). However, it develops considerations on the Chinese lexicon that are only sketched in the original contribution, while drastically shortening its managerial dimension.

implement the decisions that the discernment process would lead them to reach. Debates on cosmologies or oppositions between knowledge systems were certainly divisive. However, as they were progressively entering into contact, both traditions could not but be struck by a kind of commonality in the vision and in the means deployed towards the acquisition of moral clarity, capacity for discernment, and decisiveness. I have already noted that, at the time of the publication of the *Confucius Sinarum Philosophus* (*Confucius, Philosopher of the Chinese*, 1687), the Jesuits were paying particular attention to the *Zhongyong* and had translated it in such a way as to enlighten the description of the various motions experienced by the heart/mind as it is subjected to the action of different "spirits" (identified with the Chinese *guishen* 鬼神) evoked in the work.[171] The idea of maintaining the "mean" or "middle ground" against all external influences was reminding them of the one of "indifference" or "balance" that the "Principle and Foundation" of the *ES* incites its practitioner to maintain when confronted with decisions that involve electing among an array of means, resources and lifestyles:

> It is necessary to make ourselves indifferent to all created things in all that is allowed to the choice of our free will and is not prohibited to it; so that, on our part, we want not health rather than sickness, riches rather than poverty, honor rather than dishonor, long rather than short life, and so in all the rest; desiring and choosing only what is most conducive for us to the end for which we are created.
>
> (*ES* 23)

Jesuits were mostly interested in two aspects of the *Zhongyong:* its analysis of the various feelings that assail the mind of the subject; and the fact that the text endorses a "balance" of these various motions, organizing them around a point of dynamic equilibrium that positions the subject towards well-ordered decisions and actions (Mei 2013).

Learning to Discern: Two Sets of Resources

I have spoken of three different dimensions related to moral clarity or prudence, and each of them needs to be considered in itself. (1) Self-examination is a *habitus*.[172] (2) Discernment is engineered through a set of *procedures*. (3) The fact of taking a specific decision may be approached as a particular *event*. Clearly, these

---

[171] Mei (2013); Kim and Bae (2015).
[172] *Habitus* is to be understood here in the sense scholasticism gives to the term: an acquired quality; a disposition which has become second nature (cf. Titus 2006, 119).

three terms are interrelated: examining oneself regularly is supposed to nurture the ability to assess one's motivations and options when choices are to be made; and decisions may be reached more peacefully once the range of alternatives has been carefully discerned. In other words, not only is discernment *per se* a process but also the relationship with self-introspection and decision-making it establishes is processual in nature. Still, *habitus*, process and event are clearly distinguishable, even if the literature on "discernment" and its application to management techniques are prone to swiftly encompass them into a whole.[173] It should be added that both traditions here discussed anchor these dimensions into a preliminary education to *attentiveness*, understood as a sensitivity to motions happening within oneself and the world (natural, human, and even supernatural) that surrounds the subject. In the Chinese context, the various dimensions of what "attentiveness" refers to may be found throughout the rapprochement sometimes made between the three *jing*: respect, attention to what is taught to you and to the tasks imparted upon you (*jing* 敬); inner quietness that makes you enter into the phenomenal world without endangering the wholeness of your being (*jing* 靜); and zealous drive emanating from your inner focus (*jing* 勁). The progressive acquisition of the virtue of attentiveness, of the habitus of self-examination, of the capacity to discern and ultimately to decide governs the program of study drawn by the *Four Books*. The circle that links "study" (*xue* 學), understood as an all-encompassing process of self-discovery, with "governance" (*zhi* 治) – a circulation that the *Analects* unveil and detail – provides us with the framework into which to locate the path that leads from attentiveness to self-examination, and, from there, to decision and implementation.

The fact of focusing on the *Zhongyong* and the *Analects* allows us to approach as a textual parallel the founding document of the "Ignatian tradition", i. e., the *Spiritual Exercises*. This booklet is neither a treatise nor a spiritual meditation. The *ES* are sometimes compared, not without accuracy, to a cookbook or the libretto of an opera: their practice (during a time of retreat, or in daily life) engages the exercitant into the production of a singular "opus" (in that case, a journey of inner transformation) based on directions that are potentially offered to all (De Certeau 1973, 118). The *ES* prepare the retreatant to re-order her life and to take decisions accordingly, once she is able to embrace the greater good without letting "attachments" (tastes, repulsions, external considerations, or even scruples) impede the process and its conclusion. For reaching the full understanding of the intent and method

---

[173] See the literature review in Miller (2020), which shows that spiritual practices (prayer, meditation), daily examination, reflexive evaluation of a specific issue (both personal and collective), and "courage" in decision-taking are generally all part of what authors on the subject call "discernment".

developed in the ES, it is most useful to supplement them with two sets of writings. The first one is constituted by the other testimonies left by Ignatius, which include the dictated narration of part of his life story (see Geger 2020); a voluminous correspondence (Padberg and McCarthy 2006); and the Constitutions of the Society of Jesus (Ganss et al. 1996). This corpus offers precious examples of discernment in contexts that include financial, managerial or life-changing decisions. The second, ever-evolving textual body includes the productions of the spiritual authors who, referring to the Ignatian Tradition, have constantly renewed its expression and relevance, and continue to do so (see Fleming 1986; Fessard 1956; Demoustier 2006; Tetlow and Ackels 2007).

From the 1590s onwards, one finds testimonies showing that Ricci and his companions were giving the "First Week" of the *ES* (i.e., the part that focuses on self-knowledge and resolution to overcome one's sinful habits) to Converts. The publication of engravings illustrating the meditations proposed by the *ES* and based on Gospel narratives soon followed. *Visualization* was providing a bridge between the Buddhist/Daoist and Christian practices of meditation (Standaert 2012, 80). Partial translations of the *ES* started to appear in the 1630s or 1640s. They crystallized under the form of a booklet handed on to Chinese retreatants who were engaging into a few days of meditation (the selection was including the "rules for discernment" found in the course of the *ES*).

> The [anonymous] translator [of the *ES*] [...] had in mind the possibility of laypeople doing the exercises individually and rather autonomously. It is difficult to assert to what extent this version was disseminated, probably only in manuscript form, though nineteenth-century sources indicate that it was fairly widely available in the middle of that century.
> (Standaert 2012, 97)

A number of testimonies and correlated spiritual books testify to the success of the eight-to-ten-days format of group retreats organized by the missionaries in the early Qing period and after their return to China in 1842. The encounter between Confucian self-examination and the principles of the *ES* applied to everyday life in Chinese context led, in the mind and practices of its practitioners, to "a dynamic process of hybridization" (Song 2009, 50).

Examining Oneself: "Three Points" and "Three Times"

The topic of self-examination appears at the beginning the *Analects*, with a statement by Master Zeng 曾子:[174]

> I examine myself daily on three points. Have I advised men [of quality][175] without showing loyalty? Have I been untrustworthy with my friends? [The teaching] I received, did I fail to put it into application?
> 曾子曰：「吾日三省吾身：為人謀而不忠乎？與朋友交而不信乎？傳不習乎？」
>
> (Analects 1.4)

The meaning of this sentence is not as straightforward as it might seem. However, I gather from it that Master Zeng looks at the way he has behaved towards his *superiors*, his *equals*, and the young, i. e., *his inferiors* (he aspires to act towards the latter as was done towards him at the time the teaching was "transmitted" to him). The ternary structure of the questioning is frequent in the *Analects*, and the work also frequently mentions the duties on which self-examination focuses: loyalty governs the conduct towards superiors; faithfulness to one's words allows for easy and confident interactions within a circle of equals; and the adequation between knowledge and action is the touchstone upon which a person's character is assessed. The term "self-examination" translates the character *xing* 省, the core meaning of which is "to inspect" an administrative precinct[176] or (probably by extension) one's conduct. This lexical context conveys a sense of attentiveness, scruple, and objective evaluation: I consider myself as I would others, without partiality. (Note that the paragraph can also be interpreted as "I examine myself *thrice a*

---

[174] Zeng Shen 曾參 or Ziyu 子輿, a prominent disciple of Confucius who later taught the grandson of Confucius, who himself became the teacher of Mencius. He thus is the founder of the main branch of orthodox Confucianism.

[175] Here, the character *ren* 人 should be understood as applying not to men in general but rather to men of quality, officials, in contrast with the mass of the people (*min* 民). This can be asserted from the fact that the virtue discussed in this part of the sentence is "loyalty [*zhong* 忠]", which first applies to relationships between inferiors and superiors, as well illustrated by *Analects* 3.19. Mou's argument according to which the lesson of these two fragments would apply only "in a specific context" (Mou 2004, 237) is weak. Mou's interpretation of *Analects* 14.7 ("Can there be *zhong* which does not involve hui 誨?"), which intends to prove that *zhong* does not apply first to persons but rather to established rules, is not convincing either, as the respective position of the one who admonishes (*hui*) and the one who is admonished is not clearly specified (scholars may admonish rulers they serve). I am not arguing either that the field of application of *zhong* should be narrowly restricted. Simply, I think that this particular virtue originally applies to a superior-inferior relationship, a fact that our paragraph reflects, even if its field of application may have been enlarged.

[176] In which case the same character is pronounced *sheng*.

day…", which has sometimes reinforced the scrupulousness linked to the practice.) Two associated characters specify what is meant by *xing*: first, one must withdraw, retreat in one's innermost (*tui* 退); and, later on, one must infer, draw implications (*fa* 發) from such introspective return to the Self (*Analects* 2.9). The habit of examining oneself nurtures a regular taking of distance, which, in a second time, allows for further engagement.

Introspection also fosters humility: meeting with men of petty character, says Confucius, should lead one to engage even more attentively into self-examination, so as to avoid participating in their abasement (*Analects* 4.17). Finally, it nurtures decisiveness: if the practice of examining oneself "in the innermost" (*nei* 內) reveals no special reason for feeling guilty, then, fear and worries disappear by themselves (*Analects* 12.4). At later times, most writers of the Song period nurture a robust optimism vis-à vis human nature and advise against nurturing anguish and sense of guilt through the practice of self-examination (which they still recommend in view of self-improvement), while thinkers of the Ming-Qing period appear much more pessimistic and guilt-ridden (see Wu 1979).

Acknowledging one's mistakes should lead one to identify patterns that negatively affect our behavior, and to draw consequences from the endeavor, which may include reparations. "Alas! (Confucius says,) I have rarely met with someone who, having recognized his mistake, is able to conduct his own trial in his innermost [子曰：「已矣乎！吾未見能見其過而內自訟者也。」]" (*Analects* 5.27).

Originally, self-examination does not seem to imply any form of ritualization; its process and result are not externalized. In the course of history, the appeal exercised by the "School of the Mind" propounded by Wang Yangming (1472–1529) led to the development of the genre of written self-criticism as well as to the oral confession of wrongdoings by a student to a teacher. Moral self-scrutiny sometimes also took the form of an imaginary self-tribunal, "with the Self playing alternately the role of accuser and defendant" (Wu 1979, 27). Even Emperors – especially during the Ming dynasty (1368–1644) – used to practice self-examination and self-blame, making the latter public when disturbing natural or celestial events were taking place. Imperial practices of introspection were part of a system of guarantees upon the Emperors' performance and of restrictions upon his actions, though such demands were limited in scope (Li 2011).

The *ES* detail what they call the "Examen" in the context of a retreat in which the exercitant comes "to conquer oneself and to regulate one's life in such a way that no decision is made under the influence of any inordinate attachment" (this is the subtitle of the booklet). In this precise context, the practice may appear to an observer as extremely detailed and onerous. However, the habit of examining oneself is to be transposed into the setting of daily life in such a way as to constitute a support, and not a hindrance. During the retreat, the "particular and daily examen" is to be made "in three times" (*ES* 24–26): the morning examen is focused on awakening one's desire to go against such defect or sin that requires special vigilance; at lunchtime, the retreatant examines whether she has fallen into the weakness she is struggling against, and she renews her desire to avoid it. The exercise is repeated on the evening. The ultimate aim is to anchor into one's consciousness and habits the inner awareness and external changes fostered by the time of retreat. A freer format of self-examination will be adopted once the exercitant has returned to her daily responsibilities. Then, the time dedicated to introspection will be of around 15 minutes daily, at a regular moment of the day. The focus of the examen will vary according to changing circumstances and inner movements (Falque and Bougon 2014; Rothausen 2017; Tetlow and Ackels 2007).

Examining oneself regularly enables the practitioner to become more sensitive to whatever is happening within and around her, and to identify trends in her reactions and feelings. During the time she dedicates to the practice, and once her attentiveness has been duly awakened, the practitioner focuses on (a) first, positive events, trends and factors, so as to draw strength and inspiration from it; (b) second, factors and behaviors negatively affecting her life and duties; (c) and third, her wants and desires, in such a way as to mobilize the resources available for attaining the goal she seeks (Fleming 1996, 33; Van Breemen 1996).

Both Confucian and Ignatian models of self-examination ultimately nurture reflexivity though a *focus on particular issues, the nature of which evolves in time.* Introspection does not primarily provide the agent with a general hermeneutic of her experience. Rather, it makes her notice areas of concerns that will mobilize her attention for as long as necessary. For the Ignatian tradition, these areas of concerns need to be assessed while also paying attention to the inner peace that, in domains other than the one of concern, the agent concurrently identifies.

Assessing and Weighing

As one sees, self-examination is a practice to be maintained whether or not the need to make a particular decision is manifested. It develops the ability to remain attentive to one's inner state and proclivities and, concurrently, to better apprehend the context in which personal and professional interactions are taking place. It helps one to become a *discerning person*, but is not yet akin to a process of discernment applied to a given issue or challenge.

In the Chinese context, the *Classic of Documents* already recognizes that all human beings are endowed with a "moral standard [*zhong* 衷]" conducive to discernment, while also regulating and restricting the usage of this standard according to the special responsibilities conferred to the ruler (*Declaration of Tang* 湯誥).

The teaching of Confucius enlarges (and even rectifies) such foundational perspective in two ways: (a) while rulers are indeed entrusted with special duties, the broadening and strengthening of the moral autonomy of (potentially) every individual is activated by civilizational progress and the pursuit of study, Confucius himself dispensing his teaching "without any discrimination [of class or origin]" (*Analects* 15.39); (b) if the Mandate of Heaven is revealed directly to the ruler in the aforementioned case,[177] Confucius experiences and theorizes the internalization of the discovery of Heaven's will, imprinted into each person's moral sanctuary. The unearthing of Heaven's imprint on individual existence proceeds through learning, social interactions and the rumination of life's lessons till the day where one is able to follow one's inclinations without ever overstepping moral boundaries – but reaching such inner freedom is a goal that may be attained only when one reaches 70 years of age… (*Analects* 2.4).

This is to say that, in the meanwhile, ascertaining one's duties and calling requires the practice of discernment. Even the right understanding of what "discernment" is meant to be is already the result of a process:

> There is the one with whom you can engage into study, and yet it proves impossible to [continue to] walk together. There is the one with whom you can walk together, and yet not establish a common rule of life. There is the one with whom you establish a rule of life, and yet you cannot weigh (*quan* 權) [situations] in the same way.
> 子曰：「可與共學，未可與適道；可與適道，未可與立；可與立，未可與權。」
> (*Analects* 9.30)

The character *quan* 權 is generally understood in the sense of "exercising discretion", i.e., setting aside the rule usually followed when a compelling reason asks for such dispensation (see also *Analects* 18.8). (Below, we will find in Mencius examples of discretionary judgments and actions.) The capacity to "exercise discretion" is the result of a process that already starts with the habit of asking the master under whom one studies how to conduct oneself (*Analects* 15.6). Inner freedom grows with the ability to inquire and observe at leisure before reaching a decision (*Analects* 7.29), till the capacity to discern and strategize fully overcomes natural impulses (*Analects* 7.12). The art of discerning becomes a superior virtue when, rather than abstaining from worldly compromisses, the sage confronts situations as she finds them, determining what kind of behavior and decision such situations call for (*Analects* 18.8). Confucius insists upon the fact that confronting reality is

---

[177] The Mandate of the Heaven is generally revealed to rulers through extraordinary signs and/or divination. Divination continuously intervenes in decision-making in China, but Literati will do their utmost to "moralize" its meaning and usage.

superior to withdrawing away from it, however corrupt this world may be (*Analects* 18.8).

Two principles ensure constancy and accuracy in discernment. The first has to do with *balance*, equilibrium (*zhongyong*, cf. *Analects* 6.29). For the one entrusted with authority, "keeping balance" often means to consciously abstain from action, so as not to disrupt existing natural processes by the weight attached to one's inclinations (*Analects* 2.1; see also Slingerland 2003a, 43–75). Constancy in inclinations (which contrasts with continuous oscillations as to the object of one's interest and affections) is a sign of inner balance (*Analects* 12.10), and such constancy makes it easier to regulate the aforesaid inclinations.

Balance goes together with *detachment*, understood as possessing one thing without attaching oneself to it (*Analects* 8.18). The latter is more easily understood than practiced, since Confucius asserts that "[he has] never seen someone loving virtue more than pleasure" (*Analects* 9.18). "Conquering oneself" (*Analects* 12.1) is not an easy task. Self-conquest is powerfully helped by ritual practice (*Analects* 12.1), as the latter educates the inner self through external discipline (but this topic is beyond the scope of the present contribution). Note that Confucius constantly describes the practice of balance and self-conquest as ultimately leading to benevolence towards others (*ren*), an objective so far-reaching that words lack the one who endeavors to speak about it (*Analects* 12.3)

The Greater Good

"Discernment" is a term that is often associated with what is most specific to the Ignatian tradition; and, reciprocally, "the influence of St. Ignatius' *Spiritual Exercises* [...] pervades discernment practice and literature in the Western Christian tradition" (Miller 2020, 401). Yet, the lexical entries on discernment (Spanish: substantive *discreción*; verb *discernir*) are not very numerous in the *ES*. However, discernment certainly permeates the process the *ES* frame.

The capacity to discern is conditioned by the recognition of an *end* that I have already clearly defined, an end that I can clearly distinguish from the satisfactions associated with such or such *means:* riches may be a means towards an end oriented towards the greater good, and yet a source of satisfaction that impedes the realization of the end I had originally in mind. It is common, observes Ignatius, to put the means before the end, for example by first wanting to make a fortune and then thinking afterwards how that fortune could be placed in the service of the greater good (*ES* 169). Ignatius reasons as follows: each thing or state of things is somehow *gifted* to us as a potential means for achieving a goal which, in turn, will communicate to others the life-giving capacity that we all possess. In contrast, the abusive or possessive use of things destroys this dynamic of life and growth. We need to learn not to make any difference between things and life settings other than this one: to prefer and choose things only according to their effective capacity to nurture such dynamic, desiring and choosing that which helps us to communicate *further* (Latin *magis*) the fullness of life (*ES* 23).

The discerning process requires from us an awareness of the inner motions we experience, an awareness nurtured by self-examination. The expression "discernment of *spirits*" refers to the *sources* of the movements that agitate us, as they lead us towards "good ends" or "evil ends" – "evil ends" being sometimes reached through a path that "good intentions" contribute to draw (Fleming 1996, 243). Ignatius distinguishes two sets of "rules for discernment", the first one to be used when self-knowledge has been awakened, the second for "a more subtle discernment".

The first set of rules states that, whenever we lock ourselves into an attitude or life-style that is contrary to the life-giving dynamic described above, the evil spirit (in modern terms, it could be called for instance "the death drive") usually prompts us to persevere in this state by causing us to experience and sparkle delusional satisfactions. The good spirit, on the other hand, will make us feel our own inner discomfort and the contradictions that plague us. When, on the contrary, we strive to conform our lives to a life-giving dynamic, the tactics of the spirits are the opposite. The evil spirit saddens and discourages us, stirring up all kinds of reasons that would prevent us from continuing on this path, while the good spirit will comfort us (*ES* 314–315). It is thus necessary to discern among inner "consolations" (characterized by resolve and clarity of purpose) and "desolations" (signaled by discouragement and confusion) as well as to identify their motives. In a state of desolation, we must never change the resolutions made before we started to experience such state; for, in consolation, it is usually the good spirit who guides us, while in desolation the evil spirit very often tries to take hold of us. The evil spirit works as a skillful military leader, says Ignatius, circling enemy fortifications to find the weak point in which to concentrate the attack. Our weak points may consist of our unpreparedness and weaknesses, or, more dreadfully, our excessive self-confidence (*ES* 327).

As we progress in interior freedom we must learn to enter into a "more subtle discernment", assessing even more distinctly the actions of the spirits within us. While a state of inner comfort that has no distinguishable external cause generally comes from the good spirit, each time the consolation we feel arises from an external cause (worldly success, words we heard, thoughts that events or readings aroused), it may have its origin in the good as well as in the bad spirit. The good spirit produces in us consolation to give us strength and courage on our way; the evil spirit uses the same means to distract us insidiously from the road, generally using thoughts that first seem to be good and generous, progressively orienting them towards dubious ends. This is why we must learn to examine the course of our thoughts. If their beginning, middle, and end are all geared towards what leads us from the good to the best, this is a sign of the work of the Spirit. But if the course of our thoughts leads us at some point towards less good resolutions, projects centered on ourselves, or if it engenders a desolation that disturbs our former peace, this is a sign that the evil spirit is at work. (*ES* 331–333).

These rules apply when examining the inner moves experienced before taking a decision, be it on matters subject to change, such as the rules we fix to ourselves as to food intake (*ES* 210–217), or irrevocable, such as the sharing and dividing of one's goods (*ES* 337–344). A process of discernment is considered coming to its end once a resolution debated for some time in the innermost awakens undisturbed resolve and inner peace.

As we have seen (cf. notably *Analects* 2.4, 6.29 and 12.4), in Confucianism, peace and resolve also signal the conclusion of a discernment process. Today, contributions dealing with the practice of collective discernment have popularized the idea that the comfort awakened by a resolution (if such comfort is experienced during some period of time) is by itself a confirmation that the discernment was correct: a collective that feels peaceful about the discernment process it has led and the outcome it has produced finds in such sentiment the strength it needs for entering the stage of implementation.

A Question of Life and Death

Still, a gap remains to be filled. Discerning is one thing, making a decision effective is another one. Decision-making may be impeded by procrastination (even without any clear reason to question the decision taken) or by the fact of "loving pleasure more than virtue", as Confucius puts it (*Analects* 9.18). The Confucian tradition intends to help in the process by *radicalizing* what is at stake: virtually, every decision is about issues of life and death. Although such a trend is already at work in the *Analects* (see notably 15.9), it is Mencius who illustrates it best. Three examples will prove it.

First, there is in humankind a natural proclivity to protect and nurture life, which sometimes leads to action without even having to go through discernment: Mencius asks us to imagine ourselves suddenly noticing a child perched on the edge of a well. The very visualization of such a scene almost causes the reader to rush to lift the child off the curb – whether or not she knows the child's parents and neighbors, Mencius points out (*Mencius* 2 A.6).

The second example shows a kind of "spontaneous discernment" based on the conscious primacy given to the fact of protecting and nurturing life, even though Mencius confronts the reproach of putting "Ritual [*li*]" above all things:

> Chunyu Kun asked: "Man and woman, if they are related, cannot touch each other when they give or receive something, it is the rule [*li*, the rite], is it not?"[178] Mencius replied, "Yes, that is indeed the rule." "If your sister-in-law is drowning, will you reach out your hand to rescue her?" "Whoever does not save his sister-in-law would be a wolf. That man and woman do not touch each other if they are parents, that is the rule; as to rescuing our sister-in-law by extending our hand, that is exercising discretion [*quan*]".
> 淳于髡曰：「男女授受不親，禮與？」孟子曰：「禮也。」曰：「嫂溺則援之以手乎？」曰：「嫂溺不援，是豺狼也。男女授受不親，禮也；嫂溺援之以手者，權也。」
>
> (*Mencius* 4 A.17)

And yet, as shown by the third example, you do not protect life – at least your own life – at any price. Asked to explain why Ritual is more important than food or sexual appetite, Mencius responds:

> Suppose that by twisting your older brother's arm to take what he is eating you could get food; and you won't be able to if you don't – will you twist his arm? By climbing over the wall to the east of your property and kidnapping your neighbor's virgin daughter you could acquire a wife; you can't if you don't – will you go and take her away?
> 紾兄之臂而奪之食，則得食；不紾，則不得食，則將紾之乎？踰東家牆而摟其處子，則得妻；不摟，則不得妻，則將摟之乎？
>
> (*Mencius* 6B.1)

As we have seen in Chapter 2, Mencius makes a similar point and makes use of the same pedagogical method when speaking about justice, comparing life to a fish and justice to a bear's paw: the gourmet summoned to choose will not hesitate to sacrifice the first to keep the second (*Mencius* 4 A.10). What applies to a choice between fish and bear's paw should be true when choosing between life and justice. Mencius invites us here to enter an experiential mode of knowledge that will trigger decisiveness once what is at stake is clearly perceived. If clear and vivid, our perceptions will increase our resolve to preserve and to nurture life, or, conversely, to sacrifice one's life for the greater good. The fact that clear and vivid perceptions necessarily trigger resolution may explain why Confucius, asked about someone who used to think thrice before engaging into action, simply replied: "Twice would be enough" (*Analects* 5.20).

---

[178] In a household where an extended family resides, strict rules governing exchanges and contacts between relatives are essential to ensure the sustainability of common existence.

Radicalizing the issues at stake so as to trigger decisiveness is exactly what the *ES* also try to operate. Ignatius dedicates long developments to what he calls "the time for making election" (*ES* 169–188). I will limit myself to summarize the dimensions he stresses most during the course of these 30 paragraphs.

Whoever is finalizing a decision must be moved by a simple intention; she wants to elect what will allow her to respond more fully to the end she has elected, i.e., to choose the means best ordered to this end. Let us note that we are not speaking of deciding between right and wrong: we do not *discern* whether or not we are going to commit a crime (whether I am going or not to bribe an official for instance); we just need to refrain from committing something objectively illegal or immoral. When we are making an election, we discern between the *good* and the *better*.

The moment when to enact a decision occurs during one of the following three "times [*tiempos*]" (i.e., when we are experiencing one of the following inner states): when we realize what ought to be done "without doubting, or being able to doubt" (*ES* 175); when the experience of inner movements or "spirits" gives us sufficient light to make a choice; when I can think reflexively, without feeling any agitation, then able to make my decision according to the end towards which I am oriented.

The drive towards implementation fostered by Confucius/Mencius, on the one hand, and that fostered by Ignatius, on the other hand, look strikingly similar. Let us here remark that the factors that affect decisions in contemporary context, such as the weight now given to climate change or to the need for inclusiveness, give accrued resonance to the "radicalization" of the stakes that our two traditions deliberately operate.

Cross-spiritual Insights and Decision-making

The *Analects* and the *Mencius* speak of self-examination, discernment and decision-taking in a remarkably free, conversational and pragmatic fashion while the *Daxue*[179] and the *Zhongyong* operate a systematization of their insights and advices. Ignatius' *Exercises* may show an even greater degree of systematicity and methodological progression that these two Confucian short treatises. It would be easy to contrast the *Analects* and the *ES*, as their time and background differ to so great an extent. However, it might be more fruitful to recognize their common-

---

[179] *Daxue* (大學) or *Great Learning*: one of the 'Four Books" selected by Zhu Xi for grounding Confucian studies. The *Daxue* opens up the cursus, while the *Zhongyong* concludes it.

alities as to the process of examen, discernment and decision-taking here under study.
- Both traditions recognize that it is difficult to consistently reach and implement sound, life-giving decisions without a sustained training of the heart, the intellect and the will, a training that, taken in its integrality, constitutes what Confucius calls "study [*xue*]" and is similarly at the core of the Jesuits' educational tradition.
- Balance or prudence (an idea included within the all-encompassing notion of *zhongyong*) has often been identified as the cardinal virtue of classical Confucianism. Taking distance from our inner inclinations, for instance by suspending decision in times of desolation, constitutes the Ignatian equivalent of Confucian prudence. Resisting ingrained patterns of behavior by engaging into the way opposite to the one we usually follow – the strategy of "going against" (Latin *agere contra*) one's proclivities[180] – is also part of the Ignatian conduct for finding personal balance and preparing balanced decisions (cf. *ES* 13, 52 and 351).
- Both traditions distinguish carefully between "ends" and "means". With an optimism characteristic of both classical Confucianism and Renaissance Humanism they trust in the ability of human beings to identify and embrace objectives that are worthy of their existence and efforts, provided that the subjects' original nature has not been perverted at some point by education or circumstances.
- However, they also recognize in the variety of "means" offered to us (means being assimilated to the goods and resources at our disposal) a potential factor of disruption, which often induces us to take what should be a "means" as an "end". Overcoming our attachment to a thing or a state of thing is akin to recognize that the object of our attachment is merely a means, and to treat it (i.e., to keep or discard it) accordingly. Both traditions strongly recommend to cultivate such "detachment".
- Obviously, Confucians and Ignatian writings assess and hierarchize in their own way the potential "ends" and "means" of human existence and social organizations. For instance, for Confucius, "justice" (*yi* 義) is an end *per se* (an end higher than the conservation of one's own life, stresses Mencius), while "pleasure" (*se* 色) does not seem to be considered as one (but "joy" [*yue* 悅] certainly deserves to be seen as constituting an ultimate end). However, our two traditions, rather than coming up with pre-ordained lists of ends and means,

---

[180] I may reduce my intake of food if I show a proclivity towards gluttony, but I will increase it if I recognize in my way of fasting a form, even nascent, of self-destructive behavior.

put the stress on *mapping the process* through which individuals or organizations determine and hierarchize the ones and the others, letting them free to establish their own criteria as long as the discernment process is sincere and the result self-consistent.
- The Ignatian tradition insists upon the necessity to elucidate the inner motions that agitate or comfort us, while the Confucian tradition seems to put more stress on the immediate perception of "what is to be done" by a well-educated conscience. The commonality lies in the fact that, in both cases, conscience proves to be the ultimate judge, and thus the decision-trigger: Confucius and Mencius underline that "discretion [*quan*]" is to be exercised vis-à-vis usual rules of behavior, and Ignatius notes that the choice of the greater good may lead to electing paradoxical means, such as poverty rather than riches or shame rather than honor (*ES* 23).
- Finally, both traditions are aware that the fact of identifying what is to be done does not always provide the subject with the resolution that is necessary to make decisions become effective. They work towards overcoming such obstacle by radicalizing the issues at stake: during the last stage of the process, when issues and obstacles are already well recognized, every decision, big or small, is seen as essentially life-giving or, conversely, leading to demise. Confucius sees procrastination as detrimental (*Analects* 5.20), and Ignatius dramatizes the setting by making the subject imagine herself on her deathbed, looking back at her past decision (*ES* 186, 187).

There are still notable differences among our two traditions. For instance, the Ignatian way of proceeding relies on a representation of the Self as a locus where the agent (the subject) is led to assess the origins and effects of conflicting inclinations that both her inner world and the environment in which she is located generate (Fessard 1956; De Certeau 1973; Dunne 1996). As the quotes from the *Analects* mobilized in this article already show, the Confucian tradition represents the Self as a *knot of relationships*. Consequently, the Confucian style of introspection centers upon the conduct of these relationships as they can be observed – a process of objectification that the importance attached to ritual observances both triggers and reinforces. One could argue that the Ignatian way of proceeding relies on a "thick" conception of personhood, while the Confucian way, more parsimonious in assumptions, starts from a "thin" approach of the same, and is therefore more prone to universalization. At the same time, modernity has brought with it a number of assumptions that, in many different contexts, including the Chinese one, confers to (and requires from) the Self a degree of autonomy that stands closer to the Ignatian representation than to classical Confucianism. In today's world, and independently from the differences noted from one value system to another, are some processes of discernment more adapted than others to certain cultural contexts? This remains an open question, to which one could presumably answer more accurately by focusing on ingrained behaviors rather than on the discourses held by the agents.

Taken together, the Confucian and Ignatian traditions do not *equate* each other. But their mutual engagement through a comparative exegesis liberates resources for elaborating what could be called *a global phronesis:* in such a vision, personal growth, as it is triggered by examination and discernment, ultimately allows all the agents of a given community to become active participants in the conversational process, and decisions would thus become the end-results of interactions conducted among lucid and balanced agents, equal in status. Indeed, both the Confucian and Ignatian traditions have consistently aimed at shaping not only discerning individuals but also communities able to conduct deliberations in their midst. Chapters 11 and 12 of the *Analects*, which describe the interactions between Confucius and his disciples and among the disciples themselves, is to be read in this light. As to Ignatius, the passage from discerning individuals to discerning communities is illustrated by the way the insights found in the *ES* are furthered in the *Constitutions* of the Society of Jesus. We are here looking at the "horizon" of the dynamic process described in our research, and we thus need to remind ourselves that it is on the horizon line that mirages sometimes appear. However, by stressing the potential contagiousness of the process here described we remain faithful to the inspiration that made Confucius and Ignatius share with their friends and disciples a number of insights that, till today, appear to be loaded with some special efficacy once they are expressed and applied.

* * *

Each of the four examples developed in the course of this chapter is of a specific nature. As triggered by topics and insights found within the Chinese tradition, the focus on Ritual highlights the anomie experienced by a number of communities throughout the globe, and it suggests ways of tackling related cultural and social issues. Concurrently, it opens up ways of opening up intellectual and religious dialogue that grounds itself on patterns of interactions rather than on confrontations about words and concepts. Our second debate, which bears on meritocracy, reinterprets the Chinese experience and way of proceeding in the context of the crisis undergone by liberal democracies. The conclusions often drawn from this reinterpretation are disputed, and rightly so, but they certainly contribute to reshape the terms in which political theory is formalized. Third, looking at the way Arendt's thought has been received in China underlines the fact that a style of Western anthropological and political thinking deeply anchored in the Greek source maintains some relevance for Chinese thinkers when the latter critically assess the trends and systemic arrangements that define China's contemporary social and political space. Besides, the Chinese reading of Arendt highlights cultural and ideological phenomena that go beyond the divisions we usually draw between diverging political systems. Finally, the criss-crossing of the Confucian and Ignatian traditions on self-examination and discernment responds to a quest for sound ethical judgment and decision-making that transcends (but certainly does not abolish) differences in sensitivities and world visions.

The last example may also retroactively illuminate an aspect common to the four: they all lean towards a return to philosophy understood as a quest for wisdom. At the beginning of this book, I warned against a "cognitivist" approach of philosophy: thought systems are often described as sets of propositions that venture truth claims about "objective" realities, systems that can be conveniently opposed through landscaping operations similar to the ones we described in Chapters 1 to 3. The criticisms addressed to such cognitivist approach are many. The most important one is that no meaning should be univocally associated to a single proposition and that, in general, every single proposition meets its contrary within the system itself. These "contradictions" are not necessarily akin to logical fallacies. Rather, taking them into account helps one to assess anew the scope and ambition of a given system of thought, beyond the "summary" that the history of philosophy has provided us with. Besides, the style and context of specific assertions as well as their purported intention (exhorting, teaching, admonishing) are also to be taken into account. In other words, a cognitivist description cannot deliver a satisfactory account of a given wisdom system (Lindbeck 1984; Barret 1988).

In contrast to said approach, "philosophical wisdoms" could be defined as "idioms for construing reality". "Dialogic wisdoms" enlarge the domain they define: dialogic wisdoms are vectors that convey experience, knowledge and patterns of action in such a way as to question and (possibly) enlarge the perimeters within which the same wisdoms were meant to stay enclosed. A wisdom system can be compared to a map drafted in view of helping an intended set of people (the ones who have been trained to read the map according to the rules that govern its drawing) to travel from one place to another, at least in the symbolic ambitus that the map allows them to explore. The spreading of wisdom through dialogic transformations corresponds to the progressive mapping of a larger territory, opened to more and more people. These explorers acquire a common understanding of the rules needed for reading the maps in the very process by which these rules are being changed throughout the interactions taking place. Ultimately, our four examples testify to the fact that the traditional mappings of our positioning within the world (as well as our representations of our action upon it) are undergoing constant transformations, negotiated in the process through which our maps are displayed and studied together.

Conclusion

Should the task of enlisting Chinese philosophy into global debates be considered too serious a matter for being left to sinologists and scholars specializing in Chinese thought? The question sounds facile, but it points towards a caveat that should be kept in mind: the resources found in the various traditions of China should neither be confiscated nor monopolized under the pretext that "Chinese exceptionalism" makes their mobilization a precinct to be entered only with some kind of accreditation. For sure, and as is the case in all fields of research, the Chinese philosophical tradition needs to mobilize expertise. At the same time, insofar as one endeavors to go beyond "philosophizing" it should not be approached as being merely an object of specialized knowledge. Traditions are kept alive in the way they trigger insights that are shared, developed, put into connection with other insights, made universal through the rephrasing these insights call for.

Such conviction also leads us to avoid a dual confrontation between the so-called "Western" and "Chinese" traditions. Both have been shaped in history through their encounters with a privileged Other – with the Semitic worldview and language system in the first case; with the Buddhist/Indian logic and metaphysics (as well as with the Indo-European linguistic family they are associated with) in the second. Besides, both the Semitic and Indian corpus of thought were characterized by a remarkable diversity of opinions, richness of sources, and ductility in modes of expression: These encounters opened up new destinies to the cosmological and metaphysical systems elaborated in, respectively, the Greco-Roman world and ancient China. I am not even sure that the word "system" is here appropriate, as it tends to overlook the variety and flexibility present in these two cultural spheres. Too many historians of philosophy specialize in reconstructing a supposed overall coherence or a line of progressive evolution in the modes of thought characteristic of a given cultural sphere. But debates and dialogues have always contributed in making the art of thinking both *contextual* and *performative*. Within a dialogic performance, what we now consider as incoherencies and contradictions were not understood to be such. Answering an interlocutor's specific questions and doing so by taking into account her life setting, discoursing according to the constraints and openings attached to a given situation, making thinking and exchanging *transformational* – all of this was and remains central for what we should continue to call *the life of the mind*. Till today, once they are mobilized in a dialogic context, notions and argument assert their meaning through *performances* given in time and space. As we meet with interlocutors who come from very different horizons, we better understand the fact that parables, dialogic performances and all the other rhetorical tools meant to trigger insights and breakthrough contribute to creating communities of thought through which we discover a commonality of ends – communities that see themselves grounded not upon pre-established *identities* but on the dialogic surge of a *telos*. Let me add, evoking again Gadamer's analysis of prejudices, that this does not mean that we erase the points of departure that are ours but rather that we take them as being indeed *departures*, which, as such, determine the course of our progressive displacements.

Displacement is actually one of the *topoi* of ancient Chinese thought.[181] One of the most famous sentences of the *Analects* of Confucius says that "the wise man [*zhizhe* 知者] takes pleasure in [contemplating] the water, while the good man [*renzhe* 仁者] enjoys [looking at] the mountain" (6.23"). No opposition here: Confucius rather suggests that "wisdom" and "humaneness" complement each other, as water and mountain together compose a landscape that contents the eye and the heart. At the same time, if water provides one with a privileged metaphor for wisdom it is due to its ability to turn, to flow downhill, and to displace itself so as to adjust its course. In contrast, mountains suggest the immutable goodness of a constant heart. Mencius will reconcile the immutability of a constant heart and the adaptability of water by refining the metaphor: "Water certainly does not distinguish between East and West, but does it fail to distinguish between up and down? The goodness of human nature is like the downhill movement of water – there is no person who is not good, just as there is no water that does not flow downward" (*Mencius* 6 A.1).[182] Displacement necessarily leads us downhill, towards places where we were not thinking to go (see *Daodejing* 8).

Thought displacement is also illustrated in the ancient Chinese tradition through the usage of stories, parables, fables... Stories are a privileged vehicle for wisdom: they flow, they follow and then leave their course, like water does. They inspire the listener without obliging her to reduplicate a specific course of action. They allow her to continue the storyline, building on preceding "episodes" for inventing her own solution to the problem she is meeting with – while the decision she will take will be based indeed on the rumination of the stories heard in the past.

Said otherwise, through metaphors and rhetorical devices, Chinese thought *tends to erase and perpetually displace its own positioning*. Chinese wisdom takes its model on the infant, on the fool, sometimes on the madman,[183] and so

---

181 In the development that follows, I partly borrow from (and reformulate) a previous contribution of mine (Vermander 2016).
182 I follow here the translation of Slingerland (2011), 21. Through an analysis of this excerpt of the *Mencius*, Slingerland illustrates the relationship established between body, emotion and thought in the argumentative strategy developed by ancient Chinese philosophy.
183 See for instance *Zhuangzi*, Chapter 18.

much so because it always leads one back to the two extremes of birth and death that challenge all "positioning". It thus reveals that any true quest for wisdom is based on loss, transition and escape. Wise persons must be cautious "as the one crossing a lake in winter" (*Daodejing* 15): after all, it may be Wisdom itself that sometimes breaks down, "as ice gives way to spring" (*Daodejing* 15). Chinese wisdom locates itself just on this joint, on this passage between the solid and the fluid, at this precise moment when one may lose one's footing – and yet one has to continue. And its positioning at this passage is what makes it truly philosophical. The surrounding culture has often betrayed, distorted or contradicted the original inspiration, but Chinese wisdom still operates as a paradoxical teaching that unearths the spirit from the letter that both forwards and constrains it. The teaching of Wisdom remains for everyone to see: "Renounce your sageness and discard your wisdom [*jue sheng qi zhi* 絕聖棄智]" (*Daodejing* 19).

I find in such displacement an impetus that leads to thinking comparatively, establishing connections and tackling issues from a new angle – an impetus much greater than the one provided by the fact of reconstructing cosmological and epistemological syntheses that, anyway, remained always disputed within the Chinese tradition itself. It is through the process by which Chinese classics displace their topic, displace their wisdom, displace their readers that I am brought back with new insights towards the texts I had known (but had I *read* them?) before embarking on Chinese waters. The Chinese way of operating displacements makes me reinterpret Biblical Wisdom not through the inventory of its content but rather as a "place of confluence" (a "crossroads", cf. Prov 8:2), a fluid space, a path that develops its course throughout the upheavals of history. For instance, post-exilic wisdom cannot be equated to the teachings and experiences lived and understand prior to Exile: a collective trauma has changed its style and stresses. Wisdom appears as vulnerable as it is plural: the images that compose its ever-changing language offer to its listener approximations that need to be perpetually updated according to the course of historical experience. But Wisdom's very vulnerability allows her to be the space in which a dialogic encounter occurs and develops. And dialogue has necessarily a political dimension: "The Wisdom Books are meant to give voice back to the people, to whom the Law and the Prophets had been [unilaterally] speaking" (Beauchamp 1977, 142). For evoking another setting, Chinese Wisdom has its own way of highlighting the therapeutic dimension of Greek philosophy, the stress put by the latter on shaping both the soul and the mind (a faculty akin to what the Chinese calls *xin* 心 – the heart-mind) rather than on closing debates and perfecting systems.

These considerations have an impact on the way to assess present-day challenges and to imagine the future. They are directly related to the task of shaping a set of insights as to what it means to think, to act and to interact as human beings in today's world, and of shaping such insights in a way that makes them widely shared and creatively implemented. No need to stress the centrality of such task at a time when a "world civilization" is both in the making and at risk of disappearing even before it has fully emerged. The sustainability of any community (including the word system that gathers humankind into one) largely depends on the wisdom we devise, share and display. Ultimately, "Wisdom" deals with questions of life and death. In times of emergency, drastic decisions may be called for, and the future of the community relies on the wisdom of those called by tradition or by necessity to suggest and/or implement a course of action.

Cultures, philosophical traditions, creeds and worldviews are being presently challenged and reformulated through the interpretative resources offered by the other cultures, traditions, worldviews and creeds – and this operation happens simultaneously for all participants in the exchange. This is actually why communal identities are reasserted with such conviction and, sometimes, violence. This does not need to be the case: though identities are mobile and changeable, they are still discrete entities, and (as underlined in our fifth chapter) the solutions to our common challenges may often remain localized. However, throughout an interpretative process, these particular solutions will considerably vary from the ones suggested by the traditional understanding of one's culture and identity, and the array of solutions devised from one culture or group to another will then be legitimately understood as a correlated set of attitudes, choices and decisions.

As a "final opening", to be furthered by the reader, I will here suggest yet another way of looking at our particular traditions and at engaging them comparatively and philosophically. An ecosystemic theory of life considers "life" itself as a property of an ecological system nurtured by mutuality rather than as a consequence of the biochemical or physical characteristics of any specific organism within the system (Morowitz 1993). The lesson can be applied to the life of the mind. Let us first consider each of our wisdom traditions as a threefold "ecosystem": (a) It translates the properties of specific ecological systems (for instance, the one of the Central Plains of China, of the Mediterranean world) experientially and reflectively. In other words, it makes a community devise an adaptive strategy for the milieu in which it lives and grows, while making the properties of the natural milieu a trigger for an overall understanding of the world.[184] (b) A wisdom/philosophical tradition also meditates on its own premises and finds in itself resources for challenging both its prejudices and its conclusions. Consequently, it remains open to possible breakthrough, to far-reaching transformations that may af-

---

[184] The quasi-equivalence established by the Chinese tradition between "Water" and "Dao" is a case in point.

fect its way of dealing with the world. This "inner opening" is triggered and nurtured by the dialogic dynamic that takes place in the midst of the community. (c) Finally, a thought ecosystem can be approached as an ever-evolving endeavor for ensuring communal sustainability and shared meaning. This means that (as has been stressed from the beginning of the present work) it necessarily thinks teleologically.

These three operations occur simultaneously, and "the life of the mind" surges from the act of apprehending a milieu, of shaping rules of engagement through dialogic exchange, and of debating the ends that the community and/or the subject establish as their horizon. Historically, the whole process unfolds inchoatively, as undergoing a series of loops. The life of the mind grows throughout retroactions, the way it happens for organic life.

Today, in the net shaped by the meeting of our thought ecosystems, we still find these same characteristics: our "Web of Wisdoms" speaks to humankind of the environment that sustains its life and of the way to interact with all forms of life; of the mental ecology of our species; and of the ends we assign or should assign to ourselves. The criss-crossing of these three dimensions enables us to imagine and possibly to build a world to be inhabited together. Certainly, the tasks that such imagining imparts upon us are overwhelming. However, this global context is the one where to meaningfully locate the Chinese-Western philosophical encounter.

References

Allan, Sarah. 1997. *The Way of Water and Sprouts of Virtue.* Albany, NY: SUNY Press.
Ames, Roger T. 2005. "Getting Past the Eclipse of Philosophy in World Sinology: A Response to Eske Møllgaard". *Dao* 4 (2): 347–352.
Ames, Roger T. 2007. "'Getting Rid of God': A Prolegomenon to Dialogue between Chinese and Western Philosophy in an Era of Globalization". In *Dialogues of Philosophies, Religions, and Civilizations in the Era of Globalization* (Chinese Philosophical Studies 25), edited by Zhao Dunhua and Geroge F. McLean: 29–46. Washington, D.C.: The Council for Research in Values and Philosophy.
Ames, Roger T. 2010. "Achieving Personal Identity in Confucian Role Ethics: Tang Junyi on Human Nature as Conduct". *Oriens Extremus* 49: 143–166.
Ames, Roger T. 2011. *Confucian Role Ethics: A Vocabulary.* Honolulu: University of Hawai'i Press.
Ames, Roger T. 2016. "Getting Past Transcendence: Determinacy, Indeterminacy, and Emergence in Chinese Natural Cosmology". In *Transcendence, Immanence, and Intercultural Philosophy*, edited by Nahum Brown and William Franke: 3–33. London: Palgrave Macmillan.
Ames, Roger T. and David Hall. 2001. *Focusing the Familiar: A Translation and Philosophical Interpretation of the Zhongyong.* Honolulu: University of Hawai'i Press.
Ames, Roger T. and Henry Rosemont Jr. 1998. *The Analects of Confucius: A Philosophical Translation.* New York: Ballantine.
Amiot, Joseph-Marie. 1779. *Mémoire sur la Musique des Chinois.* Paris: Nyon.
Aquinas, Thomas. 2006. *Summa Theologica.* Blackfriars edition. New York: McGraw-Hill.
Arendt, Hannah. 1973. *The Origins of Totalitarianism.* New York: Harcourt Brace Jovanovich.
Arendt, Hannah. 1998 [1958]. *The Human Condition.* Chicago: University of Chicago Press.
Aristotle. 2004. *Metaphysics*, translated by J. Hugh Lawson-Tancred. London: Penguin.
Armstrong, David M. 1978. *Nominalism and Realism.* Vol. 1: *Universals and Scientific Realism.* Cambridge: Cambridge University Press.
Austin, John L. 1962. *How to Do Things with Words.* Oxford: Clarendon Press.
Bäck, Allan. 2008. "Aristotle's Abstract Ontology". *The Society for Ancient Greek Philosophy Newsletter*, March 20, https://orb.binghamton.edu/sagp/377, last retrieved November 15, 2022.
Baehr Peter. 2010. "China the Anomaly: Hannah Arendt, Totalitarianism, and the Maoist Regime". *European Journal of Political Theory* 9 (3): 267–286.
Bai, Tongdong 白彤东. 2009. 旧邦新命 [*New Mission for an Old Country*]. Beijing: Peking University Press.
Bai, Tongdong. 2020. *Against Political Equality.* Princeton: Princeton University Press.
Barrett, L.C. 1988. "Theology as Grammar: Regulative Principles or Paradigms and Practices". *Modern Theology* 4 (2): 155–172.
Bartsch, Shadi. 2023. *Plato goes to China: The Greek Classics and Chinese Nationalism.* Princeton; Princeton University Press.
Beauchamp, Paul. 1977. *L'Un et l'Autre Testament*, vol. 1. Paris: Le Cerf.
Beauchamp, Paul. 2005 [1969]. *Création et séparation. Étude exégétique du premier chapitre de la Genèse.* Paris: Le Cerf.
Behuniak, Jim (ed.). 2018. *Appreciating the Chinese Difference: Engaging Roger T. Ames on Methods, Issues, and Roles.* Albany, NY: SUNY Press.

Behuniak, Jim. 2021. "Sameness, Difference, and the Post-Comparative Turn". In *One Corner of the Square: Essays on the Philosophy of Roger T. Ames*, edited by Ian M. Sullivan and Joshua Mason: 5–14. Honolulu: University of Hawai'i Press.

Béjà, Jean-Philippe. 2019. "Xi Jinping's China: On the Road to Neo-totalitarianism". *Social Research* 86 (1): 203–230.

Bell, Daniel A. 2015. *The China Model: Political Meritocracy and the Limits of Democracy*. Princeton: Princeton University Press.

Bergson, Henri. 2010 [1934]. *The Creative Mind. An Introduction to Metaphysics*. Mineola: Dover.

Bernard-Maître, Henri. 1949. "Un dossier bibliographique de la fin du XVIIème siècle sur la question des termes chinois". *Recherches de Sciences Religieuses* 36: 25–79.

Berthrong, John H. 1991. "To Catch a Thief: Zhu Xi (1130–1200) and the Hermeneutic Art". *Journal of Chinese Philosophy* 18 (2): 195–212.

Billeter, Jean-François. 2006. *Contre François Jullien*. Paris: Allia.

Billioud, Sébastien and Joël Thoraval. 2015. *The Sage and the People: The Confucian Revival in China*. New York: Oxford University Press.

Birrell, Ann. 1993. *Chinese Mythology: An Introduction*. Baltimore and London: John Hopkins University Press.

Boer, Roland. 2021. *Socialism with Chinese Characteristics: A Guide for Foreigners*. Springer Nature eBook.

Boileau, Gilles. 2013. "The Sage Unbound: Ritual Metaphors in the Daodejing". *Daoism: Religion, History and Society* 5: 1–56.

Bonicco-Donato, Céline. 2022. "Les rites d'interaction : l'héritage de la conception chinoise de la face dans la sociologie d'Erving Goffman". In *Autour du Traité des rites (Liji): de la canonisation du rituel à une société ritualisée*, edited by Anne Cheng and Stéphane Feuillas: 107–123. Paris: Hémisphères éditions.

Bresciani, Umberto. 2001. *Reinventing Confucianism. The New Confucian Movement*. Taipei: Taipei Ricci Institute.

Brindley, Erica Fox. 2012. *Music, Cosmology, and the Politics of Harmony in Early China*. Albany, NY: SUNY Press.

Brindley, Erica Fox., Paul R. Goldin and Esther S. Klein. 2013. "A Philosophical Translation of the Heng Xian". *Dao* 12 (2): 145–151.

Brown, Shana J. 2011. *Pastimes, From Art and Antiquarianism to Modern Chinese Historiography*. Honolulu: University of Hawai'i Press.

Bruya, Brian (ed.). 2015. *The Philosophical Challenge from China*. Cambridge, MA: MIT Press.

Cabezon, Jose Ignacio (ed.). 1998. *Scholasticism: Cross-cultural and Comparative Perspectives*. Albany, NY: SUNY Press.

Chai, David. 2019. *Zhuangzi and the Becoming of Nothingness*. Albany, NY: SUNY Press.

Chai, Wenyu. 2013. *General Education in Chinese Higher Education: A Case Study of Fudan University*. Doctoral thesis, Hong Kong University.

Chan, Wing-Tsit, Isma'il Ragi Al Faruqi, Joseph M. Kitagawa and P.T. Raju (eds.). 1969. *Great Asian Religions: An Anthology*. London: Macmillan.

Chang, Carson. 1962. *The Development of Neo-Confucian Thought*, vol 1. New York: Bookman.

Chang, Chishen. 2011. "Tianxia System on a Snail's Horns". *Inter-Asia Cultural Studies* 12 (1): 28–42.

Chang, Kevin. 2016. "*Dongfang Xue:* European Philology in Republican China". *Geschichte der Germanistik* 49/50: 5–22.

Chemla, Karine (ed.). 1991. *Extrême-Orient, Extrême-Occident, 13. Modèles et structures des textes chinois anciens: les formalistes soviétiques en sinologie.* Nanterre: Presses Universitaires de Nanterre.

Chemla, Karine (ed.). 2012. *The History of Mathematical Proof in Ancient Traditions.* Cambridge: Cambridge University Press.

Chemla, Karine and Guo (Shuchun) (transl.) 2004. *Les neuf chapitres : Le classique mathématique de la Chine ancienne et ses commentaires.* Paris: Dunod.

Chen, Albert Lichuan. 2007. "Remarques sur les critiques chinoises du Contrat social". *Transtext(e)s Transcultures* 2, http://journals.openedition.org/transtexts/92 .

Chen, Biyao 陈璧耀. 2008. 国学概说 [*A Summary of National Studies*]. Shanghai: Shanghai Education Press.

Chen, Duxiu. 1920. "*Jidujiao yu Zhongguoren* 基督教與中國人 [Christianity and the Chinese People]". *Xinqingnian (New Youth)* 7/3 (February): 17–21.

Chen, Guying 陳鼓應 (ed.), 1983.莊子今注今譯 (*Zhuangzi: Contemporary Notes and Translation*). Beijing: Zhongguo Shuju, 1983.

Chen, Jianming. 2008. "Modern Chinese Attitudes towards the Bible". In *Reading Christian Scriptures in China*, edited by Chloë Starr: 13–31. London: T&T Clark.

Chen, Jiaren and Benoît Vermander. 2019. "Rituals, Spacetime and Family in a 'Native' Community of North Shanghai". *Religions* 10 (10), https://doi.org/10.3390/rel10100582 , last retrieved November 15, 2022.

Chen, Lai. 2009. *Tradition and Modernity: A Humanist View*, translated by Edmund Ryden. Leiden and Boston: Brill.

Chen, Lai 陈来. 2014. 仁学本体论 [*The Ontology of Ren*]. Beijing: Sanlian.

Chen, Lai 陈来. 2017. "中华文化的当代价值与意义 [The Value and Significance of Chinese Culture Today]". *People's Daily*, March 17.

Chen, Lai 陈来 and Fang Xudong 方旭东. 2018. "让西方回到西方 [Let the West Go Back to the West]". *The Paper*, 24 July, http://m.thepaper.cn/renmin_prom.jsp?contid=2286329&from=renmin, last retrieved November 15, 2022.

Chen, Xioafen 陈晓芬 and Xu Rizong 徐儒宗 (eds.). 2011. 論語、大學、中庸 [*The Analects, The Great Learning, The Doctrine of the Mean*]. Beijing: Zhonghua Shuju.

Cheng, Anne. 1984. "La trame et la chaîne : aux origines de la constitution d'un corpus canonique au sein de la tradition confucéenne." *Extrême-Orient, Extrême-Occident* 5: 13–26.

Cheng, Guangyun 程广云. 2016. "劳动、财产和自由一~在马克思与阿伦特之间 [Labor, Property and Freedom. Between Marx and Arendt]". *Marxist Theory and Practice* 马克思主义与现实2: 124–131.

Clastres, Pierre. 1977. *Society Against the State*, translated by Robert Hurley and Abe Stein. New York: Zone Books.

Cook, Scott (transl.). 2012. *The Bamboo Texts of Guodian: A Study and Complete Translation*, 2 vols. Ithaca: Cornell University Press.

Cossuta, Frédéric and Michel Narcy (eds.). 2001. *La forme dialogue chez Platon. Évolution et réceptions.* Grenoble: Jérôme Millon.

Coutinho, Steve. 2021. "Philosophy as Hermeneutics: Reflections on Roger Ames, Translation, and Comparative Methodology". In *One Corner of the Square: Essays on the Philosophy of Roger T. Ames*, edited by Ian M. Sullivan and Joshua Mason: 69–81. Honolulu: University of Hawai'i Press.

Couvreur, Sébastien (transl.). 1967. *Cheu-King* [*Shijing* 詩經]. Taichung: Kuangchi Press.

Cross, Richard. 2002. "Two Models of the Trinity?" *The Heythrop Journal* 43: 275–294.

Cullen, Christopher (transl.). 1996. *Astronomy and Mathematics in Ancient China: The* Zhou bi suan jing. New York: Cambridge University Press.

Cullen, Christopher. 2016. "The Suan shu shu, 'Writings on Reckoning': Rewriting the History of Early Chinese Mathematics in the Light of an Excavated Manuscript". *Historia Mathematica* 34: 10–44.

Darrobers, Roger and Guillaume Dutournier (transl.). 2012. *Zhu Xi Lu Jiuyuan. Une controverse lettrée. Correspondance philosophique sur le* Taiji. Paris: Les Belles Lettres.

De Bary, William Theodore (ed.). 1970. *Self and Society in Ming Thought*. New York: Columbia University Press.

De Bary, William Theodore, and Richard Lufrano (eds.). 2000. *Sources of Chinese Tradition*, vol 2. New York: Columbia University Press.

De Certeau, Michel. 1973. "L'espace du désir ou le 'fondement' des Exercices spirituels". *Christus* 20: 118–128.

De Certeau, Michel. 2013. *La Fable mystique XVIe–XVVe siècle*, vol. 2. Paris: Gallimard.

Defoort, Carine. 2001. "Is There Such a Thing as Chinese Philosophy? Arguments of an Implicit Debate". *Philosophy East and West* 51 (3): 393–413.

Defoort, Carine. 2012. "Instruction Dialogues in the Zhuangzi: An 'Anthropological' Reading". *Dao* 11 (4): 459–478.

Defoort, Carine. 2021. "Confucius and the 'Rectification of Names': Hu Shi and the Modern Discourse on Zhengming". *Dao* 20 (4): 613–633.

Dege, Carmen Lea. 2021. "'Standing behind Your Phrase': Arendt and Jaspers on the (Post-)Metaphysics of Evil". *European Journal of Political Theory*, November. DOI: 10.1177/14748851211052809.

Demoustiers, Adrien. 2006. *Les Exercices Spirituels de S. Ignace de Loyola. Lecture et pratique d'un texte*. Paris: Éditions facultés jésuites de Paris.

Denton, Kirk A. (transl. and ed.). 1996. *Modern Chinese Literary Thought: Writings on Literature, 1893–1945*. Palo Alto: Stanford University Press.

Ding, Sixin 丁四新. 2016. "A Study of the Key Concepts 'Heng' and 'Hengxian' in the 'Hengxian' on Chu Bamboo Slips Housed at the Shanghai Museum". *Frontiers of Philosophy in China* 11 (2): 206–221.

Ding, Sixin. 2019. "Huo 或 in Heng Xian of the Shanghai Museum's Edition of Chu Bamboo Slips". *Journal of Chinese Philosophy* 46 (3–4): 182–190.

Djamouri, Redouane. 1999. "Écriture et divination sous les Shang". *Extrême-Orient Extrême-Occident* 21: 11–35.

Douglas, Mary. 2007. *Thinking in Circles. An Essay on Ring Composition*. New Haven: Yale University Press.

Drury, S.B. 1985. "The Esoteric Philosophy of Leo Strauss". *Political Theory* 13 (3): 315–337.

Durrant, Stephen, Wai-yee Li, and David Schaberg (transl.). 2016. *Zuo Tradition/Zuozhan. Commentary on the "Spring and Autumn Annals"*, 3 vols. Seattle: University of Washington Press.

Elias, Norbert. 1991. *The Society of Individuals*, translated by Edmund Jephcott. Oxford: Basil Blackwell.

El-Kaisy, Maha and John Dillon (eds.). 2009. *The Afterlife of the Platonic Soul. Reflections of Platonic Psychology in the Monotheistic Religions*. Leiden: Brill.

Embassy of the PRC to the USA. 2021. "Foreign Ministry Spokesperson Hua Chunying's Regular Press Conference on February 18, 2021", https://www.mfa.gov.cn/ce/ceus//eng/fyrth/t1854866.htm, last retrieved November 15, 2022.

Fang, Thomé H. 1980. *Creativity in Man and Nature: A Collection of Philosophical Essays*. Taipei: Linking Publishing Co.
Faure, David. 1986. *The Structure of Chinese Rural Society: Lineage and Village in the Eastern New Territories*. New York: Oxford University Press.
Fei, Xiaotong. 1992 [1947]. *From the Soil: The Foundations of Chinese Society*, translated by Gary G. Hamilton and Wang Zheng. Berkeley: University of California Press.
Feng, Lisheng. 2017. "On the Structure and Functions of the Multiplication Table in the Tsinghua Collection of Bamboo Slips". *Chinese Annals of History of Science and Technology* 1 (1): 2–23.
Feng, Youlan. 2006 [1943]. *Nouveau traité sur l'homme. Introduction, traduction et notes par Michel Masson*. Paris: Cerf.
Feng, Youlan 馮友蘭. 2014 [1943]. 新原人 [*New Treatise on Man*]. Beijing: Peking University Press.
Ferro-Luzzi, Gabriella E. 1977. "Ritual as Language: The Case of South Indian Food Offerings". *Current Anthropology* 18 (3): 507–514.
Fessard, Gaston. 1956. *La Dialectique des Exercices spirituels de saint Ignace de Loyola*. Paris: Aubier.
Fingarette, Herbert. 1972. *Confucius: The Secular as Sacred*. New York: Harper and Row.
Fleming, David L. 1996. *Draw Me into Your Friendship: A Literal Translation and A Contemporary Reading of the Spiritual Exercises*. St. Louis, MO: Institute of Jesuit Sources.
Force, Pierre. 2011. "The Teeth of Time: Pierre Hadot on Meaning and Misunderstanding in the History of Ideas". *History and Theory* 50 (1): 20–40.
Foucault, Michel. 1988. *Politics, Philosophy, Culture: Interviews and Other Writings, 1977–1984*, edited by L.D. Kritzman. New York: Routledge.
Foucault, Michel. 1966 [1970] *The Order of Things*. London: Routledge.
Foucault, Michel. 2001 [1969]. "Qu'est-ce qu'un auteur ?" In *Dits et écrits I*: 817–849. Paris: Gallimard.
Freedman, Maurice. 1958. *Lineage Organization in Southeastern China*. London: Athlone.
Frye, Northrop. 1957. *Anatomy of Criticism: Four Essays*. Princeton: Princeton University Press.
Fugate, Courtney. 2019. "Kant's World Concept of Philosophy and Cosmopolitanism." *Archiv für Geschichte der Philosophie* 101 (4): 535–583.
Fung, Yu-lan [Feng, Youlan]. 1955. *A History of Chinese Philosophy*, 2 vols. Princeton: Princeton University Press.
Fung, Yu-lan [Feng, Youlan]. 1962. *The Spirit of Chinese Philosophy*, translated by E.R. Hughes. London: Routledge and Kegan Paul.
Gadamer, Hans-Georg. 1990 [1960]. *Wahrheit und Methode*. In *Gesammelte Werke*, vol. 1. Tûbingen: J.C.B. Mohr.
Ganeri, Jonardon. 2009. *Philosophy in Classical India. The Proper Work of Reason*. Delhi: Motilal Banarsidass.
Ganss G.E. et al. 1996. *The Constitutions of the Society of Jesus and Their Complementary Norms: A Complete English Translation of Official Latin Text*. St. Louis: Institute of Jesuit Sources.
Gardner, Daniel K. (transl.). 1990. *Zhu Xi, Learning to Be a Sage. Selections from the Conversations of Master Chu, Arranged Topically, Translated with Commentary*. Berkeley: University of California Press.
Gasster, Michael. 1969. *Chinese Intellectuals and the Revolution of 1911: The Birth of Modern Chinese Radicalism*. Seattle: University of Washington Press.
Geger, B.T. 2020. *A Pilgrim's Testament: The Memoirs of Saint Ignatius of Loyola*. New edition. Saint Louis: Institute of Jesuit Sources.
Gernet, Jacques. 1982. *Chine et Christianisme : action et réaction*. Paris: Gallimard.

Girardot, Norman J. 1999. "'Finding the Way': James Legge and the Victorian Invention of Taoism". *Religion* 29 (2): 107–121.
Goffman, Erwing. 1967. *Interaction Ritual: Essays on Face-to-Face Behavior.* New York: Anchor Books.
Goldin, Paul. 2008. "The Myth That China Has No Creation Myth". *Monumenta Serica* 56: 1–22.
Graham, A.C. 1986. *Yin-Yang and the Nature of Correlative Thinking.* Singapore: IEAP Monograph Series.
Graham, A.C. 1989. *Disputers of the Tao. Philosophical Arguments in Ancient China.* Chicago: Open Court.
Graham, A.C. (transl.) 2001. *Chuang-tzǔ: The Inner Chapters.* Indianapolis: Hackett.
Granet, Marcel. 1919. *Fêtes et chansons anciennes de la Chine.* Paris: Ernest Leroux.
Granet, Marcel. 1994 [1926]. *Danses et légendes de la Chine ancienne.* Paris: PUF.
Granet, Marcel. 1999 [1934]. *La pensée chinoise.* Paris: Albin Michel.
Gueydan, Édouard. 1986. *Texte autographe des Exercices Spirituels et documents contemporains (1526–1615).* Paris: Desclée de Brouwer.
Gunkel, Hermann. 1895. *Schöpfung und Chaos in Urzeit und Endzeit. Eine religions-geschichtliche Untersuchung über Gen I und Ap Joh 12.* Göttingen: Vandenhoeck & Ruprecht.
Guo, Fuping 郭福平 and Liu Yaqing 刘雅倩. 2017. "汉娜·阿伦特的 "思" 及其理论意义 [Hannah Arendt's "Thinking" and Its Theoretical Significance]". *Academic Journal of Zhongzhou* 中州学刊 5: 105–108.
Guo, Shuchun, Joseph W. Dauben, and Xu Yibao (transl.). 2017. *Nine Chapters on the Art of Mathematics.* Shenyang: Liaoning Education Press.
Habermas, Jürgen. 1987. *The Theory of Communicative Action*, translated by Thomas McCarthy. Boston: Beacon Press.
Habermas, Jürgen. 1990. *Moral Consciousness and Communicative Action*, translated by C. Lehnardt and S. Weber Nicholsen. Cambridge, MA: MIT Press.
Hacking, L. 1986. "The Parody of Conversation". In *Truth and Interpretation. Perspectives on the Philosophy of Donald Davidson*, edited by E. LePore: 447–458. New York: Oxford University Press.
Hadot, Pierre. 1995. *Philosophy as a Way of Life*, translated by Michael Chase. Oxford: Blackwell.
Hall, David L. and Roger T. Ames. 1987. *Thinking Through Confucius.* Albany: SUNY Press.
Hall, David L. and Roger T. Ames. 1995. *Anticipating China. Thinking Through the Narratives of Chinese and Western Culture.* Albany: SUNY Press.
Hall, David L. and Roger T. Ames. 1998. *Thinking from the Han: Self, Truth, and Transcendence in Chinese and Western Culture.* Albany, NY: SUNY Press.
Han, Byung-Chul. 2020. *The Disappearance of Rituals: A Topology of the Present.* Cambridge: Polity Press.
Han, Qi. 2020. "F. Furtado (1587–1653) S.J. and His Chinese Translation of Aristotle's Cosmology". In *História das Ciências Matemáticas: Portugal e o Oriente*, edited by Fundação Oriente: 169–179. Lisbon: Fundação Oriente.
Hansen, Chad. 1993. "Chinese Ideographs and Western Ideas". *The Journal of Asian Studies* 52 (2): 373–399.
Harbsmeier, Christoph. 1989. "Humor in Ancient Chinese Philosophy". *Philosophy East and West* 39 (3): 289–310.
Harbsmeier, Christoph. 1990. "Confucius Ridens: Humor in The Analects". *Harvard Journal of Asiatic Studies* 50 (1): 131–161.

Harrell, Stevan. 2013. "Orthodoxy, Resistance and the Family". In *The Family Model in Chinese Art and Culture*, edited by J. Silbergeld and D.C.Y. Ching: 71–88. Princeton: Princeton University Press.

Henderson, J.B. 1991. *Scripture, Canon and Commentary. A Comparison of Confucian and Western Exegesis*. Princeton: Princeton University Press.

Henricks, Robert G. (transl.). 1992. *Dedao [sic] jing: A New Translation Based on the Recently Discovered Mawangdui Texts*. New York: Ballantine.

Henricks, Robert G. (transl.). 2000. *Lao Tzu's Tao Te Ching: A Translation of the Startling New Documents Found at Guodian*. New York: Columbia University Press.

Heubel, Fabian. 2021. *Was ist chinesische Philosophie? Kritische Perspektiven*. Hamburg: Meiner.

Holzman, Donald. 1956. "The Conversational Tradition in Chinese Philosophy". *Philosophy East and West* 6 (3): 223–230.

Hong, Hao. 2019. "The Metaphysics of Dao in Wang Bi's Interpretation of Laozi". *Dao* 18 (2): 219–240.

Hong, Tao 洪涛. 2015. "当下语境中的汉娜·阿伦特 [Hannah Arendt in the Current Context]". *Frontiers* 天涯杂志 6: 188–194.

Hu, Xijin. 2021. "Whole-process Democracy in China Is a Great Practice of Universal Significance". *Global Times*, December 5, https://www.globaltimes.cn/page/202112/1240667.shtml, last retrieved November 15, 2022.

Hu, Xijin. 2022. "NYT's Ignorance of 800,000 American COVID Deaths Is Real 'Banality of Evil'". *Global Times*, January 14, https://www.globaltimes.cn/page/202201/1245979.shtml, last retrieved November 15, 2022.

Huang, Y.F. 2014. "Chinese Readers Digest the Ideas of Hannah Arendt". *Global Times*, January 13, https://www.globaltimes.cn/page/201401/837220.shtml, last retrieved November 15, 2022.

Hui, Yuk. 2020. *Art and Cosmotechnics*. Minneapolis: University of Minnesota Press.

Hutton, Eric L. (transl.). 2014. *Xunzi. The Complete Text*. Princeton: Princeton University Press.

Jankélévitch, Vladimir. 2015 [1931]. *Henri Bergson*. Durham and London: Duke University Press.

Jiang, Banqin 蒋邦芹. 2014. "论阿伦特对马克思劳动理论的解读 [On Arendt's Interpretation of Marx's Labor Theory]". *Academic Journal of South-Central University for Nationalities (Humanities and Society)* 中南民族大学学报(人文社会科学版) 34(3): 79–83.

Johnston, Ian (transl.). 2010. *The Mozi. A Complete Translation*. Hong Kong: The Chinese University Press.

Jones, Charles B. 2016. "Creation and Causality in Chinese-Jesuit Polemical Literature". *Philosophy East and West* 66 (4): 1251–1272.

Jones, Nicholas. 2016. "Correlative Reasoning about Water in Mengzi 6 A2". *Dao* 15 (2): 193–207.

Jullien, François. 2009. *The Great Image Has No Form, or On the Nonobject through Painting*, translated by Jane Marie Todd. Chicago: University of Chicago Press.

Jullien, François. 2015. *The Book of Beginnings*. New Haven: Yale University Press.

Kalinowski, Marc (transl. and ed.). 2022. *Maître de Huainan. Traité des figures célestes* 淮南子《天文訓》. Paris: " Bibliothèque chinoise ", Les Belles Lettres.

Kang Xiaoguang. 2018. "Moving toward Neo-Totalitarianism: A Political-Sociological Analysis of the Evolution of Administrative Absorption of Society". *Nonprofit Policy Forum* 9 (1): 1–8, https://doi.org/10.1515/npf-2017-0026, last retrieved November 15, 2022.

Kant, Immanuel. 1900–. *Kants Gesammelte Schriften* (Akademieausgabe), edited by the Königlich-Preussische Akademie der Wissenschaften, 29 vols. Berlin: Reimer and De Gruyter.

Karapetiants, Artiémiĭ M. 1991. "Modèle universel (Hong fan) et classifications chinoises antiques à cinq et à neuf termes." In *Extrême-Orient, Extrême-Occident, 13. Modèles et structures des textes* chinois anciens : les formalistes soviétiques en sinologie, edited by Karin Chemla: 101–119. Nanterre: Presses Universitaires de Nanterre.

Keck, Frédéric Keck. 2009. "Une querelle sinologique et ses implications, à propos du *Contre François Jullien* de Jean-François Billeter". *Esprit*, February: 61–81.

Keightley, David. 2000. "The Shang: China's First Historical Dynasty". In *The Cambridge History of Ancient China. From the Origins of Civilization to 221 B.C*, edited by Michael Lowie and Edward Shaughnessy: 232–291. Cambridge: Cambridge University Press.

Kim, Seonhee and MinJeong Bae. 2015. "A Religious Approach to the "Zhongyong": With a Focus on Western Translators and Korean Confucians". *Journal of Korean Religions* 6 (2): 27–60.

King, Ian T. 1991/1993. "Political Economy and the 'Laws of Beauty': Aesthetics, Economics, and Materialism in Marx". *Science and Society* 1991, 55 (3): 323–335. [Chinese translation by Li S.G. 李锁贵, in 国外社会科学 *Social Sciences Abroad* 1993, 5: 3–8]

Knoblock, John (transl.). 1998. *Xunzi: A Translation and Study of the Complete Works*. Stanford: Stanford University Press.

Koons, Robert C. and Timothy Pickavance. 2015. *Metaphysics: The Fundamentals*. Malden, MA and Oxford: Wiley-Blackwell.

L'Haridon, Béatrice. 2017. *Meou-tseu. Dialogues pour dissiper la confusion* 牟子《理惑》. Paris, " Bibliothèque chinoise ", Les Belles Lettres.

Lagerwey, John. 2010. *China: A Religious State*. Hong Kong: Hong Kong University Press.

Larre, Claude. 1987. *La Voie du Ciel (Suwen I)*. Paris: Desclée de Brouwer.

Lau, Dim Cheuk (transl.). 1963. *Lao Tzu: Tao Te Ching*. Harmondsworth: Penguin.

Lau, Dim Cheuk (transl.). 2000. *Confucius. The Analects*. Hong Kong: The Chinese University Press.

Le, Xiaojun 乐小军. 2019. "政治、意见与真理——以汉娜·阿伦特的柏拉图解释为中心的考 [Politics, Opinion and Truth: An Investigation from the Perspective of Hannah Arendt's Interpretation of Plato's Cave Allegory]". *Philosophical Analysis* 哲学分析 6: 119–129.

Le Blanc, Charles and Rémi Mathieu (eds.). 2008. *Approches critiques de la mythologie chinoise*. Montréal: Presses de l'Université de Montréal.

Lee, Junghwan. 2012. "'Jiaohua' 教化, Transcendental Unity, and Morality in Ordinariness: Paradigm Shifts in the Song Dynasty Interpretation of the 'Zhongyong'". *Journal of Song-Yuan Studies* 42: 151–233.

Lenoir, Yves and Nicolas Standaert (eds.). 2005. *Les danses rituelles chinoises d'après Joseph-Marie Amiot*. Namur: Presses Universitaires de Namur and Éditions Lessius.

Levi, Jean (transl.). 2010. *Les Oeuvres de Maître Tchouang*. Paris: Éditions de l'Encyclopédie des Nuisances.

Levi, Jean (transl.). 2018. *Les deux arbres de la Voie. (I) Le Livre de Lao-Tseu. (II) Les Entretiens de Confucius*. Paris: Les Belles Lettres.

Lévi-Strauss, Claude. 2012 [1955]. *Tristes Tropiques*. London: Penguin.

Li, Tiangang. 2001. "Chinese Renaissance: The Role of Early Jesuits in China". In *China and Christianity, Burdened Past, Hopeful Future*, edited by Stephen Huhalley Jr. and Xiaoxin Wu: 117–126. New York: M.E.Sharpe.

Li, Tiangang 李天綱. 2007. 跨文化的诠释 [*Intercultural Hermeneutics*]. Shanghai: Xinxing chubanshe.

Li, Tiangang 李天綱. 2017. 金泽 – 江南民间祭祀探源 [*Jinze. A Probe into the Origin of Jiangnan Popular Sacrificial Rituals*]. Beijing: SDX.

Li, Yuan. 2022. "The Army of Millions Who Enforce China's Zero-Covid Policy, at All Costs". *The New York Times*, January 12, https://www.nytimes.com/2022/01/12/business/china-zero-covid-policy-xian.html?searchResultPosition=1, last retrieved November 15, 2022.

Li, Zehou and Jane Cauvel. 2006. *Four Essays on Aesthetics: Toward a Global View*. Lanham: Lexington.
Liang, Shuming 梁漱溟. 1987 (1921). 东西文化及期哲学 (*Eastern and Western Cultures and Their Philosophies*). Beijing: Commercial Press.
Lieberthal, Kenneth. 1992. "Introduction: The 'Fragmented Authoritarianism' Model and Its Limitations". In: *Bureaucracy, Politics, and Decision Making in Post-Mao China*, edited by Kenneth Lieberthal and David Lampton: 1–30. Berkeley: University of California Press.
Lin, Xiaoqing Diana. 2013. "Creating Modern Chinese Metaphysics: Feng Youlan and New Realism". *Modern China* 20 (10): 1–34.
Lin, Yutang. 1959. *From Pagan to Christian*. Cleveland, OH: World Publishing Company.
Lindbeck, G. 1984. *The Nature of Doctrine: Religion and Theology in a Postliberal Age*. Philadelphia: Westminster Press.
Liu, Mengxi, 刘梦溪. 2008. 论国学 [*On National Studies*]. Shanghai: Shanghai Century.
Liu, Xiaogan 刘笑敢. 2010. 庄子哲学及其演变 [*Zhuangzi's Philosophy and Its Evolution*]. Beijing: People's University of China Press.
Liu, Xiaofeng 刘小枫. 2017. 海德格尔与中国 [*Heidegger and China*]. Shanghai: East China Normal University Press.
Lloyd, Geoffrey E.R. 2014. *Being, Humanity, and Understanding: Studies in Ancient and Modern Societies*. Oxford: Oxford University Press.
Lo, Yuet Keung. 2022. "The Zhuangzi and Wei-Jin *Xuanxue*". In *Dao Companion to the Philosophy of the Zhuangzi*, edited by Kin-Chong Chong: 447–466. Cham: Springer.
Lodge, David. 1985. *Small World. An Academic Romance*. Harmondsworth: Penguin.
Longobardo [id. Longobardi], Niccolo. 1701. *Traité sur quelques points de la Religion des Chinois*. Paris, Josse.
Lu, Jiuyuan 陆九渊. 1980. 陆九渊集 (*Works of Liu Jiuyuan*). vol.35. Beijing: Zhonghua shuju.
Lu, Miaw-Fen. 2020. "The Question of Life and Death: Li Zhi and Ming-Qing Intellectual History". In *The Objectionable Li Zhi: Fiction, Criticism, and Dissent in Late Ming China*, edited by Rivi Handler-Spitz, Pauline C. Lee, and Haun Saussy: 209–228. Seattle: University of Washington Press.
Lu, Xing. 1998. *Rhetoric in Ancient China, Fifth to Third Century: A Comparison with Classical Greek Rhetoric*. Columbia: University of South Carolina Press.
Luo, Zhufeng (ed.). 1991 [1987]. *Religion Under Socialism in China*, translated by Donald E. MacInnis and Zheng Xi'an. Armonk, NY: M. E. Sharpe.
Lynn, Richard (transl.). 1994. *The Classic of Changes. A New Translation of the I Ching as Interpreted by Wang Bi*. New York: Columbia University Press.
Lynn, Richard (transl.). 2022. *Zhuangzi. A New Translation of the Sayings of Master Zhuang as Interpreted by Guo Xiang*. New York: Columbia University Press.
Ma, Chengyuan 馬承源 (general ed.) and Li, Ling 李零 (volume ed.). 2003. 上海博物館藏戰國楚竹書 (*Chu Bamboo Writings during the Warring States Period Housed by the Shanghai Museum*), vol.3. Shanghai: Shanghai Guji Chubanshe.
Ma, Lin and Jaap Van Brakel. 2016. *Fundamentals of Comparative and Intercultural Philosophy*. Albany, NY: SUNY Press.
Major, John S., Sarah A. Queen, Andrew Meyer, and Harold D. Roth (transl.). 2010. *The Huainanzi: A Guide to the Theory and Practice of Government in Early Han China*. New York: Columbia University Press.
Makeham, John. 2008. *Lost Souls: "Confucianism" in Contemporary Chinese Academic Discourse*. Cambridge, MA: Harvard University Asia Center.

Mao, LuMing. 2007. "Studying the Chinese Rhetorical Tradition in the Present: Re-presenting the Native's Point of View". *College English* 69 (3): 216–237.

Marchal, Kai and Carl K.Y. Shaw (eds.). 2017. *Carl Schmitt and Leo Strauss in the Chinese-Speaking World: Reorienting the Political.* Lanham, MD: Lexington.

Masson, Michel. 1985. *Philosophy and Tradition: The Interpretation of China's Philosophic Past – Fung Youlan, 1939–1949.* Taipei: Taipei Ricci Institute.

Mattice, Sarah A. 2021. "Many Confucianisms: From Roger Ames to Jiang Qing on the Interpretive Possibilities of Ruist Traditions". In *One Corner of the Square: Essays on the Philosophy of Roger T. Ames*, edited by Ian M. Sullivan and Joshua Mason: 131–140. Honolulu: University of Hawai'i Press.

Maurer, Armand A. 1982 [1962]. *Medieval Philosophy.* Toronto: Pontifical Institute of Medieval Studies.

Mei, Qianli 梅谦立. [Thierry Meynard]. 2013. "从西方灵修学的角度阅读儒家经典：耶稣会翻译的《中庸》(Reading the Confucian Classics from the Perspective of Western Spirituality: The Jesuit Translation of the Zhongyong)". *Journal of Comparative Literature* 比较经学 2: 61–90.

Ménissier, Thierry. 2011. "Les humanités réactionnaires. L'usage paradoxal de l'Antiquité chez Hannah Arendt et Leo Strauss". In *Les Représentations de l'Antiquité dans la pensée européenne moderne et contemporaine*, edited by J.L. Chabot., J. Ferrand, and M. Mathieu: 189–223. Paris: L'Harmattan.

Merleau-Ponty, Maurice. 1960. *Signes.* Paris: Gallimard.

Mertha, Andrew. 2009. "Fragmented Authoritarianism 2.0: Political Pluralization in the Chinese Policy Process". *The China Quarterly* 200: 995–1012.

Meynard, Thierry (transl. and ed.). 2011. *Confucius Sinarum Philosophus (1687). The First Translation of the Confucian Classics. Latin Translation (1658–1660) of the Chinese by Prospero Intorcetta, Christian Herdtrich, François de Rougemont and Philippe Couplet.* Rome: Institutum Historicum Societatis Iesu.

Meynard, Thierry (transl. and ed.). 2013. *Matteo Ricci. Le Sens réel de " Seigneur du Ciel "* 利瑪竇《天主實義》. Paris: " Bibliothèque Chinoise ", Les Belles Lettres, 2013.

Meynard, Thierry. 2015. "The First Treatise on the Soul in China and its Sources". *Revista Filosófica de Coimbra* 47: 1–39.

Meynard, Thierry. 2018. "François Noël's Contribution to the Western Understanding of Chinese Thought: *Taiji sive natura* in the *Philosophia sinica*". *Dao* 17 (2): 219–230.

Meynet, Roland. 2012. *Treatise on Biblical Rhetoric.* Leiden: Brill.

Miller, K.D. 2020. "Discernment in Management and Organizations". *Journal of Management, Spirituality and Religion* 17 (5): 373–402.

Min, Anselm K. 2016. *Korean Religions in Relation: Buddhism, Confucianism, Christianity.* Albany, NY: SUNY Press.

Moeller, Hans-Georg. 2018. "On Comparative and Post-Comparative Philosophy". In *Appreciating the Chinese Difference: Engaging Roger T. Ames on Methods, Issues, and Roles*, edited by Jim Behuniak, 31–45. Albany: SUNY Press.

Møllgaard, Eske. 2021. "The Uneasy Relation between Chinese and Western Philosophy". *Dao* 20 (3): 377–387.

Morowitz, Harold J. 1993. *Beginnings of Cellular Life: Metabolism Recapitulates Biogenesis.* New Haven: Yale University Press.

Mote, Frederick W. 1989. *Intellectual Foundations of China.* New York: McGraw-Hill.

Mou, Bo. 2004. "A Reexamination of the Structure and Content of Confucius' Version of the Golden Rule". *Philosophy East and West* 54 (2): 218–248.

Mou, Zongshan (牟宗三), Xu, Fushan (徐復觀), Zhang, Junmai (张君劢) and Tang, Junyi (唐君毅), 1989 [1958]. 为中国文化敬告世界人士宣言—我们对 中国学术研究及中国文化与世界文前途之共同认识 (Manifesto on Behalf of Chinese Culture Respectfully Announced to the People of the World – Our Joint Understanding of Sinological Study and Chinese Culture With Respect to the Future Prospects of World Culture). In 當代新儒家 *Contemporary Neo-Confucianism*, edited by Feng Zucheng 封祖盛. Beijing: Sanlian shuju: 1–52.

Moyaert, Marianne (ed.). 2019. *Interreligious Relations and the Negotiation of Ritual Boundaries: Explorations in Interrituality*. London: Palgrave Macmillan.

Mulhern M.M. and M.H. Mulhern. 1968. "Types of Process according to Aristotle" *The Monist* 52 (2): 237–251.

Mungello, David E. 1977. *Leibniz and Confucianism: The Search for Accord*. Honolulu: University of Hawai'i Press.

Ni, Peimin (transl.). 2017. *Understanding the Analects of Confucius. A New Translation of Lunyu with Annotations*. Albany, NY: SUNY Press.

Ochs, Peter. 2022. "The Society of Scriptural Reasoning: The Rules of Scriptural Reasoning". *Journal of Scriptural Reasoning* 2 (1), http://jsr.shanti.virginia.edu, last retrieved November 15, 2022.

O'Daly, Gerard. 1987. *Augustine's Philosophy of Mind*. Berkeley: CA: University of California Press.

Onians, Richard Broxton. 1988 [1951]. *The Origins of European Thought about the Body, the Mind, the Soul, the World, Time and Fate*. Cambridge: Cambridge University Press.

Padberg, J.W. and J.L. McCarthy. 2006. *Ignatius of Loyola: Letters and Instructions*. Saint Louis: Institute of Jesuit Sources.

Palmer, Martin (transl.). 2014. *Confucius. The Most Venerable Book (Shangshu)*. London: Penguin.

Panikkar, Raimon. 1979. *Myth, Faith and Hermeneutics*. New York: Paulist Press.

Pelkey, Jamin. 2021. "Zhuangzi, Peirce and the Butterfly's Dreamscape: Concentric Meaning in the Qiwulun 齊物論". *Chinese Semiotic Studies* 17 (2): 255–287.

Peng, Guoxiang. 2018. "Contemporary Chinese Philosophy in the Chinese-Speaking World: An Overview". *Frontiers of Philosophy in China* 13 (1): 91–119.

Pfister, Lauren. 2020. *Vital Post-secular Perspectives on Chinese Philosophical Issues*. New York: Lexington.

Pfister, Lauren. 2021. "On the Demystification of the Numinous and Mystical in Classical Ruism: Contemporary Musings on the Zhongyong". In *One Corner of the Square: Essays on the Philosophy of Roger T. Ames*, edited by Ian M. Sullivan and Joshua Mason: 119–130. Honolulu: University of Hawai'i Press.

Prémare (Joseph de). 1878. *Vestiges des principaux dogmes chrétiens, tirés des anciens livres chinois, avec reproduction des textes chinois, par le P. de Prémare, jésuite, ancien missionnaire en Chine. Traduits du latin, accompagnés de différents compléments et remarques par MM. A. Bonnetty et Paul Perny*. Paris: Bureau des Annales de philosophie chrétienne.

Price, B.B. 1992. *Medieval Thought: An Introduction*. Cambridge: Blackwell.

Puett, Michael. 2000. "Violent Misreadings: The Hermeneutic of Cosmology in the Huainanzi". *Bulletin of the Museum of Far Eastern Antiquities* 72: 29–47.

Ricci, Matteo 利瑪竇. 1596. 西国记法 [*The Western Method of Memorization*], https://zh.wikisource.org/zh-hant/西國記法, last retrieved November 15, 2022.

Ricoeur, Paul. 2018 [1983]. "Préface". In Hannah Arendt, *Condition de l'homme moderne*, translated by Georges Fradier: i–vii. Paris: Calman-Lévy.

Rong, Henying. 2020. "The Reception of Leo Strauss in China: Two Chinese Straussians, between Theological Temptation and Political Criticism". *Interpretation, A Journal of Political Philosophy* 46 (2): 291–311.

Rošker, Jana S. 2021. *Interpreting Chinese Philosophy: A New Methodology.* London: Bloomsbury Academic.

Ross, David (transl.) and Lesley Brown (ed.). 2009. *Aristotle: The Nicomachean Ethics (New edition, revised with an introduction and notes by Lesley Brown).* Oxford World's Classics. Oxford/New York: Oxford University Press, 2009

Rossetti, Livio. 2011. *Le dialogue socratique.* Paris: Les Belles Lettres.

Rousseau, Jean-Jacques. 1990–2009. *The Collected Writings of Rousseau*, 13 vol. edited by Roger D. Masters and Christopher Kelly. Hanover, NH: University Press of New England.

Ryden, Edmund (transl.). 2008. *Laozi: Daodejing.* London: Penguin.

Sato, Masayuki. 2010. *The Confucian Quest for Order: The Origin and Formation of the Political Thought of Xunzi.* Leiden: Brill.

Scott, James C. 2017. *Against the Grain: A Deep History of the Earliest States.* New Haven: Yale University Press.

Sellier, Philippe (ed.). 2000. *Les Pensées de Pascal.* Paris: Le Livre de Poche.

Shaughnessy, Edward. 2007. "The Religion of Ancient China". In *A Handbook of Ancient Religions*, edited by John R. Hinnells: 490–536. Cambridge: Cambridge University Press.

Shaughnessy, Edward. 2015. "Unearthed Documents and the Question of the Oral versus Written Nature of the Classic of Poetry". *Harvard Journal of Asiatic Studies* 75 (2): 331–375.

Siderits, Mark. 2021. *Buddhism as Philosophy.* Indianapolis: Hackett.

Simionato, Alice. 2019. "The *Manifesto* of 1958: a discourse on Confucian Rationalism". *Rivista di estetica*, 72: 125–138.

Slingerland, Edward. 2003a. *Effortless Action. Wu-wei as Conceptual Metaphor and Spiritual Idea in Early China.* Oxford: Oxford University Press.

Slingerland, Edward (transl.). 2003b. *Confucius. Analects. With Selections from Traditional Commentaries.* Indianapolis: Hackett.

Slingerland, Edward. 2011. "Metaphor and Meaning in Early China". *Dao* 10 (1): 1–30.

Slingerland, Edward. 2013. "Body and Mind in Early China: An Integrated Humanities-Science Approach". *Journal of the American Academy of Religion* 81 (1): 6–10.

Slingerland, Edward. 2019. *Mind and Body in Early China: Beyond Orientalism and the Myth of Holism.* Oxford: Oxford University Press.

Solé-Farràs, Jesús. 2014. *New Confucianism in Twenty-First Century China: The Construction of a Discourse.* Oxon and New York: Routledge.

Song Kuafeng 宋宽锋. 2021. 哲学史研究方法论十讲 [*Ten Lectures on the Research Methodology of the History of Philosophy*]. Beijing: Peking University Press.

Spence, Jonathan D. 1984. *The Memory Palace of Matteo Ricci.* New York: Viking.

Standaert, Nicolas. 1988. *Yang Tingyun, Confucian and Christian in Late Ming China: His Life and Thought.* Leiden: Brill.

Standaert, Nicolas. 2008. *The Interweaving of Rituals: Funerals in the Cultural Exchange between China and Europe.* Seattle: University of Washington Press.

Standaert, Nicolas. 2012. "The Spiritual Exercises of Ignatius of Loyola in the China Mission of the 17th and 18th Centuries". *Archivum Historicum Societatis Iesu* 81 (161): 73–124.

Starr, Chloë. 2016. *Chinese Theology. Text and Context.* New Haven: Yale University Press.

Sterckx, Roel. 2007. "Searching for Spirit: Shen and Sacrifice in Warring States and Han Philosophy and Ritual". *Extrême-Orient, Extrême-Occident* 29: 23–54.
Strauss, Leo. 1996 [1958]. "The Origins of Political Science and the Problem of Socrates: Six Public Lectures". *Interpretation* 23 (2): 127–208.
Sullivan, Ian M. and Joshua Mason (eds.). 2021. *One Corner of the Square. Essays on the Philosophy of Roger T. Ames*. Honolulu: University of Hawai'i Press.
Sun Xiangchen 孙向晨. 2019. 论家: 个体与亲亲 [*On Family/Home: Individuals and Family Ties*]. Shanghai: East China Normal University Press.
Sun, Shangyang 孙尚扬. 2015. "现代社会中的意义共契与公民宗教问题——兼论儒教可否建构为中国的公民宗教 [Consensus on Meaning in Modern Society and the Problem of Civil Religion. Can Confucianism Be Constructed as China's Civil Religion?]" *Studies in World Religions* 世界宗教研究 3: 10–18.
Sun, Yat-sen 孙中山. 1986. 孙中山全集 [*Complete Works of Sun Yat-Sen*]. Beijing: Zhonghua shuju.
Tang, Junyi 唐君毅. 1989. 唐君毅全集 (*Complete Works by Tang Junyi*), 30 vol. Taipei: Taiwan xuesheng shuju.
Tang, Junyi 唐君毅. 2006 [1977]. 生命存在与心灵境界 [*The Existence of Life and the World of the Spirit*]. Beijing: China Social Sciences Press.
Tang, Yijie. 2007. "Constructing 'Chinese Philosophy' in the Sino-Euro Cultural Exchange". In *Dialogues of Philosophies, Religions, and Civilizations in the Era of Globalization* (Chinese Philosophical Studies 25), edited by Zhao Dunhua and McLean: 21–27. Washington, D.C.: The Council for Research in Values and Philosophy.
Tang, Yongtong 湯用彤. 2001. 魏晉玄學論稿 [*Essays on the Xuan School of the Weijing Period*]. Shanghai: Shanghai Guji.
Tetlow, J.A. and Carol Atwell Ackels. 2007. *Finding Christ in the World: A Twelve Week Ignatian Retreat in Everyday Life*. Saint Louis: The Institute of Jesuit Sources.
Theobald, Christoph. 2007. *Le christianisme comme style, T.I*. Paris: Cerf.
Thouard, Denis. 2002. "Qu'est-ce qu'une 'herméneutique critique' ?" *Methodos* 2, https://doi.org/10.4000/methodos.100, last retrieved November 15, 2022.
Tiles, J.E. 2000. "Quaestio Disputata de Rebus Scholasticis [Book Review]". *Philosophy East and West* 50 (10): 119–130.
Tillich, Paul. 1959. *Theology of Culture*. Oxford: Oxford University Press.
Titus, Craig Steven. 2006. *Resilience and the Virtue of Fortitude: Aquinas in Dialogue with the Psychosocial Sciences*. Washington, D.C.: The Catholic University of America Press.
Tu, Wei-ming. 1989. *Centrality and Commonality: An Essay on Confucian Religiousness*. Albany, NY: SUNY Press.
Tu, Wei-ming. 1993. *Way, Learning, and Politics*. Albany, NY: SUNY Press.
Turner, Victor. 1968. *The Drums of Affliction: A Study of Religious Processes among the Ndembu of Zambia*. Oxford: Clarendon Press and International African Institute.
Unger, J. Marshall and Chad Hansen. 1993. "Communications to the Editor". *The Journal of Asian Studies* 52 (4): 949–957.
Van Breemen, P.G. 1996. "The Examination of Conscience". In *Ignatian Exercises: Contemporary Annotations. The Best of the Review 4*, edited by David L. Fleming: 102–112. Saint Louis: Review for Religious.
Vandermeersch, Léon. 2007. "Le néoconfucianisme au crible de la philosophie analytique Feng Youlan et son Traité de l'homme". *Archives de Philosophie* 70 (3): 471–486.

Vandermeersch, Léon. 2013. *Les deux raisons de la pensée chinoise. Divination et idéographie*. Paris: Gallimard.

Van der Veer, Peter. 2014. *The Modern Spirit of Asia. The Spiritual and the Secular in China and India*. Princeton: Princeton University Press.

Veg, Sébastien. 2010. "Quelle science pour quelle démocratie ? Lu Xun et la littérature de fiction dans le mouvement du 4 mai". *Annales. Histoire, Sciences Sociales* 2: 345–374.

Vermander, Benoît. 2011. "Scholasticism, Dialogue and Universalism". *Universitas* 哲学与文化 37 (11): 23–39.

Vermander, Benoît. 2016. "Wisdom as Performance: A Dialogue Between the Chinese, Greek and Biblical Traditions". In *Cultural Roots of Sustainable Management. Practical Wisdom and Corporate Social Responsibility*, edited by Andre Habisch and Rene Schmidpeter: 89–101. Springer International.

Vermander, Benoît. 2019. "Sinicizing Religions, Sinicizing Religious Studies". *Religions* 10 (2), https://www.mdpi.com/2077-1444/10/2/137, last retrieved November 15, 2022.

Vermander, Benoît. 2021a. "Edit by Number: Looking at the Composition of the Huainanzi, and Beyond". *Dao* 20 (3): 459–498.

Vermander, Benoît. 2021b. "The Memory Palace of a Chinese Painter". In *Crafting Chinese Memories. The Art and Materiality of Storytelling*, edited by Katherine Swancutt: 25–54. Oxford and New York: Berghahn.

Vermander, Benoît. 2021c. "The Socio-Political Impact of the Bible in China". In *The Oxford Handbook of the Bible in China*, edited by K.K. Yeo: 608–626. Oxford and New York: Oxford University Press.

Vermander, Benoît. 2022a. "Self-Examination, Discernment, and Decision Making: Criss-Crossing the Confucian and Ignatian Traditions". *Journal of Management, Spirituality and Religion* 19 (5): 522–545.

Vermander, Benoît. 2022b. *Comment lire les classiques chinois?* Paris: Les Belles Lettres.

Vermander, Benoît. 2022c. "Encoding the Way: Ritual Ethos and Textual Patterns in China". *Geschichte der Philologien* 61/62: 5–31.

Vermander, Benoît, Liz Hingley, and Liang Zhang. 2018. *Shanghai Sacred. The Religious Landscape of a Global City*. Seattle: University of Washington Press.

Volkov, Alexeï K. 1991 "Recherches sur les structures des textes chinois anciens en URSS". In *Extrême-Orient, Extrême-Occident, 13. Modèles et structures des textes chinois anciens : les formalistes soviétiques en sinologie*, edited by Karim Chemla: 11–30. Nanterre: Presses Universitaires de Nanterre.

Wagner, Rudolf. 2000. *The Craft of a Chinese Commentator. Wang Bi on the* Laozi. Albany, NY: SUNY Press.

Wagner, Rudolf. 2003. *A Chinese Reading of the* Daodejing: *Wang Bi's Commentary on the* Laozi *with Critical Text and Translation*. Albany: SUNY Press.

Wang, Li 王力. 1982. 同源字典 [*Dictionary of Cognates*]. Beijing: Xinhua shudian.

Wang, Lin and Han, Zhen (eds.). 2021. *Key Concepts in Chinese Thought and Culture*. 3 Vols.: History/Philosophy/Art and Literature (Chinese-English). Beijing: Foreign Language and Teaching Press.

Wang, Q. Edward. 2001. *Inventing China Through History, The May Fourth Approach to Historiography*. Albany, NY: SUNY Press.

Wang, Yinli 王寅麗. 2017. "Postscript" to the revised translation by Wang Yilin of Hanna Arendt, *The Human Condition* (人的境况): 303–305. Shanghai: Shanghai People's Press.

Watson, Burton (transl.). 2003. *Chuang tzu: Basic Writings*. New York: Columbia University Press.

Weijers, Olga. 2013. *In Search of the Truth. A History of Disputation Techniques from Antiquity to Early Modern Times.* Turnhout: Brepols.

Winslett, Justin T. 2014. "Deities and the Extrahuman in Pre-Qin China: Lesser Deities in the 'Zuozhuan' and the 'Guoyu'". *Journal of the American Academy of Religion* 82 (4): 938–969.

Witek, John W. 1997. "Principles of Scholasticism in China: A Comparison of Guilio Aleni's Wanwu Zhenyuan with Matteo Ricci's Tianzhu Shiyi". In *"Scholar from the West": Giulio Aleni S.J. (1582–1649) and the Dialogue between Christians and China*, edited by Tiziana Lippiello and Roman Malek: 273–289. Nettethal: Steyler.

Wittgenstein, Ludwig. 1969. *The Blue and Brown Books.* Oxford: Oxford University Press.

Wittgenstein, Ludwig. 1972 [1953]. *Philosophical Investigations*, translated by G.E.M. Anscombe. Oxford: Basil Blackwell.

Wong, Peter, Yih Jiun. 2021. "Locating the 'Numinous' in a Human-Centered Religiousness". *One Corner of the Square: Essays on the Philosophy of Roger T. Ames*, edited by Ian M. Sullivan and Joshua Mason: 109–118. Honolulu: University of Hawai'i Press.

World Bank and Development Research Center of the State Council. 2014. *Urban China. Towards Efficient, Inclusive, and Sustainable Urbanization.* Washington, D.C.: World Bank. DOI: 10.1596/978-1-4648-0206-5.

Wu, Pei-Yi. 1979. "Self-Examination and Confession of Sins in Traditional China". *Harvard Journal of Asiatic Studies* 39 (1): 5–38.

Xi, Jinping 习近平. 2018. 习近平在纪念马克思诞辰200周年大会上的讲话 [*Speech of Xi Jinping at the General Assembly Commemorating the 200th Anniversary of Marx's Birth*], May 5, http://cpc.people.com.cn/n1/2018/0505/c64094-29966415.html, last retrieved November 15, 2022.

Xi, Jinping. n.d. "Classics Quoted by Xi", http://chinaplus.cri.cn/classics-quoted-by-xi/index.html last retrieved November 15, 2022.

Xinhua. 2021. *Resolution of the CPC Central Committee on the Major Achievements and Historical Experience of the Party over the Past Century*, November 16, http://www.news.cn/english/2021-11/16/c_1310314611.htm, last retrieved November 15, 2022.

Yang Huilin 楊慧林. 2012. "经文辩读与诠释的循环 [Scriptural Reasoning and Hermeneutical Circle]". *Journal of Renmin University of China* 中国人民大学学报 5: 8–15.

Yang Huilin. 2014. *China, Christianity, and the Question of Culture.* Waco, TX: Baylor University Press.

Yang Shaodong 杨晓东. 2020. 汉娜·阿伦特劳动理论研究 [*Research on Hannah Arendt's Theory of Labor*]. Master thesis, Heilongjiang University.

You, Minjung. 2018. "New Trends in Commentary on the Confucian Classics: Characteristics, Differences, and Significance of Rhetorically Oriented Exegeses of the Mengzi". *Acta Koreana* 21 (2): 503–524.

You, Xiaoye. 2006. "The Way, Multimodality of Ritual Symbols, and Social Change: Reading Confucius's Analects as a Rhetoric". *Rhetoric Society Quarterly* 36 (4): 425–448.

Yu, Jiyuan. 2014. "Is Chinese Cosmology Metaphysics?" *Journal of East-West Thought* 1(1): 137–149.

Yu Jiyuan and Lei Yongqiang. 2008. "The 'Manifesto' of New-Confucianism and the Revival of Virtue Ethics". *Frontiers of Philosophy in China* 3 (3): 317–334.

Zarader, Marlène. 2016. *Lire Vérité et méthode de Gadamer.* Paris: Vrin.

Zhang, Dainian 张岱年. 1981. "论宋明理学的基本质 [On the Basic Nature of *Lixue* in Song and Ming Dynasties]". *Philosophical Researches* 哲学研究 9: 24–30.

Zhang, Dainian. 2002. *Key Concepts in Chinese Philosophy*, translated by Edmund Ryden. New Heaven: Yale University Press and Beijing: Foreign Language Press.

Zhang, Shen 张慎. 1994. "实践先于理论，行动先于思维 – 记杰出政治理论家和哲学家哈娜·阿伦特 [Practice Precedes Theory, Action Precedes Thinking. Remembering an Outstanding Political Theorist and Philosopher: Hannah Arendt]". *Social Sciences Abroad* 国外社会科学 1994.5: 51–63; 1994.6: 65–69.

Zhao, Dunhua and George F. McLean (eds.). 2007. *Dialogues of Philosophies, Religions, and Civilizations in the Era of globalization* (Chinese Philosophical Studies 25). Washington, D.C.: The Council for Research in Values and Philosophy.

Zhao, Tingyang. 2005. 天下体系 [*The Tianxia System*]. Nanjing: Jiangsu jiaoyu chubanshe.

Zhao, Tingyang 赵汀阳. 2009. "A Political World Philosophy in Terms of All-under-Heaven (Tian-xia)". *Diogenes* 56 (1): 5–18.

Zhao, Tingyang 赵汀阳. 2011. 天下体系 [*The Tianxia System*]. Beijing: People's University Press.

Zhao, Tingyang 赵汀阳. 2012. "The Ontology of Coexistence: From Cogito to Facio". *Diogenes* 57 (4): 27–36.

Zhao, Tingyang 赵汀阳. 2013. 第一哲学的支点 [*The Axis of Philosophia Prima*]. Beijing: Sanlian.

Zhao, Tingyang 赵汀阳. 2016a. 天下的当代性: 世界秩序的实践和 [*A Possible World of All-under-the-Heaven System: The World Order in the Past and for the Future*]. Beijing: Zhongxin Chubanshe.

Zhao, Tingyang 赵汀阳. 2016b. 惠此中国 [*Blessing China*]. Beijing: Zhongxin Chubanshe.

Zhao, Tingyang. 2021. *All under Heaven: The Tianxia System for a Possible World Order*, translated by Joseph E. Harroff. Oakland: University of California Press.

Zhou, Yi 周毅. 2019. "在政治与道德之间——汉娜·阿伦特 '无思' 概念探析 [Between Politics and Morality. An Analysis of Hannah Arendt's Concept of 'Thoughtlessness']". *Tianfu New Idea* [sic] 天府新论, June: 85–94.

Zhou, Zuoren 周作人. 2009. 周作人散文全集 [*Complete Collection of Essays by Zhou Zuoren*]. Nanning: Guangxi Normal University Press.

Zhu, Xi 朱熹. 2014. 朱子语类汇校 *(Conversations of Master Zhu, Arranged Topically)*. Edited by Huang Shiyi 黄士毅. Shanghai: Shanghai guji chubanshe.

Ziporyn, Brook (transl.). 2009. *Zhuangzi: The Essential Writings with Selections from Traditional Commentaries*. Indianapolis: Hackett.

Ziporyn, Brook (transl.). 2020. *Zhuangzi: The Complete Writings*. Indianapolis: Hackett.

Zürn, Tobias Benedikt. 2020. "The Han Imaginaire of Writing as Weaving: Intertextuality and the Huainanzi's Self-Fashioning as an Embodiment of the Way". *The Journal of Asian Studies* 79 (2): 367–402.

Abbreviations

AA	Immanuel Kant, *Kants Gesammelte Schriften* (Akademieausgabe)
CPC	Communist Party of China
ES	Ignatius of Loyola, *Exercitia spiritualia (Spiritual Exercises)*
HC	Hannah Arendt, *The Human Condition*
HNZ	*Huainanzi*
KrV	Immanuel Kant, *Kritik der reinen Vernunft*
Met.	Aristotle, *Metaphysics*
OT	Hannah Arendt, *The Origins of Totalitarianism*
PI	Ludwig Wittgenstein, *Philosophical Investigations*
PRC	People's Republic of China
ROC	Republic of China
ST	Thomas Aquinas, *Summa Theologica*
UNESCO	United Nations Educational, Scientific and Cultural Organization

Note on Citations and Translations

The pinyin romanization is used throughout the book except when common usage prescribes otherwise (for instance: Sun Yat-sen) or when quotations keep specific romanizations (*Tao* for *dao* 道).

For the sake of consistency, traditional Chinese characters are the ones displayed throughout the body of the main text. In the "Acknowledgments" and "References" sections, I have made use of both traditional and simplified characters, depending upon contexts, periods and sources.

Citations originating from the received versions of Chinese classics have been checked on the reference editions published by *Zhonghua shuju* 中華書局, notably within the series *Zhonghua jingdian mingzhu quanben quanzhu quanyi congshu* 中華經典名著全本全注全譯叢書, with occasional consultation of other critical editions. This applies to the following books: *Analects, Book of Documents, Book of Rites, Classic of Changes, Classic of Documents, Classic of Odes, Daodejing [Laozi], Daxue, Guanzi, Huainanzi, Liezi,* Lu Jiuyuan's *Records of Words, Mencius, Mozi, Shuowen jiezi, Sutra of Forty-Two Sections, Mozi, Xunzi,* Yang Xiong's *Exemplary Sayings, Zhongyong, Zhuangzi,* and to the writings of Wang Bi (the latter with additional consultation of Wagner 2003). Mouzi's *Settling of Doubts* has been checked on the critical bilingual edition of the text offered by Béatrice L'Haridon (2017). Likewise, the text of the *Zuozhuan* is quoted from the critical bilingual edition provided by Durrant, Li and Schaberg (2016). The text of the *Art of Reading* and other writings of Zhu Xi has been verified on the critical edition of the *Conversations of Master Zhu* edited by Huang Shiyi 黃士毅 (Zhu 2014). The Chinese original of the excavated *Hengxian* manuscript is quoted according to the edition provided in the relevant volume of the Shanghai Museum manuscripts (Ma and Li 2003).

The quotes from the *Daodejing [Laozi]* are given according to the number of the chapter (sometimes called stanza, as these chapters are very short) in the received version. The *Analects* are quoted by chapter and section (for instance: 17.1), as is the case for the *Mencius* (the latter comprising seven books, each book divided into two parts: 6 A.2 refers to the second section of the first part of Book 6). Works such as the *Zhuangzi*, the *Huainanzi* and the *Xunzi* are referred to by chapter number followed by a section number, the way of dividing these sections differing from one edition to another. The numbering I select may depend upon the translation being referred to. For the *Zhuangzi*, by default I use the division established by

Chen (1983). One generally refers to the *Classics of Documents* and some other works by simply quoting the title of the chapter. I give the number (and sometimes the title) of the ode being quoted for the *Classic of Odes*, omitting the mention of the section to which this ode belongs.

Translations are mine each time no indication is provided. For the most important classical texts, I have checked my rendering of the texts on the following versions (full references are to be found in the Bibliography): *Huainanzi:* Major et al. (2010). *Daodejing:* Cook (2012); Henricks (1992) and (2000); Lau (1963); Levi (2018); Ryden (2008). *Zhuangzi:* Levi (2010); Watson (2003); Ziporyn (2009) and (2020). *Analects:* Chen and Xu (2011); Lau (2000); Levi (2018); Ni (2017); Slingerland (2003b). *Xunzi:* Hutton (2014); Knoblock (1998). *Mozi:* Johnston (2010). *Classic of Odes:* Couvreur (1967).

I provide the original after the translation when the excerpt is of particular importance, or when it is quoted in the framework of a lexical or conceptual discussion, or yet when its translation and/or interpretation are controverted.

Index of Authors and Works

This index refers to authors mentioned in the main body of the text, excluding References. It also refers to Chinese classics and commentarial works quoted in the book.

Aleni (Giulio)   154
Allan (Sarah)   42, 66 f., 142
Ames (Roger)   14 f., 17–20, 22 f., 27–30, 32 f., 35 f., 41 f., 44 f., 47–50, 54–56, 58 f., 64, 66–74, 98 f., 110, 155 f., 165
Analects / Lunyu 論語: 15, 28, 31, 32, 38, 45, 53, 59, 64, 66, 67, 69, 70, 74, 75, 112, 115, 116, 132, 134, 137, 141, 148, 157, 159, 160, 164, 169, 174, 189, 190, 197–198, 211, 213, 215–219, 221–223, 225, 226, 229
Arendt (Hannah):   56, 185, 198–211, 226 f., 249
Aristotle   4 f., 8, 30, 32, 39–41, 93, 112, 117, 153, 155, 158, 173, 211, 249
Art of Reading (The) / Dushufa 讀書法   169, 250
Augustine   8, 10, 29, 47, 53, 145, 203

Ba Jin 巴金   87
Baehr (Peter)   199 f.
Bai Tongdong 白彤東   118, 185, 193–198
Behuniak (Jim)   18, 20, 48
Bell (Catherine)   129, 186
Bell (Daniel A.)   193
Bergson (Henri)   8, 47
Billioud (Sébastien)   100
Boer (Roland)   201
Book of Rites / Liji 禮記   28, 77, 108, 112, 131 f., 138
Bouvet (Joachim)   63
Bresciani (Umberto)   91, 98
Brindley (Erica F.)   36, 52, 131
Bruya (Brian)   19

Cai Yuanpei 蔡元培   84, 88, 89
Cato   209
Certeau (Michel de)   168, 174, 213, 225
Chai (Wenyu)   52, 112, 145
Chan (Wing-tsit)   60 f., 73
Chen Duxiu 陳獨秀   84–87
Chen Lai 陳來   88, 100, 101–104, 105, 111

Cheng (Anne)   168, 171
Cheng Yi 程頤   91, 101
Cicero   8, 47, 173, 186
Clark (Kelly James)   19
Classic of Changes See *Yijing*
Classic of Documents / Shujing 書經   25, 40, 60, 62, 64, 115, 127, 134, 136, 140, 141, 143, 217
Confucius   15, 31, 45, 53, 58–59, 64–67, 69, 75, 83, 87–89, 96, 102, 112, 116, 119, 134, 136–137, 143–144, 146, 148, 159, 160, 164, 196–198, 212, 215–216, 218–219, 221–226, 229
Couplet (Philippe)   15
Coutinho (Steve)   68

Daodejing 道德經 / *Laozi* / Laozi 老子   1, 6, 21, 23, 27, 30, 34, 38, 45–47, 50–53, 67, 78–81, 100, 130, 133, 141, 143–144, 149, 152, 169, 172, 175, 229
Darwin (Charles)   82, 84, 121
De Bary (Theodore)   45, 96
Deleuze (Gilles)   8
Descartes (René)   8, 82 f., 112
Dewey   8, 85
Dignāga   90
Ding Sixin   52
Douglas (Mary)   132, 173, 176

Elias (Norbert)   132
Exemplary Sayings / Fayan 法言   1

Fang Dongmei 方東美   99
Fang Xudong 方旭東   101
Fei Xiaotong 費孝通   114
Feng Youlan 馮友蘭   83, 91–95, 102, 123
Fingarette (Herbert)   186, 188 f.
Forgotten Tales / Shiyiji 拾遺記   24
Foucault (Michel)   2, 6–8, 82, 197

Gadamer (Hans-Georg)   6 f., 82, 165–167, 179, 229

Index of Authors and Works

Girardot (Norman J.)   16, 21, 142
Goffman (Erwing)   129, 186, 189
Goldin (Paul)   23, 52
Graham (A.C.)   14, 36, 67
Granet (Marcel)   23f., 26, 36f., 76, 137f., 170
Gu Jiegang 顧頡剛   85
Guanzi 管子   35, 67, 131, 169
Gunkel (Hermann)   49
Guo Fuping 郭福平   203
Guo Xiang 郭象   54–55, 93
Guoyu 國語   65

Habermas (Jürgen)   82, 160
Hadot (Pierre)   21
Hall (David)   14, 17, 19f., 22f., 26–29, 32f., 35f., 41f., 44f., 47–50, 54f., 58f., 64, 66–74
Han (Byung-Chul)   186
Harrell (Stevan)   113f.
He Zhaowu 何兆武   109
Hegel (Friedrich)   8, 47, 97, 102, 112, 117
Heidegger (Martin)   8, 82, 202, 205f.
Hengxian 亙先   31, 51
Herdrich (Christian Wolfgang)   15
Heubel (Fabian)   19, 106, 111
Hobbes (Thomas)   113
Hong Tao 洪涛   205
Hongfan 洪範   25, 40, 140
Hu Shi 胡適   84, 87
Hu Xijin 胡錫進   204
Huainanzi 淮南子   23, 26–27, 34, 64, 131, 169
Hui (Yuk)   19, 53f., 83, 134
Huizi 惠子   81, 93
Hume (David)   92

Ignatius of Loyola   155, 183, 211, 219, 220, 223
(See also *Spiritual Exercises* / *Exercitia spiritualia*)
Intorcetta (Prospero)   15

Jankélévitch (Vladimir)   47
Jiang Qing 蔣慶   110, 196

Kampf (Leopold)   87
Kant (Immanuel)   2–4, 7f., 82, 92, 97, 112f., 178f., 202, 207, 249
Karapétiants (Artiémii)   25

Kim (Chin-Tai)   48, 212
Kropotkin (Pyotr Alexeyevich)   87

Laozi See *Daodejing* 道德經 / *Laozi* / Laozi 老子
Larre (Claude)   175f.
Le Blanc (Charles)   23, 38
Le Xiaojun 樂小軍   204
Legge (James)   16f., 70f., 142
Lévi-Strauss (Claude)   131
Levinas (Emmanuel)   117
Lewis (Mark E.)   140f., 143f.
Li Tiangang 李天綱   55, 118–121
Li Zehou 李泽厚   90, 120
Li Zhizao 李之藻   62
Liang Shuming 梁漱溟   85, 112
Liezi 列子   26, 27, 48
Lin Yutang 林語堂   86
Liu Xiaofeng 劉小楓   205
Liu Xie 劉勰   173
Liu Yaqing 劉雅倩   203
Livy   23, 186
Lo (Yuet Keung)   53
Lodge (David)   145
Longobardo (Niccolò)   154f.
Lu Jiuyuan 陸九淵   6, 91, 172
Lu Xun 鲁迅   85–87, 89
Lunyu See *Analects* / *Lunyu* 論語
Lüshi Chunqiu 呂氏春秋   38
Luther (Martin)   47

Ma (Lin)   19
Ma Yifu 馬一浮   91
Malraux (André)   199
Mao Chang 毛萇   137
Mao Heng 毛亨   137
Mason (Joshua)   14f., 17f.
Master Zeng See Zeng Shen
Mattice (Sarah A.)   110
McIntyre (Alasdair)   82, 102
McLean (George F.)   19
Mencius 孟子 /*Mencius*   1, 2, 15, 24, 33, 38, 42, 43, 45, 68–71, 75, 89, 93, 94, 96, 97, 111, 115–116, 120, 143, 146–150, 169, 173–175, 177, 194–195, 211, 215, 218, 221–225, 229
Merleau-Ponty (Maurice)   82, 163
Mill (John Suart)   84, 213, 219

Montesquieu (Charles-Louis de)   84
Mote (Frederick W.)   22
Mou Zongsan 牟宗三   95, 120, 123
Mouzi 牟子   118
Mozi / *Mozi* 墨子   42, 45, 76, 100, 140

Nietzsche   8, 55, 82, 87, 121
Nine Chapters on the Art of Mathematics / *Jiuzhang yishu* 九章算術   34
Noël (François)   153

Ode / *Odes* / Book of Odes / *Shijing* 詩經   24, 26, 60–61, 63, 64, 107, 115, 127, 136–138, 141, 143, 170, 171

Parmenides   29, 32
Paul of Tarsus   29
Plato   8, 93, 112, 155, 159, 197, 205
Prémare (Joseph de)   63
Puett (Michael)   27, 37f.

Qian Mu 錢穆   82, 123
Quintilian   173

Ricci (Matteo)   17, 62, 153f., 183, 214
Ricoeur (Paul)   167, 207f.
Rosemont (Henry Jr.)   14
Rošker (Jana)   5, 9, 19, 44, 59, 120
Rossetti (Livio)   158
Rougemont (François de)   15
Rousseau (Jean-Jacques)   109f., 112, 121, 162
Russell (Bertrand)   92

Settling of Doubts / *Lihuo* 理惑   118, 250
Shanhaijing 山海經   23, 24, 26
Shao Yong 邵雍   101
Shuowen jiezi 說文解字   46, 140, 143, 148,
Slingerland (Edward)   17, 32, 175, 209, 219, 229, 251
Smith (Adam)   84
Socrates   158, 206
Solé-Farràs (Jesús)   95, 98
Song Kuanfeng 宋寬鋒   95
Songs of Chu / *Chuci* 楚辭   23–24.
Spengler (Oswald)   121
Spinoza   94

Spiritual Exercises / *Exercitia spiritualia*   155, 183, 211–226
Spring and Autumn Annals / *Chunqiu* 春秋   143
Standaert (Nicolas)   131f., 155, 191, 214
Strauss (Leo)   82, 131, 206
Sullivan (Ian M.)   14f., 17f.
Sun Xiangchen 孫向晨   111–118
Sun Shangyang 孫尚揚   109
Sun Yat-sen 孫中山   87, 193
Sutra of Forty-Two Sections / *Sishi'er zhang jing* 四十二章經   117f., 250
Suwen 素問   75

Tang Junyi 唐君毅   95, 98–99, 111, 123
Tang Yijie 汤一介   82–84, 89, 90, 121
Thomas Aquinas   5f., 8, 41, 47, 191, 249
Thoraval (Joël)   100
Thouard (Denis)   166
Tianwen 天問   24
Tianzhu shiyi 天主實義   62
Tillich (Paul)   120
Tolstoy (Leo)   86
Tu Wei-ming / Du Weiming 杜維明   70, 73, 97

Udayana   90

Van Brakel (Jaap)   19
Vandermeersch (Léon)   33, 92, 94, 135

Wang Bi 王弼   53–55, 79, 172,
Wang Jia 王嘉   24
Wang Yangming 王陽明   91, 94, 101, 216
Wang Yinli 王寅麗   207
Weber (Max)   47
Wellhausen (Julius)   49
Wenxin diaolong 文心雕龍   173
Whitehead (Alfred North)   8, 30, 56, 72, 102
Wi Paekkyu 魏伯珪   173
Winslett (Justin T.)   65f.
Wittgenstein   6, 8, 160f., 187f., 249
Wolff (Christian)   3
Wong (Yih Jiun Peter)   58, 71
Wu Jingxiong 吳經熊   87

Xi Jinping 習近平   107, 110, 192, 200
Xici 繫辭   76, 135

Xie Youwei 謝幼偉　95
Xiong Shili 熊十力　83, 91
Xu Fuguan 徐復觀　59, 95
Xu Guangqi 徐光啟　62
Xu Shen 許慎　140
Xunzi / *Xunzi* 荀子　24, 28, 38, 67, 75, 77–80, 94, 108, 129–131, 136, 138, 139, 143, 186–187

Yang Huilin 杨慧林　192
Yang Tingyun 楊廷筠　62
Yang Xiong 揚雄　1, 2
Yijing 易經　31–35, 56, 63, 73, 127, 139–142, 148, 175
Yu (Jiyuan)　41
Yu Yingshi 余英時　82
Yuejing 樂經　143

Zeng Shen 曾參 / Ziyu 子輿 / Master Zeng　215
Zeno　32

Zhang (Chishen)　106
Zhang Dainian 張岱年　65, 89, 120
Zhang Junmai 張君勱 / Carsun Chang　91, 95
Zhang Shen 張慎　205
Zhang Zai 張載　101
Zhao Dunhua 趙敦華　19
Zhao Tingyang 趙汀陽　104–111, 117, 198
Zhao Zichen 趙紫宸　86
Zhongyong 中庸　56, 58, 67, 68, 69–74, 97, 107, 155, 185, 211–213, 219, 223, 224
Zhou Yi 周毅　203
Zhou Zuoren 周作人　86
Zhu Xi 朱熹　6, 34, 70, 72–74, 91, 93. 94, 96, 101, 169, 223
Zhuangzi / *Zhuangzi* 莊子　6, 23, 24, 26–27, 33, 38, 46–47, 52–54, 57, 67, 79–81, 83, 100, 128, 130, 143, 150–151, 159, 229
Ziporyn (Brook)　67, 251
Zou Yan 鄒衍　38
Zuozhuan 左傳　26, 65, 134, 139, 188, 209

Index of Subjects

Attentiveness   2, 74, 127f., 145f., 148, 152, 175, 179f., 213, 215, 217 (See also *Guan* 觀)
Authoritarianism   106, 122, 192, 200

Bentilun 本體論 (ontology)   9, 53, 102, 111
Bianming xili 辨明析理 (Analysis of principles from the viewpoint of language analysis)   93

Chaos See *Hundun*
Cheng 誠 (sincerity; integrity; rectitude)   72–73
Civil religion See *Gongming zongjiao*
Correlative thinking   8, 14, 35–39, 41, 51, 107
Cosmogony   22, 27, 52

Daoshu 道術 (the art of the Way)   150–151
Daoti 道體 (processual emergence)   93
Daotong 道統 (orthodox transmission)   82, 96, 122
Dao 道（way; the Way)   27, 31, 38, 43, 52–54, 56, 58, 60, 66–67, 71, 79, 94, 118, 119, 133, 141, 151, 159, 231
De 德 (potency; virtue)   57, 67, 99, 133, 141
Dialogic / dialogism / dialogical   5, 10, 19, 98, 127, 153, 156–167, 176, 187, 192, 203, 206, 227, 229–232
Discernment   104, 136, 155, 159, 185, 198, 211–214, 217–227
Displacement   2, 50, 136, 162, 180, 211, 229f.
Dual ontology   9, 111–113

Evil   203f., 220f.

Formgeschichte (Form criticism)   171, 173

Gongmin zongjiao 公民宗教 (civil religion)   109
Guan 觀 (to observe; attentiveness)   31, 33, 127, 148
Guishen 鬼神 (*manes* and spirits)   58, 59, 65, 119, 148, 212

heart–mind (*xin* 心)   1, 33, 57, 64, 67, 69–71, 77, 121, 230

heng 恆 [heng] (constancy; permanence; perseverance)   31, 51–52, 141
Hundun 混沌 (Chaos)   26–27, 93

Immanence   14, 21, 48–50, 52, 54f., 64, 93, 107, 109
Intercompréhension   7

Jiaohua 教化 (to educate; to civilize)   28, 72
Jing 經 (Classic, classics)   101, 142–145
Jing 靜 (rest; stillness; tranquility)   30

Language game / language-games: 160–162, 187–188
Li 理 (patterns)   32, 58, 93, 98
Li 禮 See Ritual/rituals
Logos   29, 155
lun 倫 (relatedness)   36

Meritocracy   192f., 195, 197f., 226
Ming 名 (name)   74–81

Ontology See *Bentilun*

Performative / Performativity   75–77, 128, 134. 136–138, 148, 152, 160
Phronesis   211–226
Physis   29
Process philosophy   13f., 18, 55f., 72, 123

Qi 氣 (energy; fluid; matter)   93, 131
Qinqin 親親 (mutual feelings among kinfolks)   113, 115, 117
Quan 權 See Discernment

Redaktionsgeschichte (Redaction criticism)   171
Ren 仁 (benevolence; humanity; humaneness)   58, 68–69, 102–104, 115–116, 195, 219
Ritual / Rituals   24, 28, 45, 59, 69, 75, 109, 114, 119, 127, 128–132, 134, 137–138, 141, 145, 148, 151, 169, 174–175, 185–192, 197, 209, 222

Scholasticism   2, 4–7, 54, 153, 212
Self-examination   155, 185, 212–217, 220, 223, 227
Shangdi 上帝 (Supreme deity; God)   59–60
Shu 術 (art; technique; formula)   33, 44, 127, 146, 150–151
Sinicization   109 f., 119
Substance   14, 24, 35 f., 39–41, 90 f., 161, 191, 209

Taiji 太極 (Supreme polarity)   6, 93 (See also *Wuji* 無極)
Thoughtlessness   199, 203
Tian 天 (Heaven)   25, 58–65, 70–71, 108–110
Tianxia 天下 (All Things Under Heaven)   25, 104–108, 113, 117, 150, 151
Totalitarianism   199–201, 204 f., 210, 249
Transcendence   14, 47–50, 52–55, 99, 106 f., 109, 120 f., 149

Universality   98, 157, 162–165

Vagueness   41, 44 f., 47, 55

Wen 文 (signs; characters; text)   128, 134 f.
Wisdom / wisdoms   3, 5, 15, 41, 53, 70, 102–103, 158, 182, 211, 227, 229–232
Wuji 無極 (Non-polarity)   6, 93 (See also *Taiji* 太極)
Wu wei 無為 (non-action)   31, 209

Xiang 象 (image)   32, 34, 139
Xin 心 See Heart-mind
Xing 形 (Form; forms)   34, 52, 136, 151
Xing 性 (Nature)   28, 67, 98
Xing 省 See Self-examination
Xuanxue 玄學 (arcane/mystic learning)   39, 54

Yibenxing 一本性 (single-rootedness)   96
Yi 義 (righteousness)   58, 66

Zhi 治 (governance)   213
Zhong 衷 (moral standard)   60, 136, 217

www.ingramcontent.com/pod-product-compliance
Lightning Source LLC
Chambersburg PA
CBHW050520170426
43201CB00013B/2030